C000175138

LONDON BUSES
IN THE 1960s

LONDON BUSES IN THE 1960s

Ken Glazier

Capital Transport

First Published 1998

ISBN 185414 205 4

Published by
Capital Transport Publishing
38 Long Elmes
Harrow Weald
HA3 5JL

Printed by
CS Graphics
Singapore

© Ken Glazier 1998

CHAPTER ONE
INTRODUCTION   8

CHAPTER TWO
TROLLEYBUS SWANSONG   14

CHAPTER THREE
FLEET DEVELOPMENTS   46

CHAPTER FOUR
AREA SCHEMES: CENTRAL BUSES   66

CHAPTER FIVE
GREEN LINE IN DECLINE   96

CHAPTER SIX
CHEAP FARES AND ROVER TICKETS   109

CHAPTER SEVEN
COUNTRY AREA DEVELOPMENTS   112

CHAPTER EIGHT
TRAFFIC MANAGEMENT   126

CHAPTER NINE
INDUSTRIAL RELATIONS   136

CHAPTER TEN
NEW IDEAS FOR BUSES   146

CHAPTER ELEVEN
RESHAPING LONDON'S BUSES   172

CHAPTER TWELVE
POSTLUDE   198

AUTHOR'S NOTE

This volume continues the series of books which together cover the history of London Transport from the events leading up to its formation, through the years when it remained broadly in its original form, up to the day when all was changed by the implementation of the Transport (London) Act on 1st January 1970. These last ten years were not happy ones but neither were they short of innovation. Their story takes London Transport from being a highly traditional bus operator, somewhat behind many of its contemporaries in developing new practices, to one with probably the most radical policies then being expounded. In piecing together the intricate details of this complicated story I have been able to call upon the help of many good friends, who have been generous with their time and patience. They include, in alphabetical order, Lawrie Bowles, Brian Bunker, Teresa Doherty, Martin Elms, John Gent, Dr Andrew Gilks and Malcolm Papes. I am particularly indebted to Laurie Akehurst, Derek Fisk, Dave Ruddom, Hugh Taylor and Alan Townsin who toiled through the draft text and offered many new nuggets of information and comment, as well as finding the errors. I was especially pleased that Ralph Bennett, who became a member of the Board towards the end of the period and was later chairman of the new Executive, was kind enough to take the trouble to read that part of the manuscript covering the events in which he was directly involved. He was able to give me some interesting and useful insights. Finally, I would like to record a special word of gratitude to my dear friend Dennis Odd who died from cancer at the tragically early age of 50. He has helped me with the research for this and all the earlier books in the series and has made many helpful, always pointed, comments which have helped me enrich the text. This book is dedicated to his memory.

London, May 1998   Ken Glazier

CHAPTER ONE

INTRODUCTION

The ten years starting on 1st January 1960 were the last during which London Transport remained recognisably the organisation conceived by Herbert Morrison thirty years earlier. It had lost its financial and policy making autonomy in 1948 when it became subservient to the British Transport Commission but the basic day to day business had been left intact and, twelve years later, it was still responsible for the operation of local passenger services in a huge area extending twenty-five to thirty miles from Charing Cross. This embraced not only the central area buses and trolleybuses operating largely within the Metropolitan Police District but also the extensive Country Bus system and the still intact network of Green Line coach services. In some ways the organisation was more powerful than ever. The absolute monopoly powers in the 'Special Area' conferred on the LPTB by the 1933 Act, had been inherited by the Executive in 1948 but the British Transport Commission had added

to the Executive's sphere of influence by devolving additional operating rights outside the old LPTB area, notably in Crawley and around Grays and Tilbury. By a peculiar quirk of political history, it was to regain much of its autonomy in 1963, bringing it closer in its range of power and responsibilities to the original organisation of 1933 than it had been since nationalisation in 1948.

London Transport started the 1960s in what seemed a financially healthy state, having earned a working surplus of nearly £8 million in 1960 which was enough to meet all the central charges from the Commission and leave a surplus of £1.4 million in the Executive's own accounts. Unfortunately it was not as healthy as it looked; the surplus had been earned not from flourishing trade but because costs were being held artificially low. More and more mileage was being cut arbitrarily because of staff shortages, deceptively reducing costs, but this was already causing serious disruption to bus services with inevitable loss

of business and income. London Transport's efforts to balance its duty to achieve a good financial result with trying to solve its staffing problems was to dominate events during the decade. The staffing problem was not solved; in most years recruitment was exceeded by wastage and the level of lost mileage on Central Buses for this cause alone, rarely dropped below fifteen per cent and in four of the ten years reached or exceeded twenty per cent. It was to go on dogging London Transport's fortunes until 1982, when the Executive at last realised that its mileage budget was far in excess of what could be bought with the money available.

Above **London's standard for years to come? The Routemaster had just started to go into volume service at the end of 1959 and, as the 1960s got under way, there was no sign of any rival to prevent its eventually displacing the RT family. RM 671 in original condition is seen at the Tottenham Court Road terminus of what had been trolleybus route 629.** Colin Brown

The battle to keep wages at an attractive level while avoiding unpopular fares increases proved intractable and a fresh approach was tried by the new Labour Government in 1964. As part of a strategy to encourage the use of public transport, the Government took control of the general level of fares and allowed only two increases in the next four years, at the beginning of 1966 and in the autumn of 1968, compared with the one or two increases each year which had by then become the rule. As the Board was barred by statute from running at a loss, the Government took the historic decision to provide direct grants of money to compensate for the revenue foregone. In the sense that it stemmed the haemorrhage of passengers away from public transport, the strategy worked. Between 1966 and 1968, the number of passengers carried on road services and the passenger receipts remained stable, as did the bus and coach mileage operated, but costs continued to rise and London Transport's financial performance deteriorated progressively. The Government made grants totalling over £36 million between 1965 and 1969, the annual amounts gradually increasing from £3.8 million in 1965 to £10.8 million in 1969. Despite a public perception to the contrary, these arrangements were tightly controlled and London Transport continued to manage its affairs effectively so that an average operating surplus (before payment of interest charges) of £2.4 million was earned during its seven year stewardship.

At the start of the 1960s, the Executive was behaving in a very traditional fashion. It was in the midst of replacing its trolleybuses by motor buses and the vehicle chosen, the new Routemaster, although technically very advanced, was traditional in layout and styling. The Routemaster was also intended to replace the huge RT family fleet and all seemed set for another generation of London Transport designed traditional buses. Nothing particularly radical had happened to the route network either. It had been expanded since the war to serve new areas and much work had been done by Central Road Services during the 1950s to localise suburban sections of routes particularly prone to disruption by traffic congestion but on the whole it was in its traditional mould. Much the same could be said of Country Buses, while Green Line coaches seemed almost set in aspic. Seemingly, everyone was happy to allow things to go on much as before. This impression was superficial, however and by the end of the decade the calm orderliness had been disrupted irrevocably, as old ways and old values were cast aside quite ruthlessly. By then, vehicle policy had changed radically in favour of of a substantial proportion of high capacity one-man-operated single-deckers and the route structure was being thoroughly overhauled, based on local suburban or country town networks.

London Transport's apparently timid approach to dealing with the problem of traffic congestion still seemed realistic, even as late as 1960, because the problem was still confined almost entirely to central London. The solutions then being pursued by the traffic authorities centred on restricting the number of vehicles which could park on the streets

while encouraging the provision of off-street parking. These policies were designed to improve traffic flow rather than to discourage people from bringing their cars into town and this was underlined by the widespread application of traffic management measures designed both to increase road capacity and speed up traffic. Although there was a slight temporary improvement in mileage lost by buses for traffic reasons, neither aim was in the long term interests of buses nor their passengers because they simply encouraged people to use their cars and eventually bring back the congestion which was supposed to have been cured. Between 1959 and 1969 there was a reduction of five per cent in the number of vehicles entering central London in the morning peak but the reduction in total carrying capacity of those vehicles was even greater because the number of private cars increased by twenty-seven per cent, while the number of buses and coaches dropped by twenty-three per cent. The total number of people carried into London in the

three hour period by all road vehicles fell by 69,700 (twenty-one per cent), nearly 66,000 of whom were former bus and coach passengers, an alarming thirty per cent fall in ten years.

Top **Traffic congestion was beginning to threaten the reliability of routes beyond the confines of the City and West End, at such points as 'The Nag's Head', Holloway. The virtual monopoly of the RT family in the bus fleet is clearly evident in this view showing all three main types, with RTW 472 and RTL 173 leading an unidentifiable RT. Several trolleybuses can also be seen.** Michael Dryhurst

Above **Although new legislation to abolish the British Transport Commission was being prepared in the early 1960s, the integrity of London Transport's area of operation was not under threat and the future of the Country Bus & Coach department seemed secure. RT 2516 was one of Chelsham's first, in February 1950, and was still at work in the area when photographed at Warlingham Green on route 408, which encapsulated Country Bus operations in its mixture of outer suburban and inter-urban country running.** A.J. Wild

Ewhurst was a remote Surrey outpost of London Transport's statutory area, served infrequently by route 448 which approached from the north through the picturesque but thinly populated woodland surroundings in which GS 25 is seen plying its trade. The alternative, more lucrative, direct approach to Ewhurst might have come under the Board's influence under some of the new legislative proposals following the 1954 Chambers Committee of Inquiry.
Colin Brown

Although there had been a Conservative Government since 1951, it had made no attempt to interfere with the provisions of the 1947 Transport Act relating to railways and buses, other than to abandon the planned 'Area Schemes' in the provinces. The main thrust of its transport policy had been to denationalise the road haulage industry and reorganise the railways and there had been only minor changes to the statutory framework in which London Transport had operated since 1948.

By the early sixties, the Government had decided to make further changes but these too were confined mainly to reorganising nationalised transport rather than anything more radical. The principal proposal was to abolish the monolithic British Transport Commission and transfer its responsibilities to four autonomous Boards (British Railways, London Transport, British Transport Docks and British Waterways) and a Transport Holding Company to take responsibility for the Commission's other businesses including most of its bus interests outside the London area.

Nevertheless, the Bill as originally drafted did contain one important increase of powers which was not specified in the White Paper which had preceded it. Under Clause 13 each of the new Boards and the Transport Holding Company would have been given powers to construct, manufacture and produce anything required for the purpose of their business and to sell them to one another but not to anybody else. This would have allowed London Transport complete freedom to manufacture bus chassis, bodies and major components, a substantial broadening of the limited power to build 527 bus bodies a year which had been enjoyed by the LPTB until 1947. These provisions replaced the powers held by the BTC under the 1947 Act, which themselves had absorbed the powers granted to the Board in the 1933 Act. This provision remained intact right through the Committee stage of the Bill and was within an ace of reaching the statute book, no attempt having been made to

challenge it up to that time. However, there had been representations from the road vehicle manufacturers and the railway carriage and wagon building industry which resulted in backbench pressure for the Clause to be amended. The Minister, Ernest Marples, capitulated and introduced an amendment at the report stage. In the Act as passed by Parliament the general powers remained intact in Section 13 (1) but sub-section 5 took them away again so far as the manufacture of road vehicles by the Boards was concerned. Instead, the four Boards were allowed only to manufacture road vehicle chassis or bodies and their major components for the purpose of research and development. These restrictions did not apply to the Holding Company, which became responsible for the Bristol Commercial Vehicles and Eastern Coach Works businesses.

The new London Transport Board therefore had virtually no power to manufacture buses, unlike the old Board which had had a statutory allowance of 527 bodies a year and

During the drafting of the new Transport Bill, consideration was given to the possibility of using Aldenham Works to build new buses for London Transport, resuming a tradition which ended with the Second World War, but this came to nought. The high standard of Aldenham's workmanship, which amounted almost to the creation of a new bus every three or four years, is exemplified by Middle Row's Metro-Cammell bodied RTL 655 on the Goldsmiths Arms stand at East Acton in the mid-sixties. M.E. Papes collection

the outgoing Executive which, in theory at least, could have used the powers vested in the BTC. This is an interesting episode as it is fairly clear that there had never been any intention to alter the situation as it stood in 1962 and it is certainly the case that London Transport itself had not sought any increase in its powers. What seems to have happened is that the drafters of the Bill had set out to safeguard the British Railways Board's ability to continue the manufacture of railway rolling stock but had inadvertently extended the powers to all the new Boards. Nobody appears to have noticed the oversight until the Commons backbenchers intervened at a very late stage.

These developments make fascinating comparison with some discussions a couple of years earlier when the Joint Trades Committee (representing skilled workshop staff) had approached London Transport with a request that it should resume manufacture of bus bodies. Immediately after the war this had not been practicable because the full capacity of the shops was needed to maintain the operational fleet but the completion of fleet renewal and the opening of the overhaul factory at Aldenham, combined with the diminishing size of the fleet, had changed the situation completely. Aldenham had been built to deal with a fleet of 10,000 buses requiring overhaul about every two-and-a-half years, yet the operational motor bus fleet was already down to around 7,000 and the overhaul period had stretched to three-and-a-half years. Despite the extra buses which were to be added for the trolleybus conversion the fleet was likely to go on falling in size and the period between overhauls was expected to increase further. This meant that there was a lot of spare space in the works which was never likely to be needed for overhauling buses. The Executive took the idea seriously enough to calculate that, for a capital outlay of £100,000, this space could be used to build eight bus bodies a week (400 a year), which would have covered London Transport's total needs. The manufacturing

powers held by the BTC under the 1947 Act allowed it to build one-fifth of its total vehicle requirements plus the 527 bodies inherited from the LPTB, giving a current total of about 700 bodies a year. Theoretically, therefore, the BTC could have authorised the Executive to build the four hundred bodies but this would have left the Eastern Coach Works factory at Lowestoft with a total annual building allowance of only three hundred (forty-two per cent of its capacity), at which level its business would have been uneconomic. The Tilling companies would then have been obliged to buy half their bus bodies from outside suppliers and the end effect of the change would have been to transfer manufacturing business from one subsidiary to another with no apparent gain to the Commission. Nevertheless the Executive did not dismiss the idea outright but decided to seek the views of the BTC. Not surprisingly, nothing more was heard of this project which, in any case, was overtaken by the new legislation.

Under the terms of the White Paper, the new Board was intended to inherit the operational powers which had been enjoyed by London Transport since 1933, including their complete monopoly within the Special Area but with the addition of those services running outside the old LPT statutory area which had been authorised by the Commission since 1948. London Transport had made two attempts, in 1939 and 1948, to have its area extended so that the damaging effect of the boundary on the provision of sensible bus routes could be removed. Although the area had not been altered on either occasion, the problem had been overcome in 1948 by the more pragmatic method of using the provisions of the 1947 Transport Act to allow the Executive to work beyond its statutory boundary under powers delegated from the BTC. As this method would no longer be available under the new legislation, the Executive sought again to have its area enlarged, the main basis of its argument being that the 1933 boundaries were even more inappropriate in the 1960s now that new housing and industrial developments, including the New Towns, were taking place in the belt through which the boundary passed.

The matter was taken seriously by the Ministry of Transport; so seriously, in fact, that the debate went far beyond the simple request made by London Transport and became a thoroughgoing review of not just the privileges enjoyed by the Executive but also the statutory constraints on its operations. Despite the almost unblemished accolade which had been afforded London Transport by the Chambers Committee of Inquiry in 1954, the Ministry was aware of its reputation for doing nothing in response to legitimate requests for new and improved services and its allegedly 'dog-in-the-manger' attitude to allowing other operators to run them instead. On the other side of the argument, the Civil Servants questioned the need to circumscribe London Transport now that fifty per cent of the bus industry was nationalised and suggested that more commercial freedom would help the new Board to pay its way. This culminated in an extraordinary set of proposals which would have abolished London Transport's monopoly and put it on much the same basis as any other bus operator but with a continuing duty to provide an adequate and properly co-ordinated system of public transport within the Special Area. The detailed proposals would have abolished the Consents procedure and given other operators freedom to seek Road Service Licences within the Special Area through the usual Traffic Commissioners' procedure. In return London Transport would have been set free from its duty to provide an adequate and co-ordinated service in the territory beyond the Special Area and allowed to run without restriction beyond its old boundary, subject only to the Road Service Licensing procedure. Within the Special Area, for reasons of equity, the Board also would have required Road Service Licences but its duty to operate an adequate service would have continued and this would have been a legitimate argument for opposing licence applications from other operators. The extent to which the Board's operating area should be enlarged was a

One of the ideas canvassed during the preparation of the new Transport Bill was to extend London Transport's area. London Transport had been running local services in Grays and Tilbury since 1952, taken over from Eastern National under powers delegated from the British Transport Commission, but this was to remain the only example of any substantial extension beyond its statutory operating area. RT 2254 at Tilbury Ferry represents this unique concession. W.R. Legg

A possible extension of London Transport's Private Hire area was one of the proposals considered when the new Bill which was to set up the new Boards was being drafted. The RFWs had been bought specifically for longer distance operations beyond the LT boundary but had been confined to LT's statutory area since the enactment of the 1953 Transport Act, except for staff outings. By May 1960, when this photograph was taken, RFW 5 was already nine years old and a little elderly for such duties but the class still gave a good account of itself and could no doubt have fulfilled them more than adequately if called upon to do so. A.J. Wild

matter of considerable debate. The original plan foresaw no restriction at all but with the qualification that if this were to prove politically unacceptable, the limit could be set at 100 miles from 55 Broadway and that if this too were unacceptable, the limit could be dropped to fifteen miles beyond the LPTB boundary (which is all that LT had asked for).

Enmeshed with this review was the question of what powers London Transport should have in respect of contract carriage (private hire). The original 1933 Act restrictions had been relaxed by the BTC in 1950 to allow the Executive to operate as its agent within a one

hundred mile radius of 55 Broadway but this had been withdrawn again under the 1953 Transport Act, section 18 of which expressly forbade the Commission from operating contract carriages other than staff outings except in a few specified areas, including the London Transport Area. This had effectively restored the provisions of the 1933 Act, except for staff outings which were still governed by the one hundred mile rule. London Transport wanted more freedom, arguing that if it were to be opened to competition within its own area, it should have the same freedom as others to compete more widely for contract work.

In sharp contrast with what was to happen eight years later, one of the first acts of Central Buses in 1960 was to convert route 212 from single to double-deck operation, its TDs being replaced by RTs on 6th January. The policy of the time was to convert routes to double-deck whenever physically possible. RT 741, seen at Stroud Green a few months later, was typical of its class and of the immaculate turn-out and correct 'dressing' which was then commonplace. G. Mead

Although this plea was accepted, the Ministry was worried that the sheer size of London Transport could put it in an unassailable position from which to eliminate competition completely and therefore sought to clip its wings by imposing a one hundred mile restriction. During the development of the proposals, the idea of removing the Board's monopoly powers was abandoned as being too far outside the policy set out in the White Paper, the extension of the operating area was reduced progressively, first to fifteen then finally to ten miles, and the restriction on contract operation was pulled back to seventy-five miles. Instead of abolishing the Consents procedure, the recompense to other operators was now to be a right of appeal against a refusal of consent by London Transport. In the end, none of the far-reaching extensions of powers made it into the Bill, although in mild recompense a limited new power to authorise out-boundary services was given to the Minister. On the other hand, the new procedure for appealing against refusal of consent which had been introduced as a counterweight to the widened powers did survive, so that London Transport finished up slightly worse off.

The new power to authorise the Board to run any additional services outside the statutory area now passed to the Minister of Transport under Section 8 of the Act, but in a substantially circumscribed form which effectively put an end to further expansion of this kind. The Minister was required to satisfy himself that there were exceptional circumstances which made it desirable for the Board to carry passengers on a particular route before authorising it to make an application for a Road Service Licence, whose grant was not automatic but still subject to

the normal Traffic Commissioner scrutiny. This was underlined in Section 59 where the Traffic Commissioner was prevented from granting a Road Service Licence for such a route unless existing operators in the area had either consented or had entered into a working agreement with the Board.

The Board's monopoly powers under Sections 16 and 17 of the London Passenger Transport Act were also slightly trimmed by the new appeals procedure. Appeals against London Transport's decisions could now be made to the Metropolitan Traffic Commissioner and if the appellants were dissatisfied with the Commissioner's decision, they could appeal to the Minister. For the first time since 1933, therefore, the Traffic Commissioner became involved in decisions about service provision but only where operators other than London Transport were involved and then only on appeal. For the great mass of bus operation in the Special Area supplied by the Board itself, the Commissioner's powers remained limited to the approval of the physical routes.

There was one other new provision which arose out of the prolonged debate about contract work. For the first time a statutory restriction was placed on London Transport limiting the size of its PSV fleet to what was required to meet its duties under the Act. There had been a clause in the draft Bill which gave the new Board authority to hire motor vehicles to other PSV licence holders, the intention being to allow the Board to make use of vehicles which were temporarily idle, at weekends for example. This was regarded by the Government as a sensible way of providing for the most economical deployment of the fleet but it attracted the opprobrium of the Passenger Vehicle

Operators Association who feared that the Board might set up a vehicle hiring business and undermine the legitimate trade of its members. It therefore made representations to the Minister asking him to drop the clause. Although London Transport had never shown any desire or ambition to extend its activities in the way feared by the PVOA, rather than risk losing the benefits of this clause altogether the Minister inserted the additional clause restricting the size of the fleet.

Although the shape, size and general powers of the undertaking were much the same as the old London Passenger Transport Board, there were substantial differences in the constitution of the new Board which made it a considerably less powerful organisation. Between 1933 and 1947 the LPTB had enjoyed financial independence because it had its own Stock and was also politically independent because its members were appointed by a panel of trustees. By contrast, the London Transport Board's financial requirements could be met only by money borrowed from the Minister, its members were appointed directly by the Minister and the Minister was also responsible for approving the financial framework of the organisation.

The formal structure of co-ordination and the revenue pooling arrangements with the main line railways which had been established first by the 1933 Act and then continued on the basis of common ownership under the 1947 Act, were removed by the new Act. They were replaced by a vague reciprocal requirement that London Transport should 'co-operate' with the Railways Board to ensure that railway services in the London area were properly co-ordinated. A rather loosely based arrangement was set up by the two Boards eventually but there was hardly any compulsion on them, other than their own natural preferences and historical precedent, to make the system work.

The Transport Act 1962 (Vesting Date) Order (S.I. 1962 No. 2634) was made by the Minister on 3rd December 1962 and the new Board took responsibility for London Transport on 1st January 1963. Its Chairman and full time members were the same team as had formed the Executive but with the important difference that the Chairman, who had been a member of the Commission and therefore only part time chairman of the Executive, became full-time on the abolition of his BTC job. Unlike the two previous chairmen, Alec Valentine had made his career with London Transport and was therefore in true line of succession from the Ashfield and Pick era. His was to be a short reign, however, as he retired on 31st March 1965 and was replaced by the first of a new generation of chairmen, the flamboyant Maurice Holmes. Indeed, the new Board itself, born into a period of political change, was destined to last only seven years, the shortest lived, so far, of the statutory bodies which have operated London Transport since 1933. It was nevertheless involved in some of the most far reaching changes in policy and operating methods for thirty years and it could be argued that it started the process which led eventually to the complete break up of the organisation in the 1990s.

CHAPTER TWO

TROLLEYBUS SWANSONG

Four of the planned stages for the abandonment of London's trolleybuses had already been completed by the end of 1959 and London Transport started the 1960s owning 1,199 trolleybuses to serve a maximum peak hour output of 1,010, twenty-five per cent less than a year earlier.

At this time it was still the Executive's declared policy to retain the Fulwell and Isleworth network of routes until the post-war Q1 trolleybuses, some of which were only eight years old, had reached the end of their book lives but during 1959 this plan had been under review and was about to be changed. Using the experience gained from the earlier conversions, the review team found that there was now a strong economic case for adding these routes to the end of the current abandonment programme. Although the initial cost of an early conversion would be greater, the savings in running costs which would accrue in the intervening years was estimated to be large enough to outweigh this by a substantial margin. A proposal to add a fourteenth stage to the abandonment programme, to take place on 23rd May 1962, was therefore approved by the Executive on 27th January 1960 for submission to the British Transport Commission, who approved it on 10th March. The change of plan was made public on 16th May and during the next two-and-a-half years, the whole of the remaining system was closed.

The Burnell Arms, on the corner of Plashet Grove and High Street North, East Ham, provides an unintentionally apt background to this view of L3 class trolleybus 1399 taken on 30th January 1960, the last Saturday of operation of local circular route 689, because John Burnell was Operating Manager (Central Road Services) and chaired the committee which supervised the conversion scheme. No.1399 survived this conversion, being transferred to Fulwell where it remained until the end of trolleybus operation in May 1962. *Peter G. Mitchell*

This monumental project was steered by a committee chaired by the Operating Manager (Central Road Services), John Burnell, on which were representatives of every department involved; but the design of the route network was carried out by a Traffic Sub-Committee, chaired by the Traffic Superintendent Denis Counihan. The detailed work was further devolved to a Working Party, led by Ted Leicester of the Traffic Development Office, with the assistance of Roy Smith, who later became successively Traffic Officer and Development Director, and the appropriate schedules and local managers. The partnership became legendary within the organisation for its ingenuity in balancing the conflicting constraints which faced service planners, notably the restrictive schedules agreement with the Trade Union and the need to work within ever tighter financial controls. This schedules agreement was to be one of the most onerous restrictions, as will be seen in the following account, and was to become more so over the years as more concessions were made to try to improve the attractions of the job.

Facing Page **London trolleybuses at their finest and as many like to remember them. Two of the first series of Q1 class BUTs dating from 1948 but looking practically new, are seen at the Hammersmith terminus of trolleybus routes 660, 666 and 667 in 1959. These were the smoothest and quietest trolleybuses in their day and, as sister vehicle 1768 regularly demonstrates at Carlton Colville, could still put some modern buses to shame in these respects.** Roy Hubble

Left **RM 65, running out from West Ham garage, turns right into Barking Road at the 'Green Gate' some time after the final withdrawal of trolleybuses from the area.** Colin Brown

In tackling their task, the Working Party did not have the wealth of detailed information on travel patterns which the computer revolution was to make available, almost to excess, in later years but had to rely on very basic figures showing passenger loadings at fixed points, usually about half-a-mile apart, the collection and analysis of which had to be done entirely by hand. Origin and Destination information was not part of the routine surveying procedure, although some moves were to be made in that direction during the 1960s when consultants were employed to carry out a pilot study in Newham. For normal business, surveys were carried out only when a particular need for the information arose and then only by the rather crude method of checking tickets at given key points. In practice, many new ideas were based on instinct or local knowledge of the market rather than detailed data and there was a great deal of 'suck it and see' in the process. It was surprisingly successful.

Although London Transport had been a pioneer in the art of route costing, it was still a very primitive tool and there was only limited understanding of the financial effects of service changes. It was still possible in the early 1960s for the Operating Manager to proclaim, without contradiction, that if services were reduced to allow for the increase in seating capacity of larger buses, the same number of passengers would still travel. There was also little or no knowledge of the true costs of operation outside the main Monday to Friday core period, which led to some questionable decisions about weekend and evening route withdrawals. It was within this context that the Working Party somehow had to plan a network which would meet all the passenger needs, produce the desired level of revenue (there were as yet no subsidies) and could be scheduled within the requirements of the agreement with the Trade Union. Although the arrangement of committees was unique to the trolleybus conversion, the procedures were those which were followed in all service planning by Central Road Services and, broadly, the Country Bus and Coach department and were to be the basis for the Area Schemes and Reshaping, described in subsequent chapters.

The fifth stage of the trolleybus conversion programme took place on 3rd February 1960 when routes 557, 669, 685, 689 and 690 disappeared. This seemingly ill-assorted group of routes was brought together because it enabled the overhead to be abandoned in a number of roads where other routes had already been withdrawn, notably Barking Road between Canning Town and East Ham Town Hall and the whole of Lea Bridge Road and Hackney Road. Otherwise it was much of the local network in West Ham and East Ham, covering the whole section from North Woolwich to Plaistow via Silvertown, Green Street, Plashet Grove, Plashet Lane, Portway, High Street East Ham and the last section of Romford Road between 'The Princess Alice' and Green Street. With this stage, electric traction disappeared from the streets of one more of London's former tramway operating municipalities, the County Borough of East Ham.

Two of the routes were replaced by identical motor bus services, the 669 by the 69 and the 685 by the 58, although part of the service was also met by new route 256 and an increased peak service between Canning Town and North Woolwich on the 238. In both cases the service pattern was substantially simplified and the overall level of service considerably reduced because traffic surveys had revealed that the number of passengers carried had waned so badly that the average peak hour load on the north-south trolleybus routes was only forty. In consequence, the seventy-four trolleybuses scheduled on the two routes were replaced directly by only forty-five buses, although two were also added to the 238 and perhaps four of those allocated to the 256 qualified as replacements for the Crooked Billet to Markhouse Road section of the 685. In the scheme as a whole, 107 scheduled trolleybuses were replaced by only 101 buses, which can be expressed crudely as a fourteen per cent cut in seating capacity.

As originally planned route 257 would also have been identical to the 557 but at Liverpool Street the Traffic Commissioner required a reduction in the number of buses using the turn across Bishopsgate and at Chingford Mount he reduced the number of buses authorised to stand, in both cases to less than had been acceptable for trolleybuses. About half the service was therefore extended beyond Liverpool Street to London Bridge station, incidentally helping out with the increasing number of commuters arriving at London Bridge; and between half and a third of the Monday to Saturday service was extended to Chingford ('Royal Forest Hotel'). The northern extension followed bus route 102 and thereby introduced a new 'round-the-corner' facility at Chingford Mount, which had last existed, in one direction only, in 1935.

Another device to reduce the number of turns at Liverpool Street took the form of an entirely new route 256 which ran from Chingford Mount to Moorgate (Finsbury Square) and had a portmanteau of jobs to do. It deviated from the 557/257 at the 'Crooked Billet' to follow route 685 as far as Markhouse Road, then again in Clapton where it provided a service to the Millfields Estate, running from Lea Bridge Road via Chatsworth Road and Powerscroft Road to Lower Clapton Road and finally at Shoreditch Church to run via Old Street and City Road to Finsbury Square. At Moorgate it had an interesting departure route via Chiswell Street and Bunhill Row, partly in a slightly forlorn hope that there might be some demand from new office developments at Chiswell Street but mainly to give some relief to route 170 in Old Street, where heavy peak loads were being carried towards Hackney.

Right **The driver of RM 155 explains some finer point of the Routemaster's equipment to a couple of colleagues, perhaps a trolleybus crew whose first glimpse of the vehicle this might have been. Edging past in Finsbury Square is N1 class trolleybus 1581, a 1939 model AEC 664T with elegantly curved bodywork by Birmingham Railway Carriage and Wagon Co. Ltd. Route 639 was to survive for almost another year.** C. Carter

Left **E2 class trolleybus 622 had a special place in history, having been used for the ceremonial opening of the West Ham system on 6th June 1936. It was also the last of the class to survive as it was held back when the rest were withdrawn at stage five so that it could be used in the closing ceremony too.** A.B. Cross

Below **Fresh into service, RM 168 and a K2 class trolleybus on the 649 wait at Liverpool Street terminus, to make the turn across Bishopsgate on which the Traffic Commissioner imposed more severe restrictions for motor buses than trolleybuses. The buildings on the other side of the road have long since disappeared, along with the many useful shops, under the mass of the undistinguished Broadgate development.** Malcolm Young

RM 69 had started at Poplar on 11th November 1959 but by the time it appeared in Tramway Avenue, Stratford working on the new 272 in July 1960, it had moved to West Ham.
Peter G Mitchell

One other existing bus route was involved in the conversion. Route 62 had for many years followed a curiously circuitous course which gave it a journey time of nearly ninety minutes to travel the less than three miles from Little Heath to Ilford, a condition which earned it the nick-name 'swiss roll route'. This was partly unravelled by joining the Little Heath to Barking section onto the western side of the Stratford – East Ham circulars (689/690) to form new route 162 running between Stratford and Little Heath. This provided several new through journey possibilities and strengthened the service along Barking Road from East Ham to Barking but at the expense of breaking the circle at East Ham Town Hall. The other half of the circle was covered by new route 272, which terminated at East Ham 'White Horse', except during Monday to Friday peak hours when it continued to Royal Albert Dock to give new links to the docks from Stratford and West Ham. Although there were people who used the 'round-the-corner' service, the new arrangements were judged to benefit more. The truncated 62 was simultaneously diverted intermediately between Barking and Rippleside to run via Longbridge Road and Upney Lane, to give the latter its first bus service. Even in this form, the 62 was still a very roundabout route.

Two trolleybus depôts were affected in this

stage but neither changed over completely. West Ham increased the small allocation of RMs which it had been operating since November 1959 by fifty-five, while retaining a schedule of sixty trolleybuses; and Walthamstow's forty-eight, its first assignment of motor buses, replaced about half its trolleys. Barking garage also participated with an allocation of four RTs on route 162, transferred from the 62, running alongside West Ham's Routemasters. The only other shared route was the 58 which had a small Walthamstow allocation in support of the main operation from West Ham. Only seventy-three of the RMs were brand new buses (numbered between 139 and 219) and the lion's share of these went to Walthamstow, thirty of those allocated to West Ham and one to Walthamstow being vehicles which had already seen service. Eight had been de-licensed in November 1959 after participating in the pre-conversion trials while the other twenty-two, having been used in the fourth stage of the conversion, were among those subsequently replaced by newer vehicles when the garages got into difficulty with the avalanche of engineering problems associated with the new bus.

The extension of the 272 to Royal Albert Dock proved to be a downright flop. Its future was put under review immediately but it was another eighteen months before anything was done about it, in one of the new style area schemes (see chapter four). Ironically, when the change came it re-introduced a circular operation similar to the old 689/690 but via Lonsdale Avenue instead of the main road. Passenger traffic along Upney Lane was not too brilliant either but in this case, because

it had the support of existing users of the through service, the operation proved more durable and remains part of route 62 at the time of writing thirty-six years later.

Apart from the City end, the new 256 proved to be a valuable addition to the network, so much so that during peak hours buses were carrying such good loads that they failed to provide the planned margin of capacity through Higham Hill which was supposed to cover the withdrawal of route 687 in the next stage. The Saturday operation to Moorgate was almost entirely surplus to requirements and was reduced to peak hours only as part of stage six. By contrast, the City extension of the 257 was an immediate winner as it tapped the fast developing outer suburban commuter traffic at both Liverpool Street and London Bridge. The new 'round-the-corner' link at Chingford Mount was also very popular and is another feature that has endured.

The trolleybuses withdrawn for scrap included the last twelve of the E1 class, which was particularly associated with West Ham, fourteen E2 (leaving 622 as the sole representative still licensed), seven J1 and twelve J2. Forty other withdrawn vehicles were held for 'cannibalisation': twenty-one H1, fifteen J1 and four F1. The balance of twenty withdrawn trolleybuses, comprising three H1, one J1 and sixteen J2, were stored in serviceable condition to cover failures. To cover the withdrawal of the J-class vehicles which were at Finchley and Highgate and the F1s at Hanwell, West Ham transferred twenty-six L3s to Finchley and five to Highgate, and Walthamstow sent four K1s to Hanwell and eight K1s and two N1s to Highgate.

Metro-Cammell bodied Leyland H1 class 892 waits to turn right out of Walthamstow depôt to take up an evening peak turn on route 623. The Robert Hart builder's sign, the building work between the trolleybus and the old Walthamstow Council tramway offices and the RTL trainer parked at the back of the yard, are all evidence of preparation for the imminent motor bus invasion.
E.G.P. Masterman

The sixth stage on 27th April applied to routes 623, 625, 687, 697 and 699 and completed the change-over to motor bus at both Walthamstow and West Ham. Trolleybuses were removed from twenty-three miles of road, including all remaining roads east of the river Lea, putting an end to electric traction in three more former tramway operating municipalities: West Ham, Leyton and Walthamstow. The sections abandoned completely at this stage were: the entire system between Victoria and Albert Docks and Chingford Mount via Freemasons Road, Newbarn Street and Balaam Street; also via Prince Regent Lane and Greengate Street; Plaistow Road and Stratford Broadway to the 'Thatched House'; also via Upton Lane, Woodgrange Road and Wanstead Flats; Leyton High Road, Hoe Street and Chingford Road; also via Markhouse Road and Billet Road; and the east-west trunk route from Woodford 'Napier Arms' via Forest Road to Tottenham Hale.

In no case was a trolleybus route replaced by an identical bus route, as the service planners strove to prove the greater flexibility claimed for the motor bus. The terminus at the 'Napier Arms' Woodford, flanked by Epping Forest on one side and with only limited access to the residential area on the other, had never been satisfactory but London Transport had been prevented by local objections from exercising its pre-war powers to extend the trolleybuses to Woodford Green. It was now all but abandoned by the two Forest Road routes, both of which were extended to more promising destinations further east. Route 623 was covered from

Manor House to Waterworks Corner by new route 123 which then continued via Woodford Avenue and Gants Hill to Ilford station, replacing the Monday to Friday peak hour service on route 41 but expanded to a daily operation and providing a substantial increase in the off-peak and weekend service through the area. The 625 was replaced by bus route 275, which continued beyond the old trolleybus route at both ends to run from Woodford Bridge to a rather messy variety of western terminals, Enfield Town during Monday to Friday peaks, Winchmore Hill off-peak and on Saturdays, and Turnpike Lane on Sundays. Between Woodford Bridge and Woodford Green, the 275 ran via St Barnabas Road, Broadmead Road, Fairfield Road and The Terrace, all roads previously unserved. It was also rerouted between Lordship Lane and Wood Green to run via Westbury Avenue, Turnpike Lane station and Wood Green High Road, enabling it to penetrate the shopping centre better and to have common stops in the area with other routes towards Palmers Green and Enfield.

The 697 and 699 were similarly replaced by services, respectively the 249A and 249 which, after covering the old trolleybus routes, continued further. Both were extended beyond Chingford Mount to Chingford 'Royal Forest Hotel' via route 38, replacing the localised service on that route but operating all day and, in the case of the 249, at weekends too. This re-introduced a through service from Chingford to Stratford after a lapse of twenty-five years since the former Independent route 34A (née 511) had been withdrawn. No fewer than three other routes

were enlisted to give further help in replacing these two services. The 34 was extended on Mondays to Saturdays from 'The Crooked Billet' to Leyton Green (and on to Downsell Road in peak hours), restoring the link to and from the North Circular Road which had been extinguished in the early wartime cuts of November 1939. Route 69, which had replaced the 669 trolleybus as recently as February, was extended to Chingford Mount to introduce an entirely new link across Stratford which could just as well have been operated by trolleybuses. The third helper was route 278 which nominally replaced the 687 trolleybus but followed the route through Hoe Street and Leyton High Road, rather than via Higham Hill, Markhouse Road and Church Road. It was also extended from 'The Crooked Billet' to Chingford Mount. The uncovered section of the 687 was replaced in part by route 41 which was withdrawn from Ilford and extended throughout the day on Mondays to Saturdays from Tottenham Hale via Forest Road, Blackhorse Road, Church Road and 'The Thatched House' to Stratford.

As already noted, the intention that route 256 should carry the traffic displaced from the 687 through Higham Hill had been vitiated by its unexpected popularity and it was therefore found necessary at a late stage to add some Monday to Friday peak hour shorts to route 58 between 'The Crooked Billet' and Lea Bridge Road and to restructure the Saturday service on the 256 so that the service between the same points during shopping hours was doubled. The 256 was also withdrawn on Saturdays west of Hackney (Well Street) except during peak hours.

There was also a night service which ran from Chingford Mount to the Docks by the same route as the 249 but separately numbered 299 so that night running times could be applied without violating staff agreements. It had its origins in the peculiarly trolleybus practice of operating staff trolleybuses with a conductor, so that passengers could be carried. They were not advertised but in this case the service was used by enough people to justify its being retained. It ran every night.

Many of the changes in this scheme were dictated not by passenger requirements but by a need to reduce the number of buses terminating at Chingford Mount and 'The Crooked Billet'. The end result was undeniably more complicated than was ideal and included some untidy arrangements of short-workings, some very thin frequencies on the vaunted new links and some seemingly excessive increases in service over some roads. However, matters might have been slightly more complicated had the original plans reached fulfilment. It had been hoped to extend one of the Chingford Mount routes (originally the 278, but later the 69) via Old Church Road, Endlebury Road and Simmons Lane to terminate at Chingford Hatch. Apart from opening up new territory, this was intended to give some relief to route 38 which could not always satisfy the demand from The Ridgeway. The proposal depended crucially on the removal of obstructions in Endlebury Road and the widening of the bridge over the railway in Simmons Lane. A compromise proposal which required only the removal of the obstructions, would have meant buses running in a loop from Endlebury Road via Simmons Lane, Friday Hill, Hatch Lane and Larks Hall Road. Chingford Council was not prepared to help, the proposal had to be dropped and no service has ever operated this loop.

The remarkable turn at Manor House, across six traffic lanes within yards of a major junction, slipped by the Traffic Commissioner and survived to become the western terminus of route 123. RM 147 performs the manoeuvre under the trolleybus wiring provided for its predecessors. Michael Rooum

Routemasters were normally allocated only to former trolleybus depôts, any contribution to the new routes by bus garages being confined to the existing rolling stock. Tottenham contributed to route 123 because it had taken over the eastern end of route 41, whose displaced RTWs it used, RTW 429 being seen here at Manor House about to work through to Ilford. G. Mead

The crisp, if ambiguous, 'Docks' destination carried by the trolleybuses was replaced by the more pedantic 'Royal Victoria Dock' at first but this was later replaced by other more wordy variants. The 'Royal Forest Hotel', Chingford, built in half timbered style in sympathy with the adjacent sixteenth century Queen Elizabeth's Hunting Lodge, forms the familiar background for RM 198 in September 1960. Peter G Mitchell

The theoretical schedules cost of these changes was 104 Routemasters to replace 98 trolleybuses, but on the day of the conversion Forest Gate bus garage closed and its allocations on route 25 (daily) and 40 (Sundays) were transferred to West Ham. (Route 66 went to North Street and the 86 to Upton Park.) Fortuitously, West Ham ran more buses in the morning peak, while Forest Gate had run more in the evening peak and the cross-linkings that were now possible not only reduced the RM schedule for the scheme to one hundred but also allowed the withdrawal of three RTs. The effect was to have official cross-linked allocations of RTs on routes 69 and 249A, the first cases of such mixed allocations on former trolleybus routes in one garage. The alternative of cross-linking RMs onto route 25 was not available because the stand at Victoria was not suitable for eight-foot wide buses. Routes 41 and 123 also had mixed allocations but in these cases it was because they were both operated by two garages. The trolleybus replacement share of the 41 was supplied by Routemasters from West Ham garage, while the greater part of its needs continued to be met by Tottenham with RTWs. A similar mixture of RM and RTW was to be found on the 123 which inherited seven runnings at Tottenham displaced from the 41, additional to its main allocation of RMs from Walthamstow. This arrangement, which had already been applied to route 23 in stage four, broke the policy of standardising on types by route which had been established during the post-war replacement programme, and reverted to an older one of avoiding mixed types in garages. Unfortunately for the engineers, this rule was broken in a big way with the closure of Forest Gate. The basic allocation on all the other new routes was RM, from Walthamstow on routes 249 and 275 and from West Ham on the 249, 249A, 278 and 299, while the extended 34 was given a new allocation at Leyton, using the RTs displaced from the 38.

Most of the RMs licensed for this stage were brand new (numbered between 142 and 310) and included the first of the modified design with opening front windows on the upper deck, the majority of which went to West Ham. Walthamstow had a total of forty-four RMs, of which five had been used in pre-conversion trials, and West Ham took sixty-one, of which seven were relicensed. West Ham also received sixty-eight RTs from Forest Gate to work the 25, making it the second largest garage, just behind New Cross, in terms of buses operated. Strictly speaking West Ham should have had RTLs as it was in a Leyland engineering group and it had been planned to make an exchange with Clapton, which was in an AEC group, but this was deeply unpopular with the drivers at Forest Gate and they were allowed in the end to take their RTs with them. The trolleybuses withdrawn for scrap included the last E2, 622, which had been allowed to survive the rest of the class by three months so that it could take part in the closing ceremony at West Ham, where it had been used in the ceremonial opening of the system twenty-three years earlier. The other classes now officially withdrawn were all at Highgate and Wood Green depôts and comprised the last of

Among the withdrawals in stage six were the three remaining 'B'-suffixed wartime casualties which had been rebodied by East Lancashire Coachbuilders in 1948. No.1543B had been a 'unit construction' M1 class vehicle and had therefore also been equipped with a chassis frame at the same time. There was no wired connection from Holloway Road into Parkhurst Road and trolleybuses running out from Highgate depôt on route 627 towards Tottenham Court Road, or in this case Mornington Crescent, had to go via Camden Road and Warlters Road, where 1543B is seen about to turn left into Parkhurst Road. LTPS

Also withdrawn in April 1960 were the last of the J2s, which had English Electric bodywork mounted on AEC 664T chassis and dated from 1938. Still looking immaculate, 1013 is seen in Maple Street at the Tottenham Court Road terminus of route 653. C. Carter

the Metro-Cammell bodied H1 Leylands, although two were held in reserve as serviceable spares, the Weymann J1 and BRCW bodied J2 AECs, plus twelve of the similar J3s, all dating from 1938. The H and J classes were replaced at Highgate by AEC/MCW L3, AEC/Weymann M1 and AEC/BRCW N2 classes from West Ham, and at Wood Green by K1 and K2 all-Leyland classes from Highgate and Walthamstow. Also withdrawn were the last three which had been rebuilt after being damaged by wartime bombing. All three were from the NCB batch and had lost their bodies when a flying bomb hit West Ham depôt in July 1944 (1385B, 1543B and 1545B).

The seventh stage of the conversion was in two distinct geographical parts, embracing routes 626, 628 and 630 operated by Hammersmith depôt and the 611 at Highgate. Under the criteria used to set the original 1954 staging plan, Hammersmith would have been the last depôt to be converted, in January 1962, leaving the Fulwell and Isleworth routes to continue as trolleybuses. This plan had been designed in fifteen stages starting in the east and moving progressively westward, so that the works at Fulwell would always be accessible and in a sequence which took account as far as possible of the age of the vehicles and costs of electrical distribution. It was not long before this was reconsidered in the light of two fresh yardsticks, the likely effect on the earning capacity of the routes and the extent to which overhead wires could be removed. Another factor peculiar to Hammersmith was the imminent construction of the new flyover, which would have required considerable alterations to the overhead wiring to and from the depôt. For this reason and because of the long sections of route which were operated exclusively by the Hammersmith trolleybuses, the balance was tipped in favour of an earlier conversion. Although route 611 was also shown in the first outline plan in a natural sequence grouped with other Highgate depôt routes, this was altered almost immediately to bring it forward to the fifth stage, which then incorporated routes 557, 623 and 625. This was probably related to another of the original criteria, which required account to be taken of special types of vehicle in certain areas, in this case the trolleybuses specially equipped for working on Highgate Hill. When the later reshuffle of stages took place, the 611 was added to stage seven. This took place on the night of 19th/20th July 1960.

The trolleybus overhead abandoned included the whole of the route from West Croydon to Wandsworth via Mitcham and Tooting; Brook Green Road, Shepherds Bush Road, Wood Lane and Scrubs Lane; Highgate Hill; Canonbury Road; and New North Road between Essex Road and Baring Street. The stretch from Hammersmith to Clapham Junction via Fulham Palace Road, Putney Bridge Road and Wandsworth High Street continued to be used for the time being but only during Monday to Friday peak hours by route 655. This saw the end of electric traction in the area of the last of the old smaller tramway municipalities, Croydon and over the remainder of the old South Metropolitan system from Croydon to Mitcham.

Trolleybus route 611 was replaced by an identical bus service, numbered 271, and the 626/628 by a single route 268 between Clapham Junction and Harlesden with a peak hour extension to Acton (Market Place) which differed only a little from the combined trolleybus routes. The difference was in the terminal arrangements at Harlesden, which was yet another case where the Traffic Commissioner refused approval for buses to use a turning point and stand which had been used by trolleybuses for over twenty years without any apparent trouble. Instead of running to Craven Park, therefore, the replacing buses used the long established stand at the 'Willesden Junction Hotel'.

All-Leyland class K1 1083 is about to turn into Shepherds Bush Green from Wood Lane where traffic is already tailing back as far as the camera can see. The Hillman Minx alongside the trolleybus was one of the popular family saloons which were contributing to the upsurge in traffic causing delays which may possibly explain why 1083 is turning short at Edgarley Terrace, rather than going through to Clapham Junction. D.A. Ruddom Collection

The Metro-Cammell bodied Leyland P1s dated from 1941 and were the last of the pre-war London designs to enter service, 1721 being the very last. In Butterwick on 19th July 1960, the last day of route 630, the conductor of 1721 can be seen about to pull the frog for the depôt wire for its last run-in. Butterwick itself was very new and had yet to be graced by the shelters eventually donated by the Greater London Council. Ken Glazier

The replacement of route 630 was a much more complicated matter. The southern end of the route was already suffering from the effects of serious traffic delays at the northern end and one of the aims of the service plan was to provide a more local service between Tooting and Croydon. This was done by extending route 64 from West Croydon to Wimbledon Stadium, the second time this route had been involved in a conversion. The opportunity was taken to increase the peak service between Addington and West Croydon at the same time. The main replacement for the 630 was a new bus route 220, which was extended from Harrow Road (Scrubs Lane) to Park Royal Stadium during Monday to Friday peak hours to give added support to the already very frequent service on route 12. To obtain an efficient duty schedule, the rest of the service was arranged mainly in two overlapping sections: Harrow Road to Tooting S. R. Station (with a peak hour extension to Mitcham); and Shepherds Bush to West Croydon, although there were occasional through buses. The general level of service was reduced, particularly north of Shepherds Bush where the combined peak hour frequency was almost halved, from twenty-two an hour to twelve. There was some compensation for this over the busiest section by the extension of route 71 from Brook Green to East Acton on Mondays to Saturdays, to provide the direct service to Hammersmith Hospital from the south which already existed on route 72A on Sundays. It was apparently not possible to standardise this operation on route 71 daily within the scheduling agreement. The night service, which had operated from Hammersmith to Tooting Broadway was withdrawn without replacement.

The choice of Wimbledon Stadium, rather than Tooting Broadway, as the northern terminus for route 64 was dictated by the lack of suitable places to turn in the centre of Tooting but it did have two advantages. It increased the overlap with route 220 and provided a partial replacement for the special trolleybuses which had run on Monday, Wednesday and Friday evenings when there was Speedway or dog racing at the stadium.

To build up the service to the required level, the special, unnumbered, bus service which already ran from Wimbledon Station to the stadium was extended to Tooting Broadway. Routes 628 and 630 also served two other stadiums where evening dog racing meetings were held, at Wandsworth and White City. In both cases the demand had been met by the operation of unscheduled extras and this arrangement continued in motor bus days.

Above **The 'Nags Head' Holloway, with the Gaumont cinema in full flower screening 'The League of Gentlemen', a mass of trolleybus overhead and trolleybus 1367 threading its way across the junction with Seven Sisters Road, all redolent of their respective heydays in the 1930s but all now under threat. 1367 was one of the small AEC/MCW chassisless L1 class dating from 1939, which differed from the L2s only in having the coasting and run-back brakes required for Highgate Hill.** C. Carter

Elmers End's short lived allocation of Routemasters was the first case of a former bus garage receiving the class for a full scheduled allocation. RM 283 is in Station Road, West Croydon, on its way to the new regular terminal at Wimbledon Stadium, immortalised in tram and trolleybus days as 'Summerstown'. Pamlin Prints

RM 348 revisits its birthplace, passing the functional and well tended offices of Park Royal Vehicles Ltd on an afternoon peak trip to Park Royal Stadium. In 1960 there were nearly fifty buses an hour on the joint peak hour service with route 12 from Harlesden but within a few years the Ford Prefect will no longer be alone, the neat and tidy appearance of this scene will be destroyed by the plague of parked cars and the bus service will have been halved.
Peter Mitchell

Below **RM 324 on the stand in Letchford Gardens with a group of trolleybuses on route 662, probably working a supplementary service for an event at Wembley stadium.**
F.W. Ivey

It had always been part of the conversion plan that Hammersmith depôt should close and the replacing motor buses housed at Shepherds Bush garage where an embarrassingly large amount of surplus space had existed since it had been rebuilt eight years earlier. This ready availability of an existing garage prompted a proposal in the mid 1950s to replace the Hammersmith trolleybuses with surplus RTs before it became necessary to incur the expense of putting in new and modified wiring for the opening of Butterwick and the construction of the flyover.

Fortunately for the supporters of the trolley-bus, this was found to be the less economic course of action and the routes continued for another five years. By the time the change-over did take place, matters were less straightforward because the British European Airways coaches had been transferred in the meantime from Victoria to Shepherds Bush and the space was no longer available. The depôt was therefore kept open and handed over on a five year lease to BEA as a base for the 4RF4 fleet, for which purpose £39,900 was spent on the modifications needed for an

oil operated fleet. It would be interesting to know whether these costs might have tipped the balance of the equation in favour of retaining Hammersmith as a bus garage had they been known about when the earlier evaluation had taken place.

Shepherds Bush now became the second garage to have a mixed RT family and Routemaster fleet but much more radical at the time was the appearance of RMs at Elmers End for route 64 as this was the first time that a bus garage not otherwise involved with the conversion programme had received a normal scheduled allocation of the class. The sixty-one trolleybuses scheduled for the Hammersmith routes were replaced by an additional peak vehicle requirement of sixty-three buses: fifty-two RMs at Shepherds Bush, seven RMs at Elmers End, two RTs at Croydon and two at Twickenham but at least six of these vehicles could be attributed to the augmentations and extensions not connected with the trolleybuses, so the number of buses used purely for replacement was four fewer than the number of trolleybuses. The peak vehicle requirement at Highgate was fifteen RMs, an increase of one over the trolleybuses. Sixty-nine new RMs were licensed, fifty-three at Shepherds Bush and sixteen at Highgate but the seven for Elmers End were second-hand, having first entered service at West Ham in stage six and later delicensed for one reason or another. No trolleybus class disappeared completely at this time but seventy vehicles were released for disposal from the F1, H1, K1, J2, J3 and P1 classes, either directly from Hammersmith and Highgate or from the cannibalisation and spares floats, which were topped up in turn with other withdrawn J3, K1 and K2 vehicles.

Hanwell was another depôt whose change-over had been brought forward in the programme, from the original penultimate fourteenth stage to stage eight which took place on 9th November 1960, almost certainly because of the substantial lengths of overhead which could be removed. Hanwell was responsible for only two routes, the 607 and 655, but they had little in common with each other and both ran over substantial stretches of road which were not shared with anything else, particularly the 607 which ran right out to the edge of built up London at Uxbridge. The road mileage on which the overhead was abandoned was therefore quite substantial, covering almost the whole length of the Uxbridge Road from Uxbridge to Acton Market Place and from Askew Road to Wood Lane; the stretch along Boston Road and Boston Manor Road; and the section from Hammersmith to Clapham Junction which had seen only peak hour use on Mondays to Fridays since July.

Although three bus routes were created to replace the two trolleybus services, there were fewer complications than in some earlier stages. Routes 207 and 255 were identical replacements for the 607 and 655, except that the service to Acton Vale on route 255 ran all day on Mondays to Fridays and the service between Brentford and Hammersmith was withdrawn in the evenings and on Sundays. The third route, numbered 207A, was based on some of the Shepherds Bush to Hayes End 'shorts' being diverted at 'The Grapes' to Hayes Station and, at the other end, extended from Shepherds Bush to Chelsea ('Stanley Arms') via route 49 and Kings Road. The Hayes service, which ran all day on Mondays to Saturdays, restored the connection from Ealing and Hanwell which had disappeared when route 83 was curtailed in the November 1958 post-strike cuts but it also replaced the peak hour extension of route 120, which was cut back to Delamere Road. At the eastern end it was an entirely additional service designed to give relief to the heavily used route 49, while also giving new links across Shepherds Bush. It did not run on Sundays, nor did it run between Shepherds Bush and Chelsea on Saturday evenings. There could have been further complications because the Working Party was asked to look at two other ideas: the possibility of using route 255 to give a new link from Hammersmith to Wimbledon; and to find some way of relieving the western end of route 7, perhaps by extending some shortworkings, possibly off route 207, from Acton to Paddington. The former fell because the service to Clapham Junction had to be maintained and the latter because no workable method could be found.

This pleasant sunny autumn scene at Hayes End was enacted on the last Sunday of operation for the Hanwell trolleybus routes, 6th November 1960. As yet, Q1 class 1766 was still expecting a secure future in London but the sale of the class was announced soon afterwards and their withdrawal from Hanwell proved to be the beginning of the end. *Ken Glazier*

The class associated most closely with Hanwell was the all-Leyland F1, built in 1937 and capable of notching up a lively performance on the long straight run out to Uxbridge on the 607. Their other main stamping ground was the 655, on which 695 is seen at the Hammersmith Grove terminus on 6th November. *Ken Glazier*

Route 207 continued to use the trolleybus turning circle at Frays River bridge, where RM 537 advertises the exciting innovation of non-stop flights to north America.
Malcolm E. Papes

There were again some substantial cuts in frequency and, although Hanwell's peak vehicle requirement for buses remained the same as for trolleybuses, at ninety-two, there was also a saving of one bus on the 120 at Southall and at least six of the scheduled buses were required not for trolleybus replacement but for the extensions on route 207A. Ninety-five new RMs were licensed at Hanwell and an identical number of trolleybuses was withdrawn, including the last of the all-Leyland F1 class, long associated with Hanwell. Apart from five K1s and three K2s, the most significant other withdrawal was of twenty of the post-war Q1 class whose early demise had become inevitable when the Executive announced the abandonment of the Fulwell and Isleworth services earlier in the year.

The fate of the Q1s was settled soon afterwards when a visiting team of buyers from Spain offered London Transport an attractive price for 125 of them. They wanted them quickly, so the Executive decided to withdraw the remainder prematurely and replace them with older vehicles displaced from abandoned routes. The sale became public knowledge once the Trade Union had been notified on 22nd December and the first steps were taken on 1st January 1961, when sixteen of the 1952 batch were delicensed and replaced by a similar number from the first batch. Between then and 10th January the first twenty, comprising the odd numbered vehicles between 1843 and 1883 except for 1867, were sent to Poplar garage to be prepared for shipment. This sale was completed on 20th January and was followed by two further batches of thirty each on 13th and 16th February, followed by further batches until the final sale was secured on 16th November. The vehicles were not sold directly to the companies which eventually operated them and there was a complicated series of exchanges between the official buyers and the final recipients. The two which escaped this fate were 1768, which was donated to the British Transport Museum on 31st May, and 1841, whose body shell was sold to George Cohen & Co. for breaking up but whose traction motor and gear went to Imperial College Museum.

Top **Hemmed in by its various competitors, notably the almost exclusively British built private cars, Hanwell's RM 502 waits to cross the junction at Kew Bridge. The wires are still up for pioneering routes 657 and 667, including the terminal loop curving to the left and the fog lights strung alongside the main running wires.** A.B. Cross

Centre **Route 120 was cut back to Delamere Road, giving way to the new 207A on the section to Hayes but this arrangement was also to have a short life, the northern terminus becoming Southall Town Hall in May 1963. RT 4590, still with a Park Royal body although not its original, is at Hounslow Central station.** Ken Glazier

Right **Withdrawal of the Q1s began in November 1960, confirmation of their early demise was announced in December and all had gone by the following February. Isleworth's 1866, seen here passing London Transport's Chiswick Works was uniquely fitted with one of the old silk screen printed linen number blinds manufactured at Charlton.** EATG

Between stages eight and nine the winter schedules, which came into operation on 12th October, included an important change which was directly connected with the conversion, although somewhat removed from it. All night services numbered between 284 and 299 were renumbered by the expedient of replacing the initial '2' by an 'N'. This was done expressly to release more numbers for use on new routes replacing trolleybuses. It is a pity that it could not have happened in time for the numbers 285, 287, and so on, to be used as more helpful replacements for 685, 687 etc.

The ninth stage of the conversion, which took place on 1st February 1961 again involved only one depôt but was substantially larger and more complicated. This was the second conversion at Highgate, the second largest trolleybus depôt, and covered routes 513/613, 517/617, 615, 639 and 653, leaving only a small allocation on route 627 for a few more months. Trolleybuses were removed from 12.6 miles of road, comprising: the whole of the old Hampstead network from Hampstead Heath to Kings Cross via Prince of Wales Road and Royal College Street; from Prince of Wales Road to Camden Town via Malden Road and Chalk Farm; the whole of Crowndale Road; from Parliament Hill Fields to North West Polytechnic via Highgate Road and Kentish Town; from Pentonville Road between Kings Cross Road and the Angel, Islington; and the depôt link from Kentish Town to Highgate depôt via Fortess Road, Junction Road and Monnery Road. The wiring abandoned by the 653 covered the section from Aldgate to Amhurst Park via Mile End Gate, Hackney and Stamford Hill, bringing an end to trolleybus operation at Aldgate Lay-By and to any significant electric traction in the East End, as only route 647 was left to make its brief encounter en route to London Docks.

Trolleybuses leaving Charterhouse Street circled the statue of Prince Albert at Holborn Circus before speeding through High Holborn to reach Grays Inn Road. Trolleybus 1030 was the first of twenty-five J3 class vehicles built in 1938, identical in most respects to the J2s but equipped with run-back and coasting brakes for running on Highgate Hill. The standard London seventy-seat bodywork was supplied by English Electric on AEC 664T chassis. D.A. Ruddom Collection

Routes 615, 639 and 653 were replaced by bus routes 214, 239 and 253 running between the same terminals in each case but the Holborn loop services were covered in a more elaborate way. Ever since the City of London Corporation had placed an embargo on the operation of trams within its boundaries, there had been a desire to forge a link between the northern and southern systems at this point but fulfilment of the wish had eluded the tramway authorities and London Transport until now when the change to oil-engined operation eliminated the objection. The loop working at Holborn was a compromise which had been enforced by these restrictions and had never been a particularly desirable arrangement. It was now broken and parts of the former trolleybus routes were joined to bus services from south London. Bus route 45, which had itself replaced tram route 34 just over ten years earlier, was extended from Farringdon Street via Grays Inn Road, Kings Cross, Royal College Street and Prince of Wales Road to Hampstead Heath, replacing that side of the 513/613; and the 63 picked up the Farringdon Road side of the loop and was extended to Parliament Hill Fields via Royal College Street and Kentish Town. The night service on route 513 was covered by a new route N93, which ran both ways via Farringdon Road and had a few journeys extended to Trafalgar Square.

George Cohen scrapped trolleybuses, Max Cohen Ltd were suppliers of bespoke gentlemen's suiting in an age when Aldgate was still at the heart of a thriving retail community, before the encroachment of modern developments already apparent in the background turned it into more of a wilderness. Stage nine of the conversion put an end to trolleybus operation from the extravagantly named Aldgate 'Trolleybus and Green Line Coach Station', which J2 class 989 is about to leave. RTL 767, on the left of the picture was typical of the rolling stock supplied by Camberwell for route 42. C. Carter

AEC/Weymann M1 class number 1540 threads its way through the mass of railway bridges and other railway paraphernalia in Pancras Road approaching King's Cross. LTPS

All-Leyland K2 class 1335 heads off along Holborn, where trolleybuses were not welcome in the eyes of the City Corporation and were not allowed to stop. D.A. Ruddom Collection

The Grays Inn Road routeing of the 517/617 was replaced by a new route 17, which continued beyond Holborn via bus route 45 to Camberwell Green, and the Farringdon Road service by an extension of route 143 from Archway to Farringdon Street. There was a small increase in the frequency of the main trunk of route 253 from Mile End Gate to Finsbury Park but otherwise the frequencies of the replacement bus routes were all less than the trolleybuses, the severest example being between North Finchley and Archway where the service was halved. However, the service between Camden Town and Parliament Hill Fields was built up to its former level by the extension of route 39 which was another example of a through connection being restored which had been lost in the 1958 cuts. Neither routes 39 nor 143 operated on Sundays, the latter being covered by route 133 which ran right through to Hendon Central from South Croydon. Once again, no attempt seems to have been made to tidy up this non-standard Sunday operation, probably because scheduling efficiency ruled supreme. The only other weekend variation was on route 17, which did not run to Camberwell Green, the southern terminals being Farringdon Street on Saturdays and Kings Cross on Sundays.

All the new routes were allocated to Highgate and were operated by new RMs. Six of the thirty-nine runnings on route 63 also went into Highgate, as did the whole of the revised 143, which thereby became the first route to change completely from RT to RM. The gap created in Holloway's workload was filled by route 39 which was transferred in from Chalk Farm and took over the RTs relinquished by the 143, making a mixed allocation with Battersea's RTWs. The circle

This scene at the Wellington Hospital Archway Road, with not a moving vehicle in sight except for RT 342 on the Sunday only 134A and RM 583 on the new 17, could be witnessed for less than three months between the introduction of route 17 in February and the final loss of Highgate's trolleybuses in April 1961. Trolleybus 1581, an N1 class Birmingham Railway Carriage and Wagon Company bodied AEC, is one of Highgate's Sunday only contingent on the 609 but the crew has had to dip the poles and abandon the vehicle, perhaps because the limited number of trolleybus drivers by now employed at Highgate has put a strain on their availability.

The 639 trolleybus was replaced directly by bus route 239, on which Highgate's RM 609 is seen leaving Finsbury Square surrounded by 1960-style peak hour traffic. F.W. Ivey

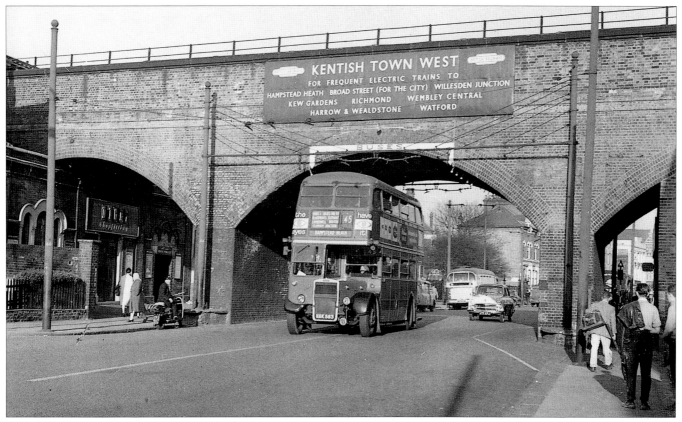

The driver of RTW 83 on newly extended route 45 takes care to position his bus accurately to follow the guidelines painted on the arch of Kentish Town West station bridge, following the traction wires which are still in place. F.W. Ivey

One of the new links forged in February 1961 was supplied by route 63 which was extended beyond King's Cross over the 513/613. The usual southern limit of journeys from Parliament Hill Fields was Honor Oak, where RT 2087 is seen sitting alongside the neatly trimmed foliage of Camberwell Cemetery, perhaps a premature destination for some of those who respond to the Player's cigarette advertisement on the side. Ken Glazier

was completed by route 45 whose new northern base was at Chalk Farm, closer to its line of route than Highgate. It too got no RMs but took over the RTWs left behind by route 39. An extra 111 buses was needed, made up of 114 additional RMs and three fewer RTWs, for which 117 RMs, with numbers ranging from 393 to 631, were licensed at Highgate.

The peak trolleybus requirement was reduced by 107 and a like number of vehicles was withdrawn. Trolleybuses sent for scrap included the last two H1s, which had been in use as spares at Stamford Hill and Wood Green, the last two J3s and the remaining twelve L1s. Small numbers of K1, K2, L3 and M1 also went for disposal but the majority of vehicles taken out of the fleet were Q1s, a further sixty-five of which were delicensed ready for shipment to Spain. They were replaced by sixty-four L3s, all of which went from Highgate to Fulwell, twenty-two of Fulwell's Q1s being transferred to Isleworth.

The operation of the new services was disrupted by cuts in service caused by staff shortage and on some routes this was exacerbated by the effects of traffic congestion. This bore particularly harshly on the wide headway sections where even the scheduled frequencies were inferior to those operated previously. On route 45 for example, late running buses in the early evening were often curtailed short of Hampstead Heath, which had only a twenty minute service at the best of times. At least at first, the new through links were not used by many passengers, leading some to question the wisdom of creating several long straggly routes. Finally, despite the heavy cuts in service between North Finchley and Archway, this stretch was still found to be badly over-bussed.

As first planned, stage ten, which took place on 26th April 1961, would have covered routes 627, 659 and 679 to complete the conversion of Holloway depôt and make a start on Edmonton but the Trolleybus Conversion Main Committee decided in October 1960 to expand its content to include route 629. This came about because the London Traffic Management Unit had devised one of its monumental one-way traffic schemes for Tottenham Court Road but could not introduce it while there were still trolleybuses at the northern end. Although the LTMU wanted an earlier date, London Transport agreed to compromise by bringing forward route 629 to coincide with the abandonment of route 627 so that the new road scheme could be introduced on 1st May. This also added Wood Green depôt, which had to be made ready for motor buses three months earlier than planned. All this was at some cost to London Transport because the separation of the jointly compiled schedules at Wood Green caused a serious loss of efficiency on the remaining 641 duty schedule which could not be rectified until November. Also, the added workload on the schedules office was accepted only on the basis that route 629 was given a straight conversion with no added complications of integration with other routes. The opportunity was therefore lost, at this time, of integrating the 629 with the closely associated bus route 29.

Above **Weymann supplied the bodywork for the N1 class AEC 664Ts which were new in 1938 and spent most of their twenty-two years at Finchley depôt. Near the end of its life 912 found itself at Wood Green and is here on the Tottenham Court Road terminal loop of route 629, about to turn from Fitzroy Street into Maple Street.** A.B. Cross

Left **RM 643 crosses Euston Road from Hampstead Road to Tottenham Court Road during the five days between the conversion and the imposition of one-way working. Behind the 269 is a 127 going through to Victoria and alongside is a 137 turning into Euston Road.**
Peter G Mitchell

Only 9.1 miles of overhead was abandoned at this stage, despite the substantial size of the routes involved, because most of the roads they used were served by other routes which were still operating. Electric traction disappeared from the section between Enfield and Winchmore Hill, from Seven Sisters Corner to Manor House, from 'The Nags Head' Holloway to Tottenham Court Road, from Pemberton Gardens (the depôt connection from Holloway Road) and between the Angel and Smithfield via St John Street. This last closure reduced the once busy five-way junction at the Angel to a single through route, the 609.

The Edmonton and Tottenham areas had been starved of direct transport to the West End for over twenty years and the Victoria Line was still only a distant dream, so one of the specialities of the scheme was to remedy the deficiency. Route 127, which covered trolleybus route 627 from Waltham Cross to Tottenham Court Road, was extended to Victoria via Charing Cross and Whitehall. It was also given a Sunday service for the first time, between Lower Edmonton Station and Victoria. Unfortunately, the consequence was a severe attenuation of route 29 south of Turnpike Lane, which left it with some very thin frequencies at off-peak times. At Victoria, eight foot wide buses could not be fitted into the bays at the bus station, so the terminal for route 127 was in the sidecourt of the garage in Wilton Road to which route 29 was also diverted so that the two routes could have a common picking up point at the station.

Wartime bomb damage and a British Road Services meat haulage lorry are both signs of the times at the Smithfield terminus of route 679 in St John Street on 30th March 1961. Trolleybus 1237 was one of the 150 all-Leyland K2 class vehicles, new in 1938, which differed from the K1 class in having English Electric rather than Metrovick controllers. Ken Glazier

The other new link had only the barest of common ground with trolleybuses and was a puny and very untidy affair. Route 276 ran nominally from Tottenham Garage to Brixton Garage, via route 627 to Camden Town then Albany Street, Regent Street, Whitehall, Westminster Bridge, Albert Embankment, Vauxhall, Oval and Brixton, but it covered these extremities only during Monday to Friday peak hours. Between the peaks it ran no further north than Finsbury Park, during Monday to Friday evenings and Saturday mid-mornings it ran only from Charing Cross to Finsbury Park and during the 'peaks' on Saturdays it ran Charing Cross to Tottenham. There was no service on Sundays nor after 2pm on Saturdays. This patchwork quilt of a service was also blessed with unattractive headways varying between fifteen and seventeen minutes at most times, improving to a mere twelve minutes in Monday to Friday peaks, which were hardly likely to attract new trade to the multitude of new links which were unique to it. It was probably doomed from the outset to wither and die, which is precisely what it did within a matter of just over two years. Ironically, route 276 achieved fame well beyond its status by being the first home of 'Silver Lady' RM 664.

The 629 and 679 were each superseded by more or less identical bus routes, numbered 269 and 279 respectively, but part of the service north of Tottenham was localised into a new route 279A running between Tottenham Hale and Flamstead End. This co-incidentally replaced the few trolleybus journeys which had run to Tottenham Hale and also provided additional capacity between Waltham Cross and Flamstead End, an area where the population was increasing and the additional passenger traffic was already putting a strain on route 205. The 279A did not run at weekends but was covered by a section of route 279 starting at Tottenham garage on Saturdays. Route 659 became bus route 259, still operating the Holborn loop in one direction only, but this did not run between Edmonton (Tramway Avenue) and Waltham Cross on Mondays to Fridays.

The peak trolleybus requirement of 138 was exchanged for one of 141 buses (144 RM minus 3 RTL) which included the extra buses needed for the three extensions beyond the trolleybus sphere of operation and therefore represented another substantial cut in both capacity and frequencies. This was particularly marked along Hertford Road, where there had been a loss of passengers to the newly electrified suburban railway services from Liverpool Street to Enfield, Hertford East and Bishops Stortford. The cuts were at their heaviest north of Edmonton, where the peak service to Ponders End was more than halved from thirty-nine to eighteen buses an hour, a capacity reduction of no less than fifty-nine per cent, yet when the operation was reviewed, it was still considered to be overbussed.

There were some unusually interesting allocations, the most extraordinary probably being the temporary move of part of route 253 from Highgate to Edmonton which was tied up with a review of surplus garage capacity. Stamford Hill was an underused site with a schedule of only forty-eight trolleybuses which had been identified as a candidate for complete or partial closure but its position in the network was ideal for efficient scheduling and it therefore earned a reprieve. Instead, it was decided to close part of the less well sited Edmonton and either lease it or use it for storage; it was eventually used to store tunnel iron for the Victoria Line. The designated home for these 253s was Stamford Hill but that would not be ready for motor buses until July, hence this temporary arrangement which in the event continued until 11th October, the official date for the closure of part of Edmonton. This operation gives an interesting insight into the defensive processes of decision making by London Transport at that time. It had been the intention that these garage journeys should run in service in the usual way but the Operating Manager thought that this might encourage people to use the through link to Hackney, which had been lost at the beginning of the Second World War, and feared that there would be strong criticism when it was withdrawn. They therefore ran 'dead' and attracted criticism for that reason instead. Nobody seems to have followed up the possibility that a permanent through link might have been worthwhile.

The 253 saga is put in an even more curious light by the fact that route 259, which terminated at or passed by Edmonton garage, was now shared by Highgate and Wood Green whereas the 659 had been an Edmonton route. The Wood Green allocation was another temporary arrangement caused by the separation of routes 629 and 641 in the conversion programme. Route 629 needed more trolleybuses on Saturdays than on Mondays to Fridays and this was helpfully balanced by the lesser needs of the 641. To bridge the gap until stage twelve in November, the 259 was called to the rescue. The 269 gave another twist to this strange set-up by having a small allocation of RMs at West Green, to balance the loss of the 29s. The 276 became the responsibility of Highgate and the 279/279A stayed in their ancestral home at Edmonton.

There was one final quirk in this stage, which would not have seemed odd anywhere outside London but which was a major breakthrough in the capital where mixed operation of any kind was anathema to the workforce. Trolleybus route 609, which was otherwise worked by Finchley depôt, had a Sunday allocation from Highgate which could clearly not continue in that form. To avoid complications in other depôts, the Highgate allocation was retained on route 609, using Routemasters, for the intervening period until stage twelve in November. This was the first and only time when motor buses working on an official schedule carried a trolleybus route number and worked alongside trolleybuses on the same route.

The imposition of route 629 made this by far the largest stage which also encompassed an unprecedented number of garages. No fewer than 147 Routemasters were licensed, seventy-three at Edmonton, twenty-three at Highgate, forty-six at Wood Green and five at West Green. Altogether 120 trolleybuses were withdrawn for disposal, the most noteworthy being the last thirty-seven of the post-war Q1s, which ran for the last time on 25th April. By that time only eleven were left at Fulwell, and these were replaced by an equal number of L3s transferred from Finchley, where their place was taken by eight M1s, an N1 and three N2s from Highgate. By contrast, at Isleworth the entire contingent of twenty-six had remained intact until the end and their substitutes were K1s released directly from Wood Green. The other eighty-three withdrawals went for scrap, and were taken from seven classes: K1, K2, L2 (including prototype 954), K3, M1, N1 and P1. Thirteen other displaced K1s, K2s and N1s were transferred into the spares float. This brought to an end the operation of the handsome Leyland/MCW P1s, which had been the last of the pre-war standard classes, actually delivered in 1941. From among all these, K2 1253 and Q1 1768 were set aside for the Transport Museum.

Apart from the Q1s, another casualty of stage ten was the stylish Metro-Cammell bodied Leyland P1 class, dating from 1941. The driver of 1697 is preparing to give a hand signal to turn across Eleanor Cross Road to the turning circle on the south side, once RT 1147 is safely past. The complete absence of other traffic is notable. LTPS

The few scheduled trolleybus journeys to Tottenham Hale were rather extravagantly replaced by a whole new route 279A, although this did also act as a localised operation and included an extension to Flamstead End. RM 720 at the Tottenham Hale end of the route in July 1961. Peter G Mitchell

A quirky allocation in stage nine was of some 259s to Wood Green garage, represented here by RM 658 in Grays Inn Road. Malcolm E. Papes

Left The 'silver lady' RM 664 was used on route 127 on Sundays when route 276 did not run, and is seen here in October 1961 already showing signs of discoloration on the roof, parked outside Highgate garage under the now disused wires. Ken Blacker

Below The operation of motor buses on trolleybus routes, other than in dire emergency, was unheard of in London but became unavoidable for the six months between stages ten and twelve, when Highgate had no trolleybuses to fulfil its Sunday commitments on route 609. Routemasters were operated on the trolleybus schedule, mingling with electrics from Finchley, with correctly printed blinds whose clarity proved that the 600 series numbers could as well have been retained for the motor bus routes. Finchley's N1 class 1538 is seen on route 609 at Moorgate passing Highgate's RM 581 on the same route. Fred Ivey

Redvers Road, Wood Green was the northern terminus of routes 543/643 which were directly replaced by bus route 243 on 19th July 1961. K2 class trolleybus 1217 was typical of Stamford Hill's highly standardised fleet of Leylands, all dating from 1938 or 1939, although it did not survive until the closure of the Kingsland Road routes, being withdrawn in April 1960. K. Glazier collection

Below The backdrop of Edwardian shops at Stamford Hill featured in many a historic tram and trolleybus picture but was about to be abandoned by the buses which preferred the sanctuary of the garage in Egerton Road. Trolleybus 1111, a K1 which was the other main class at Stamford Hill, has moved onto the terminal wire and the crew rest awhile before moving it across the Broadway to start their next journey to London Docks. Ken Glazier

The remainder of Edmonton and Stamford Hill's trolleybus routes, the 543/643, 647 and 649, were contained in the eleventh stage which took place on 19th July. Trolleybus overhead was abandoned on 18 miles of route covering the whole of the important north-south corridor from Waltham Cross to Liverpool Street, together with its surviving branches: from Wood Green to Tottenham via Lordship Lane, from Shoreditch Church to Holborn Hall via Clerkenwell and from Shoreditch Church to London Docks. This cleared away the last tiny scrap of operation in the East End, on route 647, and all remaining trolleybuses east of the line from Winchmore Hill to Moorgate.

The substitute for routes 543/643 was bus route 243, which ran between the same terminals but ran only anti-clockwise on the Holborn loop so that the whole service could be concentrated on the same stops. The night service became the N83, which was diverted at Clerkenwell Green and extended via Farringdon Street, Fleet Street and Strand to Charing Cross. Unusually, this had a Saturday night/Sunday morning service because there had been a few early Sunday morning 543s which had been covered by duties working on other routes later in the day. This was not allowed on buses under the Agreement with the Trade Union and could therefore be covered only by allocating a full duty to it. The main replacements for the other routes were both given extensions beyond the wires and all three were supported by the extension of an existing route. The 647 became bus route 67 which continued beyond Stamford Hill through Tottenham, where it branched off into previously uncharted territory along Lansdowne Road to meet route 233 head on at Northumberland Park station. At London Docks, the Traffic

Commissioner would no longer tolerate the turning arrangements, which involved a turn against the flow across The Highway, now a one-way street, and the route had to be curtailed at Cable Street. There was no Sunday service; instead, a new route 243A was invented which combined the Wood Green to Shoreditch part of Sunday only route 649A with the London Docks branch, yet another example of a weekend variation which might have been avoided had the weekday service been treated more radically.

When route 679 was running, the overhead wiring in this section of Holloway Road included a frog to enable it to turn right at the 'Nags Head' junction but once it was withdrawn all right turning trolleybuses came from Caledonian Road so it was possible to give them their own wire and simplify the special work to form a simple crossover as shown here. 1513 was one of the L3s released from Poplar and West Ham in November 1959, which replaced older vehicles at Finchley. D.A. Ruddom Collection

Below **RM 808 on the Wood Green to Bruce Grove branch of the Hertford Road route network a year after trolleybuses came off.** Peter G Mitchell

The direct replacement for the 649 was bus route 149. This already long route was given a surprisingly long roundabout extension on Mondays to Fridays (until the end of the evening peak) via Bank, Southwark Bridge, Stamford Street, Waterloo and Westminster to Victoria to serve the rapidly expanding office population along the south bank of the Thames. It was not really an extension at all but a separate route running from Stamford Hill to Victoria and numbered 149 in the interests of schedule efficiency, the idea of a crew working on two routes in the course of a duty being the last word in abomination to a London bus driver or conductor, despite the fact that they had managed to carry out such duties on the trolleybuses without being struck down.

As was now becoming the rule, the general level of service was lower than on the former trolleybus routes but the service over the busiest section was built up by the extension of route 47 from Shoreditch to Stoke Newington. Although this gave some helpful new connections from south-east London to Kingsland High Road and Dalston, the main reason for the change was to reduce the number of buses terminating at Shoreditch and Liverpool Street, where more stringent conditions were imposed by the Commissioner than had applied in trolleybus days. This whole corridor had suffered the most direct competition from the new electric suburban rail services and this was reflected in the new level of service which averaged something like nine per cent less than the trolleybuses but the service north of Tottenham was given a particularly severe caning with a cut of nearly fifty per cent as far as Edmonton and twenty-five per cent from there to Waltham Cross, adding to the severe cuts already imposed on the joint service.

The peak schedule of eighty-eight trolleybuses was replaced by an additional ninety-three buses, ninety Routemasters and three RTs. Of these, about nine were needed to cover the extensions of routes 67 and 149 and were not directly involved in replacing trolleybuses. Edmonton was allotted a further thirty-eight RMs and Stamford Hill's first motor buses were fifty-five of the same class, all brand new with numbers stretching way up to 861. The three extra RTs went to Catford for route 47. Trolleybuses withdrawn for scrap included the last eighteen of the all-Leyland K3 class, the penultimate pre-war design which had entered service for the first time in the autumn of 1940. The other sixty-seven were also all-Leyland machines, the earlier K1 and K2 classes.

Stage twelve, on 8th November 1961, completed the change-over at Wood Green and marked the first stage of conversion for Finchley. Under the original plans stage thirteen would have been another very large conversion requiring 146 buses, whereas the early conversion of route 629 had left stage twelve much smaller than average. To even these up, route 609 was added to routes 521/621 and 641, enabling 27.1 miles of overhead to be abandoned, the largest in any stage so far. The sections abandoned comprised: the whole of route 641 from Winchmore Hill to Moorgate via Green Lanes, Newington Green and Hoxton; from North Finchley to Old Street via East Finchley, Archway, Holloway, Islington and City Road; from North Finchley to Wood Green via New Southgate and Bounds Green; and from Manor House to the Holborn loop via Holloway, Caledonian Road and Kings Cross. Electric traction now ceased on the remaining sections of what had been the LCC tramway network, the nearest trolleybuses to central London now being the Harrow Road route at Paddington Green with no trolleybuses east of a line from Barnet to Childs Hill.

The service scheme was one of the most involved so far, with no fewer than eight bus routes taking part in the replacement of the three-and-a-bit trolleybus routes. Routes 521/621 were covered by a new 221 but the Holborn loop was abandoned and the new route ran via Farringdon Road to terminate at Farringdon Street. The Grays Inn Road side of the loop was served by an extension of route 168, a former tram route, from Farringdon Street to Turnpike Lane station running, like the rest of the route, on Mondays to Saturdays only. There was no through service, buses to Turnpike Lane normally starting at Clapham Junction, while those from the southern terminus at Putney Heath did not normally run beyond Farringdon Street. The Saturday afternoon and evening service via Grays Inn Road and Sunday service around the Holborn loop were withdrawn and the southern terminal of route 221 was Kings Cross at those times. The substitute for route 609 was an identical 104 but with a generally less frequent service, particularly during the peak and evenings when it was slashed to half its former level. This was compensated south of Highgate by additional buses on route 43 on which an evening service was also introduced between Moorgate and Muswell Hill (Hampden Road) for the first time since 1939.

The replacement of route 641 involved a miniature scheme of its own. New bus route 141 covered the whole of the 641 but then continued on Mondays to Fridays beyond Moorgate to serve the recently opened London Wall and its skyscraper offices and flats. After London Wall, it continued on a huge extension into the depths of south London at Grove Park, via route 179, yet another former tram route. There was no through service, however, as the Grove Park service ran only to Turnpike Lane. At this point the scheme got entangled with one of the failures from an earlier conversion, the grossly uneconomic route 48, which only a year earlier had been introduced with a great fanfare as one of the juicier fruits of the conversion. The northern

A K1 and a K2, 1116 and 1251 sweep around the turning circle at the junction of Green Lanes and Green Dragon Lane, a movement which was deemed unsuitable for motor buses at first. Until the previous April, when route 629 was withdrawn, there was a junction at this point with wiring heading off to the right for Enfield.
Ken Glazier

The number 179 disappeared for a while with the extension of route 141 to Grove Park, which is where RT 4373 was photographed the previous year.
Ken Glazier

Below With so many Routemasters running far into south London on route 141, it was necessary to seek help from RTLs to cover part of trolleybus routes 521/621, on an extension of route 168. Camberwell garage, which supplied RTL 1469, participated in operating route 168 only on Saturdays at this time. P.J. Relf

end of route 179 from Finsbury Park to St Pauls was renumbered 4A and extended via Fleet Street and Aldwych to Waterloo, replacing the busiest part of the 48 which was in turn cut back to Aldgate to run on a reduced frequency from there to North Woolwich.

During peak hours the frequency of route 269 between Turnpike Lane and Winchmore Hill was also increased. At weekends, the 141 ran only between Winchmore Hill and Moorgate and the 179 continued to run but, quite unnecessarily, renumbered 141A.

These complications were another manifestation of the problems created by the loss of joint compilation of duties, which was allowed for and widely practised under the trolleybus scheduling agreement but which was effectively banned under the Central Bus agreement (although small pockets existed at such garages as Barking, Kingston, Merton, Seven Kings, Tottenham and Upton Park). The long extension of the 141 and the involvement of route 168 were both devices to create routes of a length and complexity which would enable efficient schedules to be compiled, rather than to meet the needs of passengers, and they were to store up operational trouble in later years when traffic congestion and staff shortages played havoc with their regularity and reliability.

Ninety-four scheduled trolleybuses were replaced by ninety buses and the resulting allocations involved a few convolutions of their own. Holloway took responsibility for route 4A and also got an allocation on the extended 168. To make room, eight runnings on the 134 were re-allocated to Muswell Hill and the seven 171s were removed altogether in a messy two-way re-allocation, four to Tottenham and three to West Green, which also meant a conversion from RT to RTL. At the latter it replaced the small allocation on route 269 which went into its natural home at Wood Green, bringing to an end the short-lived operation of RMs at Willow Walk. The increase of work at Muswell Hill, which included the extra buses on route 43, was balanced by transferring the whole of route 125 to Finchley, together with its RTs. Finchley also retained responsibility for the whole of routes 104 and 221 and Wood Green took just over half the 141s, the remainder being at New Cross where it had a larger allocation than the 179.

The big event in this stage was the introduction into service of the first thirty-foot Routemasters, after a troubled negotiation the story of which can be found in chapter nine. They went onto route 104 which needed nineteen, but only fifteen were available on the starting day and the rest had to be made up with standard RMs. The required allocation was not completed until January 1962. Eighty-four standard RMs were licensed altogether, twenty-five to Finchley, which became the only garage/depôt to operate RM, RML and RT as well as trolleybuses, twenty-two to New Cross, and thirty-seven to Wood Green. Most of Finchley's RTs came from New Cross, which was also the source for some of those needed at Holloway and Muswell Hill. Among the ninety-one trolleybuses withdrawn from service were the last remaining examples of the K1, L2 and M1 classes, the others being K1, L3 and N2. Thirteen were held in reserve, the remainder going for scrap.

Another landmark associated with this stage was the appearance of lower case lettering on intermediate point blinds. This followed extensive tests which had proved to the satisfaction of the Executive that there was no loss of legibility. The greater variety of shapes was supposed to make it easier to distinguish between letters but the change was more likely to have been in response to design fashion at the time. Destination blinds remained wholly in upper case 'for greater emphasis'. The new displays appeared on all routes involved in this stage, including those operating RTs and RTLs. The style eventually caught on throughout the industry and is now almost universal.

Route 141 forged a link through London Wall to serve the still unfinished Barbican development on its long north–south trek. RM 909 is seen in the bleak new surroundings in the early days of the service. Sport & General

The penultimate trolleybus abandonment saw the completion of Finchley and the total changeover of Stonebridge but the third depôt, Colindale, was destined never to operate an oiler, as it ceased to be an operational base with the withdrawal of the trolleybuses. The conversion took place on the night of 2nd/3rd January 1962 in such severe weather conditions that the superstitious probably thought it was well identified as stage thirteen. It embraced the whole of what remained of the former Metropolitan Electric Tramways network and a small part of the London United system, comprising the North West London group of routes (645, 660, 666) and the main line route 662 along Harrow Road. These had almost no common running with any remaining routes so that the length of road on which the overhead equipment was abandoned was again considerable, at 29.37 miles. This spanned the entire stretch from Barnet to Dalling Road, Hammersmith via Finchley, Golders Green, Cricklewood, Harlesden, Willesden, Acton and Askew Road; from Cricklewood to Stanmore Circus via West Hendon, Colindale and Edgware; from Paddington Green to Harlesden via Harrow Road; and from Craven Park to Sudbury via Wembley. Heavy snow and freezing conditions made the last hours of trolleybus operation a hazardous and uncomfortable experience and despite everybody's hard work, the service was in a pretty frayed state for most of the evening. Against these odds, all the necessary vehicle transfers were completed in time for the new services to start on the morning of 3rd January.

This was another complicated scheme because the North West Group was a tightly interworked network which relied for its efficiency on the total integration of its duty schedules. All this had to be unravelled to conform with the requirements of the Central Bus Agreement and, to help with the task, four existing routes were recruited to share the burden with five new routes. Starting with the latter, new route 245 covered most of the 645, from North Finchley to Canons Park with a short extension to Stanmore station, leaving the Barnet end to be covered by another new route 260. This replaced the 660 from Hammersmith to North Finchley and then continued to Barnet over route 645 but the simple service structure of the trolleybus route was seriously disrupted. There was no service between Harlesden and Hammersmith on Sundays or outside peak hours on Mondays to Fridays and no through service on Mondays to Saturdays. To complicate matters further, there were different overlapping patterns on Mondays to Fridays and Saturdays. On Mondays to Fridays buses ran from Barnet to Willesden garage (Acton Vale, peaks) and North Finchley to Willesden Junction (Hammersmith, peaks) but on Saturdays they ran Barnet to Willesden Junction and Golders Green to Hammersmith. The 666 had a straight replacement, route 266 but with its Edgware terminal at the station, which some might feel is where the trolleybuses should have gone to in the first place. The 266 had additional shorts between Cricklewood and Hammersmith to cover that end of the 660.

Almost without exception, these new services were substantially less frequent than the trolleybuses, particularly at the outer ends where fifty per cent cuts were commonplace. Further in, there was some boosting of service levels by other services. Route 2 was extended from Golders Green to North Finchley, restoring a through connection from central London which had disappeared during the war but in doing so creating an extraordinarily long route all the way up from Crystal Palace with a running time of over ninety minutes (except on Saturdays when it came only from Victoria). The Edgware Road service received its boost from route 142, which was restructured to give extra Monday to Friday buses between Edgware and Kilburn Park, and the extension on Mondays to Fridays of route 52A from Colindale to Willesden garage via Cricklewood under the new number 292. In anticipation of the disruption which this extension might cause on a hitherto local and reliable route, the express service (also renumbered 292 but not extended beyond Colindale) was extended in Borehamwood and altered to stop at all stops in the town.

Above **The heart of the North West Group of routes was at Cricklewood Broadway where the 645, 660 and 666 met. Trolleybus 1590 has come down from Edgware and is about to turn right into Willesden Lane, leaving route 645 which turns left and joining the 660 coming from Cricklewood Lane. The N1s, the last of which were withdrawn at this stage, were AEC 664Ts with Birmingham Railway Carriage and Wagon Company bodywork, dating from 1939/1940.**
C. Carter

Overhead linesmen attend to a broken
span wire, which has caused much
concern among passers-by outside the
Granada cinema in Church Road
Willesden, while the driver of N2 class
trolleybus 1649 waits in quiet
contemplation. The N2s, whose Park
Royal bodies could be distinguished
readily by the thick corner pillars on the
upper deck, disappeared at this stage.
The tower wagon, 86Q, was one of a
batch of sixteen on AEC Mercury
chassis which were purchased at the
start of the tram to trolleybus
conversion in 1935/36. C. Carter

Paddington Green was the least
satisfactory 'London' terminus being not
only distant from the heart of town but
also in a backwater, yet the opportunity
presented by the conversion to find a
better objective was not taken and the
replacing buses continued to use it for
many years. Ken Glazier

Route 662 was combined with routes 18 and 18B as one route between London Bridge and Edgware under the number 18 but operating in two overlapping sections from London Bridge to Sudbury and Paddington Green to Edgware. The long established late evening trolleybuses between Wembley Hill Road and Scrubs Lane, which were a relic of the days when there were frequent evening events at the stadium, were not replaced, the intention being to cover the demand with special services operating when events took place. The early morning journeys on route 660 between Paddington Green and Acton Vale were replaced, as far as Acton (Gunnersbury Lane), by another new route, 293, which had to run in both peaks to fit the requirements of the scheduling Agreement.

One of the improvements which the Working Party looked at for this stage was the re-introduction of a service linking Stonegrove directly with Edgware station, which had been withdrawn when the trolleybuses were first extended to Canons Park in 1938. For some reason it was yoked to a desire to run a service to Broadfields estate where there would have been a loop working with no stand. To give staff an opportunity to get refreshments and visit a lavatory, the journey in one direction would have been broken at Edgware station which, coupled with the need for gaps in the timetable while staff took their meal reliefs, made sure that the idea was stillborn.

RM 971 leans into the turn from Glenthorne Road to Dalling Road under wires which have already been severed from those coming from Studland Street still then being used by the 667. A Thames Valley Lodekka can be seen retreating down Glenthorne Road on the Reading to London service. Fred Ivey

By the time the scrapyard at Colindale was ready to receive N1 class number 1641 all trace of trolleybus operation had been stripped from Edgware Road and it had to be towed. RM 992 is operating on the foreshortened replacement of the 645 trolleybus, on which 1641 would have run many times. Tony Belton

The schedule of 109 trolleybuses was replaced by 108 motor buses, which included about three used to increase the service between Paddington Green and London Bridge. Twenty-two of the RT family buses allocated to routes 18 and 18B were also replaced by RMs, which increased the number of scheduled Routemasters to 116. Seven garages were caught up in the chain of re-allocations set off by the closure of Colindale and the extra buses appeared in no fewer than five. The somewhat rickety policy of keeping RMs out of former Central Bus garages was finally discarded and the class now went to both Cricklewood, the original home of RM 1, and Middle Row, while yet another former trolleybus depôt got a mixed allocation, with the transfer of route 112 from Willesden (Cricklewood at weekends) to Stonebridge. Only one of the replacement services, route 260, continued to be run entirely by former trolleybus depôts (Finchley and Stonebridge). Route 18 was shared between Alperton (RT), Middle Row and Stonebridge, route 245 went into Cricklewood, the 266 to Cricklewood and Stonebridge and the 293 to Middle Row. Route 292 lost its Willesden allocation and got a bigger one at Edgware.

Although there were enough new RMs in stock to cover all the needs of this stage, the opportunity was taken to use twenty-two older vehicles, most of them former trainers, to make up the numbers. Finchley got eight new RMs and made up the balance of its needs with five which had been released from route 104 by the arrival of RMLs in December and January. Stonebridge took the lion's share of Routemasters, sixty-three, which were joined by nine transferred RTLs, for the 112. Cricklewood also took a mixture of old and new, eleven RTLs to cover the additional work on route 2 and newly allocated 142, and nineteen RMs, while Middle Row received twenty-three RMs which replaced twenty-one RTLs. The increase of eight RTs at Edgware was to cover the extra buses on route 292, which remained RT operated and lost its Willesden allocation. Alperton and Willesden were the two transit camps in this reshuffle, the latter taking over the Cricklewood runnings on the 176 and 226 to make room for some of the new work and disposing of the 112 to Stonebridge, while the former took over some of Middle Row's work on the 187 to fill the space left by the reduction of its allocation on route 18.

Top **The snow which was to cause such havoc to the north-western trolleybus services on their last evening was already evident earlier in the day when RTL 753, a Metro-Cammell bodied version, made one of the last journeys on route 18B along Station Road, Harlesden.** R. Copson

Centre **In stage thirteen of the conversion route 18 blossomed into a very long and substantial route, on which the formerly exclusive Alperton allocation became very much a minority partner and the only garage on the route not to operate RMs. Saunders-bodied RT 1771 at Edgware was typical of its contribution.** W.R. Legg

Right **RTL 1410 leaves Colindale depôt on route 52A, both of which disappeared in stage thirteen.**

Press information

LONDON TRANSPORT

55 Broadway, Westminster, London SW1

Press Office ABBey 5600

L.P.N.6
23.3.62.

MAY 9 WILL SEE END OF TROLLEYBUSES IN LONDON

THE LAST SEVEN ROUTES - 601, 602, 603, 604, 605,
657 AND 667 - CONVERTED TO ROUTEMASTER
DIESEL BUSES

NEW FACILITIES FOR SOUTH-WEST LONDON

Wednesday, May 9 will see the end of trolleybuses in London. On that day the last seven routes - 601, 602, 603, 604, 605, 657 and 667 - all of which operate in south-west London, will be switched to Routemaster diesel bus operation.

Their conversion will be made under the fourteenth and final stage of London Transport's big three-year scheme in which some 1,600 trolleybuses have been replaced by diesel buses.

In this final changeover of May 9 involving fewer than 100 trolleybuses, the routes being converted operate in a "pocket" stretching from Wimbledon and Hammersmith out to Kingston, Hampton Court, Twickenham and Hounslow. It was in this area that London's first trolleybuses ran thirty-one years ago between Twickenham and Teddington.

The seven trolleybus routes will be replaced by five new bus services - 281, 282, 283, 285 and 267, and the extension of four existing services - 116, 117, 131 and on Sundays, route 81B.

London Transport's new 64-seater Routemaster buses will be operating on all the new services and will also replace the 56-seater RT buses on routes 117, 131 and on Sundays only 81B.

The stage 14 changeover will enable London Transport to bring in a number of improved facilities including three new direct services - from the Kingston area to London Airport; from Bedfont and Hounslow to Osterley and the Great West Road factories; and from Feltham to Brentford and Chiswick. There will also be a new east-to-west service across Kingston.

The 113 trolleybuses withdrawn for scrap included the seventy-three surviving BRCW bodied AECs of the N1 class, the last twenty Park Royal bodied N2s and a further fifteen Hampton AEC/MCCW L3s. This left just the twenty-six K1s at Isleworth and seventy-three L3s at Fulwell to see out the last four months of trolleybus operation, which was now confined to 33.15 miles of road in south-west London, including the whole of the original 1931 trolleybus system and all once part of the London United Tramways network. This comprised: the routes from Shepherds Bush and Hammersmith via Chiswick to Busch Corner and onwards from there to Hounslow (Wellington Road) via Isleworth and to Hampton Court via Twickenham, Teddington and Hampton; from Hampton Court to Wimbledon Town Hall via Kingston, New Malden and Raynes Park; from Stanley Road, Fulwell to Hampton Wick; Kingston to Tolworth and The Dittons via Surbiton; and around the Kingston Hill loop via Richmond Road, Kings Road, Park Road and Kingston Hill.

On 9th May 1962, routes 601, 602, 603 and 667 were each replaced by similar bus services numbered 281, 282, 283 and 267 respectively, the only change being the extension of the 281 to terminate at the station in Twickenham, instead of continuing to use the turn across the main road in King Street. It had been planned to make a small but helpful change to the 282 so as to follow the same route as the 201 between Dittons and Surbiton, via Thorkhill Road, Ewell Road, Effingham Road and Balaclava Road but there were a number of obstructing trees whose removal would have been essential to make the roads safe for double deck operation and, not unreasonably, the Council would have none of that. The alternative of using single-deckers was one which would not even have crossed the minds of London Transport's planners in those days. On Sundays route 283 did not run and route 282 was modified to run from Dittons to Kingston serving Kingston Hill loop in both directions.

The other three trolleybus routes were covered in a more intricate fashion. The 604 was absorbed into an extension of bus route 131 to give a through route from Walton-on-Thames to Wimbledon, thereby eliminating the overlap between Kingston and Hampton Court, where buses served only tarmac and brick walls, and providing new direct east-west journey possibilities across Kingston. Another route to lose its personal identity so as to eliminate an overlap was the 657. It disappeared into a much enlarged and potentially very long 117, from Egham to Shepherds Bush, but it ran right through only on Saturdays as the Monday to Friday service was in two overlapping sections and the 117 was not extended on Sundays. Instead, route 81B ran through to Shepherds Bush, ostensibly to provide an attractive Sunday link to London Airport. The new guise for the 605 was the 285, an ambitious route which broke beyond the constraints of trolleybus operation at both ends to run from London Airport Central via Harlington Corner, route 90B to Feltham, 152 to Teddington and the 605 to Wimbledon. From there, on Mondays to Saturdays, it trod new ground through Queens Road to Haydons Road station. The 152 was withdrawn between Feltham and Teddington, except during Monday to Friday peak hours, and was further curtailed on Monday to Friday evenings and Sundays to run only between Mitcham and Hampton Court, creating another of those untidy and confusing route patterns which were beginning to be a feature of the London scene.

There was one other associated change which was only marginally connected with the conversion, as its principal purpose was to provide new links to the factories in Great West Road from places west of Hounslow, but it sneaked in because, nominally, it also helped to cover route 667 at the Hammersmith end. Route 116 was extended from Hounslow via Lampton, Great West Road and Chiswick to Turnham Green (Monday to Friday between peaks) and Hammersmith Brook Green (Monday to Friday peaks and Saturdays until early evening). Some other ideas were discussed at the time which could have become part of the scheme but were judged to be too distantly related to justify their inclusion. One was a service for the Davis Factory Estate in Cox's Lane, Hook, which was eventually served by an extension of route 281 but not for another eight years. The other idea was a direct service from Berrylands to Surbiton station, which was fulfilled more quickly, by the intervention of the Country Bus department who diverted route 418 away from Villiers Avenue in February 1964. (Villiers Avenue was left unserved until 1st July 1964, when Central Bus route 201 was diverted to cover it.)

The vestigial schedule of ninety-one trolleybuses was covered by an increase of eighty-nine buses, of which at least seven were for the extensions beyond the trolleybus system. There was also another slice of conversion from RT to RM, on routes 117 and 131, which increased the scheduled number of RMs by a further twenty-four at the expense of removing the same number of RTs. The tiny Isleworth depôt did not become a bus garage but closed its doors with the departure of the trolleybuses. Its work, now on route 117, was transferred to Hounslow bus garage where, like many of the new post-war garages, there was plenty of spare space. Allocations were further complicated by the decision to transfer some of Fulwell's work into Norbiton, which was better placed to run the 131, and the consequential shift of other work into Kingston and Merton. Apart from new routes 267, 281, 282 and 283, Fulwell took on route 206, the first case of a single deck route finding its way into a former trolleybus depôt. Route 264 moved from Norbiton to Kingston, where the tiny allocation on route 152 shifted to Merton, turning Kingston into the only all single-deck garage in the Central Bus area. Thirty-six RMs went to Hounslow, twenty-five to Norbiton and fifty-four to Fulwell, which also got six RFs.

On the whole, in the earlier stages the trolleybuses had slipped away quietly with not a lot of celebration or mourning except from staff and dedicated enthusiasts. They may have captured the imagination of Londoners in the 1930s, when they struck such an exhilarating contrast with the elderly trams which they replaced, but they did not achieve the rather false romantic status won by the trams during the war which had carried through to the celebration of many warm, emotional farewells. By the 1960s, long before most people started to worry about the effects of pollution from vehicle emissions, the average passenger probably saw little to chose between a modern motor bus and a trolleybus and were easily enough convinced by London Transport's propaganda. At first, it looked as though the same indifference might be in evidence on 8th May 1962, as the remaining trolleybuses went about their daily business unhindered by any displays of nostalgia. There had not been the build up which accompanied the final days of the trams a decade earlier, when special posters had been carried on the cars and souvenir tickets issued, but it would have been unusual for London Transport to miss an opportunity for a publicity-grabbing celebration and, sure enough, the occasion was duly marked by a commemorative run in the afternoon.

This view from outside Surbiton station shows Claremont Road, with its handsome clock tower commemorating Edward VII's coronation, along which all three local routes operated. At this point, route 602 parted company with the busier Tolworth routes and trolleybus 1437 has taken up the right hand running wire preparatory to turning into Victoria Road bound for the Winters Bridge terminus, known by London Transport as The Dittons. C. Carter

The 'Red Lion' turning circle at Tolworth, used by route 603, adjoined the Alexandra Recreation Ground, just short of the main shopping area in the Broadway. L3 1402 is about to turn right into King Charles Road to reach Ewell Road for the return journey to the Kingston loop. C. Carter

Left **Surrounded by excited crowds, laden with 'dignitaries' and threatening to collapse under the strain of it all, Diddler number 1 pauses at the Wellington Road gate of Fulwell depôt before setting off in the company of 1521 on its ceremonial run to Kingston via Twickenham.** Ken Glazier

Right **Away from the centre of excitement, route 657 saw out its last hours with quiet dignity. Outside Hounslow bus garage, which will be the new base for their drivers the next day, K1 1107 works one of the last evening peak shortworkings to Brentford Half Acre and 1101 heads for the Wellington Road terminus.** Ken Glazier

In preparation for the valedictory events, trolleybus number 1 had been brought out of the museum some weeks earlier and taken to Fulwell depôt where it was put into a fit state (just) to run under its own power as one of only two electric vehicles taking part in the procession, the other being L3 class 1521. The celebration was modest by any standards. At 2.45pm, the two trolleybuses, loaded with local dignitaries, representatives of the Press, London Transport officers and Members of the Executive, passed through the Wellington Road gates of Fulwell depôt to start a tour

of some of the capital's oldest trolleybus routes. They followed route 667 to Twickenham Junction, where they used the venerable terminal loop to take up the route of the ceremonial first run, which had taken place one week short of thirty-one years earlier. They then ran via Hampton Wick and took an anticlockwise turn around the Kingston Hill loop to finish up outside Kingston bus station where two brand new Routemasters were waiting to whisk the passengers off to their posh reception.

'Diddler' number 1 was not allowed to

retire from the event gracefully under its own power but suffered the indignity of being hitched to a lorry almost before its last passenger was off the platform, and towed away back to Clapham museum. No doubt the museum staff were greatly relieved that it had not collapsed while loaded with its distinguished guests. In all the haste, it is to be hoped that the crew of number 1 was not overlooked, driver DMI Bob Brown and especially the conductor Ron Hadland who had performed the same task on the very first trolleybus on 16th May 1931.

Left **1431 was the vehicle plated for the last run on route 604 from Wimbledon but its rôle was usurped by 1521 at the last minute. Despite that, it still completed its scheduled duty and is seen here breaking through the crowd at the Wellington Road gate of Fulwell depôt, to bump over the tram track, still visible after sixteen years of redundancy.** Ken Glazier

Right **The heavily decorated usurper, 1521, arrives to the acclaim of the huge crowd which had gathered at Fulwell for the occasion.** Ken Glazier

The official ceremonies were accompanied by some heightened public interest and seemed to spark a greater awareness of the significance of the day's events, as more and more people started to take an interest from then onwards. Isleworth depôt and route 657 were rather out of the limelight but were determined not to be outdone by big brother Fulwell. K1 class trolleybus number 1274 was held in the depôt to be specially decked out for a final run over the 657 and was generously embellished with bunting in both saloons, and draped around its windows and over its trolley booms. In this festive condition, it was brought out just after 10.30pm

and performed the last round journey to Shepherds Bush and back, by which time the last scheduled service run on the system, from Wimbledon station to Fulwell depôt at 11.46pm on route 604 was already under way. The vehicle officially allocated to this running was L3 class 1431 but, although it completed its duties, its status as London's last trolleybus was usurped by number 1521. After its ceremonial run in the afternoon, 1521 had returned to Fulwell where it had been garlanded with balloons and streamers and adorned with a commemorative plaque, ready for it to turn out at Hampton Court in time to take over the running of the last round

trip to Wimbledon, behind number 1431. At Wimbledon, there was a large crowd waiting to mark this historical event and the route back to Hampton Court and Fulwell was lined by people who had turned out specially to wave goodbye. Near Fulwell, 1521 was greeted by a group of students carrying banners reading 'The End Is Near' and at Fulwell itself there was a crowd so dense that its path was blocked. It finally managed to break a way through, an hour after the scheduled time, bringing electric road traction to an end, sixty-one years after London United had pioneered electric tramways in the capital.

Left **The accompanying Routemaster had not arrived and L3 1521 had barely done so, when the booms of number 1 were dipped in readiness for its rapid removal back to Clapham after the valedictory run from Fulwell. The Kingston Kinema provided a useful, if alarming, perch for four of the crowd of wellwishers, the rest of whom brought Clarence Street to a standstill.** M. Dryhurst

Right **All is finished. Redundant L3s parked in the yard of Fulwell depôt, their last service runs completed, await the ignominy of being hitched to a towing lorry and dragged off to Mr Cohen's torch at Colindale.** Geoff Rixon

CHAPTER THREE

FLEET DEVELOPMENTS

London Transport entered the 1960s with its latest design of bus flowing into stock at a steady rate of eight or nine a week and the Routemaster looked set fair to establish itself as the next standard type which would eventually replace the RT family. Plans put together between April 1960 and July 1961 envisaged the replacement of the RT fleet over a period of sixteen years, starting in 1962, at the average rate of about 350 a year. For the Central Area the additional capacity of the RM was to be used to make economies in peak hour operation and the number of new buses required to replace the 6,269 RT types was then estimated to be 5,806 which, with the sixty-four coaches and the trolleybus replacement vehicles, brought the potential size of the RM class up to 7,033.

The Executive was proud of its new baby and had made public its conviction, supported by detailed operational research, that it was the best design for London. The rest of the country was less convinced and many watched with some dismay as the once proud organisation seemed to be making off down a blind alley. Although there were some pockets of resistance, most operators were moving to thirty-foot long double-deckers, more and more were specifying rear engined models and even those who stayed loyal to the front engined chassis more often than not specified

Above **RTL 912 was eleven years old, already more than three-quarters of the way through its book life, when photographed at Sloane Square on a warm Tuesday in July 1961. The London Transport overhaul process ensured that vehicles remained smart and healthy, despite reaching an age when earlier generations of bus would have been overdue for retirement.** G. Mead

Left **London Transport was seemingly committed totally to the sixty-four seat rear entrance open platform double-decker at the beginning of the decade when the Routemaster had only just gone into volume service. RM 50, awaiting service in Poplar garage was typical of those already in service.** W.J. Haynes

an entrance at the front, not with any idea at that early stage of moving to driver only operation but to transfer responsibility for supervising the platform from the conductor to the driver. When RM 422 was put on display at the Commercial Motor Show in September 1960 it was completely overshadowed by innovative designs from most other manufacturers, notably Daimler showing its prototype Fleetline and Leyland which had two production Atlanteans on show. Guy had no fewer than three of its revolutionary front engined, front entrance Wulfrunians in the Hall but this design ultimately proved a disaster and helped kill Guy as an independent organisation. Even one of the Dennis Lolines on show was a unique lowbridge version for Barton Transport with an overall height of only 12ft 5ins, although this was little more than a publicity seeking artifice. What was on display was by no means a typical crosssection of what was being bought at the time, as rear-engined designs were still in their infancy. The Atlantean was already beginning to prove a particularly troublesome design and the Fleetline was also to have its problems, causing some early customers to switch back to front-engined designs for a while, but the two models established themselves as the mainstream choice by the mid-1960s. Even so, from its renowned position of design leadership, which had culminated in the RT, London Transport was now slipping into a Limbo, from which it was to spend the next twenty years or so trying to escape.

Behind the scenes, there was less confidence that the undertaking was on the right track, particularly among the younger, more junior managers but also including others in positions of greater influence. Notable among these was the flamboyant and outspoken Operating Manager of Country Buses and Coaches, Geoffrey Fernyhough, who wanted something less sophisticated, cheaper to buy and operate, for his services and managed for a long time to stave off a decision on the exact type which would be used to replace his RTs. Eric Ellen, who later became Traffic Officer (CRS) and much later Secretary to the Board but who was then Divisional Superintendent (South) in the Central Road Services department, rattled a few cages by making a strongly argued case for high capacity rear-engined vehicles. Such influence as this background rumble of dissent might have had was severely limited by the trap which the Executive had laid for itself when it first announced the Routemaster. It had then proclaimed that extensive research had shown that a sixty-four seater was the optimum size of bus for London and had used the findings to justify its decision to replace the seventy-seat trolleybuses by the smaller bus. Many must have wondered how the trolleybuses and, before them the trams, had managed to survive under this perceived burden of excessive loadings. Similar claims had been made before for the concept of a fifty-six seat standard in the 1930s but in a rather more muted fashion and not supported by scientific research. By early in 1961 London Transport was already rueing the day it had made such strong claims and began to make plans to switch to a thirty-foot version of the RM, but it was to find that it had closed its escape hatch.

Before that point was reached, however, there was an idiosyncratic little experiment which in its small way was more significant as an indicator of the way the Executive's plans might eventually develop. After six years experience with 'large saloon' (thirty-nine seater) one-man-operation, London Transport was interested in finding ways of reducing the time spent at heavily used stops, perhaps with the hope that some busier routes could then be drawn into the net but probably not yet with any idea of extending the principle to include the replacement of double-deckers on town services. For several years now, one or two of the more adventurous municipal operators had been operating OMO buses with separate entrance and exit doors, which reduced stop times by allowing boarding and alighting to take place simultaneously. London Transport decided to have some service trials with similar vehicles and placed an order for three AEC Reliances in March 1960. Fortuitously, at this very time Grimsby-Cleethorpes Transport was taking delivery of a batch of Reliances with dual door bodywork by Willowbrook and London Transport was able to secure delivery within six months of placing the order, by negotiating an extension of this production run.

The three buses were taken into stock between 30th August and 15th September 1960 and were given the fleet numbers RW 1–3, continuing the convention of the basic 'R', with W for 'wide'. They were the first eight-foot wide single-deck buses purchased by the Executive and were also the first London Transport buses to receive reversed registrations (495–497 ALH), which were taken from a batch then being allocated to the service vehicle fleet. The chassis were 2MU2RA Reliances, with Monocontrol gearboxes similar to those fitted to the RMs but without the modification for fully automatic operation, and the AH470 7.7 litre engine which normally powered this lightweight model.

The forty-two seat bodywork was of lightweight metal construction, with front and rear ends in moulded glass fibre. The front of the body was almost vertical below cantrail level and the curve of the dome was all but eliminated by a large indicator box which stretched over most of its width. There were two flat windscreens, the one on the offside being recessed. The rest of the body was less severe in appearance and the rear end in particular made a sharp contrast with the front. The curvature of the single window matched the handsomely rounded rear dome to form a kind of flattened half moon and there was only a small route number box which leaned discreetly into the centre of the dome. Unlike the standard London arrangement, the emergency exit door was in the rearmost offside bay while the two-leaf centre exit door was in the third bay on the nearside. As the Grimsby-Cleethorpes buses were intended for standee operation, there were three quarter-light windows in the cant panels on the nearside and five on the offside, another novel feature on a London bus but one which was never to be repeated. The interior was finished to the same basic specification as the Grimsby-Cleethorpes vehicles but with some standard London Transport trim. The lightweight frames of the seats had no top grab rails and their back cushions were only thinly upholstered but they were covered in the latest style of moquette as used on the RMs. This was matched by the choice of burgundy as the colour for the PVC trim below waist level but the stove enamelled window finishers were coloured grey, an interesting foretaste of the schemes to be tried by the Board later in the decade. The layout of the external livery, although still in standard Lincoln green and cream, also marked a change which was to be carried forward into later standard buses. For the first time since 1946, the thin relief band around the windows was abandoned in favour of a deeper band running right around the body below the windows and windscreens.

Newly delivered RW 3 at Two Waters garage in September 1960. LT Museum

RW 1–3 were allocated first to Two Waters garage for operation on one of the Country department's busiest single-deck routes, the 322, starting on 26th September 1960. They later spent some time at St Albans on route 355, Hertford (333/333B), and Addlestone on the 427/437/456 group before returning to Two Waters, but they did not survive to be overhauled and were withdrawn in October 1963. They had been prone to suffer from overheating, caused by the design of the transmission which brought together the engine, fluid flywheel and gearbox, unlike the RT and earlier designs where the gearbox was mounted separately, further down the chassis. This was a taste of what was to come with rear engined designs in later years. The Reliances were also disliked by the drivers, who found the cab layout haphazard compared with standard London Transport designs and also complained about difficulties with the centre door in narrow country lanes. All three were bought by Chesterfield Corporation who ran them for fourteen years. RW 2 has survived as a preserved vehicle, owned by Graham Batten.

RW 2 in St Peters Street opposite St Albans garage during its spell on route 355. The uncompromisingly flat front contrasts with the much softer, curved outline of the rest of the bodywork. They were not liked by drivers who found the cab layout inconvenient and also found the centre exit troublesome at some stops. Colin Brown

Left This view of RW 2 reversing at Warners End on its first Sunday in service, shows the rather old fashioned look given to the rear end of the Willowbrook bodies by the shape of the window, although the design was pleasantly rounded. The position of the wide emergency exit door in the rear overhang gave rise to a very small window at the extreme rear of the offside, giving a rather untidy look from this aspect. As London's first purpose-built full size OMO single-deckers, the RWs were the first to be fitted when new with reversing lamps and were also the first to have Routemaster type direction indicators from new.
Ken Glazier

Above **RW interior view, showing the windows in the cant panels and the provincial style seat frames.**

RW 3 on route 456 at Weybridge during its stay at Addlestone garage. M. Dryhurst

Attention now turned to the development of a thirty-foot version of the Routemaster. London Transport was obliged to tread carefully for reasons which are covered in detail in chapter nine and confined itself at this stage to a trial batch of twenty-four. It also seemed to put off any further move to the larger vehicle for at least four years by seeking approval from the British Transport Commission to purchase a further 1,340 RMs, at a cost of £8,479,000, to replace 1,488 RT family buses between 1963 and 1966. This submission was made on 26th July 1961, by which time the first of the longer vehicles was already in stock.

The new model was hardly a radical departure from the Routemaster concept but it was a wonderful demonstration of the innate flexibility of the design. It was, in effect, merely a standard 8/5RM5/8 with a half-length bay measuring 2ft 4ins inserted into the body structure at its mid-point to increase the overall length to 29ft 10⁹⁄₁₆ ins (but always referred to for simplicity as 30ft). This allowed an additional row of seats to be provided on each deck, increasing the seating capacity by eight to seventy-two. This method was chosen because it was much quicker than redesigning from scratch and also more economical as most of the structure was unchanged. It was therefore possible to use almost entirely standard Routemaster parts and the minimum of re-tooling was required. At the time, many thought this upset the symmetry of the original design but it came to be accepted over the years and has been imitated in some other models, notably

perhaps the classic Northern Counties bodywork of the period which had a number of visual resemblances to the RM. The new bus was identical mechanically to the short version with CAV electrical equipment, SCG automatic transmission and Lockheed hydraulic brakes. Even the 9.6 litre AV590 engine was retained, despite an increase of seven hundredweight in the unladen weight. The only differences in the mechanical

specification were the longer propeller shaft needed to accommodate the increase in wheelbase from 16ft 10ins to an unusually long 19ft 2ins, and an increase in tyre size on the front wheels from 9.00–20 to 10.00–20. The smaller tyre size had been a London Transport standard, intended to give lighter steering but this had ceased to be a limiting factor once power steering had been adopted as standard. The completed bus was coded 7RM7.

Above and Below **The exceptionally long wheelbase of 19ft 2ins is underlined in these views of RML 885 at Finchley on changeover night and RML 890 in the garage yard. Although the inserted bay looked untidy to eyes accustomed to equal length windows, the greater length suited the Routemaster design, giving it a sleeker appearance, and the arrangement soon came to be accepted as satisfyingly symmetrical.** Sport & General/Michael Rooum

The greater length of the RML required the fitting of a second emergency exit, towards the front of the lower deck.

The completion of RM 1000 on 16th October 1961 was marked by a small ceremony attended by Lord Brabazon (left) and Alec Valentine (right), Chairmen of ACV and London Transport respectively.
Capital Transport collection

The interiors were identical in overall appearance with the same trim and furnishings, the most noticeable difference being the short window half way down the saloon. In the second offside bay of the lower saloon there was a hinged push-out window which could be opened by a rather clumsy looking rod and lever device. This was required under the Construction & Use Regulations on vehicles longer than 27ft 6ins to provide a second means of escape from the lower saloon in an emergency. A less remarked feature which was never modified, either on later production buses or during the refurbishment programme in the 1990s, was the absence of a vertical grab rail in the short central bay. This left a gap in the sequence of stanchions which has caught out many an unwary passenger in the intervening years and one can only speculate on how it managed to escape the notice of the vehicle examiners.

For this experimental batch it was decided to use a rather cumbersome method of construction, known as 'knife and fork' in the trade, as it would have been too expensive to set up a new production line for such a small number. The bodies were first built as standard Routemasters but were then taken aside to be split apart so that the extra section could be inserted. They were therefore completed at a very slow pace and it took from 10th July 1961 to 8th January 1962 for the complete batch to be delivered, during which period over two hundred standard RMs were received. At first the new model was given the classification ER (Extended Routemaster) and the first four were delivered as ER 880–883 but all were reclassified RML on 30th August and this was the code carried by all subsequent similar vehicles. The reason for this is explained later. The first fifteen (RML 880–894) went into service at Finchley garage on 8th November 1961, where they were joined by RML 895–897 on 1st December and RML 899 on 2nd January 1962 to complete the number needed for route 104.

As this was the only route on which the RMLs could be operated, the rest spent a long time languishing at Aldenham and it was not until 1st May 1964 that the last two (RML 898 and 902) were finally licensed for service at Finchley. This was a less than distinguished start to the career of a bus which was to become one of the most enduring variants of a marque which itself was to establish new records for longevity. Fortunately it was possible to find some work for the unwanted vehicles because London buses were still a popular choice for overseas promotional tours, usually in association with 'British Weeks'. RML 898 made two visits to the United States, to San Francisco in 1962 and to New Orleans and Memphis in 1963, RML 902 made two to Europe in 1963, first to Munich and then to Zurich and RML 903 went to the 'Exposition Britannia' in Philadelphia in October 1963. After that, the RMLs were getting too old to make a good show and the job was taken over by new RMs. Instead, many of the thirty footers found themselves in the undignified role of training buses and so it was to remain until the Industrial Relations climate changed in the second half of the decade.

The decision to reclassify the ER to RML was connected with an important change of vehicle purchasing policy. Since the early post-war years London Transport's policy had been to maintain at least two sources of supply for chassis and bodies and this had been the philosophy behind the sharing out of the prototype Routemasters between AEC and Leyland for running units and between Park Royal, Weymann and (less convincingly) ECW for the body structures. It had then been the intention to place twenty-five per cent of the orders for running units with Leyland, the other seventy-five per cent being the proportion which had to be placed with AEC under the terms of the long-standing manufacturing agreement with that company. It soon became clear, however, that it would be hopelessly uneconomic for Leyland to produce this specialised vehicle in such small numbers and, after a failed attempt to phase the building programme to Leyland's satisfaction, the conclusion was reached that it would be unrealistic to try to split production. Instead, the Executive decided to maintain the principle of an alternative supplier by having a proportion of RMs equipped with Leyland engines. As this removed the need for a separate Leyland classification, RML 3 was reclassified as RM 3 and CRL 4 became RMC 4, leaving the RML classification available for the long version of the type.

The initial contract with Leyland was valued at over £320,000 and covered the supply of 406 of the highly regarded O.600 engine and the spare parts to go with them. Delivery of the main batch was scheduled to start in the summer of 1962 and applied to RM 1255–1452 and 1521–1719 which was actually a continuous series of 397 straddling sixty-eight coaches. Six engines were to be held as spares and the remaining three were supplied for pre-production trials of the installation. RM 632 was earmarked for the first experimental installation and was sent to Self Changing Gears at Coventry in January 1961 for four months before going to Leyland to have its AEC engine replaced. In line with normal London Transport practice, the output of the 9.8 litre O.600 engine was derated to 115 bhp at 1,800 rpm and a number of other alterations were made. These included omission of the air filter, a fitting not favoured by London Transport as it was inclined to become clogged and create a fire risk. This decision created the only feature which enabled the Leyland engined RM to be distinguished from its siblings without looking under the bonnet, its distinctive and noisy deep-throated roar. Despite the importance of this variation, no separate type code was applied to these buses, which were given the same classification as equivalent AEC examples. AEC did make a distinction in its unit classification, however, by adding a prefix '2' and making them 2R2RH

RM 632 entered service at Hanwell on 21st June 1961 and was joined there by the first to be fitted with a Leyland engine from the outset, RM 870, in September. The third trial bus was RM 1009 which was licensed at Hanwell in March 1962. Three months later, on 5th June, just as the production batch began to flow, Leyland Motors Ltd and the ACV group, the parent company of AEC,

The second prototype, RM 2, was withdrawn from passenger service on 31st October 1959 and, still in original condition, was relegated to training duties on which it is engaged here at Neasden. It was fitted with a standard radiator in 1964. Tony Belton

RML 3 had a spectacularly short operational career, having been demoted to training duties in November 1959 following dynamo and fan problems, which it shared with the other three prototypes. Now, with the decision not to purchase Leyland running units for production buses, it was renumbered RM 3. It was destined to remain as a trainer until the end of March 1972. Later in 1963 it was taken out of use for remedial work and overhaul, during which it lost its original front grille and wings in favour of the standard type.
Tony Belton

announced that they were to merge and the whole point of ordering Leyland engines was nullified. It was obvious that negotiations for the merger must have been going on for some time and London Transport, particularly Mr Eric Ottaway who had led the negotiations as Chief Supplies and Services Officer, felt badly betrayed.

Nevertheless, a second contract was signed for a further 175 engines to be installed in RM 1811–1985 between January and July 1964 but these were the last; London Transport announced officially at the end of 1965 that no further orders would be placed for Leyland engines in Routemasters. Like its RTL predecessor, the Leyland engined Routemaster was a more troublesome animal than the true bred AEC version, with a tendency for oil to leak from the injector pipe into the engine and with an intractably erratic idling motion.

Once the trolleybus conversion was completed, the flow of standard RMs into service suddenly dried up while the arguments with the Trade Union about the way in which they

were to be used rumbled on. Apart from a handful licensed to cover accident losses, none entered service for six months and the next major influx of Routemasters was therefore the sixty-eight coaches. The experimental running of CRL (later RMC) 4 had been so successful that it was the only prototype still in service in 1961 and proved subsequently to be one of the longest lasting short wheelbase Routemasters in passenger service. It had been popular with passengers who were particularly drawn to the sightseeing benefits of travelling on the upper deck. This breakthrough, following several failed attempts in the past, could almost certainly be put down to the road holding qualities and general stability of the Routemaster which gave upper deck passengers a feeling of security and comfort when travelling at speed which earlier, and many later, types were unable to deliver. Add to this the need for London Transport to make operating economies and the attraction of a vehicle with a payload nearly fifty per cent greater than the Green Line RF becomes clear.

At its meeting on 25th January 1961, the Executive authorised the purchase of sixty-eight 'CR' type coaches at an estimated total cost of £484,000, and the news was made public during the following summer. The classification CR was a natural derivation as the basic AEC version of the Leyland CRL, but by the time the new coaches were delivered the policy had changed and they were numbered RMC 1453–1520 with the type code 6RM6. The basic body shell was the standard Routemaster design and differed little in external appearance but there were many alterations for coach work. Their frontal aspect was distinguished by double headlamps on each side, the inside one of each pair raised slightly above its partner to fit neatly into the sloping wing moulding. The other change at the front was a modified indicator display incorporating a single aperture box for both route number and intermediate route details, the same as the layout already carried at the rear of the standard type. The main differences at the back were the electrically operated double jack-knife doors and the attendant hinged emergency exit door, both similar to the arrangement on RMC 4 except that the emergency door handle was at floor rather than waist level. The side route indicator box had to be raised to make room for the access flap to the door operating mechanism, which was immediately above the entrance, and the blind changing handle was therefore on the upper deck instead of the platform. They were finished in an attractive version of the Lincoln green livery, with light green reliefs between the decks and on the thin moulding around the saloon windows in a style similar to the RFs. In the tradition of Green Line, they carried no advertisements and the between-decks panels were adorned instead with the by-now orthodox Green Line bullseye.

The important differences from standard were to be found in the passenger saloons and in the detailed specification of the running units. Unlike the RT 'coaches' at Romford and Grays, the RMCs were fitted out fully as coaches, with deeply upholstered seat squabs, higher than standard seat backs, ash trays on the upper deck seat backs and parcel racks above the seats on both decks. The seats were also more widely spaced, one complete row being omitted on the upper deck and the longitudinal seats on the lower deck being reduced in length to give a total capacity of fifty-seven (thirty-two up; twenty-five down). The pattern of the moquette was a style recently introduced on the Underground and comprised a geometrical blend of grey, black and maroon, in rather sober contrast to the bright Sung yellow of the window surrounds and the white ceiling panels. The backs of the seats were covered in red Rexine to match the panelling below the windows and around the rear upper deck emergency exit, on which the same burgundy finish was used as on the bus version. The brighter interior was further enhanced for night time running by the provision of fluorescent lighting for the first time as standard on a London bus. The parcel racks were of stainless steel tubing with red nylon netting and the cove panels above them were protected from the ravages of turbulent luggage by being finished in matt grey. Two other standard coach features were the absence of upright stanchions and the use of brown Treadmaster tiles instead of wooden slats on the saloon floors. The overall effect was cheerful and luxurious.

The changes to the running units were all related to the higher service speeds and longer journeys undertaken by the coaches. To improve passenger comfort, air suspension was employed on the rear sub frame although coil springs were retained at the front. The engine was the same AV590 9.6 litre unit as on the standard vehicles but the rear axle ratio was set at 4.7:1 to enable higher road speeds to be attained and, as there was far less gear changing than on buses, the automatic facility was omitted. To meet the needs of the higher daily mileages performed by Green Line vehicles, the RMCs were also equipped with larger, 41-gallon, fuel tanks.

CRL 4 was also reclassified in August 1961, becoming RMC 4 but unlike the other three prototypes it survived to become part of the main fleet, remaining in passenger service until May 1979, after which it was preserved by LCBS. In original condition but after reclassification, RMC 4 is seen at Golders Green during its time on the 716 and 716A. The flat profile of the front hub is clearly visible in this unpainted condition. Fred Ivey

RMC 1453 was taken into stock on 28th June and was used in a substantial publicity campaign in which it featured in a splendid colour photograph taken against a delightful wooded background, a brave start which helped gloss over the fact that things were not all that well in the Green Line camp. The main production run started with the arrival at Aldenham of RMC 1454 on 18th July and continued at the rate of three or four a week until 20th December. The first routes to receive the new coaches, on 29th August, were the 715 and 715A, among the busiest of Green Line routes and therefore a prime target for the economies of scale represented by the Routemasters. Only twenty RMCs were needed for the less frequent service, eight at Guildford and twelve at Hertford, to replace twenty-five RFs. The introduction of the remaining RMCs took place in three further stages, starting on 24th October when routes 718, 720 and 720A changed over and another twenty-five RFs being substituted by nineteen Routemasters, twelve at Epping and seven at Windsor. In the last two stages there was a straight one-for-one conversion, first on 21st November, when Garston garage received nine RMCs for route 719 in exchange for a like number of RFs and finally on 2nd January 1963 when the sixteen RFs needed for routes 716 and 716A were replaced by seventeen RMCs, nine at Addlestone and eight at Stevenage. Although seventy-five RFs were made redundant, only the ten short-wheelbase former Private Hire vehicles (RF 16–25) were discarded immediately, although twenty-four thirty-footers were eventually sold in 1964 and 1965. The impact of this programme on service levels and the development of Green Line are studied in detail in chapter five.

Stocks of paint left over from the unsuccessful experiments with a light green livery were used up by tolerating compromise liveries such as this, where the relief band is finished in the darker main body shade of the experimental scheme in combination with standard 'Lincoln' green, giving the vehicle a distinctly sombre look. RF 94 is seen on route 715 at the 'Toby Jug', Tolworth in the kind of heavy Kingston By-Pass traffic which played such havoc with timekeeping. A.J. Wild

The short-wheelbase former Private Hire coach 1/1RF1/3s were the principal casualty of the arrival of the RMCs and were sold out of service. Because of their provenance, these were unique in having glass roof panels, which also dictated a different design of luggage rack, but in other respects they were similar to the standard version. RF 23 is on the north side of Eccleston Bridge in June 1961, behind it the newly built shelters which were to have a very short life. G. Mead

The basic structure of the RMC body was identical to the bus version, the main external differences being the simplified blind layout, the twin headlamps and the special version of the Green Line livery, but internally the appointments were to full Green Line specification and underneath there was air suspension on the rear sub frame. Gleaming with deep gloss Lincoln green paintwork, RMC 1455 was one of Hertford's twelve, although it lacked a garage stencil plate when photographed on its first day in service in Upper Regent Street.
Ken Glazier

The first day in service for Epping's twelve RMCs on routes 718, 720 and 720A was 24th October 1962; RMC 1474 is seen during the summer of 1964 after transfer to the new Harlow garage and following the modification of the air intake grille above the cab.
Capital Transport

About half way through the construction of the RMCs, another faltering step was taken towards a more up-to-date vehicle design when Park Royal started work on a modified version of the RML with a forward entrance and staircase. London Transport had begun to realise that some compromise was going to be necessary if they were to persuade the staff to accept a larger vehicle and the opportunity to transfer some responsibility for boarding and alighting passengers from the conductor to the driver was seen as one possibility. There does not appear to have been a lot of conviction on the part of the Executive, however, and it seems more likely that it was responding to pressure from AEC and Park Royal who were anxious to increase the model's potential for sale outside London where a number of BET companies had adopted the forward entrance layout as standard. The new bus, numbered RMF 1254, was handed over to London Transport on 18th October 1962 but its first public appearance had been on the Park Royal stand at the Commercial Motor Show at the end of September.

Like the RML, it used a high proportion of standard Routemaster parts and had the classic appearance of the class. The main external differences were the repositioned entrance and staircase immediately behind the front bulkhead, a fully enclosed rear end and a revised design for the radiator grille. The new grille incorporated the familiar AEC triangle at the top of the centre strip, instead of the embossed bullseye hitherto carried on the bonnet lid and this proved to be a foretaste of a change which was adopted as standard the following summer. The electrically operated twin folding doors, supplied by Deans, were an improved version with each fold having a single glazed section to help improve the driver's visibility. The hinged emergency exit door was in the rearmost offside bay, leaving space at the back for a single piece lower saloon window which was the same depth as the side windows and therefore shallower, as well as wider, than on the rear entrance variety. A standard set of route indicator boxes was supplied at the front and rear and the offside route number box moved forward with the staircase but there was no nearside indicator, presumably because it would have been too close to the front blinds for it to be worthwhile.

One of the reasons why the forward entrance layout did not find universal favour was that it was intrinsically a less efficient user of internal space than either a front or a rear entrance design. RMF 1254 had two upper deck and one lower deck seats fewer than an RML, giving it an overall capacity of sixty-nine, only five more than a standard RM. Adherents to the rear engined concept were quick to point out that the potential capacity of an Atlantean or Fleetline was seventy-eight, although it is unlikely that London Transport, at that time, would have contemplated cramming in so many. Apart from the desire to retain a seat pitch which maximised passenger comfort, the Executive would have had one eye on the reaction of the Trade Union to such a big increase. The staircase, which was directly opposite the front of the doorway, was also considered by

some to be less satisfactory than the usual arrangement on rear entrance buses, as it rose towards the rear through a complete half circle, making it more difficult to negotiate and potentially more hazardous if the bus stopped sharply when anyone was on it. The passenger doorway was slightly narrower than on an RM but, most crucially, also lacked the cutaway section which served to increase the space available for boarding and alighting passengers on an open platform. There was barely room for two slimmish people to go through the gap side by side, unless they were extremely friendly. Interior furnishings and finishings were identical to other bus Routemasters, except for the omission of the polished metal strip above the windows, a change which was about to be adopted as standard.

Mechanically, RMF 1254 differed from the RMLs only in having stronger rear springs, and its weight and performance were also much the same. The completed vehicle was classified 1/7RM8, its running units being regarded as a modified RML, while the body was given its own classification. It was finished in standard red and cream and was a well balanced and elegant design which put to shame many of the cruder efforts then beginning to gain currency outside London.

While it was on display at Earls Court, RMF 1254 was dressed for route 104 and there was a general expectation that it would go into service at Finchley once the show was over. Not only did it not do so but, in the absence of acceptance by the staff, it was destined never to operate as a bus for London Transport. It did see some service quite soon, however, as it was sent to Liverpool for demonstration service between 26th October and 26th November. It then languished until 1st March 1963 when it went down to Canterbury for service with East Kent, who tried it out on route 4 between Canterbury and Herne Bay from 4th to 20th March. In passing, it is worth noting that the possibility of selling the rear entrance version had not been abandoned. For two weeks in February 1963, RM 1414 ran for Manchester Corporation, whose vehicle policy at that time was similar to

London Transport's, based on short-wheel-base rear entrance double-deckers. The availability of the Leyland engine no doubt increased its attraction for Manchester but there was no order.

After returning from East Kent, RMF 1254 disappeared from view for over a year, during which it was used as a guinea pig for a new design of front headlamp panel, without ventilation grilles and whose lower edge lined up with the bottom of the radiator grille. This was eventually adopted as standard on the production run of RMLs. Meanwhile, British European Airways was interested in replacing its 4RF4 airport coaches with double-deck vehicles towing trailers, instead of devoting valuable internal space to luggage. RM 8 had been used to test the practicability of the idea and the next phase in the trials gave RMF 1254 some useful work for the first time. It was modified to accept a trailer and put into trial service between Gloucester Road Air Terminal and Heathrow Airport, starting on 4th August 1964. Shortly afterwards, between 15th and 30th August, it went north to Halifax in its third stint as a demonstrator. The General Manager at Halifax, the renowned Geoffrey Hilditch, reporting on the comparative trials in 'Bus and Coach', gave RMF 1254 high praise for its suspension and described it as giving 'the best ride of any double-decker in which I have ever travelled'. He also praised its stability, ease of maintenance and good visibility for the driver, although he had some doubts about the vacuum brakes, perhaps because of earlier experiences of them on the Daimler CD 650. Unfortunately, the price made the Fleetline or Atlantean seem a more economical proposition and, as on the two previous occasions, no orders were forthcoming. The RMF remained on the BEA service until the Corporation's own version of the Routemaster went into service, after which it was delicensed, on 24th October 1966 and once again went into store. A month later, it was sold to Northern General Transport where it joined the similar vehicles which represented the one and only provincial sale of the model.

During its stay with East Kent, RMF 1254 ran on route 4 between Canterbury and Tankerton, where it is seen in drenching rain on 9th March 1963. The company has taken the trouble to put a number blind in the offside aperture, a detail which most other operators would have disdained. The intermediate style of radiator grille, with a triangle at the top but still with brake ventilator grilles in the wing housing, was still intact at this stage of its career. *Ken Glazier*

The only service work by RMF 1254 in London was carried out on behalf of the British European Airways Corporation to test the practicality of hauling a luggage trailer instead of having purpose-built airport coaches. The main modifications involved the fitting of a towing eye and overrun brake for the trailer but the rear row of seats in the lower deck was also removed to make space for hand luggage. Another alteration, visible in this photograph taken at London Airport (Heathrow) three weeks after it entered service on 4th August 1964, was the addition of a second nearside mirror to help the driver see the platform and lower saloon. A.J. Wild

Northern General Transport was the only provincial operator to buy the Routemaster, taking fifty in two batches of eighteen and thirty-two in 1964 and 1965. No. 2109 was in the second batch which differed from the first in having the shallower heater intake grille and blanked-off brake cooling grilles, the main difference from the London model being the sliding vent saloon windows. Gerald Mead

Below RMF 1254 found work and a permanent home in November 1966 with the Northern General Transport Company, in whose fleet it took the anagrammatical number 2145. It was fitted with a Leyland O.600 engine to bring its mechanical specification into line with NGT's own fifty, but differed from them in having wind down opening windows, rather than sliding vents, and the newer style of wing. Opening windows were also retained on the front upper deck windows, which were fixed on the company's own batch. Another difference which can be detected in this comparative view with 2122, was that the RMF retained the double nearside driver's mirrors which had been fitted for its BEA service. The Omnibus Society

While London Transport battled over the future of its double-deck bus replacement policy, the last of its vertical engined full size single-deckers were quietly withdrawn. The last official allocation of a 15T13 class AEC Regal III, on routes 352 and 387 at Tring, ceased on 23rd May 1962, when an RF took over, but Crawley retained one which it used to cover the single conductor-operated running on its works supplementary schedule and the 434 at weekends. T 787 was delicensed on 13th August 1962.
D.W.K. Jones

Meanwhile, mainstream developments had not been going to plan. With the completion of the trolleybus conversion on 9th May 1962, a start should have been made on the replacement of the RT family. Although many of the oldest examples had already gone, having been sold prematurely following the service cuts of the 1950s, the oldest of those still in stock were now fifteen years old. There had been a review of the depreciation provisions in December 1960 when the Executive had decided that the RT family should be replaced at an even rate of between 350 and 375 a year so as to achieve a more balanced age profile for the fleet and a more even flow of work through the overhaul shops at Aldenham Works. This meant that 2,685

(43%) would get three overhauls and be replaced after a service life of sixteen years, 1,718 (27%) four overhauls and go after twenty years and 1,866 (30%) would get a fifth overhaul and last for twenty-three years, the last RTs being withdrawn in 1977, RTLs in 1976 and RTWs in 1972. This compared with the original book life of fourteen years and represented a considerable vote of confidence in the reliability and durability of the RT.

This was already showing in the substantial savings in maintenance costs achieved through extending periods between docking and overhauls and it had even been possible to close down the special docking units at Camberwell and Norbiton which had been

built in the 1950s as part of the post-war garage plan. Unfortunately, as will be seen, London Transport's engineering organisation became so heavily dependent on RT standards of reliability that it was quite unprepared for the more daunting task of maintaining an inherently less reliable modern fleet in later years. All classes were covered by the depreciation review but, of the others, only RF buses and RLHs had their book life extended, from fourteen to seventeen years, which made the RFs due for replacement between 1969 and 1971 and the two RLH batches in 1967 and 1971. The life of RF coaches remained at fourteen years, leaving them due for withdrawal in 1965–66 and all other single-deckers remained at twelve years.

The other remaining front engined single-deckers were TD class Leyland Tiger PS1s with Mann Egerton bodywork almost identical to the 15T13s. A handful survived into the 1960s, at Kingston on routes 215, 215A, 218 and 219 and at Edgware on route 240A. The 218 and 219 received RFs displaced from route 212 at the beginning of 1960 but the Cobham to Downside section of the 215A was not approved for RFs until 1962, the TDs being replaced on 28th February. The last ten at Edgware were replaced by RFs on 10th October 1962. TD 104 is seen next to the railway bridge at Mill Hill.

The financial case for the first 1,488 was based on the assumption that peak service levels would be reduced to take account of the extra capacity of the RM but this had failed to gain acceptance from the staff and while the negotiations about the intended first stage at Harrow Weald rambled on through the summer of 1962, no new standard RMs went into service. They continued to arrive from Park Royal at the rate of seven or eight a week and by the beginning of December there were 178 in store, under cover at Edmonton, Willesden, Holloway, Hanwell, Hendon and Finchley and in the open at Stonebridge and Walthamstow. In the end the idea of making economies in this way had to be abandoned and the programme took the form of a straightforward like-for-like replacement concentrating first on the busiest routes where the extra capacity might produce extra revenue.

The joint management/Trade Union Bus Allocation Advisory Committee, met on 19th November 1962 to consider proposals from London Transport for the first phase of the revised replacement programme, covering the allocation of 519 scheduled RMs. The routes proposed were those with the highest revenue per car mile and the order of priority took account of any existing inadequacies in service, particularly where using the larger bus would avoid the need to schedule a more frequent service. They were, in order, routes 73, 24, 9, 37, 15, 30, 6, 14, 7, 52 and 137, which would have displaced sixty-three RTs, 308 RTLs and 148 RTWs. Based on its recently revised depreciation policy, London Transport expected the RTWs to be retained in service until 1972 and the last of the RTLs until 1976. The programme therefore included the redeployment of all the displaced RTWs. Those from route 24 at Chalk Farm were to go onto route 171 from Tottenham and Walworth, both garages which already operated the class, Upton Park's were to move over from the 15 to route 101, those from route 6 were to go to Cricklewood for route 16 and Putney's were to go to Camberwell for route 196. This was immediately challenged by the Trade Union, whose officers foresaw adverse reaction at garages where RTs were withdrawn in favour of Leylands. They were also concerned about the continuation of mixed allocations left over from the trolleybus conversion on routes such as the 41, and also about the operation of mixed types on parallel routes. A sub-committee was therefore set up to consider these matters and in the meantime conversion of the RTW operated routes was deferred.

Above right **Although the new RMs swept the RTLs off the 37 on most days, they were still required on Saturdays when the allocation was greater by no fewer than twenty-three buses. Fresh out of Aldenham, RTL 659 was one of the 450 Metro-Cammell bodied examples which were proving to be fully up to the high standards of manufacture and durability for which that company was famous. The bus is parked on the stand at Wakefield Road, Richmond.** A.J. Wild

Right **The first RTWs to be toppled by the RM were those on route 14 from Putney garage, which were replaced in one swoop on 2nd October 1963. RTW 381 is seen in Gower Street on 16th September.** Ken Glazier

A revised programme was agreed to clear the immediate backlog of vehicles and during December no fewer than 179 brand new Routemasters suddenly swept onto the streets. The great majority of them were licensed on 12th December when 119 scheduled runnings on routes 37 (Putney and Stockwell) and 73 (Mortlake and Tottenham) changed overnight from their long lasting RTL operation. Londoners were now treated to their first taste of the Leyland engined variety which made a mass debut and constituted the majority of the new buses, only those at Putney and eleven of Tottenham's having the familiar AEC unit. The small allocation of RTs on route 73 from Hounslow had been replaced by second hand RMs a week earlier on 5th December and an interesting little quirk of the complete change was that the whole of the bus service along Upper Richmond Road was now operated by the type and that, from 2nd January 1963, they were joined by RMCs on Green Line routes 716/A to make the road entirely Routemaster operated, except on Saturdays. Another overnight change took place on 17th December when the thirty-three RTs on route 13 from Hendon and Rye Lane garages were replaced by the more sweet toned AEC engined type. The last twenty to be licensed in 1962, a mixture of AEC and Leyland engined models, went to Cricklewood on Christmas Eve, where they represented a little over one-third of the number needed to complete route 16. The remainder went into service on 1st January 1963, the first new buses to be licensed by the new Board. By now the accumulation of vehicles had been cleared and the programme proceeded in a more normal manner with the big allocations at Rye Lane and Peckham on the 36 group being tackled in a changeover which took until 1st April to complete.

RM 1772 and Metro-Cammell bodied RTL 561 approach Ladbroke Grove station in December 1963, during the transition to RM operation on route 7. Fred Ivey

The sub-committee recommended that the problem of redeploying the RTWs could be toned down by adjusting the overhaul programme so that the 268 AEC RT8s due for disposal in 1963/1964 would be given a fourth overhaul and the like number of RTWs, due for their fourth overhaul should be withdrawn in their place. This was an expensive proposal because, whereas the RTWs had received a third overhaul to a standard which assumed a further ten years in service, the RTs had been given lighter attention. Under the revised proposals, it was still planned to redeploy all the RTWs displaced in 1963 but the proposed routes were changed. The new plan was to send Putney's and Upton Park's to Brixton for routes 95 and 109 respectively, Chalk Farm's to

Southall, where they would have reappeared on routes 92/A and 105 after a lapse of twelve years, and those from route 6 would also have gone to Southall to complete its entire allocation with the class. Only the allocation to routes 95 and 109 survived the negotiating process. Routes converted during the remainder of 1963 were, in sequence, the 9 (Mortlake and Dalston garages), 81B (Hounslow), 43 (Muswell Hill), 63 (Peckham), 85 (Putney and Norbiton), 85A (Putney), 14 (Putney), 24 (Chalk Farm) and finally route 7 (Middle Row) which was not completed until January 1964. The appearance of the 81B near the top of this list is an indication of how important this route had become as a link between the Piccadilly Line at Hounslow West and Heathrow Airport.

Routemasters swept into central London in December 1962 and two of the routes to receive them are illustrated here. RM 1801 passes the Hilton Hotel followed by another on route 73, in an uncannily deserted Park Lane. Capital Transport

Conversion of the Mortlake allocation of route 9 gave that garage the distinction of being the first old Central Bus garage, as distinct from former trolleybus depôt, to operate entirely Routemasters. Another landmark came, at last, with the conversion of routes 14 and 24, the first routes operated by RTWs to receive Routemasters but this unexpectedly marked the beginning of their withdrawal from passenger service. As planned, some of Putney's were transferred to Brixton for use on route 95, but the remainder went, not onto route 109 but as trainers, establishing them in a rôle which was to become more familiar in subsequent years. The idea of restocking Southall was quietly abandoned. Earlier transfers to the training fleet had been from the RTL class,

replacing the RT2 trainers the last of which, green RT 79, was delicensed at Dunton Green on 13th February 1963, just short of twenty-three years after it had first entered service at Chelverton Road. Some of the newer RTLs displaced by the conversion of route 9 were also despatched to Brixton, where they anticipated the arrival of the 'wides' by five months and were allocated to routes 50 and 57, and to Cricklewood, already a 'balancing' shed operating both AECs and Leylands, for route 60. To replace the older RT3 and RT10 bodied vehicles in the Country Area, a programme of repainting red RTs with RT3/1 bodies was started at the end of 1963. These gradually eliminated the roof box from Country Bus service until the last two were withdrawn on 1st February 1964.

Above Left Routemasters first appeared on route 85 in August 1963, using vehicles made surplus by the withdrawal of route 276, but this study of RM 1000, with its unique registration letters, was taken in Alton Road, Roehampton a couple of years later, by which time it had been decided to discontinue the use of the offside route number. Ken Glazier

Above An early Leyland arrival at Brixton was RTL 1556, found here in South Lambeth Road on 21st October 1963. G. Mead

Withdrawal of the 2RT2s which survived on training duties began in the summer of 1962, the last being delicensed on 13th February 1963. For a timber framed vehicle which was over twenty years old RT 130, photographed in Parliament Street, was in remarkably good condition, bearing testament to the durability of the original design and workmanship. Ian MacGregor

More radical vehicle developments were subdued during 1963 but an indication of the direction preferred by the Country Bus department was given in February with the arrival at Northfleet garage of the AEC Renown demonstrator 8071 ML. This was a new low floor chassis which AEC had developed to replace the unsuccessful chassisless 'Bridgemaster'. Like Routemasters, 8071 ML (known unofficially as RX 1) was powered by the AV590 engine and its transmission was through a Monocontrol gearbox, but it had a conventional beam axle and leaf-spring front suspension while using air suspension at the rear. There was also a synchromesh version which was not tried by London Transport. The Park Royal bodywork was a far cry from the elegance of the London Transport design produced by the same manufacturer, although with the benefit of hindsight it can be seen as of quite a high standard compared with what was to come out of that factory in later years. The frontal appearance was particularly ungainly, with a single skin dome, chunky corner pillars and a poor match between the high bonnet line (which was made lower on production models) and the low cantrail giving a rather cramped appearance to the driver's windscreen. The forward entrance layout was always a problem with low floor chassis, but the Renown was designed to give a reasonably tidy arrangement and was quite successful in this respect. By London standards it was a very high capacity bus, with a total of seventy-six seats (forty-four up; thirty-two down), which was no doubt an attraction for the busier double-deck services.

It went into service on the busy Thames-side route 480 in February 1963 but ran only for four months before being returned to Chiswick on 24th June. London Transport showed no further interest in the model and neither did very many other operators, who by now were far more likely to adopt a rear engined model to achieve the low height which was the Renown's main selling point. For London Transport, it offered little if any advantage over the RM in terms of economy of operation and could have been more costly to maintain. Geoffrey Fernyhough, the Country Bus Operating Manager, would probably have preferred a vehicle with a more simple specification, including a synchromesh gearbox and perhaps he would have done better to have pressed for a Regent V but this proved to be his only opportunity to win the argument and it was not to be long before the Routemaster was adopted as the standard vehicle for Country Buses.

Following its satisfactory experience with the saloon heater installations in the Green Line RTs, London Transport had decided in 1960 to equip all Country Area buses, covering a total of 991 vehicles in the RT, RLH, RF and GS classes. The programme started in September 1961 and was completed during 1963. At its meeting on 26th June 1963, the Board decided to extend the programme to the Central Area and authorised expenditure of £166,720 to equip a further 2,144 vehicles with a life expectancy of at least eight years, in effect the RFs and younger RTs.

In its prototype form, the AEC Renown had a higher bonnet line than was to appear on the production vehicles, giving it a rather clumsy looking front end, hardly enhanced by the graceless style of bodywork then standard for Park Royal's customers outside London. Although in London Transport Country Bus livery and bearing garage code and running number stencils, the status of this vehicle as a demonstrator is revealed by the illuminated advertisement for itself and the County of Middlesex registration, 8071 ML. A.J. Wild

There were no significant new vehicle developments at all during 1964, although decisions were taken during the course of the year which would have a fundamental effect on the future composition of the fleet. A total of 316 RMs was added to stock, continuing the replacement of the RT family throughout 1964, the last full year of standard RM production. A further report from the Bus Allocation Advisory Sub-Committee had recommended the complete withdrawal of all RTWs from passenger service by 1966 and their transfer to the training fleet where the use of eight-foot wide vehicles was considered more appropriate. The Board also yielded to the pressure from the Trade Union to eliminate mixed operation of types on one route and the first routes processed at the beginning of the year were therefore those which had been involved in the trolleybus conversion but had retained a partial allocation of RTs. They were the 18 (Alperton), 23 (Barking), 41 and 123 (Tottenham) and 64 (Croydon). The twenty-seven RTWs released from Tottenham were transferred to the training fleet. It is of interest to note in passing that it had been the intention to replace the RTs and RTLs used in the first three stages of the conversion, at Carshalton, Bexleyheath, Clapton, Lea Bridge, Bow and Ilford, as a first call on the new buses, once all trolleybuses had been replaced. This had been stated in all the early documents concerned with the replacement programme but appears quietly to have dropped out of the reckoning as a result of the change of policy at the end of 1962.

Other routes converted during the year were the 15/100 (Upton Park), 30 (Putney and Hackney), 134 (Muswell Hill, Holloway and Potters Bar), 130 group (Croydon), 137 (Victoria and Norwood) and 3 (Norwood and Chalk Farm). Route 15 was another important RTW route and, in line with the original plan, the forty-three vehicles displaced by the RMs were sent south of the river to Brixton for routes 57A and 109, joining those sent there from Chalk Farm the previous year and completing Brixton's switch to Leyland vehicles. Another similar switch took place at Rye Lane in June, when route 12 changed from RT to RTL using vehicles dislodged from Putney by the conversion of route 30 but in this case the rest of the 'all-Leyland' element consisted of Leyland engined RMs. Rye Lane was the last garage to receive a new allocation of RTLs as the Board had again changed its policy on disposals away from the oldest buses, irrespective of type, towards the rapid withdrawal of the unpopular Leylands of both classes. This had the interesting side effect of introducing into the fleet twenty-three roof-box bodied RTLs, as the older bodies were switched to the Leyland chassis during their final overhauls. As a consequence, during 1965 no fewer than 194 RTLs and 249 RTWs were withdrawn.

Operation of RTs on route 18 by Alperton garage had continued after its expansion to replace trolleybus route 662 but was brought to an end following the agreement with the Trade Union to eliminate these pockets of mixed operation, RMs being substituted on 11th March 1964. RT 285, still carrying an RT3 body, was photographed at Edgware before any of these developments, in September 1961. G. Mead

RT 1596, with RT3 bodywork, makes the time-honoured sweep around the full width of Oxford Circus, before the major works on the new Underground station for the Victoria Line changed its appearance for all time. RTs and RTLs were eliminated from route 137 during October and November 1964. A.B. Cross

There were several detailed changes to the specification of new standard RMs during 1963 and 1964, starting with RM 1662 at Peckham in August 1963 which was the first production bus to have the new triangular motif at the top of its radiator grille. Later in 1963, RM 1743 appeared at Chalk Farm on 12th November, without an offside route number blind. This now became the standard and instructions were issued to all garages to discontinue the display of offside route numbers on all buses immediately. Most did so with great enthusiasm but some continued for a while, the most notable being Harrow Weald which seemed to take pride in turning out its buses with full displays, including, where fitted, the RT3 style nearside pillar plate. Starting with Upton Park's RM 1902 in May 1964 vehicles were delivered with the cooling grilles in their wings replaced by a blank plate and, in November, RMs from 2063 upwards had a shallower external heater grille and a continuous cream band around the front.

More significantly, on 1st June, RM 1923 entered service at Putney carrying an illuminated offside advertisement display, the first of two hundred similarly equipped vehicles which went into service between then and February 1965. Depending on the electrical equipment carried, this variation was coded 2/5RM9 or 11/5RM9/2. The prototype was RM 1577 which had been used to demonstrate the principle to potential advertisers whose response was sufficiently enthusiastic to encourage London Transport to order a production batch (RM 1923–2121). All also had an illuminated panel above the windows on the lower saloon front bulkhead, which caused the removal of the heater control switch onto the top of the heater ducting panel, where it was fitted vertically instead of horizontally and replaced the (nearly always unused) advertising panel. This feature was adopted more quickly than the exterior illuminated panels, appearing from February on RM 1800 and 1810–1922 (coded 2/5RM9/1), and was fitted to all subsequent bus Routemasters from new. The Commercial Advertising department required that the exterior advertisement buses should operate on central London routes, as this was the most fruitful area for attracting advertising. In consequence, the allocation to route 130 at Croydon was made up of second hand vehicles from Dalston and Hendon, who received the new buses to run on West End routes 9 and 13. Second hand RMs were also used for the conversion of route 40 at Camberwell and Upton Park on 27th January 1965, using buses saved on other routes in the big scheme scheduled on that day.

Above **The normal rolling stock for the 8 group before the arrival of Routemasters in the first quarter of 1965 was the RTW type, like RTW 174 in the background of this view of the terminus at Old Ford, but on this occasion Bow has put Metro-Cammell bodied RTL 571 out to work the Sunday morning market service on route 8A, perhaps because they were proud of this smart new arrival from Aldenham.** A.J. Wild

Left **An older type of Country Bus could still be seen along tree-lined bus routes until 1963, albeit in this suitably lopped form for lopping trees. 971J was one of five so modified in 1953, before which it had been STL 1470. They were replaced by a like number of purpose-built Ford Thames vans.**
Colin Brown

Production of the standard RM came to an end in May 1965 with the delivery of RM 2217 from Park Royal. The only specification change to take place during this period was a minor livery alteration, first tried on RM 2128 which was allocated to Bow in January and then adopted as standard from RM 2210 onwards. The use of cream for the relief band, which had been standard since it had itself replaced white in 1945, was now discontinued in favour of 'flake grey' which was considered to be a more modern colour and more likely to brighten the appearance of the bus. Nearly all those licensed between January and May were allocated to routes 6 and 8, starting at Bow in January and February, then Willesden between February and April and finally Hackney in April and May. These two routes needed 104 buses between them and from this it will be evident that the rate of production had slowed markedly to only five or six a week. This lower rate was to continue during the delivery of the remaining 543 Routemasters, reflecting the period of extreme uncertainty into which London Transport's vehicle buying policy had now plunged. The history of those last Routemasters is inextricably linked to the next phase of vehicle development and is covered in chapter ten.

Above **RMs delivered after August 1963 had the new radiator grille with the triangle motif at the top but RM 1939, one of the batch delivered to Hackney for route 30 in July 1964, had already received one of the earlier type, leaving it bereft of any identity at the front, by the time it was photographed on newly converted route 6A at the Law Courts in April 1965.** G. Mead

Route 1 became the last recruit to the RTW class on 25th January 1965 when it took over the Saturday Willesden allocation. The association lasted less than a year as RTLs had replaced the RTWs by the beginning of 1966. RTW 8 is seen at the Willesden end of the route awaiting a through journey to Catford.
Capital Transport

CHAPTER FOUR

AREA SCHEMES: CENTRAL BUSES

During the period of the trolleybus conversion, London Transport had developed a taste for the idea of comprehensive reviews of service provision in given areas. Not that there was anything new in the approach. The LPTB had carried out a whole series of such reviews immediately after it was first formed in 1933 and then again during the tram to trolleybus conversions between 1936 and 1940 but these had been for the specific purpose of co-ordinating disparate operations and had fallen out of favour once their designated purpose had been achieved. A similar approach had been appropriate when it came to dismantle the trolleybus network but while they were working on this project, the service planning team came to realise that there was considerable scope for the principle to be extended to the rest of the Central Bus network. In fact, some changes which they had identified as desirable during that review were not followed through because they were deemed to be outside its scope. The idea was particularly attractive at this time as there was immense pressure to find ways of saving money, while still trying to give improvements for which the public was asking. Although demand had been falling for some years, there were still places where persistent inadequacies existed and areas where new housing and industrial

developments were still taking place. The concept of comprehensive reviews was given added momentum by the decision to replace the RT fleet by Routemasters on the basis of ten new buses for eleven old, which would require careful planning of peak hour resources where, as in the majority of cases, the newly converted RM services would cover roads shared by routes remaining RT. It was therefore decided that a small team of investigators would work on a continuous programme of such reviews, working around London with special attention to the heaviest loss-making services. Although the 'ten for eleven' principle was toppled by the Board's failure to secure an agreement with the Trade Union, the idea of area reviews survived and eventually became the basis of the Reshaping Plan (see chapter eleven).

As will be seen, the planning team often had great difficulty in arriving at simple solutions to some quite straightforward problems. At the root of their difficulties lay the workings of the scheduling agreement with the Trade Union which contained a complex set of rules governing the maximum length of duties, how long individual spells of duty could be, in what proportions duties could be early, middle or late turn, the proportions of duties which could exceed various levels of

spreadover and the way in which work could be rostered through the week. The complications were further exaggerated by the fact that different rules applied on Mondays to Fridays, Saturdays and Sundays and it was this aspect of the agreement which led to different route patterns being adopted at weekends. None of this was unique to London Transport, except in the detailed application of the rules, but any other operator would have overcome the restrictions by adopting joint compilation, London Transport's jargon for the widely used method of working crews on a variety of routes during their duty so as to achieve an efficient mixture of journey lengths. Unfortunately this method was barred to London Transport except by specific agreement in each case, agreement which was rarely conceded and therefore rarely sought. The person who paid for this was the passenger because London Transport created jointly compiled schedules simply by joining routes together and creating the sort of non-standard route patterns which were becoming all too common. The staff still had to work over the combination of routes which joint compilation would have given but as they carried a single route number everybody, except perhaps the passenger, was happy.

An early example, introduced on 12th

Facing Page **Route 162 was diverted into Mayesbrook Park Estate on 11th October 1961, in a scheme which had considerable local ramifications in West Ham. RT 2146 is at the western end of the route, Stratford Broadway.** A.B. Cross

Left **In the localisation scheme of 12th October 1960, route 108A was scaled down to a peak hour only service, leaving Eltham to be covered by the 228/A. RTL 1480 is in the new approach road to Blackwall Tunnel, part of a greater scheme which was to lead to yet more changes to the route structure at the end of the decade.** A.B. Cross

October 1960, was actually a continuation of the series of route 'localisation' schemes which had been set up during the 1950s but was more complicated than most and therefore effectively an area scheme. The aim was to improve the quality of service south of the river on the routes operating through Blackwall Tunnel which at this time consisted only of the original single bore with one lane of traffic in each direction and with several severe bends which limited vehicle speeds. There were two routes through the tunnel, the long established 108 running between Bromley-by-Bow and Crystal Palace and the more recent 108A between Bromley-by-Bow and Eltham (Southend Crescent). The latter had been treated to a localisation of its own in March 1953 when route 70 had been extended from Greenwich to Eltham, an arrangement which made sense in the traffic conditions of 1953 but which was now beginning to suffer from traffic delays on the long drag from Victoria. The 70 was therefore withdrawn from this section, the 108 was withdrawn between Lower Sydenham (Fairlawn Park) and Crystal Palace and the 108A reduced to a peak hour only service.

The Crystal Palace service was covered by a new route 108B, which started on the south side of the tunnel at Greenwich ('Star in the East') and followed the same route as the 108 except that it was rerouted between Blackheath 'Royal Standard' and Prince of Wales Road to run via Delacourt Road and Shooters Hill Road to give some relief to route 89. Roughly the same level of peak service was maintained over each section but between Blackheath and Lower Sydenham the off-peak service almost doubled, because the shortworkings on route 108 to Fairlawn Park had run only in peak hours.

The Eltham service was covered in a way which looks surprising to the modern eye but which looked reasonable in the conditions of the early 1960s. Route 228 was given a two-pronged extension from Eltham (Well Hall Station), as 228 to Surrey Docks covering route 70, and under the new number 228A to Greenwich ('Star in the East'), covering route 108A. In effect, a lot of the journeys which previously terminated at Rochester Way were linked with the 228s at Well Hall, which led to a substantial improvement in the peak service across this gap.

When double-deckers replaced single-deckers on its West Drayton to Hounslow section from 15th March 1961, the route number 222 disappeared. RF 508 was one of the thirty-seven which had been modified for one-man operation in 1959, the newly fitted platform doors being visible, open, behind the windscreen in this view at Uxbridge bus station. W.R. Legg

For reasons which are not clear, routes 161/161A were withdrawn between Woolwich Road (Victoria Way) and Greenwich Church as part of this scheme, although they approached this area from Eltham by an entirely different route. Their removal did help to keep the cost of the scheme down, however, and two fewer buses were needed to run the new pattern of service. Room had to be found in south London garages for the work transferred from Athol Street and this led to a chain of re-allocations. The eight runnings on route 108B were allotted to Catford, which lost its allocation on route 94 to New Cross, dislodging a like number of 163s into Camberwell, who sent eight 40s to Athol Street. The seven runnings lost at New Cross on route 70 were partly compensated by an allocation of five on route 228. As all these changes were confined to the Monday to Friday routes, they introduced yet another case where a completely different pattern operated at weekends, with Eltham served by both the 70 and 108A on Saturdays and the 108A alone on Sundays and Crystal Palace by the 108 on Saturdays and Sundays.

There was another scheme on 15th March 1961 which was again for a specific reason, in this case the completion of work on the bridge at West Drayton station which allowed double-deck buses to pass underneath. The two routes which ran under the bridge were the 222 and 224, both of which also passed under the low bridge in Yiewsley High Road which carried the Western Region Uxbridge branch, then still operating. To take full advantage of the new facility, therefore, it was necessary to indulge in some route restructuring. Route 222 was withdrawn altogether and replaced south of West Drayton by an extension of double-deck route 223. The section between Uxbridge and West Drayton was covered in a characteristically complicated way. Extra shortworkings were scheduled on route 224B on Saturdays and on the 224 on Sundays but on Mondays to Fridays a new route 224C was introduced, chiefly to maintain the peak hour link from Cowley and Yiewsley to the Bath Road factories. This ran from Uxbridge to West Drayton most of the time but with a half-hourly extension via former route 222 to London Airport North and then continuing through the tunnel to London Airport Central.

The changes in route lengths apparently gave the opportunity for a bit of tidying up on the section between Uxbridge and Ruislip which had been shared between routes 204 and 223 on Mondays to Fridays and Sundays. Apart from a few school journeys on the 204, this now became exclusive to route 223 once more.

All this huff and puff gave rise to an increase of a mere three in the number of RTs scheduled and a cut of four RFs. However, this proved to be a temporary arrangement as the Yiewsley bridge was altered to enable double-deckers to be substituted on routes 224A, 224B and 224C from 9th May 1962 without any change of schedule, in anticipation of the closure of the Western Region branch service between West Drayton and Uxbridge (Vine Street) on 8th September 1962. Route 224 itself remained single-deck for a further year.

RT 2921 makes an unscheduled appearance on RM route 238 heading for Becontree, from which the route was withdrawn in October 1961.
Peter G Mitchell

The first two of the true 'Area Schemes' were introduced with the Winter Programme on 11th October 1961 but one of these really arose out of a review of the new services introduced in the East and West Ham areas as part of the trolleybus conversion. Two new areas were blessed with a bus service as a result of the east London changes: Mayesbrook Park, Becontree and Lonsdale Avenue, East Ham; but the ramifications went far and wide in a complicated set of changes involving routes which were less than two years old. Route 5, already a long route by any standards, was extended on Mondays to Saturdays from Barking Garage to Becontree (Chittys Lane) to replace that section of route 238. The 238 was in turn diverted and extended to Little Heath ('Haw Bush') over the route of the 162 via Barley Lane, while the 162 was withdrawn from Little Heath on Mondays to Saturdays and diverted into new territory at Mayesbrook Park via Lodge Lane.

At this point the complications began to set in. Route 238 did not run on Sundays, so the service to Little Heath continued to be supplied by route 162 but renumbered 162A to distinguish it from the weekday operation. There was presumably some technical scheduling reason why the 238 could not have covered Mayesbrook Park to avoid this unnecessary complication. Further convolutions involving the 238 entered into the arrangements for the service for Lonsdale Avenue. This was carved out of route 272, which now became a circular service on Mondays to

Saturdays, from Stratford via West Ham Lane, Plashet Grove, East Ham, Lonsdale Avenue, Green Street and West Ham Lane. The peak hour operation to Royal Albert Dock, which had proved such a flop, was withdrawn at the same time. To maintain the correct levels of service on Saturdays, it was necessary to introduce the further complication of withdrawing route 238 between East Ham and Canning Town and diverting it via High Street North and Plashet Grove to Stratford Broadway, with the number 238A.

The other element of the scheme was unconnected with these changes, apart from being in the same area and providing some of the savings which helped to pay for the new facilities. It had the merit of tidying up a rather messy Monday to Saturday service pattern on routes 249 and 249A and substituting a more efficient arrangement. Both routes had infrequent through services from Chingford to the Docks, augmented by short-workings from Stratford, an arrangement which made it impossible to schedule proper interworking on the timetable. To overcome this the 249A was replaced south of Stratford on Mondays to Saturdays by the extension of route 41 to Victoria and Albert Docks. The service north of Stratford on the 249A was linked to the shorts on route 249 to give a stronger through service, the total effect being to double the frequency of buses across Stratford Broadway. Unfortunately, the pattern did not lend itself to this treatment on Sundays as route 41 did not run east of

Tottenham Hale, so the 249A had to continue to operate on that day.

The other scheme was a fairly modest affair aimed primarily at dismantling the circular operation on route 156, one of the old established Morden station feeder routes. The section between Sutton Common Road and St Helier had never been developed and was now never likely to be, whereas there was a section of unserved hinterland at Sutton Common whose residents had long been clamouring for a service. A new route 286 was therefore created, running between Raynes Park station and Belmont ('California') via Worple Road, Wimbledon, South Wimbledon, Morden, Sutton Common Road, Collingwood Road and Sutton, which replaced the south-eastern side of the circle while omitting the undeveloped section of Reigate Avenue. The other side was covered by the extension of route 151 from North Cheam to Sutton Garage via Cheam and Sutton High Street.

This was a good example of how the method was supposed to work. The scheme as a whole saved money, three fewer peak buses being needed for the revised services, but an important section of road got a new bus service and there were several new links, including a direct service from Worple Road, Wimbledon to the industry between South Wimbledon and Morden and onwards to Sutton. This was paid for by some quite severe cuts, notably along St Helier Avenue which not only lost the whole of the 156 but also got a less frequent 151.

There was one running cross-linked from route 25 on the new circular route 272, which explains the presence of RTL 1423 at Stratford. West Ham's RTs were replaced by RTLs when West Green garage closed on 3rd January 1962. M. Dryhurst

Approval was given in October 1961 to the use of RFs on route 215 runnings which did not operate on route 215A, followed in February 1962 by the clearance of route 215A as well, RFs displaced from Hounslow being used to replace the Tigers. TD 54 was the lowest numbered one still running when it was photographed at Esher. A.J. Wild

The Monday to Saturday service on route 213 between Sutton and Belmont was replaced by double-deck route 151 from 3rd January 1962. RF 523, which had started life as RF 304 before being renumbered in 1956, was one of the original 1959 conversions for Central Bus one-man operation but was still in use as a two-man bus, theoretically with the doors kept open, when photographed at New Malden on one of the Sunday runnings supplied by Kingston garage. Ken Glazier

The newly introduced route 286 was extended to Kingston via Coombe Lane on 3rd January 1962, although its blinds were not printed in the new lower case style, suggesting that they had been prepared for an earlier operational date. RT 1692, under the wires in Worple Road Wimbledon on the last Saturday of trolleybus operation, was one of the rare examples of a vehicle which retained its original body. It had been one of the quartet that had toured Europe in 1950 to advertise the Festival of Britain which had been adorned with commemorative plaques as well as GB plates. A.J. Wild

Even while the ink was drying on the new schedules, a further stage to this scheme was being planned for introduction on 3rd January 1962, when parts of routes 200 and 213 were double-decked. Neither route could be changed over completely. Route 200 had no low bridges to cope with but the introduction of double-deckers to the leafy heights of Wimbledon had been resisted by a high powered local residents group and London Transport had yet to win the argument. The main obstruction on route 213 remained the low bridge at Worcester Park and as there was no practicable way of splitting the service anywhere between Kingston and Sutton, double-deckers on this section were still ruled out. There was now a long overlap with route 151 from North Cheam to Sutton, however, and the new pattern of service opened the way for the Belmont service to be tackled by switching the ends of the two routes. The 151 was withdrawn from the section between 'The Grapes' and Sutton Garage and rerouted to run over route 213 through Carshalton and Staplehurst Road, to Belmont ('California'). The Belmont service on route 213 was withdrawn on Mondays to Saturdays and diverted to finish with the rest of the service at Sutton Garage. This represented a substantial cut in service to Belmont, varying between a quarter and a half of the total but there was a countervailing increase through Sutton High Street to the garage, so no buses were saved and only one running changed from RF to RT. Once again, as the 151 did not run west of Morden to Cheam and Sutton on Sundays, there was no change to the Sunday pattern of service.

In the case of route 200, the short section from Raynes Park to Copse Hill was not involved in the dispute with local residents and was selected for conversion, the newly born 286 providing the means. The opportunity was also taken to link this isolated area with its nearest major commercial centre by extending the 286 through to Kingston, introducing buses to the hitherto unserved section of Coombe Lane and joining route 213 at Traps Lane. As the bridge at Norbiton station was too low for double-deckers, the 286 had to run via Gloucester Road, another first for buses, and then Kingston Hill. To keep a standard route to and from Kingston, the 213 was similarly diverted. Two extra RTs replaced the one RF saved on the 200.

The former Admiral garage in Willow Walk, known as West Green, ceased operation after the close of traffic on 2nd January 1962. It had been a Leyland shed but in the last few days some RTLs were exchanged with RTs from West Ham, in anticipation of the complete swap on the day of the closure. One of these was RT 1822, seen entering the garage in flight from the severe weather which afflicted London in the early days of 1962. A.B. Cross

Although not an Area Scheme, the changes connected with the closure of West Green garage on 3rd January 1962 were an example of another important strand of the Executive's strategy for saving money. West Green garage, situated in Willow Walk near West Green Road, was one of the most solid surviving reminders of the Independent bus era in London, dating from 1923 when A. T. Bennett had converted part of the family's extensive engineering works on the site to a bus garage to house his 'Admiral' fleet. It had passed to the London Public Omnibus Co. in 1927 and then to the LGOC in December 1929. It was a medium sized garage with a scheduled peak output at the end of 1961 of sixty-five buses but its fate was sealed when Wood Green trolleybus depôt became a motor bus garage as, like many depôts, Wood Green had a considerable amount of unused parking space and was able to absorb most of West Green's work. The allocations on routes 29, 144, 217, 231 and 233 moved up the road in

their entirety, while route 29A switched to Palmers Green and the 171 to Tottenham, which already had a small allocation. Tottenham also took over the Wood Green allocation of route 259, acquiring in the process its first Routemasters. West Green had been one of the first two garages to operate production RTLs at the end of 1948 and was now the longest serving operator of the type but Wood Green was in an AEC engineering group and the Leylands had to go elsewhere. As recorded in chapter two, when West Ham garage had taken over the work of Forest Gate garage in April 1960, it should have received RTLs as it was in a Leyland group but the staff had persuaded the management to allow them to keep the RTs. Their time now ran out as a double switch was made in which West Green's Leylands went to West Ham, whose RTs went to Wood Green, some operating at West Green for a few days first.

The Harrow area review which came to grief when the Executive failed to secure a

new agreement with the Trade Union, covered routes 114, 140, 158 and 230. The review team apparently found that there was no need for any restructuring but they were able to redeploy some of the resources to provide a new Monday to Saturday service between Harrow Weald Garage and Northwick Park Station, serving College Avenue, College Hill Road and the section of Kenton Lane from there to Christchurch Avenue for the first time. It was numbered 230A despite having only a tenuous connection with route 230 from which it further differed by being officially allocated two RTs. In practice it was treated as a buffer route and it was common for spare RLHs to be operated. The 230A survived the mayhem which accompanied the introduction of the new schedules on 10th October 1962 but it was a frail thing operating in unpromising territory and it was not long before, on 14th August 1963, it was reduced to a Monday to Friday peak hour only service.

Route 209 was not affected by the planned changes in October 1962 but would have become Harrow Weald's only wholly RT route had the scheme gone through. In the midst of the conflict on 13th October, RT 4598 graces the calm suburban surroundings of Long Elmes. Peter G. Mitchell

Widespread changes on 27th February 1963 designed to move services into garages nearer their line of route, caused route 205 to be reduced to a Sunday only service. A few years earlier, with trolleybuses still running, RT3-bodied RT 799 heads east along Eleanor Cross Road. A.B. Cross

The Routemaster connection having been cleared away, work now concentrated on pure service reviews and one of the first of significance came to fruition in the Enfield and Waltham Cross areas on 27th February 1963. One of the aims of the scheme was to obtain more efficient garage allocations, notably on routes 205 and 242 which were both remote from their Enfield base. In the case of route 205, the solution was rather drastic as it was withdrawn entirely on Mondays to Saturdays. To cover the service north of Waltham Cross routes 279 (Saturdays) and 279A (Mondays to Fridays) were extended beyond Flamstead End to Hammond Street, although to maintain the level of service south of Flamstead End this was done by extending shortworkings from Waltham Cross. The Chingford service was covered by route 242, which was withdrawn between Waltham Abbey and 'The Wake Arms' and extended via Sewardstone Road to Chingford ('Royal Forest Hotel'). The Epping Forest arm of the 242 was replaced by a new route 217A from Alexandra Park ('Victoria'), formed by the extension of shortworking 217s from Waltham Cross to 'The Wake Arms'. Routes 205 and 205A continued to operate on Sundays between Flamstead End and Chingford or Hammond Street and 'The Wake Arms' respectively which, with the already existing 242A (Upshire – Potters Bar), gave an entirely different network to the area on that day of the week. The 242A was also extended in Potters Bar from the garage to 'The Lion' so that it could connect with route 29. There was another long overdue improvement on route 121 which was extended daily from Ponders End to its obvious local objective at Enfield Town and in Chingford from its unique terminus at the station to the main terminal in the town at 'Royal Forest Hotel'. It lost its Saturday only projection to Enfield Chase.

The operation of routes 242 and 242A was transferred from Enfield to Potters Bar, setting up a chain of re-allocations in which part of route 134 was transferred into Muswell Hill, the whole of the 251 from Muswell Hill into Edgware and the Edgware allocation on route 107 into Enfield. To facilitate the 107 re-allocation on Saturdays its duty schedule had to be combined with the 107A and as this was outside the terms of the Schedules Agreement the whole operation had to be absorbed into one route. The projections beyond Ponders End to 'The Alma' and Ponders End station were withdrawn and the 107A was nominally extended from Enfield Chase to Queensbury, although the only structural change was in the early morning when the Enfield Lock to Enfield Chase service was extended to Arkley. Other changes associated with the scheme involved the 217 and 231, which lost their Wood Green allocations in favour of an increase at Enfield, to make room for which the 102 went from Enfield into Palmers Green and the 29A from there into Wood Green. On Sundays the 102 went into Muswell Hill for the first time. Wrapped up in all this were frequency reductions, particularly on route 107 and between Turnpike Lane and 'The Cambridge' which gave a net saving of three peak buses, nearly four per cent of the number involved.

Route 242A stayed in place in the Waltham Cross area changes on 27th February 1963 but was re-allocated to Potters Bar and given a short extension from the garage to 'The Lion' to connect with route 29. RT 2662 is at the Upshire terminus displaying its new Potters Bar High Street destination. Peter G Mitchell

Judging by the movement of the driver's overcoat there is a chill wind blowing around RT 2787 at route 194B's exposed temporary terminus, Broom Road, on the first day of the new service to Shrublands Estate, 27th February 1963. P.J. Relf

There was another small scheme on the same day which included the inauguration of a service for the Shrublands estate, tucked away in an isolated corner of Shirley, close to the Kent/Surrey border. It was actually an extension of some of the many shortworkings which terminated at Monks Orchard Road but these were shared in a complicated way between the 194 and 194A and it was therefore necessary to make changes to both routes, although in the case of the 194 it amounted only to a reduction in its share of the shorts. Route 194A, on the other hand, as well as losing some shorts, yielded the section between Croydon (Katherine Street) and Thornton Heath, which had been introduced only in May 1962, to new route 194B. This ran from Thornton Heath (High Street peaks and Saturdays/Garage Monday to Friday off-peak) via route 194A to Shirley Park, then Wickham Road and Bridle Road to Broom Road, which became its a temporary terminus until access to its final terminus at Bramble Close became available a year later. The new route was allocated to Elmers End, which supplied eight RTs, six of which had been gleaned from the 194/A.

Other Croydon area routes included in this review were the 68, 75, and 196 but the ramifications extended also to routes 70 and 188 and the re-allocations even further. The aim of this part of the scheme was to strengthen the basic Monday to Friday service on route 68 throughout the day and a handsome increase of fifty per cent was achieved. To help pay for this, route 75 was withdrawn between West Croydon station and Croydon garage and the 188, outside peak hours on Mondays to Fridays, between Euston and Chalk Farm. The 188 and 196 also contributed with frequency reductions, partly compensated in the case of route 188 by the extension of some shorts from Surrey Docks to Greenwich. Even so, the scheme as

a whole needed five extra buses, two for the Shrublands service and three for the improvements to route 68, all in recognition of the gradual growth in importance of Croydon as a commercial centre. The extra workings on route 68 were shared between Chalk Farm, where they picked up the buses and staff shed by the 196, and Croydon where room was made for them by transferring some 12s to Rye Lane. The 173 moved on Mondays to Fridays from Rye Lane to Peckham, where the reduction on route 188 had left space for it.

The biggest scheme so far came with the summer schedules on 8th May 1963 and involved a major restructuring of routes in the Woolwich area. This stemmed from a review of the routes introduced at stage one of the trolleybus conversion which themselves had added substantially to the complications of the network. One of the principal aims of the scheme was to eliminate the unsatisfactory arrangement whereby route 126 terminated from the south at Plumstead Common, tantalisingly short of the main local objective at Woolwich. This had its origins in the necessary pennypinching of the early post-war years when the route had first been extended to serve the estates north of Falconwood but it is surprising that no earlier opportunity had been found to rectify so obvious a flaw.

Inevitably, so it seems, the remedy was not a straightforward extension of route 126, most probably because this would have created an inefficient route length for duty scheduling purposes. Instead it was cut back, to Welling Station on Sundays and to Eltham on Mondays to Saturdays. Instead of using its pre-1951 terminus at Southend Crescent, however, it was diverted away from the High Street shopping centre to finish at Well Hall station, where canteen facilities existed for the staff. It was replaced in two parts. Between Eltham and Welling it was covered by

a Monday to Saturday extension of route 124, which then continued via Wickham Lane and Plumstead to Woolwich (Parsons Hill) to cover this section of route 195. The rest was replaced by route 241 on Mondays to Saturdays, 51 on Saturdays and Sundays and 51C on Saturdays, all of which were extended from Welling to Plumstead Common and then onward to Woolwich (Parsons Hill) via Burrage Road, over which section they covered the withdrawal of routes 54 and 180. All three were further extended in peak hours to Woolwich Road (Victoria Way), a further complication introduced in connection with changes to routes 177 and 180.

Route 180 took a key step towards its eventual role as the principal route on the Abbey Wood – Greenwich alignment by having its Monday to Friday peak hours only extension from Woolwich to Plumstead Common withdrawn, enabling the entire route to be extended on Mondays to Saturdays from Woolwich to Abbey Wood garage. It did not follow route 177 along McLeod Road but instead absorbed this end of route 177A and continued beyond its Grovebury Road terminus to bring buses to Sewell Road and Harrow Manor Way for the first time. The frequency of route 180 between Woolwich and Greenwich was also increased and the extension of routes 51, 51C and 241 also provided extra mileage as far as Victoria Way. Otherwise, route 177A was not replaced west of Woolwich and there were accompanying frequency reductions on route 177 which added up to a cut of about fifty per cent between Greenwich and New Cross. On the other hand, there was a one-third increase in the peak hour service to the Abbey Wood Estate.

Although route 180 did not run on Sundays, it would have been quite logical simply to renumber the 177A, which operated only between Woolwich and Abbey Wood Estate on that day; but that was perhaps too simple. Instead, Sunday only route 163A was withdrawn between Woolwich and Woodlands Estate and extended via the weekday 180 to Abbey Wood. (The two early morning journeys which had continued beyond Camberwell Green to Kennington ('Horns') were taken off at the same time.) This did have one merit, as it provided the opportunity to standardise the service to Woodlands Estate, which was now covered on Sundays, as on other days, by route 192, extended from Woolwich. Coincidentally, the Lower Sydenham end of the 180 had its Sunday service restored with an extension of route 160 from Catford, adding one more to the list of non-standard routes. This example was reinforced by a diversion at the other end which switched the terminus from the 'Guy, Earl of Warwick' at Welling to Plumstead garage and by the decision to renumber the route to 160A. The diversion to Plumstead garage was no doubt to enable crews to reach refreshment and toilet facilities which were notoriously unavailable at Lower Sydenham.

This leaves one link remaining to be forged in this chain of changes, the fate of route 195, although the section between Woolwich and Welling has already been mentioned in connection with route 124. The rest, from Welling to Eltham, was covered by the extension of route 89 in a huge hairpin loop via Bexleyheath, Bexley and Blackfen to Well Hall where it was within just over a mile of itself at Shooters Hill having taken nearly an hour to complete the journey. It is difficult to see what benefit such an arrangement had over the old circular working on the 132, confusing as that might have been, which the 195 had been designed to unravel. The new schedule on route 89 gave a slightly less frequent service between Welling and Lewisham and this was compensated by an increase on route 192, which also contributed to the overall level of service between Woolwich and Plumstead Common. The extension of route 89 did at least run daily and there was one other small change which ran counter to the general trend of Sunday variations. Route 122A was reinstated on Sundays and the extraordinary Sunday extension of route 53 beyond Plumstead Garage to Erith was withdrawn. It could be, perhaps, that the reinstatement of the 122A and the diversion of the 160A were intended, taken together, to cover the Sunday operation of the 195 from Welling to Woolwich but if so it was a clumsy and unhelpful way of doing so.

Route 177A had been a spin-off from the trolleybus conversion in March 1959, running between Abbey Wood estate and Woolwich until being extended to New Cross in May 1962 and then replaced by the 180 in May 1963. RT 3068 climbs to cross the railway in Eynsham Drive, with new housing going up in the background, while working on the short route.
Peter G Mitchell

Route 195 was introduced at the time of the conversion of the Bexleyheath trolleybuses in March 1959, amalgamating part of route 696 with the eastern side of the 132 loop. Four years later, as part of the big scheme of changes in the Woolwich area on 8th May 1963, it was withdrawn. RT 2813 is at the Parsons Hill terminus at Woolwich, about to work a short to Bexleyheath. W.R. Legg

The Sunday extension of route 53 to Erith, covering the 122A, had been an early example of this type of economy, dating from October 1956, but it was dismantled as part of the Woolwich area changes. Plumstead's RT 2582 is leaving the Elephant & Castle stop in New Kent Road on the last Sunday of this operation, 5th May 1963.
Ken Glazier

The inevitable alterations to garage allocations brought about some interesting new features. Route 180 filled the gap left at Abbey Wood by the withdrawal of the 177A, including four runnings transferred from Catford to make room there for the additional work on routes 124 and 192. Balance was achieved at Catford by switching a couple of 47s to Bromley to provide a cushion against the cut on route 126. To cover the loss of the 195 Bexleyheath garage acquired an interest for the first time in routes which had no trolleybus associations. It took some of the extra runnings on route 89, shared with New Cross, and the whole of route 132 which was transferred from its traditional, inefficiently remote, base at Sidcup where room had to be made for the extra work on route 241.

Much of the complexity of the Woolwich scheme could be ascribed to the curbs imposed by the scheduling agreement and it was these that helped create the further muddle in the Uxbridge Scheme which was also launched on 8th May. A core aim in this case was to replace the single-deckers on route 224 with double-deckers, now that approval for their operation south of Harmondsworth had been secured. As it would have been impracticable to reduce its already low frequency, route 224 itself was unchanged, but some economies were needed on the high frequency section between Uxbridge and West Drayton. A simple reduction in frequency of the joint 224A/B/C was apparently not feasible and it was found necessary to involve route 204 but only on Mondays to Fridays. The residual journeys still operating beyond Uxbridge to Ruislip on those days were withdrawn and transferred to route 198 (a.m.) and 224 (p.m.) so that the 204 could be used to twist back on itself, 89 style, and run via Cowley to West Drayton. In peak hours it continued further, to London Airport Central, replacing the 224C. Some shorts previously numbered 224C were renumbered 224B on Mondays to Fridays but on Saturdays it was found more economical to run a slightly more frequent service on both 224A and 224B and withdraw the shorts altogether. The Saturday service on route 204, which still ran to Ruislip, was renumbered 204A and the section of route through Ickenham was now served, variously, by routes 198, 204A, 223 and 224.

Other changes in the Uxbridge area were only loosely associated with the 224 but, as often happened, were done at the same time to avoid disturbing the duty roster too often. The 98 group, which was already a fair muddle, was given a shake up and came out in an equal state of confusion. Saturday only route 98 (Hounslow Garage to North Harrow) was given a Monday to Friday service, but only between Hounslow and Hillingdon with a peak hour extension to Ruislip Station. This was, in effect, the 98A renumbered, reduced and diverted to run direct in Hillingdon via Long Lane, instead of via Windsor Avenue and Granville Road. This loss was made up by diverting the 98B away from Long Lane. The 98B, which was already a long route running from Feltham (in peak hours) or Hayes to North Harrow was also given a short peak hour extension from North Harrow to Rayners Lane (which became all day in the Winter schedules from 9th October).

The other member of the group was the 198, which ran from Hounslow West on Mondays to Fridays and Hayes on Saturdays, to Uxbridge, also serving Windsor Avenue in Hillingdon. This was withdrawn between the peaks between Hounslow West and Hayes but also extended to Hounslow garage at other times on Mondays to Fridays. All this was designed to save money and took place alongside an approximate cut in frequency of about twenty-five per cent which gave a saving of five buses.

In the absence of an agreement for one-man operation in the Central Area, converting single-deck routes to double-deck on reduced frequencies was still considered worthwhile, even as late as May 1963 when route 224 was given the treatment. RF 533, seen in Bakers Road Uxbridge on 16th April 1963, was one of six which had been transferred from Country Buses in December 1956 following a row with the staff, and had been fitted with doors for the second time when it was converted for one-man operation in 1959. Ken Glazier

RT 1595 at Uxbridge station on one of the proliferating weekend variations, the Saturday only 204A, renumbered from 204 when the Monday to Friday service was extended to West Drayton and London Airport. A.B. Cross

Some of the savings from these changes were used to provide a new service for the post-war estates north-west of Northolt Station. This was accomplished by joining together routes 225 and 232 between their less than satisfactory terminals at 'Eastcote Arms' and Greenford ('Civil Engineer') respectively, forging some useful new north-south links at the same time. Route 232 was extended via Yeading 'White Hart', Church Road, Northolt, Mount Farm Road and Eastcote Lane, where it picked up the route of the 225 to Northwood station (continuing to Mount Vernon Hospital on Sundays). It had been hoped to take the more direct route through Ealing Road (later renamed Kensington Road) to Northolt but there was a five ton weight limit on the bridge over the Grand Union Canal in Ealing Road and London Transport had been unable to persuade the authorities to make it suitable to take a bus.

The re-allocations which flowed in the wake of all these changes had some surprising consequences. There was a net saving of three buses from all this huffing and puffing (six fewer RFs, three additional RTs) but the only garage to lose work was Hounslow, whose disappearing allocation on the 98A was not replaced. Route 232 remained allocated wholly to Southall and to make room for its extra buses, part of route 97 was transferred into Hanwell, introducing RTs to that garage for the first time. The balance was completed by the transfer of eight runnings on route 207 from Hanwell to Uxbridge garage, bringing Routemasters to this Buckinghamshire outpost which was not, however, new to the route as it had been running RTs on Sundays since October 1961.

Route 225, a rare wartime innovation, had one more day of its nineteen year life to run when RT 2804 made this journey down Joel Street, approaching Wiltshire Lane, on its way to the 'middle-of-nowhere' terminus at the 'Eastcote Arms'. Ken Glazier

RT 1674, pulling away from Eastcote station in unfamiliar territory for route 232, has an RT3/3 body built by the resoundingly named Saunders Engineering and Shipyard Company, its canopy route number plate gleaming as though illuminated. Peter G Mitchell

Another double-decking which took place in the same 8th May programme caused less upheaval but is worth mentioning as it was really a delayed part of the Sutton Area scheme already described and in a way constituted a miniature 'scheme' in its own right. The route concerned was the 213 which was itself converted from RF to RT on a drastically reduced frequency but this was substantially restored over most of the route by a new 213A which provided a service for some previously unserved roads. This ran between the same terminals as the 213 but deviated from the main route in Norbiton to continue through Gloucester Road, Kenley Road and Clarence Avenue, regaining the old route in Coombe Road. The presence of route 286 in Coombe Lane was an obvious help in serving the traffic displaced from the 213 and the reasoning behind the earlier extension of route 286 now became a bit clearer. The 213A also took over the Sunday extension from Sutton to Belmont. Even this little change had its allocation quirk. The normal Monday to Saturday allocation on the 213 had been shared by Norbiton and Sutton but on Sundays Norbiton ran no single-deckers at all and the 213 was run by Kingston on that day. Kingston could hardly run double-deckers only on Sundays but there were no single-deckers to exchange with the 213, so the solution was to put double-deckers back into Kingston, after a lapse of just twelve months, and transfer Monday to Saturday route 264 from Kingston to Norbiton in exchange for the 213.

The next scheme was one of a sequence stemming from reviews of services along the major corridor, known in shorthand as

'Brixton Road' but extending all the way down the Brighton Road to Croydon. This particular phase, introduced on 14th August 1963, had at its core the hapless route 276 which had never prospered since its introduction at stage ten of the trolleybus conversion

and had already lost its Saturday service in October 1962. It was now withdrawn completely and its essential elements covered in various ways which allowed for increases on the hard pressed London to Streatham and Wandsworth corridors, where inadequacy was occurring because of the considerable increase in newly built office accommodation on Albert Embankment. Route 39, another ill-fated route in these troubled times, was completely altered north of Charing Cross, on Mondays to Fridays only, to run via Oxford Circus, Albany Street and Camden Town to Finsbury Park. There was a peak hour extension to Tottenham, a town it had last served in October 1938 when, ironically, it had been rerouted in connection with the introduction of trolleybuses.

Above **The new abutments of the railway bridge, built when the roadway was lowered to accommodate double-deck buses, can be seen behind RT 3736 on the 213A at New Malden station eight months after the route was inaugurated.** Ken Glazier

Left **The absence of a Sunday service on route 194B led to strong pressure for one to be provided for Shrublands estate. The pressure was resisted but a concession was made from 18th August 1963 with the diversion of route 194 to follow the 194A routeing through Shirley Way, bringing it a little closer to the estate in Bridle Road. RT 1562 appears in the new guise as route 194C at East Croydon.** Peter J. Relf

This sustained the Tottenham to West End link, while the service between the West End and south London was maintained by a massive rescheduling of routes 59A and 159. This included the withdrawal of the 59A between Streatham and Thornton Heath but increased the peak hour service between Trafalgar Square and Brixton garage above the previous combined level of the three routes. The former route of the 39 was taken over by another new route, 156, which ran on Mondays to Fridays only, from Parliament Hill Fields via Camden Town, Tottenham Court Road and Trafalgar Square, then via route 77A across Lambeth Bridge, to Clapham Junction with a peak hour projection to Wandsworth. This was accompanied by a reduced service on routes 77 and 77A, although there was a small net increase in service along Wandsworth Road. The overlap between the localised and in-town sections of route 77A between Clapham Junction and Wandsworth was also eliminated to save money. There were no structural changes to weekend services, so the 39, still working over its old route, had to be renumbered 39A.

Not directly connected with all this but linked to it by interlocking garage re-allocations was a restructuring of routes 74 and 74A, which resulted in the diversion of the latter away from Marylebone Station to run to Camden Town, and the introduction of a new route 74B. This was introduced as much as anything for operational reasons and was a device to get the Riverside allocated buses closer to the garage for relief purposes. It was, in effect, an extension of half the shortworking buses from Earls Court to Hammersmith Broadway via Lillie Road and Fulham Palace Road.

Taken as a whole, there was an increase in the peak vehicle requirement of two buses. The saving of one bus on the 74 group had been used to finance an increased service on route 85A, which kept the allocation at Chelverton Road at the same number, although there was some transfer from the 74 to the 74A. Chalk Farm took over the 39 from Holloway and therefore lost both its small allocation on the 74 and all its share of the 196. The 196 moved into Highgate, taking its RTLs with it and introducing the RT family to yet another former trolleybus depôt. Part of its Camberwell allocation also moved over to make room for the extra buses now needed on the 59A but at Streatham the extras needed on the 159 were just added. At Holloway the loss of the 39 was made up by providing half the requirements for route 156 and the transfer of some 27s from Riverside, where they made way for the extra 74Bs. The remainder of the 156 was put into Stockwell, where more than enough room was created by the reductions on routes 77/A.

The Winter Programme on 9th October 1963 contained a massive dose of weekend changes, all aimed at achieving mileage reductions of one per cent on Saturdays and five per cent on Sundays compared with the winter of 1962. Most of the cuts were straightforward reductions in frequency but there were a number of changes which added to the increasing list of route patterns which differed at weekends. One curiosity was the 265, which already did something different on each of the weekend days, running in two unconnected sections on Saturdays (Copt Gilders to Kingston/Kew Green to East Acton) and only between Copt Gilders and Kingston on Sundays. The Saturday service to East Acton was now replaced by the extension of route 7 over its own former route, giving this section three different routes: 265 on Mondays to Fridays, 7 on Saturdays and 15 on Sundays. The Copt Gilders operation was not touched on Saturdays but on Sundays it was replaced by new route 65A, which was an extension of shortworking 65s from Kingston.

A second involved yet another group of routes which were of recent origin and saw the withdrawal of route 239 (Moorgate – Hampstead Heath) in its entirety on Saturdays and Sundays. Route 63 was also withdrawn between Kings Cross and Parliament Hill Fields so that it could be diverted over the 239 to Hampstead Heath, taking the number 63A. Some compensation was provided on route 214 to build up both the Moorgate and Parliament Hill Fields services. Curioser still were the alterations to route 142, which was withdrawn on Sundays between Edgware and Kilburn Park while the emphasis of its Saturday operation was switched towards the Kilburn end, when half the service between Edgware and Watford was absorbed into a long extension of Saturdays only route 292A. This gave the route the shape of a deranged horseshoe and the distinction of completing a journey from Borehamwood to Bushey Heath in forty-eight minutes, compared with thirteen by country route 306.

RM 1675 heading south at Ludgate Circus on route 63A, one of the new routes invented to cover the weekend withdrawal of route 239, which by chance re-introduced the pre-war route of the 63 to Hampstead Heath.
Malcolm E. Papes collection

Facing Page The number 156 came back on 14th August 1963 for what was to prove a fleeting appearance between Parliament Hill Fields and Clapham Junction with a peak hour extension to Wandsworth, on which Stockwell's RTL 1591 is working. The Skyways advertisement for its coach/air service to Paris at £9 return shows how the value of money has changed in the intervening thirty years, although it was cheap even by 1963 standards. G. Mead

Left The number 65A was given to an amalgam of shortworking 65s and the Sunday rump of the 265 as one of the economies instituted in October 1963. Both routes are illustrated in this view of the Argyle Road terminus, Ealing – RT 839 on the 65A and RT 2241 on the 65.
Peter G. Mitchell

By far the greater number of route changes in the programme evolved from another huge review of east London services, although many of these too were concentrated in the weekends. The theme this time was 'localisation', although in a couple of cases the validity of this label might appear difficult to justify. The biggest example was route 25, which already had an infrequent 'local' service on Mondays to Fridays between Bow and Becontree Heath. The entire Monday to Friday service was now split so that buses from Victoria went no further than Ilford and a very much reduced Becontree Heath service started from Aldgate in peak hours and Bow at other times. The balance of the service east of Ilford was made up by extending route 150 to Becontree Heath. On Sundays route 150 already had an extension beyond Ilford to cover route 147 to East Ham and this now had to be renumbered 150A.

Above right The 292A had been introduced in June 1962 as a Saturday only version of the 292 running to Edgware instead of Colindale and was extended on to Watford in October 1963. It would not be long before the vantage point for this photograph of RT 3838 in Barnet Way, Mill Hill, would become lethal for the photographer, once the road had been widened and become a super-highway. Colin Stannard

Yet another Sunday only route number came into being on 9th October 1963 when the Sunday service on route 150 had to be renumbered 150A. In this timeless view at Chigwell Row, RT 2209 shares the stand with RT 3769 on a more venerable Sunday variant, route 62A. The encroachment of cars around the buses illustrates one of the causes of fading demand and loss of revenue. J.G.S. Smith

RT 294 uses part of the new ring road at Romford on its way to Upminster Park Estate, which it reached as a 'localisation' of route 86 in October 1963. Colin Stannard

Another number to resurface after a short absence was the 179, which popped up in east London on 9th October 1963 as an amalgamation of parts of routes 145 and 193. Half the Thames View Estate service started from Barking, where RT 867 lays over on the London Road stand. Cigarette advertising was still acceptable at this time and bus sides were a popular choice for most of the big tobacco companies. P.J. Relf

It is an interesting indication of the traffic conditions of the time that London Transport still found it possible to achieve an effective improvement in reliability by creating quite long rambling new routes across large tracts of suburban London, provided they were isolated from central London or a few key sections of trunk main road. The changes surrounding the localisation of route 145 fell into this category, the purpose being to isolate the service east of Ilford from the ravages of traffic delays encountered on the Southend Road between Woodford and Gants Hill. A straightforward splitting of the route was eschewed in favour of a greater upheaval stretching right over to Upminster to include a service east of Chadwell Heath free from the delays in Stratford and Bow. Apart from a few school journeys, route 145 itself was simply withdrawn between Chingford and Ilford but the replacement was a new daily

route 179 which continued beyond Ilford to Thames View Estate via route 193. The 193 was withdrawn only between Barking and Thames View so as to retain the link from Ilford Lane towards Seven Kings, and the bulk of the compensating cut between Ilford and Barking was made on route 169. Route 193 did not get shorter, however, as it was simultaneously extended from Chadwell Heath to Upminster Park Estate as a localisation of route 86. The 86 was nominally withdrawn from the short section between Upminster Station and the estate, but in fact half the service was cut back to Chadwell Heath. As the 193 ran daily, Upminster Park Estate got a Sunday service and in consequence route 248 was withdrawn between Hall Lane and the station and shrank to a one bus operation with meal relief gaps in the timetable. The scheme as a whole spread to many more routes in the area, but other changes to the route structure were confined to Sundays, notably between Aldgate and Poplar where there was still a very frequent service during the hours of the Petticoat Lane market on no fewer than five routes (5B, 9, 15, 40 and 95A). Changes were made to the frequency patterns of routes 5B, 9 and 15, including the withdrawal of a number of shorts on route 9, to make way for an extension from London Bridge to Poplar of route 44, which was already a non-standard route on Sundays as it had been covering the 77 to Wallington since November 1958. The extension was designed to provide connections to the market from more parts of south London but, unlike the 95A, the 44 ran for the whole traffic day and not only during market hours. Part of the same scheme but quite separate from these changes was the introduction of a full circular service on route 272 on Sundays, making it a daily operation.

Among other weekend economies was the withdrawal of route 148A on Sundays, itself an amalgam of Monday to Saturday sections of routes 147 and 148. The service to The Drive, Ilford, was maintained by extending route 145 to Leytonstone under the number 145A. The 32, whose introduction in stage three of the trolleybus conversion had always seemed one of the more pointless inventions of that programme, also disappeared on Saturdays to be replaced by the extension of shorts on route 25 from Aldgate to Victoria, a few extra morning buses on route 26 and some 10s extended from Leytonstone to Stratford. The route was withdrawn altogether in November 1964.

Eleven buses were distilled out of these schedules, a cut of nearly five per cent on the 230 buses involved in the scheme and there were the usual re-allocations to balance the ups and downs of work among garages. Route 86 lost its North Street allocation, to make room for 175s switched from Hornchurch which took over part of the 193 and some extra 86s. Route 145 was removed from Upton Park but its replacement route 179 was found a more economical home at Barking, where room was made for it by transferring some 169s to Seven Kings and the whole of the 162 into West Ham. The space at West Ham was made available by the cuts on route 25, and at Seven Kings by a cut on route 148.

The number 213B was applied to the Sunday route through Clarence Avenue, Malden, when the 213A was extended from Sutton to Wimbledon on Mondays to Saturdays in January 1964. RT 4289 is on the Wood Street stand at Kingston, to which the 213 group had been diverted when the Kingston one-way system was introduced on 14th July 1963. A.J. Wild

Upminster station became the eastern terminus of route 86 when the 193 was extended to Upminster Park estate in October 1963. RT 2776 was one of the trio of vehicles which had visited the United States in 1952 and had been equipped with additional ventilators in the front dome to overcome the heat of the southern states. Gerald Mead

The next big programme of new schedules came into operation during the week commencing 29th January 1964 and was of particular note to the staff as it included new duty schedules and rosters which reduced the proportion of Saturday work. It also covered the closure of yet another small garage, the former trolleybus depôt at Carshalton. The main Area Scheme was a further stage in the Brixton Road/Croydon review and included another example of long-legged localisation, this time applied to route 133 which was withdrawn on Mondays to Fridays between Thornton Heath (High Street) and South Croydon garage. It was replaced by a new 133A which ran from South Croydon to Kennington Church, with a peak hours extension to Embankment (Horse Guards Avenue) via Lambeth Bridge and Millbank, theoretically covering for route 50 although by an almost entirely different route. The peak hours only extension of route 50 from Stockwell to Horse

Guards Avenue (via Vauxhall) was withdrawn and a Monday to Saturday extension to Victoria installed in its place. This in turn covered the 57, which was cut back to Stockwell, except outside peak hours on Mondays to Fridays, when it was further curtailed at Brixton Garage. At the other end, the 57 was given a huge extension, which has endured until the time of writing, from Tooting Broadway to Kingston, following route 155 to Wimbledon and then replacing the two-year old route 286.

The 286 was withdrawn entirely on Mondays to Saturdays and its other end was replaced by an extraordinary extension of route 213A from Sutton garage to Wimbledon Station. The planning team apparently baulked at the idea of running it all the way back to Kingston but seem to have been resigned to having to create this extremely indirect route, which bore all the hallmarks of a combination of bits and pieces designed

around the efficiency of the duty schedule. The 286 continued to run on Sundays only between Kingston and Belmont and the 213A, which covered the Belmont service via Carshalton on Sundays, had to be renumbered 213B on that day. As the 57 had already been bastardised into the 57A some time earlier, the non-standard Sunday pattern was complete.

Some beneficial side-effects of these changes included a substantial increase in service to Victoria and lesser increases on the Stockwell–Brixton–Streatham–Thornton Heath alignment and between Kennington and Brixton. On the other hand, there were hefty cuts between Kennington and Liverpool Street, Vauxhall and Horse Guards Avenue and between Thornton Heath and Croydon. The latter was based on the theory that a more reliable localised service would deliver more buses than the unreliable, theoretically more frequent, through service.

In the Croydon area, the main thrust was a re-organisation of the services between Croydon and Thornton Heath designed to give New Addington estate a direct service to the Purley Way factories. This was done by re-routeing the Monday to Friday peak hour extension of route 130A to Thornton Heath (High Street) to run via Waddon and Purley Way, instead of direct via Broad Green. The off-peak service to Thornton Heath was cut back to West Croydon and the whole of the operation renumbered 130B. The former 130A service was replaced by route 194A which was extended on Mondays to Fridays from Katherine Street to Thornton Heath garage and on to the High Street in peaks, a section it had abandoned only eleven months earlier. To complete the circle, the 119 was withdrawn in peak hours between Thornton Heath garage and High Street. As part of this scheme, Lisson Grove and Rossmore Road Marylebone, which had been served on Mondays to Fridays by a diversion of route 59A since November 1958, were given a weekend service for the first time. As the 59A did not operate at weekends, the Saturday service was supplied by diverting half the 159s, renumbered 159A, and on Sundays, when there was no 159 either, the 59 was diverted instead, a model example of a non-standard weekend pattern.

The net effect of all these changes was to increase the peak vehicle requirement by two buses, not a bad result at a time when services generally were being cut. There were also some interesting allocation changes, made more extensive by the coincidental closure of Carshalton garage. Carshalton's routes were shared by Sutton (154) and Merton (157) but Sutton was perennially cramped for space and had to relinquish its allocation on route 115 to Thornton Heath. There was also a reshuffling of work between Sutton, Kingston and Merton which gave route 213A an exclusively Sutton allocation. There was quite an upheaval at Brixton which lost both routes 50, to Streatham, and 57, to Merton, their place being taken by route 133 which lost both its Croydon and Streatham allocations, except on Saturdays when Croydon still had a stake. This pattern did not fit so well at weekends when it was necessary for Thornton Heath to help out on route 154 and, on Saturdays, Elmers End on the 157. This sparked off a chain of re-allocations, with the 75 moving into Catford, the 94 to New Cross, more 141As into Holloway, the 39A into Chalk Farm, the 196 into Highgate and Camberwell, the 168 from Camberwell and Wandsworth into Stockwell and some 77s and 88s into Merton, where they collided with the arrival of the 157s to give a net increase in its allocation.

The biggest impact of the new Saturday scheduling agreement on route patterns was in the Hackney area, where there was also a small scheme on Mondays to Fridays. This included the localisation of the Chingford Hatch service on route 35 on Mondays to Fridays to start from Dalston Junction after the end of the morning peak, except that an infrequent through service was retained in the evening peak. The buses which previously ran to Chingford Hatch were cut back to Clapton, Kenninghall Road, creating an overlap which cost two buses. The basic service remained at roughly the same level but the same could not be said of its companion routes along Lea Bridge Road, the 38, 170 and 257 all of which sustained cuts which, combined, took off eighteen peak buses an hour on this road, with lesser cuts extending to Victoria on route 38 and Liverpool Street on the 257. The 170 was involved in a more radical change at the same time which stripped it of all but a handful of the shorts which had run east of Bloomsbury to Hackney, Clapton and Leyton on Mondays to Fridays and of its entire Saturday service. This was partly cushioned by new route 253A which ran on Mondays to Saturdays from Bloomsbury to Finsbury Park Station, following the 170 to Clapton and then the 253, over which it was a wholly additional service.

The farewell party was already in full swing when RT 2659 was welcomed home as the last bus to run into Carshalton garage early in the morning of 29th January 1964. Carshalton had been a bus garage for less than five years but its history went back to 1906 when it opened as a tram depôt for the SMET Company, becoming a trolleybus depôt in 1936. D.M. Stuttard

Saunders bodied RT 1054 rounds the bend into Brixton Road at Kennington Gate on route 159A, which provided the Saturday service for Lisson Grove from 1st February 1964.
Colin Stannard

The RMs allocated to Croydon for the 130 group in September 1964 were also used to cover Sunday only route 59, which provided the Sunday service for Lisson Grove from 2nd February. RM 373 is seen in Baker Street crossing Marylebone Road, followed by some of the ever increasing motor car population.
Capital Transport

On the group of routes contained in this scheme there was a reduction of nearly 3 per cent, cutting six buses from the schedule. There were also some re-allocations either to balance the share of work between garages or to put services into garages nearer their line of route, notably the withdrawal of the entire Clapton allocation on route 38A. This was transferred into Leyton, where it replaced the 34 and 106. The 34 went into Walthamstow, which thereby acquired its first RTs, and the 106 into Clapton. The loss of the 170 at Clapton had been balanced, more or less, by the 253A but the 106 did not make up for the 38A so Clapton also gained some work from Poplar with the switch of some mileage from route 56 to the 277.

The other Saturday changes were designed to get route lengths which suited the new scheduling agreement and involved radical changes to routes 6, 256 and 257 creating a veritable 'dog's dinner'. In fact, all three routes were withdrawn. To cover Hackney Wick, route 6A, which had run only until lunch time between Waterloo and Hackney Wick, became an all day service but with two-thirds starting at Liverpool Street. The Kensal Rise service still operated as far as Hackney but was then diverted to follow route 257 to Chingford Mount, being renumbered 6B in the process. There was also a section of 6B from Liverpool Street to Chingford 'Royal Forest Hotel'. The 256 was replaced between Chingford Mount and Hackney by new route 256A, which continued to London Bridge, replacing that part of the 257.

Amidst general retrenchment, a considerable boost was given to the level of service between Hackney and Finsbury Park from 29th January 1964 by the introduction of route 253A. RTL 1475, seen at Finsbury Park, was one of twenty-three of the class which came out of overhaul during 1964 with RT10 roofbox bodies, following the decision to bring forward the withdrawal of the Leylands. Michael Beamish

A Saturday only route that emerged from the upheaval caused by the new Saturday working agreement was the 256A, a combination of parts of the 256 and 257. The tower of Guy's Hospital looms over this peaceful scene in London Bridge station forecourt where the specially designed LGOC iron stop posts, original though by now displaying modern signs, and the London Bridge Station Tearooms serve as reminders to RTL 1407 of a bygone age. Vectis Transport Publications

The summer programme for 1964 was delayed by the protracted negotiations which took place following the publication of the Phelps Brown Report (see chapter nine) but when it did materialise, on 1st July, it contained three Area Schemes of varying size and impact, covering Barnet, Hampton and south-east London. The smallest was the Barnet scheme, a modest affair amounting to a localisation of route 34, which was beginning to feel the effects of congestion on North Circular Road. It was a straightforward exchange of the New Barnet station to Chesterfield Road section with route 261 to give a more local route between Arnos Grove and Chesterfield Road. Five Palmers Green runnings switched from the 34 to the 261. The 34 was simultaneously withdrawn on Saturdays between Leyton Green and Downsell Road. There was a consequential benefit to route 261's passengers, as the enlarged duty schedule provided scope for the elimination of the gaps in the timetable which had been necessary to accommodate the crews' meal reliefs.

The core of the slightly larger Hampton scheme was the extension of route 111 on Mondays to Saturdays until about 7pm from Hanworth 'Brown Bear' through hitherto unserved roads to Hampton station, via Bear Road, Swan Road, Hanworth Lane, Nightingale Road, Broad Lane and Percy Road. It was further extended on Saturdays to Kingston via Hampton Court, replacing a Saturday only extension of route 71 which had itself replaced shorts on the 216 in the May 1959 aftermath of the abortive attempt to introduce one-man operation to Central Buses. Route 111 was also withdrawn on Mondays to Fridays, except during peak hours, between Cranford and Hounslow being replaced by an extension of the 110. Yet again, a simple route running between the same terminals daily was distorted into one that did something different in the peak and off-peak and on Saturdays and Sundays. One extra bus was needed.

The newly served area was not one which had developed recently but an old established tree-lined suburban area which still contained some of the market gardening with which much of Middlesex had once been covered. The residents of this sleepy area did not take kindly to the sudden imposition of double-deck buses onto their semi-rural idyll, without their being consulted. Their vigorous protest culminated in an approach from the MP to the Chairman of London Transport but such protests rarely achieved anything in those days and the service continued to operate, gathering strength over the years to become an important inter-suburban service.

Above right **Palmers Green's RM 790 is seen approaching Barnet Church on the Chesterfield Road extension of the 261, a section of route formerly covered by the 34.** Capital Transport

Right **RT 2099 is ignored by passengers and staff alike while laying over at Hounslow bus station on route 111, newly extended to Hampton station.** Tom Maddocks

The big scheme in south-east London was another example where routes were revisited almost before they had had time to settle down, in this case only a matter of fourteen months after they had last been changed. One of the central features was another attempt to sort out the 2 group, which at that time included the 186, an improbably straggly route from Woolwich to Victoria via Crystal Palace. Passenger carryings on the route over Tulse Hill were still increasing as more blocks of flats were built in place of the old villas and the service level was becoming seriously inadequate. The suburban end of the 186 was also beginning to suffer from irregularity caused by traffic congestion in town and the radical solution was to withdraw the 186 and cover it by changes to routes 2, 2A, 2B and 122. Route 2B was a Sunday only route which already stood in for the 186 between Crystal Palace and Victoria on that day but then continued to Golders Green as part of the total 2 group service. The same principle was now applied to Mondays to Saturdays and the 2B became a daily route, except that it did not run north of Swiss Cottage on Saturdays. The rest of the 2 and 2A was re-organised from what was already a complicated, but fairly tidy, service into an even more complicated and messy agglomeration of short-workings.

The other half of the 186 was absorbed into a vastly changed route 122. This inoffensive little route which had been plodding its way up and down between Woolwich and Bexleyheath for twenty-eight years was now rudely jolted with an extension at both ends which more than doubled its size and completely changed its nature. It was extended from Woolwich to Crystal Palace daily, to cover the 186, and from Bexleyheath to Slade Green Station on Mondays to Saturdays, giving a service to Colyers Lane for the first time. To give the required level of service to Crystal Palace on Sundays, the 122A was extended from Woolwich, only fourteen months after it had been instrumental in eliminating a previous non-standard Sunday working. The net effect of this part of the scheme on service levels was to provide an increase between Victoria and West Norwood, particularly in the off-peak, which was concentrated mainly on the Tulse Hill route. There was also a general increase in the evening service between Golders Green and Crystal Palace. On the 122, the peak service between Woolwich and Bexleyheath station was cut. Two extra buses were needed.

The 51 group was the subject of some tidying up, including the absorption of the anachronistic 241 into the group. The 51 itself was now extended on Mondays to Fridays from Sidcup to Woolwich, with a further extension to Victoria Way during Monday to Friday peak hours, to replace the 241 but for some pedantic reason, the shortworkings to Sidcup garage (a minute variation) were given the separate number 51B. This in itself was designed to confuse because there was an existing 51B between Eltham and Orpington station, which was withdrawn at the same time. The 51 was also altered at its southern end so that a couple of journeys were extended in the evenings on Mondays to Saturdays and on Sunday afternoons from

Farnborough to Hayes Station via Locksbottom, Croydon Road and Baston Road to give a link from Hayes to Farnborough Hospital. To accommodate this without running foul of the 'no bifurcation' agreement, buses working the Sunday extension to Bromley garage were curtailed officially at Locksbottom, whilst actually continuing to run to the garage out of service. The former 51B was effectively extended to Green Street Green as part of

the 51A and the spur working to Orpington station was withdrawn. This was replaced by route 94 which was extended on Mondays to Saturdays from Petts Wood Station via previously unserved Queensway and Towncourt Lane, to Orpington (St Andrews Drive) and then in peak hours to Sidcup Station. There was also a general reduction in service levels on the 51 group which helped remove three buses from the peak requirement.

Above **RT 1358 sets out along Vauxhall Bridge Road on one of the last runs through to Woolwich on 30th June 1964, after which its rôle was usurped by the 2B and 122.** Ken Glazier

Saunders bodied RT 2385 at Bexleyheath garage on the newly extended route 122 to Crystal Palace. W.R. Legg

Another Orpington route was involved in the next segment of the scheme, the 229 which lost its peak hour extension from Woolwich to Victoria Way and suffered the loss of all its shortworkings between Woolwich and Bexleyheath. The level of service was restored by the extension of route 132 on Mondays to Saturdays (except in the evenings), from Bexleyheath Garage to Woolwich (Parsons Hill) with a peak hour extension to Victoria Way, creating yet another hairpin route in this area. This little re-jig, perhaps with some judicious trimming of journeys, saved three peak buses, bringing the saving for the whole scheme to six buses. There were two significant re-allocations, among the mass of small adjustments caused by the scheme. The Camberwell allocation on route 163 was removed to New Cross, which became its sole supplier, and the gap at Camberwell was filled by the 168, which lost its Stockwell allocation to accommodate the 2B.

The summer programme as a whole saved nine double-deck and eight single-deck buses. The latter came from route 211 which was converted from RF to RT and extended to Ruislip in place of the 97, recovering its pre-1952 route. This was the last summer in which a full programme of seasonal extensions and increased Sunday services was operated. Although the scale of such operations had gradually diminished over the years, ten extensions or special routes still survived in 1964 and there was a five per cent increase in Sunday service levels compared with the winter of 1963. By 1965 the staffing crisis had become so serious that the Board decided that all resources should be concentrated on maintaining the basic network. Only two extensions operated that year (routes 14 and 38) and there was no general increase in Sunday services. With the withdrawal of these extensions in the winter programme of 1965, this forty year tradition came to an end.

One of the casualties of the summer programme in 1964 was the short Saturday only route 263 between Coulsdon North and Clock House Farm Estate, which was replaced by a Banstead Coaches service which also ran on Mondays to Fridays. RT 742 is at the outer terminus at The Mount.
A.J. Wild

Double-deckers took over route 211 in July 1964, enabling it to regain its pre-1952 projection to Ruislip and continuing the policy of converting busy single-deck routes. RT 765, seen in Drayton Bridge Road, carries an RT10 roofbox body of the type with which its number-sake started life at Mortlake in August 1948.
Colin Stannard

The winter programme of 1964 was also delayed by disagreements with the Trade Union and did not take place until 18th November. There was yet another east London scheme involving routes which had already had attention in recent times but the main thrust of the programme was a massive onslaught on weekend services with cuts of nearly five per cent on Saturdays and nearly seven per cent on Sundays. Localisation was again in the air, this time applied to route 10. Although the Abridge service had for very many years operated only from Leytonstone for most of the day on Mondays to Saturdays, this was no guarantee against delays being transmitted from the London end of the route as individual duties could be scheduled to operate on both sections. The local operation was therefore formalised by the creation of a route 10A, which was formed by the Leytonstone to Woodford Bridge and Abridge shortworkings being extended via Whipps Cross to Leyton Green. The rest of the 10 remained as it was, running between Victoria and Woodford Bridge with a few morning peak and afternoon journeys continuing to Chigwell. There was no change to the Sunday operation. Alongside this, what remained of the 32 was finally withdrawn, stripping another six peak buses an hour from the Aldgate – Wanstead corridor and bringing to an end the short and dismal career of this extraordinary invention of the trolleybus conversion. Extra buses on route 25 between Victoria and Aldgate covered the important end.

The localised section of route 10 took on a new identity in the winter programme of 1964, becoming 10A on an extended operation to Leyton. RT 2330 appears to have been baulked by parked vehicles as it loads in the middle of the road at Chigwell. Colin Stannard

The number 39A, used on Saturdays only, disappeared in November 1964 with the loss of the Parliament Hill Fields variation on that day of the week. RTL 551 is in Victoria Street on its way to the southern terminus at Southfields. Capital Transport

The localised section of route 35 also became a separate route, taking the identity 35B in recognition of its intermediate diversion between Dalston Junction and Lea Bridge Road to run via Graham Road and Millfields Estate. It was also extended beyond Chingford Hatch to Chingford ('Royal Forest Hotel') to supply Friday Hill with its first bus service, twenty-five years after it was first mooted. By thinning out the service on route 35 it was possible to provide the new service without cost and the net outcome of the whole scheme was a saving of four buses. Route 10 abandoned its traditional base at Leyton for a new allocation of RTLs at Bow, although the new 10A remained loyal. Bow relinquished most of the 26 in favour of Leyton but this careful balancing act did not prevent a loss at that garage because route 144 was transferred to Walthamstow. It was fortuitous that this was nearer its line of route, as the true reason for the transfer was to release space at Leyton for building work to start on its modernisation.

Although not an area scheme, the weekend changes to the network in this programme, as distinct from the widespread and general reduction in service levels, were so extensive that they deserve a special mention. The only route to be withdrawn in its entirety was the Saturday service on route 189 but the number 286 also disappeared in changes to the 213 group. Parts of three more routes were lost on Saturdays, two more on both Saturdays and Sundays and nine more on Sundays, many of them by the creation of new weekend or Sunday only services. The opposite was the case with the Sunday 8B and Saturday 39A, which were withdrawn respectively between Willesden and Alperton and between Victoria and Parliament Hill Fields, enabling the numbers 8 and 39 to be restored on those days. The 213 scheme similarly allowed the pattern to be tidied up and standardised on the Monday to Saturday pattern, with the 213 being restored to Belmont, the 213A introduced between Kingston and Morden and the 213B withdrawn.

The Saturday and Sunday services on routes 226 and 245 were substituted in part by the 245A which was an amalgam of the 226 between Golders Green and Cricklewood and the 245 from there to Stanmore, leaving the Anson Road and Robson Avenue routeing between Cricklewood and Harlesden unserved and the route through Childs Hill and Chichele Road to route 260 alone. The 44 between Wallington and Mitcham and the 115 were treated similarly on Sundays, with new route 115A following the 44 as far as Hackbridge and then the 115 to Croydon Airport. Another pair welded together in this way were the 172 and 188, whose northern and southern ends respectively were joined at Kingsway to form a new route 188A from Archway to Greenwich Church. Finally, the 56 was withdrawn on Saturdays and the 277 extended to Poplar, as it already was on Sundays.

Among several stretches of road from which buses were now withdrawn on Sundays was Victoria Embankment east of Horse Guards Avenue, routes 155 and 177 having been cut back to Kennington and Elephant & Castle respectively.

The diversion of the localised section of route 35 via Millfields Estate, Hackney, in November 1964 provoked its renumbering to 35B as displayed on RT 4647, the number 35A still being in use for the summer Sunday route to Chingford. Colin Stannard

RTL 1446 on route 188A, one of a glut of new Sunday only routes which appeared in November 1964. C. Holt

One of the biggest programmes so far was launched on 27th January 1965 and its main aim was clearly economy as no fewer than fifty-four buses were removed from the peak requirement. It contained three distinct schemes but these covered so many routes and so much of London that it can be difficult to see where one scheme ends and another begins. By far the largest of the three was yet another attack on east London which contributed thirty-one of the buses saved from the fleet as a whole, partly in response to the decline in importance of the London docks which was already beginning to become evident. One of the main elements of restructuring was the further localisation of route 40, which was linked to yet another attempt to find a more economical way of covering the 48, resulting in changes which were very complicated. The number 40 was retained for the route running from Wanstead Flats to Aldgate, continuing to Herne Hill in peak hours but on Saturdays and Sundays it continued to run to Wanstead station, although now diverted via Dames Road and Lake House Road instead of Woodford Road and the southern end of Blake Hall Road. It also ran to London Bridge on Saturday mornings and to Norwood Junction on Sundays. The south London end was covered by a new 40A between Herne Hill and Poplar, with peak extensions to North Woolwich to replace the remaining vestiges of the 48. On Saturdays this route ran via Loughborough Junction and Milkwood Road, in place of the 42 and therefore took the number 40B.

The Wanstead section of the 40 was covered on Mondays to Fridays by changes to route 162. This was withdrawn between Green Street and Stratford and diverted over the new route of the 40 to Wanstead. On Saturdays it continued to run to Stratford, being renumbered 162A, but was intermediately diverted via East Ham High Street North and Plashet Grove in connection with changes to the 238. Route 238 was withdrawn on Mondays to Saturdays from the section between Upton Park and North Woolwich and diverted instead via Green Street and Plashet Road to Stratford Broadway. The Saturday 238A also took over the route of the 162 between East Ham and Stratford so that it became the same as the Monday to Friday route and took the number 238. The existing Sunday route 162A was now the same as the 238 and was renumbered accordingly. This was a crisp illustration of the extent to which services in this part of London had been turned over, as the 238 was now identical to the 162 as originally launched in February 1960. The North Woolwich service of the 238 was not completely covered but route 33 was extended on Mondays to Fridays to Canning Town, continuing in peak hours as far as Silvertown, on lower frequencies. The 33 was withdrawn on Saturdays, being covered in part by the extension of route 5B (renumbered 5C) from Barking garage to Becontree Heath.

Decline in traffic to the docks was so severe that not only was the 238 not fully replaced but there were also sharp cuts on routes 40A, 58 and 69 which totted up to a total reduction in peak service in excess of twelve buses an hour at North Woolwich.

Left **RM 327 is seen at Blackwall Tunnel, the main eastern terminus of route 40B, the Saturday version of 40A, which replaced the southern end of route 42 on Saturdays.**

Below **RM 242 bumps along in typical East End surroundings alongside still evident wartime bomb damage on route 5C, the number chosen to identify the variation caused when the 5B was extended to Becontree Heath on Saturdays in January 1965.**
G. Mead

The Victoria and Albert Docks also took a caning with twenty per cent cuts in the basic service on routes 41, 249/B and 278 and the loss of all the shorts on routes 249/B between Plaistow and the Docks. The number 249B disappeared at this time, as the route was withdrawn between Chingford Mount and Yardley Lane Estate, leaving what remained to become shorts on the 249. Yardley Lane was served instead by an extension of route 278 which was able to operate the longer route with one less bus. In the reshuffle of mileage on Saturdays route 278A was withdrawn.

A tiny fraction of the savings was reinvested to allow the introduction of a bus service to South Park Drive, Barking. This was done by extending route 129, on Mondays to Saturdays, from Ilford to Barking (Blakes Corner), at a cost of four buses. As a consequence, the unchanged Sunday service to Little Heath was renumbered 129A. Allocation changes included the removal of routes

5 and 238 from Poplar, the 33 from Barking into Upton Park, the 40 from Camberwell and the 147 from Seven Kings. The loss of route 5 from Poplar had its origins in a proposal to extend route 5A from West India Dock to Poplar via Poplar High Street, which did not materialise because route approval for this very narrow and tortuous road was refused by the Traffic Commissioner, as was the possible alternative of Saltwell Street which actually survived long enough to appear in the publicity leaflet for the scheme. The associated reduction in frequency on route 5 and balancing increase on the 5A was retained in the final scheme, despite the fact that the 5A would not then provide back-up to Poplar.

The second major scheme had ramifications from Farnborough in the south to Borehamwood in the north and, for once, involved some simplification of earlier complications while introducing some new ones of its own. This too was designed for economy and

resulted in a saving of nineteen buses. Route 199 (Waterloo to Farnborough), which had been introduced as an earlier example of localisation, was withdrawn and replaced by changes to the routes from which it had been carved. Route 1 took over the Monday to Friday operation from Waterloo as far as Bromley Garage but was extended only as far as Catford Garage on Saturdays. It was also extended from Marylebone to Willesden on Saturdays in place of the 176. The Farnborough service became a more suitably localised operation on route 47 from Lewisham on Mondays to Fridays but was a straight extension of the through service on Saturdays. On Mondays to Saturdays the 47 was also extended from Stoke Newington to Stamford Hill, bringing it into line with Sundays. The peak hours only extension of route 60 from Waterloo to Surrey Docks was also withdrawn, leaving this section solely to route 1 instead of the three routes on which it had previously relied. Rather tenuously linked with this part of the scheme was the withdrawal of route 124 between Welling and Woolwich, except for a few journeys in each peak.

The 60 was the link to the changes in the north, as it was simultaneously extended from Cricklewood to Colindale Station. This was related to the withdrawal of route 292 between Colindale and Willesden garage on Mondays to Fridays, when the express service was also withdrawn. Route 142 was also recast to run in two sections all day on Mondays to Fridays (Watford – Edgware or Colindale/Edgware – Kilburn Park), instead of just in peak hours, and this had the effect of reducing the frequency south of Colindale. The peak hour extension of route 52 to Borehamwood (Drayton Road) was also withdrawn, although there were still some journeys to Rossington Avenue and the Sunday service to maintain the link first established during the war. The level of service between Cricklewood and Kilburn Park was topped up by route 16 on which the localised service between Kilburn Park and Sudbury Town was restored, after having been withdrawn surprisingly in July 1964. This had been one of the earliest examples of localisation.

Top **When the 199 started in October 1957, its number could well have been chosen as a little joke, being at the opposite extremity of the old double-deck series from the 1 whose outer end it replaced, but the fun petered out on 27th January 1965 when the 199 was withdrawn. Saunders bodied RT 1268 looks smart but forlorn and deserted in this view at Cornwall Road stand, Waterloo in June 1963.** G. Mead

Centre **A casualty of the new schedules on 27th January 1965 was the express service on route 292, which had started as 52A in November 1955. It was now incorporated into the stopping service in compensation for the loss of route 52 north of Mill Hill 'Green Man', which is where RT 2651 was photographed entering Selvage Lane in May 1962.** Peter G. Mitchell

Right **The link from the heart of the West End to Bermondsey and Surrey Docks was severed in January 1965 when route 60 was cut back to Waterloo. Cricklewood was entirely responsible for the route, RTL 1323, seen leaving Waterloo Bridge, being typical of its rolling stock.** A.B. Cross

One other minor change was the diversion of the Catford garage service on route 176 to Lewisham (Rennell Street) and there were also frequency cuts on this and routes 12, 184 and 185. Barely related to all this was the localisation of the Croydon service on route 12 on Mondays to Fridays. The already complicated series of overlapping sections was now joined by a new one from South Croydon to Peckham (with shorts to Norwood Junction), the service from Oxford Circus being cut back partly to Norwood Junction and partly to Forest Hill. None of this applied at weekends.

The final, smaller, scheme also concerned the withdrawal of a route of recent provenance, the 156 which had started only in August 1963 when it had helped replace another short-lived route, the 276. One of the objectives of the scheme was to provide a service from Waterloo station to the newly developing offices along Albert Embankment, while at the same time strengthening the service along Stamford Street which was another area where offices were blooming. This was done by diverting the Turnpike Lane to Clapham Junction service on route 168 to run via Blackfriars Bridge, Stamford Street, Waterloo and Lambeth Palace Road under the new number 168A. Additional shorts were added to the 168 between Farringdon Street and Clapham Junction and the whole route was diverted between Vauxhall and Victoria Embankment to run via Lambeth Bridge, Millbank, Whitehall, Horse Guards Avenue and Whitehall Court to cover this part of the 156 and to give common southbound stops with the 77 group at Westminster. Whitehall Court had always been a sensitive road and the operation of buses, particularly in the evenings, had attracted opposition from the well-heeled residents from the day it had started on 1st

New route 168A supplied the first direct connection between the new offices on Albert Embankment and Waterloo station, continuing over Blackfriars Bridge to and beyond Ludgate Circus, where RT 3839 was photographed. Malcolm E. Papes collection

October 1950, so it was not long before this new arrangement stimulated their wrath. The route was therefore altered in the winter programme to run via Trafalgar Square and Northumberland Avenue, a better objective but a rather roundabout alternative in the direction of Farringdon Street.

The Parliament Hill Fields service of the 156 was covered by an unlikely extension of route 163 from Westminster, another novelty which was to prove to have a short life. Five buses were saved in this scheme and route 168 once again lost its Camberwell and Holloway allocations (and therefore RTs) whilst

being restored to Stockwell. Holloway took responsibility for the whole of the 168A. No changes were made at weekends other than to divert the 168 to follow its Monday to Friday route. Whether by chance or design, this had the effect of leaving St Thomas's Hospital without a Saturday service from the Vauxhall direction. As this was an important part of its catchment area there was soon an outcry and the matter was put right on 6th March when routes 77 and 77A were diverted on Saturdays to follow the Sunday routes via Millbank or Westminster Bridge and renumbered 77B and 77C respectively.

Yet another attempt to find a satisfactory way of linking Parliament Hill Fields with the West End was made with the extension of route 163, simultaneously giving it a better in-town objective than the marginal Horse Guards Avenue terminus. It was probably touch and go whether RT 4403 would ever reach its advertised terminus as it set out from Plumstead to tackle all the intervening traffic hazards.
Colin Stannard

The last old style double-decking took place on 25th August 1965 when route 200 lost it Regal IVs, like RF 321, and was allocated RTs instead, at a time when comparable routes elsewhere were being converted to one-man operation. R.D. Hyslop

The agreement to introduce a shorter working week was implemented on 17th March 1965 and put a stop to further major changes until the new duty schedules and rotas could be scheduled with the winter programme. The new style rosters triggered a historic change to the day of the week on which service changes were made, from Wednesday to Sunday and this programme was introduced on Sunday 3rd October. There were some conversions to one-man operation in east London, including the first examples of double-deck routes being tackled (see chapter eleven) but the main plank of the programme was a massive area scheme in west London. One of the items was a second attempt to localise the Teddington service on route 27. Like the 16, the 27 had been localised for many years by route 270 between Kensington and Teddington but this had unaccountably been dismantled in February 1963. The new idea was to link the Monday to Friday East Acton to Kew Green section of route 265 to the Teddington service under the number 27A, with compensating reductions on the 27 west of Turnham Green. The 265 was withdrawn north of Richmond and the peak hour extension from Kingston terminated at Dee Road.

Further thinning out of the service between Turnham Green, Kew Bridge and Brentford was contributed by changes to route 255. This was now withdrawn altogether at weekends and all but withdrawn between Turnham Green and Acton Vale on Mondays to Fridays, being reduced to an all day service between Clapham Junction and Hammersmith, continuing to Turnham Green until early evening and Hanwell in peak hours. The Hanwell to Brentford segment was covered by a controversial daily extension of route 83 from Ealing Broadway, which introduced the residents of Boston Manor to the irregularities caused by delays suffered at

such places as West Hendon, Wembley and Hanger Lane. The section along Uxbridge Road to Acton Vale was covered by an extension of the 268 from Harlesden or Acton to Hanwell garage in a kind of tail chasing exercise which saw its simultaneous withdrawal between Fulham (Edgarley Terrace) and Clapham Junction on Mondays to Fridays, where it was covered by the 255. The 268 continued to operate between Harlesden and Clapham Junction at weekends.

A form of localisation was initiated on route 105 which was withdrawn on Mondays to Saturdays between Southall and Hayes North (except for a few peak hour journeys to Blyth Road). Its replacement was a new route 195 which was planned to go beyond Hayes North to Charville Lane estate but the Traffic Commissioner would not approve the operation of buses along Charville Lane and Romney Road and, until they could be made ready, the service was temporarily curtailed at Hayes North. The extension did not take place until 30th May 1967. At the other end, the peak service continued beyond Southall to Perivale. Additional help in building up the service between Southall and Greenford was supplied by route 120, which was extended on Mondays to Saturdays to Greenford station but via Lady Margaret Road, Somerset Road and Allenby Road, the latter new to buses.

Over seventeen years after the nationalisation of the railways, the station sign at Richmond still displays the old company names as Twickenham's RT 4701 passes on new route 27A which localised the northern end of the 265 and the south-western part of route 27. John Gascoine

Following the continuing drain of suburban factory traffic away from buses there were also substantial cuts in the peak hour service between Park Royal and Greenford and this was also a feature of the changes to the 112, another route which served a disproportionately large number of factories. In this case, the cuts in the basic service were associated with the extension of the Hampstead Heath to Park Royal service on the 187 to Brent station, absorbing 112 shorts. It was therefore renumbered 187A and the Monday to Friday service on the 187 was reduced to the section between South Harrow and West Kilburn. The total service between Shepherds Bush and East Acton was maintained at this time but was to take its share of the cuts in January 1966 when route 71 was cut back to Brook Green. To maintain the connection to Hammersmith Hospital, route 72 was diverted via Ducane Road in its place, leaving the 105 as sole proprietor of Westway. This lasted until 19th June 1967 when a new local route 295 was introduced between East Acton and Hammersmith, as part of a programme of restoring some of the more drastic cuts of the intervening eighteen months.

The final change in this scheme was a localisation of a localised service, an indication of the way traffic delays were spreading ever further outwards. The Hounslow service on route 73 was thinned out beyond Twickenham on Mondays to Saturdays and replaced by the extension of half the service on 281. This had the effect on Mondays to Fridays of splitting the 73 into three overlapping sections (Stoke Newington – Richmond; Kensington – Twickenham; Brook Green – Hounslow). The 281 extension was to prove to be a valuable addition to the network and it has endured into the 1990s as one of west London's major trunk services.

No fewer than twenty-four buses were saved in this scheme and there were many allocation changes. The chain of re-allocations which compensated for the loss of route 255 from Hanwell to Riverside and the loss of most of the 105 at Shepherds Bush extended as far east as Walthamstow in the following epic sequence: route 73 withdrawn from Hounslow into Tottenham, some 123s to Walthamstow, whole allocation on route 34 to Palmers Green, where route 112 had been reduced. The work removed from the 112 re-appeared at Middle Row (187A), which sent 28s to Wandsworth; 168s went to Stockwell, 88s to Shepherds Bush. Other 88s went from Riverside to Shepherds Bush, where work transferred from route 105 to the 120/195 went into Southall, which sent the 55 to Hanwell.

The next round of schedule changes came on 23rd January 1966 and included an immense programme of Sunday changes which cut the prodigious total of 368 buses (over thirteen per cent). Eleven routes were withdrawn outright on Sundays and parts of ten more also disappeared, among them the Elephant to Horse Guards Avenue section of route 184, bringing to an end all day Sunday operation on any part of Victoria Embankment. There were also cuts on Mondays to Fridays and Saturdays but these were modest by comparison, amounting to twenty-five and thirty-four buses respectively.

One of the Sunday economies in the programme of changes introduced on 23rd January 1966 was the withdrawal of route 181. The section from Tooting Bec to Streatham was covered by the extension of route 19, bringing it back to its historical Sunday terminal after a gap of nine years, but by a different route. RTL 1629, displaying 'Streatham via Tooting Broadway', passes one of the new BESI scanner posts at Hyde Park Corner. A.B. Cross

The main feature of the programme was a scheme centring on Mill Hill, where the low railway bridge had been rebuilt as part of the work associated with the southward extension of the M1 motorway from Berrygrove to Hendon. The foremost benefits were the restoration, after an absence of twenty-five years, of the through service from Golders Green to Edgware on route 240 and the creation of a new cross-suburban through service on route 221, whose Turnpike Lane to North Finchley 'shorts' were extended on Mondays to Saturdays via Woodside Park, Mill Hill East and route 240A to Edgware station. The service beyond North Finchley to Woodside Park, Mill Hill East and Golders Green on route 125 was withdrawn altogether on Monday to Friday evenings and Saturdays and reduced in frequency at other times. Route 240A continued to operate on Sundays but was now double-deck and was extended to Golders Green so that the service

Saunders RT 4654 works on the Hampstead Heath to Park Royal station peak hour section of the newly created 187A, which took over the Park Royal to Brent service of the 112 in October 1965. Michael Beamish

Although route 240A continued to run on Sundays after January 1966, it lost its single-deckers in favour of RTs and scenes like this, showing RF 468 at Mill Hill East station on 15th January, ceased to be. Ken Glazier

At 'The Green Man', Mill Hill RM 1001 weaves its way across the now staggered junction of Hale Lane and Deans Lane on the new extension of route 221 to Edgware. Colin Stannard

The changes in January 1966 brought forth new route 104A to provide a localised service simultaneously to routes 102 at Golders Green and the 104 north of East Finchley. The attenuated 104 supplied the rolling stock, like RML 903 seen on Barnet Hill displaying the special destination blind designed to warn intending passengers in Finchley Road that it was not going directly to Barnet. J.G.S. Smith

via Bittacy Hill on route 240 could be reduced. Almost imperceptibly associated with these changes was the introduction of new route 104A on Mondays to Fridays between Golders Green and North Finchley via Hampstead Garden Suburb and East Finchley. This replaced the year old local peak hour service on 102 between Golders Green and Muswell Hill and gave a local service to the 104 north of East Finchley. The 104 was severely reduced, particularly outside peak hours. The change to route 221 resulted in the loss of a common stop at North Finchley for buses towards Bounds Green as the Traffic Commissioner would not approve the operation of buses across Ballards Lane from Nether Street into the bus station. An alternative route through Birkbeck Road and Dale Grove was proposed, so that buses could approach the bus station from Ballards Lane, but this was opposed by the council who objected to buses using residential roads.

Also as part of the road scheme a bus station, of sorts, had been provided in gloomy conditions under the motorway viaduct alongside Mill Hill Broadway station. The removal of the height restriction enabled route 140 officially to end its historic exile in Bunns Lane and run under the bridge to terminate closer to the heart of Mill Hill shopping centre, although this had to be deferred until 15th July 1967 because the bus station was not finished. A more radical change was made to route 52 which was withdrawn from Deans Lane and diverted to Mill Hill Broadway via Deansbrook Road, giving that road its first bus service and the 52 a more useful objective than the middle-of-nowhere terminus at 'The Green Man'. Until the bus station was ready, it stood in Brockenhurst Gardens, using the old stand for double-deck route 240. The two school journeys to Borehamwood followed this new route, then ran via Watford Way to Apex Corner but the through service on Sundays continued to run via Deans Lane and was therefore renumbered 52A.

Route 140 also took part in some changes in the Harrow area, which included the exchange of routeings west of Harrow on routes 114 and 158, not in response to any newly discovered passenger demand but in pursuit of schedule efficiency. The change enabled the round trip times from the relief point at Harrow Weald to each of the terminals to provide various combinations which allowed the length of duty spells to be closer to the limits imposed by the scheduling agreement. The 114 now ran via Lower Road and Bessborough Road to Ruislip Lido and the 158 via Porlock Avenue to Rayners Lane station. The 140 was simultaneously diverted via Porlock Avenue as there was a greater demand there than along the direct route.

These new schedules sparked off the worst dispute with the staff since the strike of 1958 and the messy sequence of events described in chapter nine put a stop to any further area schemes for the rest of the year. By that time attention had turned to the Reshaping Plan and the concept of Area Schemes took on a new and very different character.

CHAPTER FIVE

GREEN LINE IN DECLINE

At the beginning of 1960, the basic network of Green Line coach routes had changed hardly at all since their restoration in 1946. The only radical departure had been the introduction of the highly successful peripheral route 725 in 1953 but this had not been followed by any others or by any other novel ideas. During the 1950s there had been new routes to serve the New Towns and out-county estates, adding the numbers 715A, 716A, 719, 720A, 723A and 723B to the canon, but there had been no structural changes nor any significant alterations to the basic timetables. The substantial increases in population in the Home Counties during the 1950s had encouraged passenger traffic to grow progressively and by 1959 twenty-eight per cent more vehicles were needed to meet the peak demand than in 1950. Most of this had been met with scheduled duplication, a large share being entrusted to RT type double-deckers which, with the higher capacity of the RFs, elevated the increase in capacity to nearly fifty-two per cent. At the end of the decade London Transport was still forecasting a continuing increase in demand, although the amount of increase had been reduced substantially compared with the assessment made in 1955. On the face of it, all

looked quite rosy but more recent trends in coach traffic had been less encouraging. The modernisation of British Railways services, particularly the electrification schemes, had already begun to attract traffic away from the coaches onto the faster, cleaner and more reliable new trains. Green Line coaches would have been vulnerable to this competition in any case but were becoming more susceptible as the relentless build up of road traffic and the wider spread of traffic congestion gradually undermined the reliability on which much of the system's reputation rested.

In 1960, during which diesel trains replaced steam on the St Pancras to Bedford services and the Metropolitan Line was electrified between Rickmansworth and Amersham, the number of passenger journeys on the coaches increased slightly (0.3 per cent), but passenger mileage fell by 3.3 per cent, an indication of the loss of longer distance travellers to the railways. In the first half of 1961, following the electrification of the Bishops Stortford and Hertford East services in November 1960, passenger journeys fell by an average of 3.5 per cent, the worst loss occurring on route 715A which shed seven per cent of its trade. Other reasons given at the time for the accelerating downward trend were:

that cheap return fares were available on the railways but not on most Green Line services; new shops were gradually opening up in the New Towns, making shopping trips to London less necessary; and delays caused by traffic congestion. By the end of the year a new reason had been found when demand on routes 709, 710 and 711 along Uxbridge Road slumped. This time it was blamed onto the greater comfort offered by the new Routemasters on route 207, compared with the trolleybuses, and in particular the fact that they had heaters. This echoed a similar finding in 1938 when traffic on coaches between Golders Green and Barnet was said to have been attracted onto the new trolleybuses. Over the whole of 1961, the losses averaged 5.2 per cent, the worst day of the week being Saturday (6.3 per cent).

Above **One of the great successes of the early post war years was the peripheral route 725, which was still being heavily duplicated at busy times. RF 180 is at the Worcester Park station stop on 4th August 1962 on a busy Saturday journey to Gravesend.** A.J. Wild

In the background, the British Transport Commission, ever vigilant about coach competition with the railways, had set up a study to investigate the extent to which Green Line extracted traffic from rail. The study was conducted by the Commercial Manager of London Transport and the Chief Commercial Officer of the Southern Region, using routes 710 and 715 in a comparative study with their parallel railway routes. Their findings were that ninety-three per cent of rail passengers travelled distances of between ten and thirty miles, whereas over fifty per cent of Green Line passengers travelled less than ten miles. On route 710 more than sixty per cent used stops not directly served by rail. Their conclusion was that Green Line served different passenger needs and did not affect the use of railways, which was probably true but the evidence used to support the argument seems very flimsy. The report was submitted to the London Transport Sub-Commission but no more seems to have been heard of it.

Meanwhile, the haemorrhaging of traffic was beginning to cause serious concern. A major poster and newspaper advertising campaign, pitting the merits of the Green Line against the disadvantages of the car, was launched in May 1960 but seems to have had little impact. By the spring of 1962, thoughts began to turn to making drastic economies in the off-peaks on Mondays to Fridays by standardising on an hourly frequency, rather than the thirty minute headway scheduled on most routes, but nothing happened immediately. At this time it was still being stressed that the system remained highly profitable.

In fact the only serious changes to Green Line in 1960, which were introduced on 23rd November, were positive and designed to open up new areas to the network. Route 712 was diverted intermediately between Radlett and St Albans to run via Park Street and Chiswell Green instead of Shenley, and changes were made to the 716 and 717 to increase the penetration of Hatfield and Welwyn Garden City New Towns. The 716 was re-routed between Welwyn and Stanborough 'Bull' to run via Digswell, Knightsfield, Peartree Lane and Broadwater Road, instead of the direct route along the A1 which the 716A was left to serve; and route 717 was diverted between Hatfield and Welwyn Garden City to run via Hertford Road, Chequers, Howlands, Hollybush Lane and Ludwick Way to Welwyn Garden City station. This gave the more populous Knightsfield, Longcroft Green and Howlands areas new coach services and the centre of the New Town twice the frequency, at the expense of withdrawing from Valley Road and reducing the service along the A1. As it happened this also proved to be the last year during which the summer only route 726 served Harold Hill. It ran for the last time on 11th September 1960 and was cut back to Romford for the 1961 season.

Little thought seems to have been given at this time to the effect on Green Line's fortunes of the vehicles used. Fine though the RFs were, they were now beginning to be a little long in the tooth for a front line high quality service and their livery was at best staid; perhaps, some thought, even dreary. Added to this, the use of ordinary RT buses

for most duplication work in the pursuit of efficiency, had rather adulterated the glamour of the name. The first signs of an attempt to improve the appearance of the fleet came in August 1960 when the first of twenty-eight RTs came out of Aldenham wearing the Green Line livery, complete with side bullseye transfers as carried on the Grays fleet. Intended to replace the bus RTs on regular duplication work, they were also fitted with saloon heaters and were therefore identical in all essentials to the Grays and Romford coach RTs. In this guise they presented a distinctive image more in keeping with their rôle but were still buses in all but name.

Above **RT 4749 on local route 395A will pass most coaches working on the 715 at this spot in Hertford bus station while shuttling between Hertford and Ware, but it will be at least six hours before it sees RF 25 again. Meanwhile, the coach will be away on its one hundred mile round trip to Guildford and back. The RF, delivered in 1951 as a Private Hire coach, was one of ten which were converted for Green Line work in 1956 and which were now about to be evicted by the RMCs.** John Fozard

In the same month, an attempt was made to find a brighter, more modern colour scheme for the coaches, to replace the 'traditional' Lincoln green. Sixteen RFs and the prototype CRL 4 were repainted in two lighter shades of green, with black trim on their front wheel nut rings and on the rear wheel discs. At first they retained the green and gold side route boards but these were later given a black background with the lettering changed to yellow. The RFs were allocated to High Wycombe and Reigate garages for operation on route 711 but after two years it was decided to carry on with Lincoln green as the main body colour, although the lighter relief colour was retained. It was characteristic of the way standards were slipping that, when the experiment was finished, stocks of unused paint were used indiscriminately, creating a series of compromise colour schemes.

The lighter coloured greens used in the livery experiments on Green Line RFs and CRL 4 are illustrated in this view of RF 33 taken some time later when it was on loan to Central Buses on route 206 at Hampton Court. A.J. Wild

Below **RF 103 at Hemel Hempstead bus station in 1965 has received a coat of the porcelain green relief colour first used on RMC 1469.** Malcolm Young

Hopes for future regeneration were now invested in the new Routemaster coaches, described in chapter three, which were launched on 29th August 1962 in a blast of publicity exuding untarnished confidence in the future. Unfortunately, the changes made to the first routes to receive them, the 715 and 715A, were indicative of a different prognosis. Route 715 was one of the most frequent coach routes, with a basic twenty minute headway from end to end, augmented by the hourly service on route 715A between London and Hertford. It was also the most heavily duplicated Green Line route at its northern end, with five double-deckers allocated to the 715 and two to the 715A on Mondays to Fridays, almost enough to double the peak hour frequency. Taking full advantage of the higher capacity of the double-deckers, the through service on the 715 was reduced to give almost the same number of seats each hour but with the consequence that the headway was increased by fifty per cent from every twenty minutes to half hourly. The 715A remained hourly but was stripped of its duplication and one of the Hertford duplicates was removed from the 715. In all, seven vehicles and twenty crews were saved and mileage was reduced by twenty-eight per cent. There was an immediate loss of traffic amounting in revenue terms to twenty-eight per cent of the gross saving but the Country Bus and Coach Operating Manager was well satisfied because the savings which had been achieved amounted to £33,600 a year compared with the original estimate of £24,500. Unhappily, the longer term effects do not seem to have been recognised. Although the larger vehicles may have been capable theoretically of carrying the traffic, the loss of frequency made the service less attractive and the removal of the duplicates eliminated a source of punctual departures from central London in the evening peak. The combined effect was a serious loss of quality and, ultimately, of passengers.

The next batch of RMCs went to Epping and Windsor for routes 718, 720 and 720A, where they entered service on 24th October. No change was made to the basic half hourly frequency of route 718 but all scheduled duplication, two at Epping and one at Windsor, was removed. Route 720 suffered a fifty per cent cut in frequency from half hourly to hourly, a widening of its headway by one hundred per cent, but the 720A remained hourly, so that the cut between Aldgate and Potter Street was proportionately less, at thirty-three per cent. Route 718 enjoyed a slight increase in passenger traffic (less than half per cent) but, between them, the 720 and 720A lost nearly eleven per cent of their passengers. The loss was particularly heavy between Potter Street and Bishops Stortford and it was claimed, without supporting evidence, that many of these had transferred to route 396.

The next conversion showed that there was a more positive way of doing things. Route 719 received RMCs at Garston garage on 21st November, without any change of timetable, the only saving being the removal of one duplicate. Traffic immediately increased by nearly fifteen per cent and it would be nice to think that this influenced the decision not

to make any savings when routes 716 and 716A received their RMCs at Addlestone and Stevenage on 2nd January. Even the duplicates were retained on these routes but subsequent events suggest that the message seems to have been lost on those looking for salvation.

Above **RMC 1467 at Hertford when still less than a month old in September 1962.** Malcolm Young

Below **Heavy New Town traffic to Harlow justified the conversion of route 718 to RMC in October 1962. RMC 1476 is posed at the town's new bus garage.** LT Museum

Further attrition came on 22nd May 1963 when new timetables were introduced on routes 723, 723A and 723B which more or less halved the service between East Ham Town Hall and Aldgate. This was in response to the severe loss of traffic which had followed the electrification of the London Tilbury and Southend line the previous year. In the latter days of steam, the LT&S had been notorious for its general dowdiness and unreliability and there can be little doubt that this had been beneficial to the Green Line. The transformation wrought by the new faster, more frequent trains was a great success with the public and their switch of allegiance was to prove a mortal blow to the coaches in the long run. On the positive side, in Welwyn Garden City, route 717 went in search of more new traffic with a diversion along Howlands and Cole Green Lane, instead of Hollybush Lane, to serve what was then known as Hatfield and Welwyn New Hospital, later the Queen Elizabeth II Hospital.

The arrangements for serving Whipsnade were also changed in pursuit of new traffic and economies. Route 726 was re-instated on Sundays from 26th May and on Mondays to Fridays from 3rd July but there was no Saturday service this year, or ever again. Instead, from 25th May, a couple of Saturday journeys and four on Sundays were diverted off route 712 at St Albans to run non-stop to the Zoo under the number 712A. This was a device to give the Whipsnade service some more useful central area picking up points than the rather remote Baker Street stop and proved to be a success. Another economy measure on the 712 was an intermediate diversion between Park Street and North Orbital Road to run via the more direct route through Park Street Lane and Tippendell Lane. This avoided the low bridge over the A5 on the St Albans Abbey branch at Park Street and enabled double-deckers to be used for duplication.

A more sweeping approach to the search for new traffic was tried on route 705 from 28th August 1963 when the section between London and Windsor was converted to an express operation with only fourteen instead of forty-eight intermediate stops. The route was also diverted between Hammersmith and Chiswick to run via the newly completed section of Great West Road and the Chiswick flyover, instead of King Street and Chiswick High Road; and via Colnbrook By-Pass instead of Colnbrook village. This made it a hybrid of normal limited stop and express operation, which led to the rather curious arrangement whereby a normal black-on-amber blind was displayed between Sevenoaks and Victoria and a white and blue 'Express' blind west of there. Special slip boards were also carried.

Nineteen minutes was lopped off the running time and the average scheduled speed went up from 19 to 25 mph. but the faster operation was not only meant to be more attractive to passengers. It also saved money as the new schedule required one RF fewer at Windsor for the same level of service. Inevitably, there was also detriment as the stopping service between London and Windsor suffered a fifty per cent cut which cannot have helped its long term health.

The opening of the new Dartford Tunnel on 18th November 1963 appeared to present a golden opportunity to tap a new market for the Green Line and route 722 was accordingly extended from Corbets Tey to Dartford via the Ockendons, Belhus and Aveley. Perhaps because it was not the most inspired choice of route to extend, perhaps because the potential was not there in the first place, or perhaps because of the severe traffic congestion which was encountered on the extension, it was hardly used and ran for the last time on 3rd November 1964. The companion bus service 300 fared a little better, lasting until being downgraded to GS OMO in May 1965 but even this disappeared in May 1967.

Route 726 lost its Saturday service in the summer of 1963, a portent of its eventual withdrawal altogether after 1968. RT 3232, now thirteen years old but in sparklingly good condition, passes through Allsop Place at Baker Street on a northbound journey. Ron Wellings

RT 3251 arrives at Market Street Dartford bereft of passengers after its journey through the Dartford Tunnel on the unpropitious extension from Corbets Tey. Between it and the RT on former trolleybus route 96 in the distant mist, a traction standard survives as a support for a street lamp. A.B. Cross

The next new idea to be tried was to cash in on the M1 motorway, which at this time came only as far south as Berrygrove on Watford By-Pass. When it re-appeared for the 1964 summer season on 10th May, route 726 followed a completely new route between Temple Fortune and Friars Wash, via North Circular Road, Great North Way, Watford Way, Watford By-Pass and the M1 motorway. It was the first London Transport route to use a motorway and ran non-stop from Temple Fortune to Whipsnade Zoo. Later in the year, with the winter programme on 4th November, came a much bolder venture which also made use of the M1. An entirely new Green Line route 727 was introduced on Mondays to Saturdays between Tring garage and Victoria, serving Northchurch, Berkhamsted and Hemel Hempstead New Town before joining the motorway for a fairly fast run to Watford By-Pass then through Hendon Central and Golders Green to Baker Street. After that there was another bold stroke with the route through central London which went via Marylebone Road, Oxford Circus, Piccadilly Circus, Trafalgar Square, Parliament Square and Victoria Street.

This broke the embargo on the use of certain streets within central London which had been laid down by the Amulree Committee in 1932 and overrode the long time objections of the Traffic Commissioner to any increase in services through Oxford Circus and Regent Street. Another milestone was the experimental removal of the restrictions on the use of the stops in Regent Street at Piccadilly Circus, which also benefited the 709, 710 and 711. These were another Amulree measure and had been in force since 1933, their effect being to limit the times of operation to Monday to Friday evenings, Saturday afternoons and evenings and all day on Sundays. (The similar restrictions on the stops for routes 715/A in Oxford Street at Selfridges were removed from 8th February 1965.) Unfortunately, the good intentions came to nothing as route 727 survived only until 30th October 1965 when it was withdrawn in the wake of insurmountable irregularity. Its poor performance was not helped by the sudden and unexpected closure of the M1 south of its junction with the M10 in May 1965 which enforced a diversion through Bedmond and Garston, nor by the heavy congestion encountered on Watford By-Pass, nor by the delays caused by works on widening Finchley Road. It probably did not help, either, that the rolling stock used were the standard thirteen year old RF coaches whose top speed was 40 mph, not quite what the customers might have expected of travel in the motorway age.

Other changes on 4th November were directed at economy. The depredation of traffic on route 703 caused by the electrification of the Metropolitan Line Amersham service had by now become intolerable and the route was withdrawn completely, although the service between London and Wrotham was retained by a straight extension of route 717. The route was simultaneously converted to double-deck operation, the RFs at Hatfield and Swanley being replaced by RMCs acquired from Harlow, where routes 720 and 720A were converted back to RF, without benefit of any increase in frequency. A different approach

Another fruitless attempt to stimulate traffic by speeding up the service was made on route 709 between London and Uxbridge from 4th November 1964. RF 105, displaying the special slip boards, passes the Old War Office in Whitehall about ten months later when its failure was about to be rewarded by withdrawal. Ken Glazier

The front page of Modern Transport for 12th December 1964 was given over completely to a feature about new route 727, apparently indicating the importance of the event in the eyes of the editor. However, it was not what it appeared to be but an advertisement by AEC, one of their odder ideas at this time being to extol the virtues of obsolete types. RF 90 is shown on the starkly new, featureless Motorway which it shares with very little other traffic. Capital Transport collection

Modern Transport

VOL XCII No. 2377   DECEMBER 12, 1964   1s 6d

AEC Green Line coaches shorten Tring-West End Journey by 15 minutes

Despite increasing traffic congestion, London Transport is finding new ways of offering Green Line passengers faster services.
Linking Tring, Berkhamsted and Hemel Hempstead with the heart of the West End and Victoria, the new 727 route is London Transport's first all-the-year-round Green Line service

to use a motorway. The journey time is cut by nearly a quarter of an hour due to the higher operating speeds and the fact that the coaches run non-stop for the 14 miles between Hemel Hempstead and Apex Corner, Mill Hill.
The AEC-powered RF coaches operating on this route are distinguished by yellow and black destination

boards, which are among the first of this type to be introduced and which denote express services.
Other AEC RF vehicles operate on route 709 (Chesham—Godstone) where the travelling time from Chesham to Oxford Circus has been cut to 86 minutes—a saving of 20 minutes.

Advertiser's announcement

Above **The special slip board advertising the limited stop operation between London and Windsor can be seen below the nearside windscreen of RF 189 at Butterwick, Hammersmith. The white on blue 'Express' blind, displayed west of Victoria, shows the open style of bullseye which was adopted for a time during the 1960s.** Colin Brown

Left **RF 228 in Brent Street Hendon shows the unified route board for the 712 and 713 which allowed coaches to change route during a duty without compromising the information displayed.** Ken Glazier

was tried on the alternative routes to Amersham, with another example of express operation. Route 709 was re-routed between Shepherds Bush and Uxbridge to use Western Avenue as far as Swakeleys and then via Park Road and Belmont Road. This was altered on 2nd December to be via Long Lane and Uxbridge Road to improve joint stopping arrangements in Uxbridge. It was also withdrawn on Sundays between Baker Street and Chesham, the service to Chesham being covered by the extension of hourly route 710 which was also left to serve the road through The Chalfonts.

The combined Monday to Friday service on routes 712 and 713 was reduced to being basically hourly, with alternate journeys working via Chiswell Green and Shenley, although there were some additional peak journeys between London and both Dorking (numbered 713) and Luton. A similar hourly service operated on Sundays but with additional hourly journeys between London and St Albans. The various combinations to which this gave rise required the introduction of new route numbers 712B (Dunstable via Park Street) and 713A (Luton via Radlett) but this messy arrangement was simplified on 14th April 1965, when the numbers 712 and 713

were used to indicate the route south of St Albans, whatever the northern destination. This revised and reduced pattern of service, which later spread to other routes, was a rather inefficient and hollow form of economy. There were no vehicle savings and, although three duties were removed on Mondays to Fridays, the money saving was considerably off-set by the addition of spread-over payments to three other duties. The amount saved was out of scale with the loss of goodwill and almost certainly led eventually to a self-defeating loss of passengers.

Apart from the curtailment of route 722, already mentioned, there were other economies in east London. Route 723 was re-routed

between Rainham and Grays to follow the 723A via Belhus estate, the 723A was extended from Grays to Tilbury via Dock Road and the 723B was cut back to Grays. The effect of this restructuring was to reduce the service via Purfleet by one coach an hour daily and between East Ham and London by one an hour in the peaks and two on Saturdays. With some trimming on the 721, the Grays and Romford changes saved nine RTs.

Despite all the economies, there was a fractional increase in mileage on the Green Line network in 1964 but this was to be the last time that an increase was to be recorded. From now on, the volume of service was to shrink relentlessly year after year.

THE NEW GREEN LINE COACH

This experimental coach is running every half hour on Route 705 between Sevenoaks and Windsor

It has the following features:

- Quieter and smoother ride
- More seats
- Luxury seats with footrests
- Wide-view windows
- Fluorescent lighting
- Luggage racks
- Adjustable air-conditioning for each passenger

Take a trip on it. If you have any comments please send them to the Public Relations Officer, London Transport, 55 Broadway, S.W.I

Left **An official photograph of RC 1 was used in this poster which was displayed widely to publicise the new AEC Reliance coaches. The bodies supplied by Willowbrook were based on the styling of the contemporary BET Federation standard design, other notable innovations being the new livery of pastel grey with a wide green waistband and, inside, coach type seats. A minor point of interest is that the registration numbers on these coaches were adrift from the fleet number by two, because they took the numbers following on immediately from the eight XFs.**

Above **The 30ft long Routemaster coaches were purchased for the Romford and Grays Green Line services so the 715A was never intended to have RCLs in the first place and they were fated not to stay with it for more than a year. Newly into service, RCL 2249 is seen at Marble Arch.** Capital Transport

During 1965 steps were taken to improve the quality of the vehicles used on the Green Line. The thirty-foot long version of the Routemaster coach, the RCL, was used to replace the RTs at Grays and Romford, starting with the 721 on 2nd June, then the 722 on 16th June, routes 723/A on 1st July and finally the 726 on 14th July. Route 723B was to have received RCLs at the same time but it was found that they could not go under the railway in London Road South Stifford, as their longer wheelbase straddling the dip in the road brought their roofs too close to the bridge for safety. The five RCLs intended for route 723B were therefore sent to Hertford to work route 715A, in exchange for five RMCs.

A more fundamental change took place on 28th November 1965, when the fourteen new AEC Reliance RC class coaches, described in chapter ten, entered service from Dunton Green and Windsor garages on route 705. They were not to be followed immediately by fresh orders as the Board was uncertain about the future prospects of the network and had already decided to investigate the desirability of refurbishing the RFs to give them a few more years front line life. Following the successful launch of RF 136 on 15th March 1966, the refurbished coaches went into service between August 1966 and September 1967.

Meanwhile, the network suffered a minor wound on 26th September 1965 when the

massive one-way system was introduced at Victoria, making Eccleston Bridge part of the south-east to north-west through route while traffic in the other direction was routed over Elizabeth Bridge. Eccleston Bridge had been virtually the private domain of Green Line since 1933 and was its principal central London stopping place. As recently as 1961 the passenger shelters on the bridge had been renewed completely and a new enquiry office opened on the north side. The new traffic arrangements undid this cohesiveness by forcing the transfer of southbound coaches to new stops in Buckingham Palace Road, leaving the new enquiry office isolated on the wrong side of the road well into LCBS days. Although this was less satisfactory, it is perhaps a minor miracle that the London Traffic Management Unit was prepared to countenance a large number of coaches continuing to have the exclusive use of one lane on its new fast through traffic route, rather than banishing them to some obscure backwater.

There was an increasing tendency from about this time for bus routes which paralleled Green Line services to be withdrawn on Sundays and for a special scale of fares to be introduced on the coach route, lower than normal but still higher than the bus scale. For example, on route 710 between Uxbridge and Gerrards Cross and 711 onwards to High Wycombe, there was a lower minimum fare to cover the absence of route 455 on Sundays. This was to become increasingly common as the Sunday bus network withered away and by the summer of 1968 there were special scales on routes 702 (Sunningdale to Virginia Water), 704 (Riverhead to Tonbridge), 705 (Westerham to Sevenoaks), 706/707 (Tring to Northchurch), 708 (Godstone to East Grinstead), 711 (Uxbridge to Beaconsfield), 716 (Hitchin to Potters Bar, also Saturdays only Hatfield to Ganwick Corner), 716A (Stevenage to Welwyn Garden City, Welham Green to Potters Bar and Addlestone to Woking) and 720 (Bishops Stortford to Old Harlow). In some cases there were special scales on all days, either where there was no longer a bus route or where the bus service had been heavily reduced. These applied on routes 701/702 (Ascot/Sunninghill to Virginia Water), 704 (Farnborough to Sevenoaks), 706/707 (Chelsham to Westerham/Oxted), 712/713 (Radlett to Borehamwood), 715 (Cobham to Burpham),

717 (Swanley to Wrotham), 718/725 (Windsor to Staines) and 721 (Brentwood to Romford). Of these, the 717 was unique in having the normal bus scale of charges, these having been introduced as far back as 23rd April 1952. The only case of a coach route being extended to cover a withdrawn route was initiated on 3rd October 1965, when route 707 was extended from Oxted to Holland (Coldshott) on a specially reduced fare scale, to cover the withdrawal of routes 464 and 465.

Although this arrangement appeared to make sense economically, it could have an adverse effect on punctuality. Before local fares were introduced, coaches delayed on their journey through London could make up time on the outer section of a journey, between Staines and Windsor for example, where there was little intermediate traffic. Once the lower fares were introduced, coaches would be obliged to make frequent stops and the opportunity to recover time was lost.

A new way of overcoming unreliability was tried on routes 701, 702 and 714 from 1st November 1965. They were split in London on Mondays to Fridays, the 701 working Ascot to Victoria and Hammersmith to Gravesend, the 702 Sunningdale to Victoria and the 714 was split end on at Baker Street. Through tickets continued to be issued on route 714 and a system of transfers was introduced,

which also allowed travel on appropriate parts of route 716 and 716A. No transfers were allowed at first on routes 701 and 702, presumably because the overlap was considered adequate to meet most needs but this was relaxed from 22nd November. A system similar to that operating on route 714 was then introduced, with transfers at Hammersmith and Victoria.

Meanwhile, one of the two express operations, the 709, had failed to deliver the desired improvement and suffered the ignominy of losing the whole of its western end from Baker Street to Chesham from 1st November 1965, becoming an hourly service between Godstone and Baker Street only. Route 710 was extended to Chesham daily and a few additional peak journeys were put on between Amersham and Lambeth North, where a new stand was appointed in Hercules Road. For some reason these were shown in timetables as terminating at Trafalgar Square. Route 720A was also withdrawn, the Harlow New Town section being covered by the intermediate diversion of route 720. The hapless route 722 was also withdrawn on Saturdays, Sundays and Monday to Friday off-peaks, leaving the peak service to struggle on for a few more years. Finally, the off-peak service on route 719 was cut to hourly. These cuts, together with the loss of the 727 already mentioned

Facing page **Romford's first scheduled single-deckers on Green Line work since 1939 helped launch the highly successful cross-country route 724 on 10th July 1966. For this first one-man operated coach route standard RF2/1s were modified, these being the only examples of OMO coach RFs which were not also modernised. RF 204, allocated to Romford garage, was one of them.** Ken Glazier

Left **RF 141 at Hertford bus station after the reversion of route 715A from RCL to RF operation. It displays the new style of destination blind introduced the year before this photo was taken in July 1966.** J.G.S. Smith

By the time this photograph was taken, modernised RF 153, seen on its way to the new summertime terminus at Chartwell, had already been downgraded to bus status, although being used as a coach. It is performing a movement which would become impossible a few years later, turning from Stockwell Road into Brixton Road at Brixton Police Station. Colin Stannard

and seasonal frequency reductions on route 718, helped produce a 5.2 per cent cut in annual Green Line car mileage. This was the largest so far, just exceeding the 4.5 per cent of 1963, but was the first of a succession of years during which recession became increasingly rapid.

The continuing loss of trade on routes 715A and 722 led to them both losing their RCLs on 12th June 1966. Route 715A received RFs and the 722 reverted to RTs, which was not exactly a vote of confidence, while the RCLs were moved to Tunbridge Wells and Windsor to serve what was considered more promising territory on route 704.

The most portentous event in Green Line terms during 1966 took place on 10th July when a new peripheral route was opened between Romford and High Wycombe, via Epping, Harlow, Ware, Hertford, Welwyn Garden City, Hatfield, St Albans, Watford, Rickmansworth and Amersham, a distance of seventy miles. Numbered 724, it was only the second such route in Green Line history and came no less than twenty-three years after the successful pioneering route 725. However it was not in this respect that it was a portent but because it was the first to be one-man operated. Until then London Transport had been wary of upsetting the standard of operation of the coach routes by adopting this

form of economy but the Reshaping Plan, which was by now being drafted, was to enshrine the principle of universal one-man operation, and the Prices and Incomes Board report which followed the disputes in early 1966 included provision for its introduction on Green Line. Even so its first application was confined to a route which did not enter central London. The 724 was, without doubt, the most fertile of the new ideas tried out at this time, was to become an established part of the network and still exists, in modified form, at the time of writing.

Another novel approach to the development of the network appeared the following Saturday, when route 706 was given a seasonal extension to Chartwell, the home of Sir Winston Churchill who had died a year earlier. This operated on Saturdays and Sundays in its first season but when it re-appeared for the 1967 season on 25th March, Wednesdays and Thursdays were also included. The Chartwell operation was also destined to endure, outlasting the disappearance of the main service by many years.

Although they were left until the last day of the year, when schedules based on the new five day week were introduced, 1966 did not escape its share of service cuts. Route 710 was cut back from Chesham to Amersham on Mondays to Fridays and lost its peak hour

Amersham to London shorts, the ailing routes 715A and 723B were withdrawn on Sundays and outside peak hours on Mondays to Fridays, the latter also being cut back from Aldgate to East Ham, and the 723A was withdrawn altogether. Route 709 was also all but withdrawn, the service being reduced to two up and two down peak hour journeys and two rounders on Sundays to serve St Lawrence's Hospital, Caterham. The 'dead' running against the peak flow was apparently always ignored by at least one crew, who worked in service whatever their route card told them. In any case, it lasted only until 24th February 1967, after which the journeys carried passengers officially. Two of the RCLs displaced from Grays were allocated to the maimed 709 at Godstone in place of RFs. There were one or two positive elements in this programme: route 711 was diverted to serve Banstead Village, via Garratts Lane, Banstead High Street, Sutton Lane and Downs Road, instead of the mainly unpopulated Brighton Road; the through service on route 714 was restored, although the Sunday service was cut to hourly; and routes 714 and 718 were both diverted via Oxford Street and Portland Place to serve Oxford Circus. This was a further breach of the 1933 embargo on Green Line operations in central London but alas too late to be of any significant help.

Enthused with the success of route 724, the Country Bus and Coach department decided to try another peripheral route, again one-man operated, this time linking the two main London airports at Gatwick and Heathrow. Route 727 started on 13th May 1967 and ran from Luton Station to Crawley via St Albans, Watford, Rickmansworth, Uxbridge, West Drayton, Heathrow Airport, Hanworth, Teddington, Kingston, Tolworth, Epsom, Tadworth, Reigate, Woodhatch and Gatwick Airport. It was not able to serve Luton Airport because London Transport was severely restricted by statute in what it could run in the Borough of Luton. The 727 covered a distance of seventy four miles in just under three-and-a-half hours, making it both the longest and, at an average speed of over 21 mph, the fastest Green Line route. As traffic to and from the airports was the main target of the service, the eleven modernised RFs allocated to it were provided with a makeshift luggage compartment by removing the rear row of seats, reducing their seating capacity to thirty-five. The scheduled allocation was shared equally between Reigate and St Albans garages, four each, but the elderly Regals were hard put to keep up the necessary performance and no fewer than three spares were held at St Albans to cover late running and breakdowns. It was to prove another inveterate success which, although itself later reduced to a more local operation south of Kingston, lived on in spirit in the form of Jetlink 747.

On the same day that this exciting new project was launched, route 718 had its Monday to Friday frequency north of London reduced to hourly, except for some peak hour shorts between London and Harlow, although the seasonal half-hourly service was re-introduced on Sundays. This proved to be a stepping stone to making the entire service hourly from 7th October.

A new agreement on annual leave which came into force on 22nd May 1967 granted staff with more than five years service an extra three days leave, two of which added to the main summer holiday, which then ran from a Saturday to a Sunday, covering three weekends. This put a strain on staff availability, particularly on Saturdays and led to staff shortages. As a direct result of this, route 702 was withdrawn on Saturdays between Sunningdale and London from 12th August until it could be restored, after the end of the summer holiday block, in the winter programme on 7th October. Route 714 also had to be reduced on Saturdays for the same reason from 22nd July until the winter programme, in this case by cutting the through frequency to hourly and operating hourly shorts from Luton to London. Unfortunately the resulting timetable gave uneven intervals, with headways at worst of 15/45 minutes, which was hardly likely to encourage or retain traffic. This poor timetable was operated again from 18th May 1968 until the route's conversion to one-man operation. Cuts continued to be the order of the day on other routes in this programme. Meanwhile, the M1 motorway had been extended southward from Berrygrove to Brockley Hill and route 726 was diverted to take advantage.

The long journeys made by Green Line coaches made them particularly vulnerable to disruption in snowy weather. This appears to have been the reason why RF 152 was to be found at St Albans bus station on 8th February 1969 working an unscheduled short to Heathrow. J.G.S. Smith

On 2nd December the need for economy caught up with the small garage in Whitefield Road Tunbridge Wells, which had been opened by Autocar in January 1930 and had always worked the London coach route. Reductions in service had made space available at Dunton Green, into which route 704 was now transferred. The combined timetable with route 705 was also restructured to give a twenty minute service between Windsor and Bromley Common, with one coach an hour running as a 705 via Westerham to Sevenoaks and two (at uneven 20/40 minute intervals) as 704s to Sevenoaks. The service beyond Sevenoaks to Tunbridge Wells became hourly. The express service on route 705 between Windsor and London was also discontinued and coaches returned to their old route along the same roads as the 704. There had been plans to retain the express operation and use the time saved to divert route 705 via Heathrow Airport, which would have enabled the twenty-minute headway to be maintained at Windsor and Victoria, though not intermediately. The Board gave authority for the installation of luggage racks in place of the offside longitudinal seat in the lower saloon of the twelve RCLs and at least one coach was modified. The plan was dropped, for reasons unknown, but both routes were diverted to run via the East and West Ramps of the airport perimeter road, where they were able to make connections with bus services into the airport.

Left **In a complicated set of moves at the end of December 1967, route 708 exchanged its RFs for RMCs, enabling it to be reduced to an hourly service. RMC 1505 is in the revised livery introduced with the RCLs.** Colin Stannard

Right **Route 714 was in the first phase of the programme of conversions to one-man operation on 23rd November 1968, when its service was also cut. Just over a year later on 2nd December 1969, in the dying days of London Transport's hegemony, RF 122 arrives in a cheerless Luton.** W.N. Jackson

Conductors on the Green Line were never exactly overworked but the duties on the much curtailed 709 must have been among the easiest, despite the size of the vehicle. The conductor of RCL 2226 is taking his ease on the back seat as it cruises into Regent Street from Piccadilly Circus, on an evening peak dead run to Baker Street. *Colin Stannard*

All this was made possible by replacing the RC single-deckers on route 705 by RCLs, acquired from Grays garage whose waning routes 723 and 723B were downgraded to RMC. The RCs, which had given much mechanical trouble since their début in March 1965, were withdrawn for an extended period of examination (see chapter ten). The RMCs for Grays came from Stevenage garage and were made available by another cut on the same day when route 717 was withdrawn between Welwyn Garden City and London. Its route between Welwyn Garden City and Little Heath was covered by the intermediate diversion of route 716A, which was also re-allocated from Stevenage to Hatfield garage. The London to Wrotham portion, operated by

Swanley garage, also lost its RMCs on 30th December in favour of RFs, the same day that a similar conversion of Garston's route 719 took place. The double-deckers were transferred to East Grinstead and Two Waters garages for route 708 so that it too could be reduced to an hourly service. Some of these changes were related to the intention to start the conversion of the coach routes to one-man operation. The first stage should have taken place on 7th October 1967 and would have included routes 701, 702, 714, 719 and 720 but was delayed by the protracted Union negotiations covering the whole question of OMO and the Reshaping Plan. Under these plans route 717 would not have survived in the truncated form and route 719 would have

run through from Hemel Hempstead to Wrotham, hence the coincidence of the vehicle changes at Two Waters and Swanley. The number 717, rather than 716A, was to have been allocated to the revised route from Stevenage to Woking.

The following year saw further inroads into the coach network, starting on 18th May 1968 when the Monday to Friday off-peak service was withdrawn from route 702. This left only two peak hour journeys, although the service continued to run on Saturdays and Sundays. Through running on the 701, which had been extended in Ascot meanwhile to Heatherwood Hospital (on 30th December 1967), was re-instated at the same time. A month later, on 15th June, the 707 was withdrawn on Sundays between Chelsham, Oxted and Holland leaving the latter without a Sunday service of any sort; and route 715A lost its Saturday service. The 722 finally gave up the ghost on 2nd August, what little traffic was left being served by a peak hour extension of Central Bus route 150 from Becontree Heath to Romford (North Street), and the 723B breathed its last on 4th October. Another route lost in this period was summer service 726 which was doomed never to re-appear after it was withdrawn at the end of the season on 6th September. Sadly, it had been diverted to serve Oxford Circus to give it a more attractive central London picking up point as recently as 3rd June.

Staff shortages again took their toll during 1968 and route 715 was reduced for this reason at short notice on 24th August. The Oxford Circus to Guildford service was cut to hourly during the off-peak on Mondays to Fridays, and on Saturdays and Sundays three gaps of an hour were made in the basic half-hourly service. The full service was resumed on 5th October.

On 23rd November 1968, Green Line finally surrendered to the inevitability of one-man operation. Seven routes were converted on that day, two more than had been in the October 1967 programme, the 701, 702, 714 and 720 on their existing routes, although the 714 was cut to hourly on Mondays to Saturdays, and three others with modifications. In line with the 1967 plan, route 719 was now extended to Wrotham, absorbing the 717 and bringing this stretch of route its third number in four years. The two extra routes were the 710 and 711. The 710 was drastically curtailed to run only between London (Baker Street) and Amersham, losing both the short section from Chesham to Amersham and the entire route south of London to Crawley, although this was partly compensated by the operation of an additional peak journey on the 709 for which Godstone was allocated another RCL. In London it was diverted via Bayswater Road and Oxford Street, in another belated breaking of the 1933 Amulree embargo. A double run was inserted into route 711 at Gerrards Cross to boost the service at 'The Packhorse' but it was also reduced to a basic hourly headway, boosted to half-hourly during peak hours and Saturday shopping hours. With the new OMO timetables, running times varying by time of day and day of week were re-introduced for the first time since 1942. The principle was also applied to the remaining two-man operated routes in 1969.

The Whipsnade service became a daily operation when routes 712 and 713 were converted to one-man operation on 15th February 1969. RF 194 is at Epsom on 7th April 1969. G. Mead

Not a common event, but one which would never occur again after 31st December 1969, was the substitution of Central Bus vehicles for disabled coaches. On this occasion, Cricklewood rushed RT 780 out to Golders Green to cover a working on route 717, even taking the trouble to transfer the blind from the RF to the RT, although leaving it looking a little crumpled. Ken Glazier

The rest of the single-deck operations followed on 15th February 1969, when routes 706, 712, 713 and 725 changed over. Route 708 was also converted, losing its double-deckers after only fourteen months, this apparently having been a late addition to the conversion programme. The plan had been to keep two-man operation on the 708 until it was found that the longer OMO running times on the 706 would play havoc with the regularity of the joint timetable. Route 706 was withdrawn between Chelsham and Westerham, except for Monday to Friday peak hours and the summer journeys to Chartwell. Route 707 was withdrawn between Oxted and Chelsham and the service north of there was incorporated into the 706. The Saturday service beyond St Albans to Luton on the 712/713 was also withdrawn but the summer journeys to Whipsnade now became daily, in

place of the 726. Route 715A was also withdrawn in this programme. The only routes which were not one-man operated were the double-deckers: 704, 705, 709, 715, 716, 716A, 718, 721 and 723. This meant that there was no coach work available for the RMCs displaced from route 708, which were therefore redeployed as buses. Most went to Hatfield, where they provided a welcome improvement for users of routes 303/A, and three to Addlestone for route 461A, although two of these were passed on to Grays for route 370 in May. With the withdrawal of route 707, appropriately amended side route boards were produced in the normal way at Aldenham but these turned out to be the last. None were produced by LCBS, although some were crudely amended at garages, and eventually this characteristic feature of the Green Line fell into disuse.

As though the Green Line did not have enough problems, severe staff shortage at Windsor led to the introduction of emergency schedules on route 704 from 19th April 1969. This was done rather crudely and simply involved the withdrawal of those Windsor to Sevenoaks journeys staffed by Windsor crews, which ensured an irregular service north and west of Bromley. This lasted just over five months but when new schedules were introduced on 4th October, they did not restore the old pattern but went further to reduce the whole basic service to hourly, giving a joint half-hourly with route 705 between Windsor and Bromley. This released six RCLs which went to their natural home at Grays to operate on route 723 once more, in company with three RMCs. The RMCs displaced from the 723 remained at Grays and were switched to bus routes 370/A, with some journeys on other routes.

These were the last changes made in 1969 and the last by London Transport, who relinquished control of the Green Line to London Country Bus Services Ltd on 1st January 1970. In its last decade under London Transport's stewardship Green Line had suffered a catastrophic decline in fortune. Between 1960 and 1969 no fewer than forty-two per cent of its passengers had deserted for other means and those who remained made journeys with an average length of less than ten miles compared with over eleven, so that the volume of business fell by forty-nine per cent. This may be compared with volumetric losses of twenty-four and twenty-nine per cent by Country and Central Buses respectively. It also needs to be set against the background of a growth in population in the outer country area of no less than twenty-seven per cent. There can be little doubt that most of the decline could be attributed to the phenomenal growth in car ownership and usage, which not only took people away from the coaches but also created congested traffic conditions which were fatal for a service which thrived on reliability. The spread of railway modernisation also had its effect but some of the policies followed must also take their share of the blame. Many reductions in service were made on routes which were still well used and, even in the off-peak, passengers were often left behind which, on an hourly service, was an invitation to try other means of travel. The attenuated services were also more vulnerable to the effects of traffic delays and the loss of punctuality was made worse by the loss of empty duplicates starting on time in London and by the carriage of local passengers on the rural sections. Timetables were often badly co-ordinated too, a particularly bad example being departures from East Grinstead where the hourly 409, the hourly 708, and even the hourly train, left the town within three minutes of each other. Perhaps more could also have been done to make the system more attractive, including a more dynamic approach to fares policy than the rather timid improvements described in chapter six, circumscribed as they were by policies which limited competition with the railways. Nevertheless, the network handed over to the National Bus Company at the end of 1969 still required 217 peak vehicles and still turned out sixteen million car miles a year.

CHEAP FARES AND ROVER TICKETS

As London Transport's fortunes sank more and more into serious decline, the Executive and later the Board turned increasingly to new ways of stimulating business. By 1960, annual increases in fares had become commonplace but the big increases in costs which were shouldered in the fight to make bus work more attractive to new recruits, soon made more frequent assaults on the passengers' pockets necessary. The one increase in 1960 took place on 8th May and applied to the 4d and 5d fares for 1½ and 2 miles which were increased by 1d. By the end of 1960, after two substantial wage increases for bus staff as well as improvements for others, the Executive found it necessary to seek approval from the Transport Tribunal for another rise in fares, which was approved by Order dated 21st November 1960. The increases were not applied until 15th January 1961, which laid the foundations for this to be the first year when fares went up twice. The January changes applied to fares of 7d and above,

which were increased by between 1d and 5d on buses and up to 1s 4d on coaches. These same fares, except for the 8d rate for two miles on buses, were increased again on 30th July, this time by 1d. On some coach routes this would have eliminated fares below one shilling, which would have taken them out of the stage carriage category for licensing, and in these cases one fare was held at 11d. In 1962 there were increases on 15th March and 3rd June, by which time fares for journeys over two miles had increased by between 3d and 10d in a matter of eighteen months, the heaviest proportionate increase of forty-two per cent falling on the lowest fares. Early Morning Single fares were also withdrawn on 1st January 1962 and even Rover and Twin Rover tickets were increased by 1s (twenty-five per cent) and 1s 6d (fifteen per cent) respectively from 1st March 1962.

The first sign of a move towards new discounted fares was in the summer of 1961, when an experimental 'Bus-About' ticket was

issued for travel on Central Buses and trolleybuses. Unlike the Red Rover which was not available on Mondays to Fridays, the new ticket was valid for one day's unlimited travel on any day of the week in July, August and September. It was a great success and secured an increase in the sale of rover tickets from 39,000 in August 1960 to 182,000 in 1961. It was repeated the following year but not in 1963 when Red and Twin Rovers were made available instead after 9.30am on Mondays to Fridays during August. From 1964 onwards these two tickets were available throughout the day on Mondays to Fridays in July, August and September.

Above **The price of Rover tickets went up from five to six shillings on 1st January 1962 and remained at that level for most of the 1960s. RF 413 advertises the Central Bus version of the Rover as it roams the back streets of Ealing.** Colin Brown

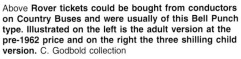

Above **Rover tickets could be bought from conductors on Country Buses and were usually of this Bell Punch type. Illustrated on the left is the adult version at the pre-1962 price and on the right the three shilling child version.** C. Godbold collection

Centre **It was eventually found possible to issue Green Rovers through Gibson machines, using the class code 'EMS' (originally Early Morning Single but redundant since January 1962).** C. Godbold collection

Right **Central Bus conductors would not issue Rover tickets, which therefore had to be obtained from Underground stations or garages and were in this more substantial card form. Those illustrated are child examples of the pre-1962 half-crown ticket and the later three shilling version.** C. Godbold collection

On 1st January 1962 special Cheap Day Returns were introduced on the northern ends of routes 703, 709, 710 and 711 to encourage shoppers to use the coaches when going to the West End for the January sales. They were valid on Mondays to Fridays during the month of January for journeys to London after 9.30am, but could not be used for return on coaches leaving town between 4.30 and 6.30pm. The arrangement was apparently not a success and was not repeated in subsequent years. Something rather more substantial was offered in a new type of ticket called the 'Ranger' which was launched on Good Friday, 20th April 1962. This was valid on both Country Buses and Green Line coaches and offered twenty-five shillingsworth of travel for £1 over a period of seven consecutive days. The ticket was a three page document (two for the children's version) which had a grid showing fare values, rising at 1d intervals up to 25s and another showing fare stage numbers. The conductor was required to clip the ticket at the appropriate point, adding the amount of the fare to the value at the previous cancellation, and write in the number of the fare stage. It was available after 9.30am on Mondays to Fridays and all day at weekends until 30th September. This too did not re-appear.

To help reduce the time lag between increases in costs and the introduction of higher fares, Section 48 of the Transport Act 1962 provided a new quick procedure, by notice in the London Gazette, for fares increases which were estimated to yield a less than ten per cent increase in revenue. The first increase made under this procedure was on 23rd June 1963, when the higher fares in the scale were again increased by between 1d and 7d. As required under the new statute, these were

confirmed by Order of the Transport Tribunal on 19th December 1963, following a public inquiry. There were two increases in 1964, both using the new procedure, which tackled the lower rates for the first time for some years. The 3d minimum, unchanged since 1957 when the infamous 'Suez halfpenny' was imposed, went up to 4d on 1st March, then fares of 6d and above went up by 2d or 3d on 19th July.

An application was made to the Transport Tribunal for an increase which the Board planned to introduce on 2nd May 1965 but, at the request of the Minister of Transport, London Transport undertook not to increase fares before the end of 1965, while the whole future of the undertaking was reviewed. The deferred increase was implemented on 16th January 1966 when the 6d and 10d fares for 1½ and 2½ miles respectively were withdrawn and therefore effectively increased by 2d, and the four, five and six mile fares were increased by 1d, 2d and 3d respectively. This was to be the last increase for two-and-a-half years, the deficiency being made good by government grants under the authority of the Transport Finances Act 1966.

Another attempt at Cheap Day Returns on the Green Line was tried from 26th April 1965, once more on routes 709, 710 and 711 and now also on the 712, 713, 714, 715 and 715A but again only on the sections north of London. Unlike their predecessors, these were available for return journeys originating in London as well as from the outer ends and could be bought after 9.30am on Mondays to Fridays with no return from London allowed in the evening peak. They did not generate much demand and were discontinued when another new type of return was introduced on 6th June 1966. These were eventually,

though not at first, called 'Greenliners' and were available on all routes, except the 722, 725 and 726. They gave a discount of thirty per cent on journeys of ten miles or more into central London after 9.30am on Mondays to Fridays, with the usual evening peak restriction. These were supplemented from 3rd July by special Sunday cheap returns on the three routes to Dorking for the summer period until 25th September. All these tickets continued to exist for the remainder of London Transport's tenure.

There were two innovations relating to Green Line during 1967, both specific to a particular route. From 24th March, maximum fares of 10s single and 15s return were introduced on route 724 and, when route 727 was introduced on 13th May, through road/rail tickets between Heathrow Airport, the Midlands and the North were made available via Luton and Watford.

The most ambitious rover type ticket to be launched so far and also by far the best bargain, was the 'Weekender' which was introduced on 25th March 1967. This cost £1 (10s child) and was available on Central Buses, Country Buses, the Underground and on British Rail trains where they used the same lines as the Underground. They could not be used on the Red Arrow, suburban flat fare, Green Line or booked excursions, nor on the 405/B between Crawley and Tilgate or Furnace Green but, unlike other special tickets, they could be used north of Rickmansworth on the Metropolitan Line. They were normally available for a Saturday and Sunday but at Bank Holiday weekends could also be bought for use on Sunday and Monday. Even when their price was increased to 25s from 29th June 1968, they maintained their excellent value because they were made available on the whole Green Line network at the same time. Other Rover tickets were also increased in price on 29th June, Red and Green Rovers by a shilling (to 7s) and Twin Rovers by two shillings to 12s. Red Rovers were again made available after 9.30am on Mondays to Fridays during the three summer months but this year the arrangement was allowed to continue for another three months and eventually became permanent.

Fares increases came back into vogue in 1968 when, as part of the agreement under which control of London Transport was to pass to the Greater London Council, the Board was required to return to a working surplus of £2 million by 1970 by a mixture of service economies and substantial fares increases. Since 1967 it had been government policy to refer all price increases proposed by nationalised industries to the National Board for Prices and Incomes but this put transport operators in double jeopardy as they also had to get the necessary authority from the Traffic Commissioners or Orders from the Transport Tribunal. Proposals submitted to the Minister in June 1967 by London Transport were designed not only to raise extra revenue but also to facilitate the introduction of automatic fare collection by creating a simplified scale rising in 3d steps for journeys up to thirteen miles and in sixpenny steps for longer journeys. This required an increase in the minimum 4d fare to 6d, double what it had been four years earlier. There was a delay of four months before the proposals were referred to the NBPI and another five months before that Board's report No. 56 was published in March 1968. This confirmed the fares increases as being necessary if London Transport was to attain the financial viability which was now essential. London Transport's immediate application to the Transport Tribunal was considered at a Public Inquiry in April and May and the Tribunal's decision was dated 24th June. They refused to approve the application in full but agreed to the minimum fare being increased from 4d to 5d and the two mile fare from 8d to 9d with smaller increases than had been applied for on higher values. The effect of the ruling was to reduce the estimated net yield of the increases from £8.6 million to £5.8 million; it also prevented the simplification of the fare structure. The increases were introduced in two stages on 5th August and, coinciding with the first stage of Reshaping, 7th September 1968.

This left London Transport still needing to raise an extra £8 million to reach the financial target set by the Greater London Council and a further application was submitted to the Minister, this time using procedures sanctioned by Section 27(2) of the new Transport (London) Act (1969) which did not require Transport Tribunal approval. The National Board for Prices and Incomes, to whom the application was referred, again concluded in Report No. 112 that, subject to minor modifications, the proposals were desirable in current circumstances. They were approved by the Minister and introduced on 7th September 1969. An important innovation contained in the changes was the introduction of a higher rate of charge for journeys in the 'Inner Zone', which approximated to the area

RT 2256 at the East Grinstead terminus of the 424 advertises the country bus version of the Rover ticket. E. Shirras

within the Circle Line, where the Board claimed that it cost more to provide the service and that there was also a higher standard of service. This was done by shortening the distance between fare stages from half-a-mile to about five-sixteenths of a mile, which meant a double increase for some passengers. The minimum fare was increased to 6d and fares for journeys of over five miles were increased by 6d in the Inner Zone and 3d elsewhere.

The scale based on 3d steps in the lower ranges lasted less than three months because London Transport found itself still with a gap of £1.5 million because of increases in wages and National Insurance contributions. Application was made for a further increase of 3d on the two and four mile fares, which had not been increased in September, and this

was approved after consultation between the Minister, the Board, the Greater London Council and the National Bus Company, without further reference to the Prices and Incomes Board. The new rates were introduced inside the Special Area on 30th November. This put the entire scale onto 6d steps upward from a 6d minimum fare, a near perfect scale for automatic collection of fares but in depressing contrast to the 3d minimum and steps of one penny which had existed only ten years earlier. The Traffic Commissioner approved similar increases outside the Special Area and these were introduced on 28th December. This must have been the last occasion on which the status of the Special Area came into play as it, along with the Board, expired at midnight on 31st December 1969.

The seven shilling Rover came in June 1968, when its availability was also extended to Mondays to Fridays all year round. In 1969 London Transport also bent to heavy criticism of its refusal to allow their use on flat fare buses and removed that restriction too. RT 2051, apparently abandoned by staff and passengers alike outside Loughton garage, carries an advertisement proclaiming both improvements, as well as twin fronts announcing the opening of the Victoria Line. J.G.S. Smith

Left **Route 330 had the distinction of linking three New Towns, Welwyn Garden City, Hatfield and Hemel Hempstead, where this photograph was taken. RT 4586 was one of a number which were given experimental cream coloured fleet names when overhauled in 1966.** Colin Brown

Below **RF 584, seen at Hertford bus station, represents the standard large saloon which, with the RT class, dominated Country Bus operations in 1960. The RF-operated services in the north-east changed several times during the decade in the constant pursuit of economy, the 393A being a new route which emerged from the restructuring of 7th June 1961. It ran via Nazeing Gate rather than Leaside Nurseries but was otherwise the same as the 393, with which it replaced routes 372/A between Hertford and Welwyn Garden City.** Colin Brown

CHAPTER SEVEN

COUNTRY AREA DEVELOPMENTS

The history of the Country Bus department in its last ten years was one of mixed fortunes. The population in the area it served continued to increase, particularly in the New Towns, an extra half million people (nearly twenty-seven per cent) being added between 1960 and 1969. Services were expanded to meet the new demand but Country Buses was not immune from the country-wide movement of people away from public transport into private cars and was therefore concurrently making cuts in existing services to cope with the falling demand. These opposing factors enabled bus mileage cuts to be held at 13.6 per cent, compared with the 19.5 per cent of Central Buses and a fleet average of twenty per cent. It was also beset by staff shortages and industrial strife, although to nothing like the extent experienced by Central Buses. Because the services it ran were generally at lower frequencies than those of Central Buses, the Country Bus and Coach department was obliged to react more promptly and with greater finesse to the shifts in demand and availability of staff to ensure that it met its budget targets. In this account, developments will be covered area by area followed by a more general review of the process of contraction and other changes.

Route 809 reached Warwick Road, Pestcotts, on 7th June 1961, sixteen months after being introduced as far as Pankhurst Crescent. On 27th January 1962, the Saturday before it was extended again, to Chells, RT 4775 was photographed on the Warwick Road stand. The abandonment of intermediate point blinds in favour of the universal 'Town Service' was intended to speed up turn round times at terminals when buses switched between routes.
Peter G Mitchell

The first New Town to record a development was Stevenage, on 3rd February 1960, when new route 809 began to serve the newly occupied area of Pestcotts in the east of the town. The 809 followed the 392A from the bus station to Bedwell and then branched off along Six Hills Way and Chells Way to Pankhurst Crescent. There were some works journeys to Gunnels Wood Road and the opportunity was taken to divert other works services to pass the bus station in Danestrete from the same date. The 809 was extended further in Pestcotts via Chells Way to Warwick Road on 7th June 1961, then on 31st January 1962 to Chells (Newton Road), where it was joined by 801 school journeys, and finally to Hudson Road, Mobbsbury Way on 21st May 1963. In the meantime, the opening of a new section of Monks Wood Way to forge a link with Great North Road allowed the diversion of routes 303, 303A, 315A, 390, 716 and 716A to serve this part of the New Town from 24th October 1962.

On 29th July 1964, an area to the west of Chells, known as Pin Green, got its first bus service and the section of Shephall Way between Longmeadow and Bandley Hill was given its first full time service. This road had been covered until then only by hospital service 808 which had been extended to Bandley Hill on 25th October 1961. When planning the alterations to provide these services the Country Bus planners seem to have abandoned any attempt to give each one a distinct identity and present a system which passengers could be expected to understand. Instead they introduced complications into the local network which were to be compounded as the new areas continued to develop until almost every route variation was covered by the same group of numbers. The underlying reason for this was the need to compile efficient and cost-effective schedules while respecting the requirements of the Trade Union agreements but Stevenage stood out as exceptional, better solutions being found elsewhere. Routes 392A

and 801 were combined into a circular operation from the bus station via Bedwell, Bandley Hill, Longmeadow and Monks Wood, numbered 800 clockwise and 801 counter-clockwise. Three prongs, numbered 800 or 801 depending on what they did in the south of the town, continued northwards from the bus station: to the railway station; to Hitchin (Mondays to Saturdays); and, also Mondays to Saturdays, to Pin Green (Lonsdale Road/Archer Road), which was reached via Fairlands Way and Lonsdale Road. Works journeys from the south to Gunnels Wood Road were numbered 800A or 801A and there was a new 802A from Pin Green to Gunnels Wood Road. All four routes were extended in Pin Green to the Archer Road shopping centre on 16th June 1965 and then onwards to Webb Rise from 15th May 1966, when a Sunday afternoon and evening service was also introduced.

From the latter date another prong was added to the network serving a new area north-west of Pin Green called Almond's Spring, part of the 800 group being extended from the bus station to Almonds Lane via Sish Lane and Grace Way, and a new 802B works service introduced from Gunnels Wood Road. This was of particular interest as Sish Lane had been one of the first roads in the New Town to be served by buses but had been without an all-day service since October 1958. The three routes were extended further east to Sishes End via Vardon Road on 13th May 1967. They were joined there by routes 384 and 386 which were diverted through Letchmore Road, Walkern Road, Almonds Lane and Vardon Road resuming something resembling the traditional route which they had been forced to abandon four years earlier while the road system was being rebuilt. One of the new roads which came into use in the early 1960s was Fairlands Way and the opportunity had been taken from 23rd November 1960, to divert route 386 along it and St Georges Way to serve the bus station. This left route 384 to look after the Letchmore Road route until it too had to be diverted, from 15th April 1963, because Almonds Hill was about to be severed. The former route was then bereft of buses until the new Almonds Hill restored the physical link, albeit on a more northerly alignment. The final link in the local network was established on 15th June 1968, when the Pin Green services were extended northwards to Martins Wood (Derby Road) via Webb Rise and Fairlands Way. As this was only a stone's throw from Sishes End, it is a wonder that the temptation to join the two prongs to form yet another loop was resisted.

Stevenage New Town's original route, the 392, ran for the last time on 14th May 1966, leaving Greydells Road and Haycroft Road uncovered, the area being served from the next day by the new section of routes 800/801 through Sish Lane. RT 2175, at Stevenage bus station, was one of a number in red livery on temporary loan to Country Buses in the mid-sixties which were replaced on 20th March 1965 by green ones released from Garston by the arrival of RMLs. J. Gascoine

Above **How Wood estate was reached by route 355A on 13th April 1960 and the route survived until the end of London Transport days, by which time former Green Line RF 242, at Park Street, had been demoted to a bus.** J.G.S. Smith

Above right **Route 391 was extended to Mile House estate in May 1960 and was still going there, using the same type of bus but now one-man operated, when this photograph of RF 693 was taken in Victoria Street, St Albans, on 8th February 1969.** J.G.S. Smith

Right **The destination of Green Line RT 650 is Marshalswick Chandlers Road which, to avoid any doubt, is mentioned three times on this incorrect combination of blinds. Chandlers Road was reached in June 1960 and route 354 was still chugging around the circuit when photographed in St Peters Street nine years later, by which time the offside route number fitting had been replaced by a plain panel.** J.G.S. Smith

St Albans, although not a designated New Town, had expanded considerably since the end of the war and was continuing to do so, although the three areas which, during 1960, had reached a stage where a bus service was needed, were the only ones to be served newly during the decade. The first was How Wood estate, to the south of the town, west of Park Street. A route 375 from St Albans to the estate appeared in the timetable for 14th October 1959 but did not operate and the area had to wait until 13th April 1960 when some journeys on route 304 were diverted and a new route 355A was introduced. This ran from St Albans garage via Holywell Hill, Watling Street and Park Street Lane to terminate at Birchwood Way and was operated by one OMO RF. With the summer programme on 25th May 1960, routes 391/A were extended from Hill End to a new housing area called either London Road or Mile House Estate (depending on your source), via Drakes Drive, Cell Barnes Lane, Grasmere Road and Thirlmere Road. From 23rd June, yet another newly developed neighbourhood was able to enjoy its first bus service, with the completion of road improvements in Marshalswick. Route 354 was withdrawn from its established terminal at Chestnut Drive and extended via Marshalswick Lane and The Ridgeway to Chandlers Road. There were a couple of further developments to the How Wood route, starting with the withdrawal of the 355A and its replacement by a new route 361 on 16th June 1965. This reached How Wood by a different route through Chiswell Green and Tippendell Lane and ran in a loop via Penn Road, How Lane and Park Street Lane. A Monday to Friday extension to Radlett was introduced on 2nd December 1967.

Below **Route 361 served How Wood by an alternative route, through Chiswell Green, from June 1965, being extended to Radlett station in peak hours from December 1967. The blinds on RT 2369, on layover at Radlett station, are interesting as both are 'lazy' displays but the one on the side continues to act as an intermediate point blind by referring to Chiswell Green.** J.G.S. Smith

In an attempt to find a more acceptable use for them, eighteen RTLs were operated by Country Buses from Hatfield garage from July 1960, but they were unpopular with drivers and engineers and lasted for just short of a year, all having gone by 30th June 1961. RTL 1277, painted green and with fittings in place to receive trafficator 'ears', is outside the old garage on the south side of St Albans Road which had been vacated in 1959. Ironically the garage became a Used Car sale room, capitulating to the competition which has led to the poster campaign for the Green Line. Michael Rooum

Below The 'Cherry Tree' was near the hub of the complicated little network of routes known as the 340A, on which RT 3654 is working a journey to the Haldens branch, first reached by the 340B in June 1961. The 'via Welwyn Garden City Station' display was meaningless as this was the terminus of all the variants.
Colin Stannard

In Welwyn Garden City new development was now concentrated in the area to the north of the town centre on each side of the East Coast Main Line. A new shopping centre opened at Knightsfield, west of the railway, in the spring of 1960 and route 324 was extended the short distance from its original 1957 terminus at Harwood Hill on 25th May. To meet the increasing demand a few extra peak hour buses were scheduled, but residents had to wait just over a year for the big improvement which the area's increasing status justified. On 7th June 1961, routes 303 and 303A were removed from their long established route through Valley Road and the leafy glades of Great North Road and

diverted instead through the Knightsfield area, running via Digswell Road, Ingles, Digswell Road, Bessemer Road and Hertford Road to rejoin their route at Welwyn By-Pass. This gave not only an extra two buses an hour to the area but also direct links beyond the bounds of the Garden City to Barnet, Potters Bar, Hatfield, Stevenage and Hitchin. The main road was covered, somewhat sporadically outside peak hours on Mondays to Fridays but rather more solidly during peaks and on Saturdays, by a new route 315A. This ran only from Hatfield station to Knebworth on Mondays to Fridays, comprising mainly existing shortworkings taken over from the 303, but continued through to Hitchin on

Saturdays when it absorbed the afternoon extension of route 340B from Welwyn Garden City. The Great North Road was no longer fertile ground for bus traffic and this fragile looking arrangement soon withered under the pull of the New Town and the general decline in demand. The Saturday extension was cut back to Mardley Hill within sixteen months (24th October 1962) and all but the peak hour service was withdrawn in the major changes of 31st December 1966. In the meantime routes 303 and 303A were diverted more deeply into the new housing at Digswell on 22nd May 1963, using a newly completed section of Knightsfield between Shoplands and Bessemer Road.

By early 1961 new areas of housing were being occupied on the east side of the tracks, alongside Bessemer Road which was served by a handful of journeys on route 388 passing through on their way to Tewin and Hertford. The first frequent all-day service to the neighbourhood was supplied in the same small scheme of alterations as the 303/A on 7th June 1961. Route 340B was diverted intermediately via Handside Lane instead of Stanborough Road and then extended on Mondays to Saturdays from the station to a terminus at Blythway, known as 'Haldens' on publicity and blinds, via Bridge Road and Bessemer Road. By 22nd May 1963, when route 315A was extended to Haldens, the 340B had been diverted along Haldens itself to terminate at another part of Blythway. The Handside Lane diversion in June 1961 was associated with the withdrawal of routes 372/A as part of a wide ranging cost-cutting scheme in which routes 381, 388, 390 and 393 were restructured and new routes 380 and 381A were introduced. Out of all the upheaval, Beaconsfield Road estate in Epping got a bus service, by the diversion of route 381 and the new 381A; and links from the west to Harlow New Town were slightly strengthened by the extension from Hertford via St Margarets of route 390, one of the four routes used to replace the 372.

One section of road in Hatfield which lost its bus service in this period was Great North Road between St Albans Road and Longmead. This had nothing to do with subtle route developments but took place suddenly on 20th February 1966, when Wrestlers Bridge, which carried the road over the railway just north of St Albans Road, collapsed. It was demolished and has never been replaced. The 340B and Birch 203 were diverted via Hertford Road and Mount Pleasant Lane.

In the massive upheaval associated with the introduction of the five day week on 31st December 1966, the 340 group was restructured. The 340B was reduced to a peak and lunchtime service between New Barnet and Birchwood Estate and the Haldens service became part of a new 340A from South Hatfield (Northdown Road) which, in the developing tradition of the New Towns, was really three routes. Its 'main line' from South Hatfield took a completely different route from the 340B between Hatfield station and Welwyn Garden City, following the 717 via Mill Green and introducing buses to Chequers before making a wide sweep through Howlands, Cole Green Lane, Ludwick Way and Bridge Road to reach the station. A new 'branch' was introduced to serve recently completed housing at Panshanger, which was reached from the station via Bridge Road, Heronswood Road, The Ridgeway, Herns Lane and Daniels. The Haldens 'branch' was also extended in a loop to serve Sloansway, Lumbards and Rowans for the first time. The use of the same number for three such disparate operations was dictated by the way in which the buses were scheduled. Each bus would operate the following three hour cycle: South Hatfield to Welwyn Garden City station; lay over; the Haldens loop, back to the station, then to Panshanger; lay over; back to the station; the Haldens loop, back to the station, then to Panshanger; lay over; back to the station; lay over; station to South Hatfield. This was no doubt good for scheduling efficiency but, apart from being confused by the route numbering, passengers also had to suffer an irregular 20/40 minute headway on both loops. The service lost from Handside Lane was compensated by the diversion of one bus an hour on route 330, renumbered 330A.

Hatfield New Town shared many routes with the Garden City and got caught up in most of the changes associated with that town but it was smaller and the only area of its own to be opened up to buses during the 1960s was the eastern side of South Hatfield. This came about on 22nd May 1963 when new daily route 341B started work between Marshalswick Estate, St Albans and South Hatfield (Northdown Road). It was really the existing 341A diverted via Queensway and Woods Avenue instead of running direct via Bishops Rise, although the 341A continued to operate on Saturdays until November 1964. The area served was enlarged slightly on 31st December 1966 when the route was altered to take in Travellers Lane and Lark Rise but that was all.

At Harlow, the other big New Town in the north-east, the major transport development of 1960 was the arrival of the electric train in November when the services between

Route 341B was ten days old when this photograph of RT 1036 was taken in Hatfield on 1st June 1963. G. Mead

Liverpool Street, Hertford East and Bishops Stortford were modernised. Among the many improvements was a new station at Burnt Mill which was given the new name Harlow Town to confirm its enhanced status as the main railhead for the town. The original station in London Road, near the old centre of Harlow, was renamed Harlow Mill to avoid confusion. The first routes to serve the new station were the 805 and 806 which were re-routed between the bus station and Canons Gate via Fifth Avenue, Elizabeth Way and The Hornbeams, instead of the southern end of Hodings Road. At first they got no closer than Burnt Mill roundabout but from 7th June 1961 they, and the journeys on route

396A which already passed this way, were diverted into the station forecourt. At this time the town was still developing rapidly, south and south-westwards, and most of the remaining gaps were filled in during the ensuing ten years. Latton Bush was served by a two-stage extension of route 804 beyond its 1959 terminus at Bush Fair, to Tysea Road from 25th May 1960 and then in a loop via Commonside Road, Trotters Road, Southern Way and Tawnays Road from 7th June 1961. There was then a pause until 28th March 1962 when route 396A was extended from Hare Street to Passmores, a district so new that the road used to reach the terminus, now Partridge Road, had not yet been named.

RT 604 at Harlow bus station working on the new Latton Bush extension of route 804. A.B. Cross

The next round of changes co-incided with the commissioning of the new garage in Fourth Avenue on 22nd May 1963, following a formal opening ceremony the previous day conducted by the MP for Epping, Graeme Finlay. Following the example of Stevenage and Hatfield, the main shed, which could house forty-five buses, was a simple steel framed structure with curtain walls, and the canteen and administration block was a single storey building facing the main road. There was a spacious parking and standing area alongside, where a further nineteen buses could be kept in the open. The new premises replaced those at Epping which had been London Transport's first new garage in September 1934. At that time it was ideally placed for the Green Line services which were its predominant responsibility but by 1963 coach work had become less significant and the centre of gravity of the new network had moved a crucial seven miles north to Harlow. Harlow's starting stock comprised twenty-five RTs for routes 339, 396 and the new 397 group, sixteen RMCs for the 718, 720 and 720A, seven bus RFs for the 381, 381A, 390, 393 and 393A and two coach RFs which were late running spares for the 718.

The route alterations included another bout of restructuring for the country routes which no doubt had cost reduction through improved scheduling efficiency as one of its aims but which also had the beneficial effect of introducing direct links from the surrounding villages and towns to the shopping and other commercial facilities of the New Town. Route 380 (Hertford – Sawbridgeworth) disappeared, to be replaced as far as Eastwick by the extension of route 388 from Hertford to Harlow bus station, and onwards to Sawbridgeworth by the diversion of route 390 at Harlow bus station via Gilston. Route 381 was similarly diverted at Tylers Cross to Harlow. Substantial alterations were also made to the town services, causing the disappearance of the pioneering 396A, in number if not in spirit. The Passmores to Bishops Stortford leg was renumbered 397, associated works services becoming 397A/B, and the Epping service was swallowed up by the extension of route 339. The main drag of Tendring Road got its first bus service, but only during Monday to Friday peak hours on new route 804A (Latton Bush – Templefields – Harlow Mill) while Tumbler Road and Traceys Road in Brays Grove benefited from route 805 being

re-routed through the area, although a year later, half the service was restored to Tillwicks Road and Bush Fair.

The new housing around and to the south of the old village of Great Parndon was still served only by rural routes 381, 390, 393/A as late as the spring of 1964 but its lack of a town service was remedied in the summer programme on 6th May. Route 804 was extended from the bus station to the new district of Stewards, south of Southern Way, via Hare Street, Great Parndon and Kingsmoor Road but this appears to have been premature as it was cut back to Staple Tye (Ployters Road) on 3rd October 1965. After many deferments it was also intermediately diverted via Abercrombie Way and Pyenest Road to serve the Hollyfield neighbourhood from 24th January 1966. The May 1964 programme also included an interesting experimental route introduced at the request of the local council which gave the rest of Southern Way its first bus service. Route 389, which ran from Potter Street to Harlow Town Station via Southern Way, Abercrombie Way, Third Avenue and the town centre, was unusual in being operated by two GSs, a class very much in decline but the nearest thing to a minibus then available. It did not prosper and ran for the last time on 12th January 1965, after earning a two month reprieve while the Traffic Commissioner heard objections to its withdrawal.

Another, more enduring, experiment was tried on 15th May 1966, the idea this time being to go more deeply into some of the more established areas with a shopping hours service, in the hope that this would stimulate off-peak demand. Route 380 was one-man operated, using two RFs, and ran from Mark Hall North to the bus station via Momples Road and Maddox Road. This was an idea which was to gain ground particularly in the 1970s and more recently with the 'midibus revolution' in the 1980s but was novel, at least to London Transport, in the 1960s. It is of interest to note in passing that a similar experiment started in Ware on the same day on route 389, which completed a circuit incorporating Kingsway and Tower Road for the first time.

A service to Stewards was restored, this time by the extension of route 397 from Passmores, first as far as Longbanks in Parnhall Road from 31st December 1966, then in a loop via Paringdon Road back to Southern Way on 27th April 1968. The latter date also

Above left **When Epping garage closed at the end of traffic on 21st May 1963, the resulting route restructuring included the extension of route 339 to Harlow in place of the 396A. This side-by-side parking of RTs 1089 and 643 at Epping seems symbolic in the circumstances.** J.G.S. Smith

Left **The country routes around Harlow were restructured in May 1963, bringing the 381 into the New Town. Two years later, from 16th June 1965, it was extended to Eastwick, where it turned in a loop with journeys in one direction broken at Harlow. RF 308, originally a green bus numbered RF 527, then a Green Line coach under the new number from 1956 and finally a bus again, is seen at The Lion Inn Eastwick on 12th April 1969.** Michael Rooum saw the diversion of route 804 away from Ployters Road to Staple Tye shopping centre, the Ployters Road rump being taken over by new route 804B, with an extension onwards to Kingsmoor (The Maples) in Paringdon Road.

Not much was added to the network at Hemel Hempstead during the 1960s as most of it was already in place but there were some developments in the south-west and in the north-eastern corner. Although no new roads were served when route 302 was extended from Longlands to Bennetts End on 7th June 1961, an all-day bus service was introduced for the first time to the section of Bennetts End Road between St Albans Hill and Howe Road, previously served only by works service 334, while Windmill Road and White Hart Road had seen only 719 Green Lines until then. A more noticeable addition to the map on the same day was the first service along Queensway, a new road which swallowed up Queen Street and the western end of Highfield Lane before carving a great sweep around and across Highfield Lane to meet Swallowdale Lane at a new roundabout. Works route 314B was diverted to run this way, instead of Adeyfield Road. A little further north on 17th January 1962, the 322 was extended along a sequence of new roads from Highfield (Bathurst Road), via the extension of Fletcher Way, Solway and Jupiter Road to a new terminus at Deimos Drive, with works journeys continuing to Maylands Avenue via Swallowdale Lane. Highfield got its second bus service on 20th March 1966 when route 301C was renumbered 312 and extended from St Pauls Road via another new road situated to the west of the old Redbourn Road, then called Catsdell but whose identity over this section later changed to Allandale. The terminus was at Bellgate in the northern section of Redbourn Road which later became Cambrian Way. The final link was forged on 9th December 1967, when route 344 was extended to Grove Hill (Washington Avenue) via Queensway (its first all day service) and High Street Green.

Other new estates in the northern country area which got bus services in this period included: Oakfield Estate, Hitchin (383 extended December 1960); Molewood Estate, Hertford (333 diverted May 1964); Hilltop Estate, Chesham (336 extended, May 1964) and Hicks Farm Estate, High Wycombe (new 442, October 1965).

Top **The juxtaposition of lower case lettering on intermediate point blinds with the use of stencil plates for garage codes was a rare event as the former did not begin to appear until November 1961 and the latter were replaced by painted codes in 1961 on Central Buses and in the second half of 1962 on Country Buses. The combination appears on RT 4730, working on the new extension of route 302 to Bennetts Gate, which started on 7th June 1961.**
M.E. Papes collection

Centre **RF 566 at the Watford Junction terminus of route 322, which was extended in Highfield, Hemel Hempstead to Deimos Drive on 17th January 1962.** J.G.S. Smith

Right **RF 578 is seen on Route 344 which, when introduced between the bus station and Grove Hill on 9th December 1967, completed the Hemel Hempstead network for the 1960s.** J.G.S. Smith

The only New Town in the south was Crawley, which was also the only one where local services were shared with another operator. The old town of Crawley had been at the southern tip of the London Passenger Transport area and was small enough for the boundary to cause no problems for the route network, but the New Town straddled the boundary. When the British Transport Commission reviewed the problems caused by the 1933 boundary in the late 1940s, Crawley was identified as one of a number of towns where the boundary should be redrawn to concentrate local services in the hands of one operator. In the case of Crawley the chosen operator was London Transport and the boundary revisions would probably have coincided with the implementation of one of the Area Schemes envisaged in the 1947 Transport Act, but these were abandoned by the new Conservative administration in 1951. At Grays, the only area where the results of the boundary review had been applied, it had been possible to do so under the new government's policy because the other operator in the town, Eastern National, was already wholly owned by the BTC and so London Transport was able to operate under delegated powers. At Crawley, the situation was different because Southdown was a BET company which could operate freely, subject only to the constraints of the licensing system. To avoid a split network, with some areas denied direct access to the main centres of employment in the north of the town and at Gatwick, the Executive had entered into an agreement with Southdown Motor Services to share the services on an equitable mileage basis.

It was one of the sectors allocated to Southdown under this agreement, Gossops Green lying south of the Horsham – Crawley railway line, that was being developed at the beginning of the decade and to which the first new services had been introduced in 1959. This had started modestly on 31st August 1959, with a peak hours only service, numbered 76, which ran from Gossops Drive (Medway Road) to the industrial area at Gatwick Road (Rutherford Way), operating subject to workers' demands. The main route from Gossops Drive to the town centre, numbered 79, had started on 10th December 1959, and avoided contact with London Transport local routes by using the By-Pass and Ifield Avenue. This was extended on 27th May 1962 to give a service to Buckswood Drive, then via Horsham Road and Ifield Road to become a circular service. The reason for Southdown's not using the more direct route via Ifield Road became apparent in 1961, when access to Ifield Road from the By-Pass was severed. From 1st March, routes 426, 426A and 852 had to be diverted via Warren Drive and Ifield Avenue, route 426A regaining its route through West Green Drive via Ewhurst Road. From the same date the new area north-east of Three Bridges station was served by a further diversion of route 426A via St Mary's Drive, Chaucer Road and Grattons Drive, instead of Worth Park Avenue. Although it was an infrequent country route, the loss of the 426 from the eastern end of Ifield Road was not popular and it was reinstated from 23rd May 1962, using Ewhurst Road to regain Ifield Avenue.

There was a comprehensive network of works services in Crawley giving access to the industrial area from all points of the town and they were still very busy in the early years of the decade. Its steamed up windows indicate that RT 4171 had already done good business before picking up a new load at Three Bridges station. A.B. Cross

Expansion was now taking place beyond London Transport's statutory boundary in the south-eastern wedge of land between the Horsham and Brighton railway lines, a district known as Furnace Green. Under the stricter rules imposed on the new Board by the 1962 Act, the area would not have been open to them but for the existence of the agreement with Southdown, which the Minister accepted as good enough to allow him to give his consent. The Executive was therefore able to introduce new Monday to Saturday route 476B from the town centre (with works journeys from Manor Royal) to the junction of Furnace Drive and Weald Drive, via Southgate Avenue and Hawth Avenue, from 17th July 1963. The network here was completed on 3rd October 1965, when route 476 was extended from Southgate via Ashdown Drive and Weald Drive to complete a loop back to town via the 476B, which was reduced to a works service only. The only other new roads to be opened up under London Transport's stewardship were the north ends of Weald Drive and Hawth Avenue over which works journeys to Rutherford Way on routes 405B and 476 were diverted from 23rd November 1968.

Other new estates in the southern country area which got bus services in this period included: St Mary's Estate, Swanley (route 423 diverted, March 1961); Batts Hill estate (447 diverted, May 1963); Joydens Wood (new 401A, peak hours October 1963, all day Mondays to Saturdays January 1964); Imberhorne estate East Grinstead (new 435, December 1964); Botleys Park, Holloway Hill (new 474, November 1965); Downs estate and the north-eastern side of Temple Hill, Dartford (new 499, May 1966); and Manor Farm, Byfleet (427 journeys, June 1968).

Below left **RT 3211 makes its way through older parts of Dartford on route 499 which gave Downs estate in eastern Dartford and Henderson Drive their first bus service when it was introduced in May 1966.** N. Rayfield

Below right **The route which bore the number 499 before May 1966 was the short Bow Arrow Lane service, on which RT 4512 is seen at Dartford Market Place in April 1965. The use of the same number for two entirely different routes on consecutive days in the same town was one of those confusing things which Country Buses seemed to like doing.** Capital Transport

Route 441 was typical of trunk Country Bus services in suffering heavy off-peak cuts between 1960 and 1969, its basic service being halved, while maintaining much the same peak service. In the absence of a comparable Green Line route, a Sunday service was also retained. RT 988 is at Staines Central station at the beginning of this period, 1st May 1960. A.J. Wild

Centre **The first bus service to Hicks Farm Estate, High Wycombe, was operated by a GS when it started on 3rd October 1965, but this was soon replaced by the larger Regal IV. RF 612 is seen loading in High Wycombe town.** E. Shirras

A rough and ready guide to the amount by which the New Towns bucked the trend of general decline can be provided by a comparison of the peak vehicle requirement at the five garages serving them with that for the rest of the fleet. The five New Town garages enjoyed an increase of thirty-two peak buses (twenty per cent) between January 1960 and December 1969, compared with a reduction of 109 (thirteen per cent) in the other garages. Even on Sundays, when the New Towns were just as vulnerable as anywhere to the flight of passengers to the private car, the cut in the number of buses scheduled was held at thirty-six per cent over the ten years, compared with an awesome sixty-two per cent at those garages lacking the cushion of an increasing population.

At the beginning of the decade the degree of retrenchment in bus services was comparatively modest. Between January 1960 and the summer of 1962, four routes and four sections of routes were withdrawn on Sundays, one on Saturdays and part of one on Monday to Friday evenings. Mileage remained fairly stable on Mondays to Fridays, while the reduction on Saturdays was less than four per cent and on Sundays less than five per cent. Then, in just one programme for the winter of 1962, on 24th October, there was a three per cent cut in Saturday mileage compared with the previous winter, and a ten per cent cut on Sundays. This included the withdrawal of one route on Mondays to Fridays only, parts of two others on Saturdays and five whole and four parts of routes on Sundays. This set the trend, with further cuts in every succeeding programme, at first concentrated on the weekend but increasingly spreading to Mondays to Fridays as time went by.

Below **Route 327 was one of the first double-deck routes to be converted to RF one-man operation, on 4th November 1964, and one of the large number which lost their Sunday service on 31st December 1966. RF 86, lacking its 'Pay as you enter' sign, is at Broxbourne station on 12th April 1969.** J.G.S. Smith

GS 19 in Shire Lane, Farnborough, on the short-lived Biggin Hill to Orpington route 479 on 25th May 1963 which was later taken up by the Orpington Rural Transport Association. Ken Glazier

Another of several brave attempts to stimulate bus usage was this local circular route for shoppers in Belhus estate. GS 34 did have one passenger on this journey from Derwent Parade on 2nd October 1962 but business was too poor for the route to survive. Ken Glazier

Extra pressure was put on the need for economy as the wages of bus staff rose and a series of improvements was made to their conditions of service. One of the biggest improvements was the move to a five-day week, which was incorporated into duty rosters from 31st December 1966. The new schedules introduced at the same time contained substantial cuts in service and the virtual elimination of single-deck two-man operation, which was reduced to just four scheduled buses on Mondays to Fridays. Four small routes were withdrawn altogether, another six on Saturdays and fifteen on Sundays, although some of these were covered in part by adjustments to other services. There were also three sections of route from which Sunday services were withdrawn and there were many frequency reductions and examples of off-peak and evening operations being abandoned. Six routes, or groups of routes, were converted to one-man operation with spare RFs, including double-deck routes 323 (group), 374, 431 (group) and 460, and the high frequency town services on the 391/A and the 447 group. Twenty-six fewer double-deckers were scheduled on Mondays to Fridays, balanced by an increase of six single-deckers (twelve extra RFs, six fewer GSs), there was a total cut of thirty-eight on Saturdays (twenty-four double-deck, eight RF and six GS), and twenty-five on Sundays (twenty double-deck, three RF and two GS). By the end of 1969, compared with 1960, seventy-seven buses had been stripped from the Monday to Friday schedules (eight per cent), 233 from Saturdays (twenty-six per cent) and 273 from Sundays (fifty-eight per cent). By this time the Sunday network had been reduced to main roads and town services and there were three garages which ran no Sunday bus services at all (Dunton Green, East Grinstead and Tring), while even Hatfield had only one bus in service.

Some attempts were made to drum up new business, particularly from the potential of shopping trips. The first example of such an experiment was at Belhus estate, where a local circular route, numbered 372, served Avontar Road, Daiglen Drive, Afton Drive and Broxburn Drive, alternately clockwise and anti-clockwise, every thirty-minutes each way. One GS and one driver, supplied by Grays garage, were able to give a service from 10am until 12.30pm and from 2.15 until 5pm on Mondays to Fridays only. It started operating on 20th June 1962 but failed to ignite public interest and ran for the last time on 23rd October. An entirely different experiment was tried in Kent, in response to local requests for a service linking Biggin Hill with the shops at Orpington. Route 479 ran on Saturdays only, starting on 16th February 1963, and used one GS from Dunton Green. It was hardly a promising time of year to start such a service and it was no surprise when it suffered the same fate as the 372, being withdrawn after 15th June. This stirred the Orpington Rural Transport Association into action and they started a service of their own quite soon afterwards. It has survived the years and at the time of writing is, ironically, part of the London Transport network. The other similar experiments in Harlow and Ware have already been described.

Above **The Buntingford branch line has closed and passengers must now transfer to substitute bus route 351 at Ware station, where RF 653 is seen picking up a peak load.** J.G.S. Smith

Above right **To avoid leaving the village of Stanwell Moor isolated when the West Drayton to Staines railway line closed, a two days a week service on new route 444 was provided. RT 3508 inaugurated the route and was photographed in Church Street Staines on the first day, Tuesday 30th March 1965. Note the continued use of 'West Station' as the Staines destination.** Ken Glazier

Right **Central Buses provided route 225 as the main replacement service for the Staines West branch but it was to spend most of its time, like this one, transporting fresh air around Middlesex. RT 4649 had been a green vehicle but was one of those repainted red in the programme to eliminate roofbox buses from the Country Area which started in 1963.** Colin Stannard

Another small area of new business owed its origin to the modernisation plan for British Railways, which has immortalised the name of its then chairman Dr Beeching, under which several branch lines in the Country Area closed, spawning a number of replacement bus services which BR were required by statute to secure. The first to go was the line from St Margarets to Buntingford, which had intermediate stations at Mardock, Widford, Hadham, Standon, Braughing and West Mill served by nine Monday to Friday and eleven Saturday trains. The last trains ran on 15th November 1964 and the Monday to Friday service was replaced by a new limited stop bus service numbered 351, running from Much Hadham to Buntingford via Widford, Wareside (for Mardock), Ware, Standon and Puckeridge. Two one-man RFs from Hertford garage supplied a roughly comparable peak and evening service but the daytime journeys were not covered. The 351 did not run on Saturdays, the only additional service being an earlier journey to Buntingford on route 331.

The former Great Western branch from West Drayton to Staines with intermediate stations at Colnbrook Estate, Colnbrook, Poyle Estate and Poyle and for many years the home of its characterful pre-war diesel railcars, closed after business on Saturday 27th March 1965. Most of the stations were in remote, largely uninhabited areas and served mainly industry, the principal areas of habitation being at Colnbrook and Poyle Estate close to existing bus services at Colnbrook, and at Stanwell Moor. The service was roughly at hourly intervals on Mondays to Saturdays, with extra peak hour trips (including one through train to Paddington) but the replacement bus services were considerably more restricted because it was claimed that much of the through traffic could be carried equally well on existing route 224. Both Country Buses and Central Buses participated in the replacing services. The main service was covered only during Monday to Friday peak hours by Central Bus route 225, using two RTs from Uxbridge, but the isolated community at Stanwell Moor, whose nearest

public transport had been at Poyle Halt, was given an entirely new shopping hour service on Tuesdays and Saturdays only. Route 444, operated by Staines garage also with an RT, linked the village with Staines on a circular route from Church Street via London Road, Stanwell New Road, Horton Road and Hithermoor Road. Somebody seems to have overlooked the fact that Wednesday, not Tuesday, was market day in Staines but this was rectified in the winter programme on 3rd October.

The line from Welwyn Garden City to Luton, which had stations at Ayot, Wheathampstead, Harpenden and Luton Hoo, closed after 24th April 1965. The substitute bus route 366 was one-man operated and ran express between the two towns stopping only at Wheathampstead, Cherry Trees, Batford Corner (for Harpenden) and Newmill End (for Luton Hoo). It was a service of rather greater substance than its predecessors, needing no fewer than four RFs from Luton garage, and was the only one to have a long-term future.

Left **Route 438A was inaugurated to cover the closure of the Three Bridges to Groombridge branch, also taking some 424 special journeys under its wing. RT 3053 is on the stand at Three Bridges station.** Colin Stannard

Below left **London Transport gave up its share of route 316 in May 1964, leaving Rover Services to enjoy a monopoly. GS 51 is seen a year earlier on the road from Lye Green to Bovingdon.** Ken Glazier

Below right **Rover Services Bedford OB LBH 757 in the bus station at Hemel Hempstead on its version of route 316 to Chesham via Latimer.** Ken Glazier

The only line in the south to close in this period was the Three Bridges to Groombridge service, with stations within the London Transport area at Rowfant, Grange Road and East Grinstead which enjoyed an hourly service every day of the week. Routes 434 and 473 already linked all these stations and were considered adequate to carry all but the displaced peak hour traffic, with only two extra journeys needed on Sunday mornings. To meet the peak demand, new route 438A was introduced between East Grinstead and Crawley but via Copthorne and Crawley Down rather than following the route of the railway. This was the route already followed by the existing special journeys on route 424 which were therefore renumbered 438A too. Two additional RTs, one each from Crawley and East Grinstead were needed. Beyond East Grinstead, Maidstone & District took responsibility but there was an ironic sequel eighteen months later at the first station, Forest Row. Until then London Transport route 409 had used the forecourt as a stand but was not allowed to carry passengers beyond 'The Swan'; the rules were now changed to allow passengers to travel to the closed station from 14th June 1968.

Another minor expedient adopted by London Transport to relieve itself of unremunerative services was to pull out of joint operations, leaving other operators to carry on alone. The first to go was the 316 between Hemel Hempstead and Chesham via Bovingdon and Lye Green, which was shared with Rover Bus Services. The Sunday service was an early casualty, on 12th October 1960, and the rest went on 6th May 1964, although by then the number 316 was being used for the local Sunday service between Amersham and Ley Hill. Curiously, in the same programme, United Counties withdrew its half share of route 359 (Amersham – Aylesbury), leaving the remaining two-hourly service solely in the hands of London Transport.

The next handover had a special poignancy as route 448 had been the subject of a particularly bruising dispute with Tillingbourne Valley Services Ltd in the early days of the LPTB, which had culminated in a rare working agreement between the operators. From 12th August 1964, the Board withdrew from route 448 (Guildford – Ewhurst) and handed over the local Guildford route 448A to Tillingbourne Valley, leaving them in sole command of both. Finally, from 4th November 1964, routes 350/A were replaced in Bishops Stortford between Station Road and Havers Lane Estate by Eastern National route 309. There was one more countervailing exchange when the business of Bream Coaches was taken over on 30th December 1967. They had operated two routes, Hemel Hempstead bus station to Apsley Mills via Long Chaulden and Warners End (numbered 314 by London Transport) and a works service from Long Chaulden to Maylands Avenue (314C). This unexpected reversal of trend was no doubt acceptable because the operations were in an expanding New Town and could be integrated with the rest of the network to make the whole operation more economical.

There was one long overdue move in the opposite direction when London Transport entered into a joint running agreement with the Thames Valley Traction Company in Slough, one of the towns which had suffered most from being split by the LPTB boundary. A new cross-town service, numbered 407, started on 22nd January 1966 connecting Langley in the east with Cippenham (Mercian Way) in the west by a combination of mileage culled from route 417 and Thames Valley 61. There was also a variant via the Trading Estate numbered 407A, which followed route 61A. In exchange, Thames Valley extended its routes 60, 60A and 69, each coming from different parts of Maidenhead, from Slough to Langley Village. Season Tickets issued by Thames Valley were valid for travel on routes 407 and 407A but London Transport Rover tickets were not valid west of Salt Hill and could not be used on the company buses.

Towards the end of the 1960s the new ideas which were to lead to some exciting experiments during the following decade, began to germinate and it was one of these which the Country Bus department produced at the very end of its mandate just in time to bequeath to the new London Country Bus Services Ltd, although it was not meant to be such a close run thing. Called the 'Blue Arrow' it had been planned for introduction early in 1969 but had run into resistance from the staff. At one stage the factory owners in Stevenage threatened to introduce their own buses and London Transport then considered using a private operator to run the service under contract, but all came right in the end. The Blue Arrow was one of many ideas floated at that time which had their origins in north America, where the desire to resuscitate public transport was beginning to take hold. It was aimed at giving the same convenience as the private car by supplying a service on which a seat was guaranteed to season ticket holders, who could be picked up at a pre-arranged point close to their homes and returned there at the end of the day. It ran between Chells and the industrial area at

London Transport surrendered its rights on route 448 to Tillingbourne Valley from 12th August 1964, after which scenes such as this showing GS 26 at Peaslake, became a thing of history, although GSs continued to be around for some time because some were bought second-hand by the company. A.J. Wild

Stevenage and was timed to meet shift starting and finishing times, including journeys for those who went home for lunch. Three XFs were painted in a blue and silver livery and were the first buses to carry the fleet name 'LONDON COUNTRY' but the service started on 29th December 1969 and was run for its first three days by London Transport.

The routes of the long established local operator, Bream Services, were acquired by London Transport on 30th December 1967. No vehicles changed hands and this Bedford's work was taken over by standard RFs and RTs. Ken Glazier

One of the oddest services ever run by London Transport was the cycle transporter route through Dartford Tunnel, which was operated on behalf of the Dartford Tunnel Joint Committee who owned five of these Thames Traders with specially designed Strachan bodywork. There were racks for twenty-three cycles in the open sided lower section and space in the rear compartment for tricycles and tandems. Seats for thirty-three on top, allowed for a rather improbable number of tandems. The designers obviously assumed that cyclists were by nature athletic and supplied a very basic means of access to the upper deck from both sides. The service was operated from Dartford Garage but was poorly used and was eventually replaced by Land Rovers operating on demand. J. Tilley

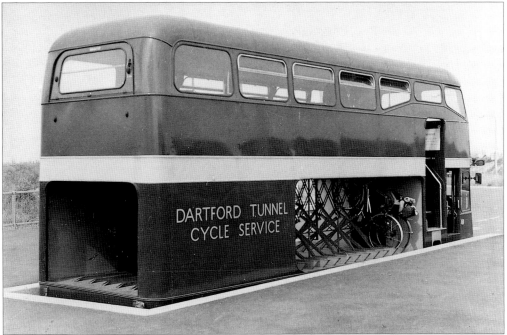

XF 6 in the special blue and silver livery invented for the Blue Arrow service at Stevenage, evinces the swansong nature of the event by unveiling the new 'LONDON COUNTRY' fleet name while necessarily retaining legal lettering for the London Transport Board. LT Museum

CHAPTER EIGHT

TRAFFIC MANAGEMENT

During the 1950s there had been an increase of over 170 per cent in the number of private cars licensed in the London Transport Area and the proportion of households owning a car rose from about fifteen per cent to sixty-five per cent. The use of all these extra cars began to have such a serious effect on traffic conditions in central London that the Government had felt obliged to introduce legislation in the Road Traffic and Road Improvements Act which became law in 1960. This allowed the rapid installation of Parking Meters throughout central London, following a successful experiment in Mayfair which had been operated under emergency traffic orders since July 1958. A force of Traffic Wardens was to be created to take over from the Metropolitan Police, responsibility for enforcing parking regulations and provision was made for automatic fines by ticket. Income from the meters was to be devoted to the provision of off-street parking. The expectation was that road capacity could be increased by between fifteen and twenty-five per cent if the streets

were cleared of parked vehicles other than at parking meters. The 'road improvements' part of the Act related to a £120 million programme of improvements designed to increase the capacity of specific roads and intersections by about fifty per cent over volumes recorded in 1956. At the same time, the Minister of Transport, Ernest Marples, set up the London Traffic Management Unit with a brief to speed up traffic by the use of traffic engineering techniques. It can be seen that the thrust of all these policies was to speed up traffic and make room for more, a process which was bound in the end to be self-defeating. At this stage, however, they had the support of London Transport who saw them as a way of speeding up bus services.

Parking meters were installed in another large part of the West End and in the West Central postal district during 1960 and the immediate effect was favourable, London Transport's claiming that bus journey times in the area concerned had been reduced by four per cent. By the end of 1962, the whole

of the area bounded broadly by Whitehall, Pall Mall, St James's Street, Piccadilly, Park Lane, Edgware Road, Marylebone Road, Southampton Row, Theobalds Road, Old Street, Bishopsgate, Cheapside, St Pauls, Fleet Street, Arundel Street and the river was covered by the parking meter zone and similar schemes had been installed in Croydon, Kingston and Woolwich. Apart from some rounding off of the area of central London covered by meters, no more schemes were introduced for another six years. The change of Government in 1964 and the concurrent establishment of the new Greater London Council with London-wide responsibility for highway management, brought a change of emphasis.

Above Ill-matched 'Except Buses' plates have been attached to the 'No Left Turn' and 'No Entry' signs at the corner of Piccadilly and Berkeley Street, allowing a Bow RTL on route 32 to run northwards along London's first 'contra-flow' bus lane which came into being on 14th October 1962. London Transport Museum

In 1965, the Minister of Transport set up a working party of representatives of the Greater London Council, the Metropolitan Police and London Transport, under the chairmanship of the Council's Director of Highways and Transportation, to consider and report on ways in which traffic management could help improve bus services. Its most important finding was that a radical improvement in road conditions for buses was possible only if the volume of other traffic using bus routes at busy times was restricted. Meanwhile, the Ministry of Transport had started a study of possible ways of restraining urban traffic, with special attention being given to London, and the working party looked to this group to find the long term solutions. Specific proposals made by the working party were for the introduction of sixteen new urban clearways, a further twenty-six controlled parking zones and twenty-seven more major one-way traffic schemes but it emphasised that these could, at best, only prevent conditions getting worse. The recommendations were endorsed by the Greater London Council in November 1965 and, in February 1966, the Council announced its intention to create an Inner London Parking Zone covering forty square miles. Progress was slow and little had been done about parking controls by the end of the decade, although some of the other traffic management measures were realised.

Although a number of important new major road schemes were completed during the 1960s, the most widespread and outwardly obvious demonstration of the measures taken to assist traffic was the abundance of 'Traffic Management Schemes' which were, almost without exception, one-way traffic systems. They varied in size and complexity from simple 'round the block' arrangements to massive plans covering miles of road, but in every case their aim was to increase both the speed of traffic and the capacity of the road system. In some cases the roads into which traffic was diverted were barely suitable for large and heavy vehicles and many of them were residential streets whose use would certainly have been denied in more sensitive times twenty or so years later. As nearly always happens when an agency is created to carry out a task which, once finished, becomes somebody else's responsibility, it will look around to find new ideas to occupy its time. The LTMU was not immune to this temptation and some of its schemes looked like barrel scrapings.

Many of the larger schemes did no service to the cause of public transport as they took buses away from the centres of activity to which their passengers wished to be taken, vitiating the benefits of improved reliability which, in any case, proved to be ephemeral. These inconveniences were heightened by the fact that Bus Maps were not altered until anything up to two years after the event. Because each scheme was nominally experimental the wise men of the Publicity Department decided that they would not go to the expense of changing maps until permanent Traffic Orders were made. As the information was also omitted from amendments leaflets and even from London Transport's own official timetable booklet,

A Metro-Cammell bodied RTL on route 30 serves one of the temporary stops in South Carriage Road, Hyde Park while the eastern end of Knightsbridge is closed for the construction of the new road tunnel. The temporary flyover which carried westbound traffic in the park over the eastbound flow from Knightsbridge can be seen rising on the left and one of the temporary street lights is behind the shelter. On the right, Decimus Burton's screen and Robert Adams's Apsley House have survived until the present day, but the buildings on the left were swept away in the wake of the widening and re-alignment of Park Lane, being replaced by the Hilton and Intercontinental Hotels.

strangers trying to find their way about could be led badly astray, hardly an encouragement to use buses. The improvement in traffic flows and the increased road capacity simply encouraged more people to drive into these areas, with the result that surrounding roads became more congested. By 1969, London Transport had begun to campaign for bus priorities and traffic restraint, but the lesson is one which politicians have found difficulty in learning over the years.

Major road schemes nearing completion at the beginning of 1960 included the Hook underpass on Kingston By-Pass which opened on 12th February and the new northern access to Blackwall Tunnel (26th June) while work continued throughout the year on the huge Elephant & Castle roundabout project, which was not to be completed until early in 1967, and the Hanger Lane underpass and gyratory. On the same day that the Hook underpass opened, an urban clearway was installed in Putney High Street which provided a good demonstration of the mixed blessings such schemes could bring to buses. In the interests of traffic movement, the use of the stops near Chelverton Road was banned during peak hours, while those serving the shops and residences at the northern end of the High Street were moved permanently onto Putney Bridge, remote from their objectives and in less congenial, not to say bleak, waiting conditions. A different approach was tried at Shoreditch Church from 24th February, when a tidal flow scheme was introduced, using movable traffic islands in Old Street and Hackney Road.

Meanwhile one of the smaller and probably more effective LTMU schemes came into operation at Brixton on 25th April, when

one-way operation was instituted around the triangle occupied by St Matthew's Church. A more ambitious scheme started on Sunday 23rd October 1960 when Park Lane became southbound only and the East Carriage Road in Hyde Park was devoted to northbound traffic but neither road was altered in any significant way and northbound buses and coaches therefore entered the park through the gates at Hyde Park Corner, leaving through those at Marble Arch. Whereas in the Brixton scheme, buses and coaches were still able to stop close to their objectives, the Park Lane scheme put northbound vehicles into the park, some way from the major objectives to the east. To this day these stops are used by far fewer than use the comparable stops in the present-day southbound carriageway of Park Lane.

The 'Hyde Park Boulevard' project which created the modern arrangements in Park Lane was still some way in the future but an associated scheme was the Hyde Park Corner tunnel linking Knightsbridge and Piccadilly, the biggest road project in central London for many years, work on which started in February 1961. While the work was going on, the eastern end of Knightsbridge was closed and traffic diverted, from Sunday 5th February, via a section of the South Carriage Road. New slip roads were built from Knightsbridge into the South Carriage Road immediately east of the French Embassy, from the southern end of Park Lane into East Carriage Road and from Hyde Park Corner roundabout into the East Carriage Road east of Apsley House. A temporary viaduct for westbound light traffic was built across the slip road from Knightsbridge to give through traffic a free run.

A little earlier, on 11th December 1960, there was a small scheme at Russell Square, which was unexceptionable but another small one in Culling Road, Rotherhithe, which started in February 1961, was controversial. Culling Road linked Lower Road with Jamaica Road near the entrance to Rotherhithe Tunnel and its use by northbound traffic was designed to reduce congestion caused by traffic waiting to enter the tunnel. Unfortunately, it was a very narrow street with a sharp acute bend and was barely adequate for large vehicles, which made its use very unpopular with local residents. Another system which squeezed traffic through extremely narrow streets was introduced at Aldgate on 19th March. This was more modest than the system introduced later and concentrated on the north-south flows through the area. Middlesex Street and Mansell Street were reserved for northbound traffic, except that on Sundays when Petticoat Lane market was in operation Dukes Place, Bevis Marks and Camomile Street, at some points barely wide enough to take a bus, were used instead. Southbound traffic used Houndsditch and Minories. Right turns out of Commercial Road were also banned. The immediate effect was to create severe congestion in Aldgate High Street as the heavy flows of northbound traffic waited to turn right across the eastbound flow, a situation so serious that both the Police and London Transport wanted the scheme abandoned immediately. They were persuaded to agree to its continuing while better traffic signs were tried and the situation was later eased by allowing right turns into Commercial Street at Gardiners Corner.

The LTMU was not the only organisation which saw one-way systems as an answer to traffic problems. They were very much in vogue all over the country and an example in London Transport's outer area was initiated at Rickmansworth on 16th April. This made the High Street one-way eastbound between Rectory Road and Station Road and westbound only between the By-Pass and Station Road, an arrangement which allowed buses to continue to serve the heart of the town in both directions, although the 335 and 336 towards Watford were diverted via the By-Pass to avoid having to loop through the town.

The next major scheme, at Tottenham Court Road which came into operation on 1st May 1961, was not only one of the most damaging to bus traffic but, as mentioned in chapter two, also caused a change to be made to the trolleybus abandonment programme. The section of Charing Cross Road north of Cambridge Circus and the whole of Tottenham Court Road became northbound only, and southbound traffic was banished to Gower Street, Bloomsbury Street and Shaftesbury Avenue or, in the case of route 73, St Giles's High Street which was also used by westbound routes from New Oxford Street to Oxford Street. This took southbound buses away from a busy shopping thoroughfare and put them into a backwater instead, the most damaging sacrifice being the removal of the very busy stops at the Dominion Theatre from which there was an immediate loss of passengers.

The Operating Manager (Central Road Services) was moved to reflect on what might have been the effect on the two-way system had special measures been taken instead,

including a total ban on parking. The unsatisfactory nature of this scheme continued to rankle over the years and there were even suggestions at one time that the position could be at least ameliorated if buses had offside passenger doors, so that they could stop on the western side of Gower Street, nearer the shops. Agreement was later secured for a contra-flow bus lane to be provided in Tottenham Court Road and Charing Cross Road but it was to be thirty years before this was even partly realised. There was one small benefit of the scheme, however, in that northbound buses on routes 22, 38 and 38A now ran via Charing Cross Road and New Oxford Street, rather than slipping through the back via Shaftesbury Avenue. To enable the scheme to be implemented quickly, London Transport was persuaded, at no small financial cost, to bring forward the conversion of trolleybus route 629 from November to 26th April, and electric traction was removed from the area.

Another damaging central area scheme, introduced for a week's experiment on 15th July 1961 and re-introduced permanently on 26th November, was the Piccadilly/St James's Street gyratory, which removed the westbound route 9 from Piccadilly Circus and imposed a long detour via Pall Mall on routes 14, 19, 22, 38 and 38A. Two weeks later, the system at the 'Marquis of Granby' junction in New Cross which had been tried in part eleven years earlier, was introduced as a permanent arrangement. Less damaging than many, it brought Lewisham-bound buses to New Cross station and created common stops in Lewisham Way for services bound towards central London.

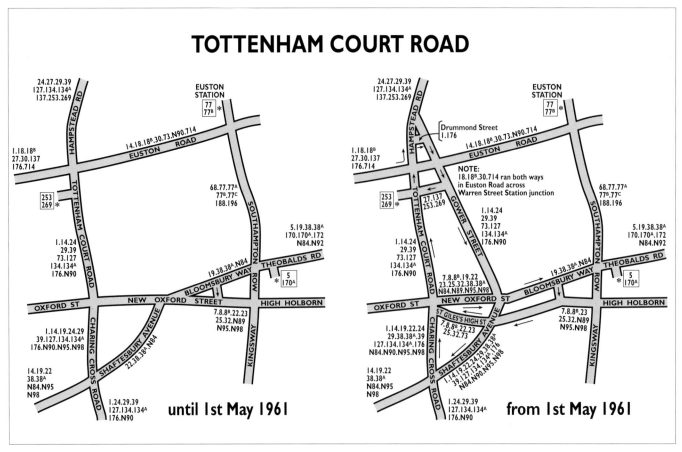

TOTTENHAM COURT ROAD

until 1st May 1961   from 1st May 1961

Nothing in this scene was to survive a sequence of road schemes and building developments over the succeeding thirty years, not even the recently built blocks in the background. The scene is the junction of Hampstead Road and a surprisingly narrow Euston Road, looking north with RT 1126 on route 1 turning from Euston Road into Tottenham Court Road. The approaching RM 648 on route 269, with destination blind already changed for its return journey, signifies that it is one of five days between the removal of the trolleybuses and the introduction of the Tottenham Court Road one-way system on 1st May 1961 when southbound buses were banished to Gower Street. Capital Transport collection.

RT 356 swings around Cambridge Circus on its way from Charing Cross Road into Shaftesbury Avenue while work takes place on the preparations for the new traffic scheme. Capital Transport collection

In the south-western suburbs, the narrow streets of Richmond were turned into a traffic roundabout from 28th August 1961, effectively removing westbound buses and coaches on routes 33, 37, 714, 716 and 716A from the centre of the town into Paradise Road and Red Lion Street. The next scheme, whose purpose seemed somewhat obscure in any case, proved to be an outright failure almost from the moment it started. On 5th October southbound buses (but not trolleybuses an route 609) were diverted away from Upper Street, Islington to run along and stop in the northern section of High Street, presumably to clear Upper Street for moving traffic. The catastrophic congestion, which developed immediately, caused a change in the stopping arrangements within two hours. After a few more days of struggle, the whole thing was called off on 9th October, the declared intention being to 'try again when road works have been carried out'. It has never again been tried.

The biggest scheme of any so far was instituted on 11th October 1961 stretching in Hackney from Mare Street to Hackney Wick and affecting east-west traffic. Westbound traffic was split between Victoria Park Road and Wick Road, while eastbound ran via Well Street and Cassland Road. In an attempt to continue serving as much of the old routes as possible, routes 6 and 6A were split between the two westbound routes at first but this created more problems than it solved and was later modified. During November 1961, no fewer than eight schemes, including two new sections of road, came into operation. The new roads were the Hammersmith flyover (16th) and Staines By-Pass (18th). Traffic management schemes included a ban on right turns from Upper Woburn Place into Euston Road (1st), a further stage in the Elephant & Castle project which introduced a massive gyratory system encompassing Westminster Bridge Road, St Georges Road, London Road and Lambeth Road (13th); Clapham Common North Side/The Avenue/West Side (18th); Baker St/Gloucester Place (26th); and Woolwich Road/Tunnel Avenue/Denman Street (27th).

There was then a lull until May 1962, when another major scheme outside the LTMU's area was instituted in Watford. A section of High Street between Clarendon Road and Market Street was closed to through traffic and a one-way circuit introduced through Market Street, Exchange Road, Upton Road, High Street, Clarendon Road, Beechen Grove, then either Derby Road and Water Lane or Queens Road. Once again the effect was to take some buses out of the main shopping area altogether in one direction. There were two LTMU schemes on 27th May, the more important of which created a one-way system encompassing Grays Inn Road, York Way, Wharfedale Road, Caledonian Road, Kings Cross Road and either Swinton Street or Acton Street. Westbound buses from Pentonville Road ran via Penton Rise to join the system at Swinton Street. The lesser scheme was a ban on right turns from City Road into Goswell Road, which pushed southbound buses down to Wakley Street. This was later (6th October 1963) consolidated into a triangular one-way system for all traffic.

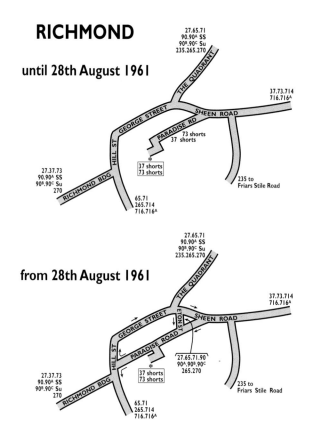

RICHMOND

until 28th August 1961

from 28th August 1961

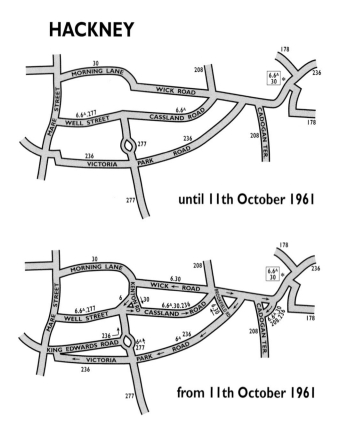

HACKNEY

until 11th October 1961

from 11th October 1961

Two small schemes at Esher and East Acton were followed by a further section of the Elephant & Castle system, covering Lambeth Road and Garden Row, all in June 1962, before the next major project in Earl's Court and Kensington was put into effect in two stages, the northern end on 10th and the rest on 30th September. The complete scheme made the sequence of roads from Gunter Grove to Holland Road, as far as Addison Crescent, one-way northbound, while the southbound sections were Addison Road and Earl's Court Road south of Pembroke Road. Northbound buses were removed from the very busy and important centre around Earl's Court Station and exiled to distant and difficult to reach stops a block away on the other side of a busy road. The system was further extended four years later, on 23rd October 1966, to include the whole of Holland Road. Southbound buses then ran via Holland Park Avenue and Addison Road but, because of a right turn ban, also ran via Royal Crescent between 7am and 8pm on Mondays to Saturdays.

A small but more significant alteration took place on 14th October 1962 when Old and New Bond Streets became one-way southbound and routes 25 and 32 were diverted northbound via Berkeley Street and Davies Street. Berkeley Street was also one-way southbound at its southern end and its use was a special concession to enable buses to observe the Green Park station stop. The effect was to introduce London's first contra-flow bus lane (but not known as such at the time), indeed London's first bus lane of any sort. Major road schemes completed during the second half of 1962 included Stevenage By-Pass (opened 27th July), South Mimms By-Pass (25th July) and the Hyde Park Corner tunnel (17th October).

One proposal which never came to fruition, although it was given serious and detailed consideration at about this time, was to make Blackwall and Rotherhithe tunnels one-way in opposing directions. Blackwall was still a single bore tunnel and was inadequate for contemporary demands, whereas Rotherhithe was considerably underutilised. Such a plan would have had a disastrous effect on the three bus routes which used the tunnels (82, 108, 108A) as they would have been subjected either to a substantial and crippling diversion or to being cut back on each side of the river. Fortunately, the limitations imposed in particular by the narrowness of Rotherhithe and also by the severe bends in Blackwall eventually killed the scheme.

In May 1962 the first stage of the Watford one-way system was introduced, bringing buses and other traffic to the hitherto quiet purlieus of Beechen Grove in time for the arrival of the Routemaster coaches, like RMC 1506, six months later.
Capital Transport

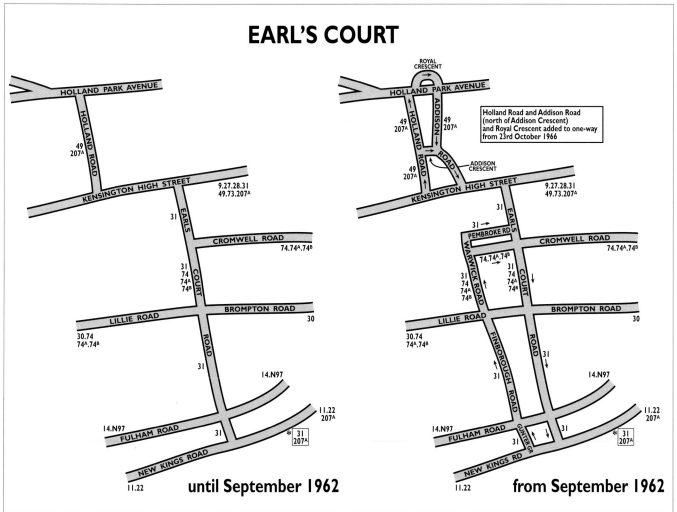

EARL'S COURT

until September 1962   **from September 1962**

Holland Road and Addison Road (north of Addison Crescent) and Royal Crescent added to one-way from 23rd October 1966

The pace at which new Traffic Management Schemes were introduced began to ease in 1963 but the size of those which did materialise was not necessarily diminished. Kingston was subjected to a massive one-way network from 14th July 1963 encompassing Clarence Street (south- and westbound), Wood Street (north- and eastbound), Cromwell Road and Queen Elizabeth Road (east- and southbound) and London Road (westbound). Wood Street became another of those increasingly familiar outposts, remote from and on the far side of fast moving traffic from the shops. To avoid excessive gyrating by routes 85, 213, 213A and 286 coming in from the east, these were transferred from the bus station into Wood Street lay-by and routes 406, 406A and 418 from there into the bus station. For inward passengers on the four Central Bus routes, this was actually an improvement as they now had stops within the shopping area, rather than in Cromwell Road. Two further schemes in September applied one-way working to Royal College Street and Camden Street (1st) and on the Queens Road, Kender Street, New Cross Road circuit, with a short cut for eastbound buses through Besson Street (7th). The last scheme of 1963, on 8th December, was an urban clearway around Shepherds Bush Green and, although this did not alter any bus routes, it did require the removal of standing buses. These were deported to back street stands in Richmond

Gardens (route 49), Roseford Gardens (81B, 117) and Rockley Road (207, 207A), a good illustration of the lack of sensitivity to local residents displayed in so many of these schemes. Three years later, the clearway was strengthened by rescinding the long-standing arrangement whereby traffic was allowed to turn right from Goldhawk Road into Shepherds Bush Road. Route 11 and shorts on the 220 and 268 now had to make a complete circuit of the green to complete this turn.

When the road around Camberwell Green became a gyratory on 16th February 1964 the associated measures included a banned right turn from Denmark Hill into Coldharbour Lane and routes 35, 42 and 45 were therefore further diverted through Orpheus Street and Daneville Road. A bigger scheme was imposed on Barking town centre from Good Friday, 27th March, embracing London Road, Broadway and East Street. This included a ban on the turn from Ripple Road into East Street which forced routes 23C, 87, 106 and 179 to trek all the way around the triangle. Harlesden, which came next on 14th June, was another example of buses being taken from the heart of a shopping area and consigned to a back street with stops on the far side of a busy road. High Street became west- and northbound only, southbound buses used Manor Park Road, and routes 187, 220, 226, 268 and 293 approaching from

Acton Lane or Station Road used Tavistock Road. This was followed on 5th July by a scheme at South Kensington, encircling Old Brompton Road, Glendower Place and Harrington Road which, although small, had the unfortunate effect of pushing the nearest stop to the station for southbound 49s and 207As, to Onslow Square, two hundred yards away and across a busy road. This was eventually put right by diverting both routes via Thurloe Place and Exhibition Road to a stop in Thurloe Street. Then, on 19th July, the Camden Town system was enlarged to make Camden High Street one-way north-westbound. South-eastbound buses from Chalk Farm ran via Hawley Street, Hawley Road and Camden Street to Camden Road, where they were joined by all other southbound buses through Bayham Street and Crowndale Road. Parkway also became one-way, north-eastbound, and southbound routes 3, 39, 53, 253B, 715, 715A and 718 all left the main system at Bayham Street to run through Pratt Street and Delancey Street. To avoid a crippling diversion on departure from their respective stands at Buck Street and Greenland Road, the 74 was transferred to Greenland Road and the 31 to a new position in Bayham Street. Like many of the changes enforced in this period, the latter was to prove unpopular with local residents who have kept up a vociferous, but so far unsuccessful, campaign ever since to have the buses removed.

Routes 406/A and 418 vacated Wood Street lay-by to make room for routes 85, 213, 213A and 286 when the Kingston gyratory scheme was introduced on 14th July 1963. RT 3667 stands where now there is a huge road underpass. W.R. Legg

Following small schemes at Blackbird Cross (6th December) and Old Town, Clapham Common (31st December), the next major project was centred on the 'Nags Head' junction at Holloway and came into operation on 31st January 1965. This was one of the bigger schemes, confining Parkhurst Road and Seven Sisters Road as far as Isledon Road to northbound traffic and consigning southbound buses to the backwaters of Isledon Road, Tollington Road and Camden Road. This was the route followed in both directions by Green Line coaches and it was a slight irony that these pariahs were therefore brought onto the more important thoroughfare on their northbound journeys. The portion of Caledonian Road between Camden Road and Hillmarton Road also became oneway, buses in the reverse direction using Hillmarton Road and Camden Road and losing their ideally sited stops in Holloway Road. Right turns at the 'Nags Head' and Jones's Corner were also banned and route 279 was therefore given a further northbound diversion via Camden Road, Warlters Road and Parkhurst Road, while southbound routes 17 and 143 had to run via Seven Sisters Road, Hertslet Road and Tollington Road, all three also losing their stops alongside the shops in Holloway Road. Another incidental change was to route 14, which continued along Hornsey Road on southbound journeys to Tollington Road.

Another big system was installed on 5th February, this time encompassing the triangle of Great Eastern Street, Old Street and Shoreditch High Street. Northbound buses making for Kingsland and Hackney were allowed a short cut through Curtain Road, while a similar concession was granted to routes 8, 8A, 47 and 78 which were able to use Holywell Lane to reach Bethnal Green Road. Some of

the same routes were involved again from 5th April, when Stoke Newington High Street became northbound only, buses in the opposite direction using a circuit around Northwold Road, Rectory Road, Manse Road and Evering Road. Routes 73, 106 and 106A, which had used Northwold Road in both directions, took a different route to regain the High Street, through Brooke Road.

The stand for route 74 at Camden Town was moved from Buck Street to Greenland Road, where RTW 312 stood amidst a baffling lack of traffic on 7th November 1965.
Ken Glazier

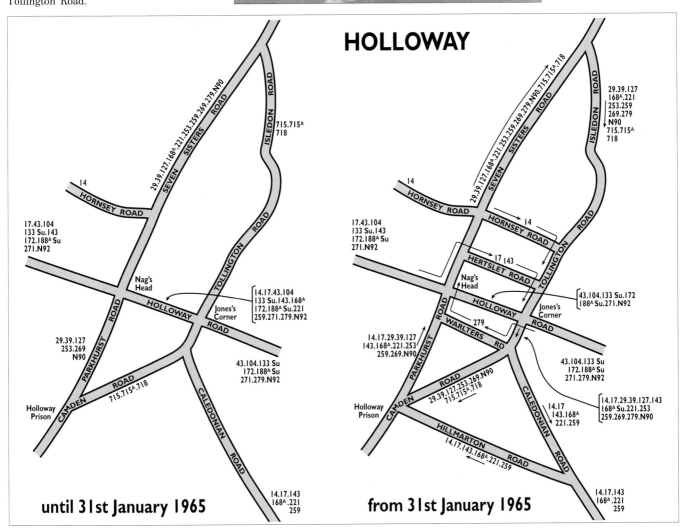

HOLLOWAY

until 31st January 1965

from 31st January 1965

VICTORIA

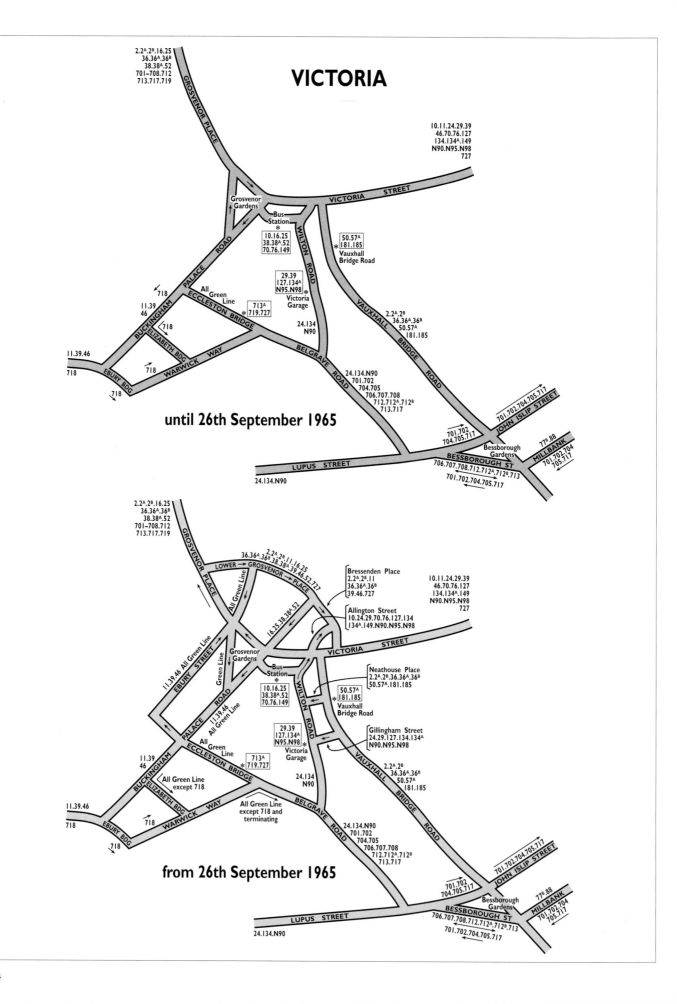

until 26th September 1965

from 26th September 1965

Surely the biggest scheme of any was the one introduced in the Victoria area on 26th September 1965. The core of the system was made possible by the construction of a new road, named Bressenden Place, across the former Stag Brewery site from Buckingham Palace Road to Victoria Street which opened officially on the day the new traffic scheme started. This, together with the nearly new Neathouse Place which linked Vauxhall Bridge Road with Wilton Road, enabled a clockwise circuit to be designed using Neathouse Place, Wilton Road, Victoria Street, Grosvenor Gardens (north side), Grosvenor Place, Lower Grosvenor Place, Bressenden Place, Victoria Street and Vauxhall Bridge Road. Buckingham Palace Road also became one-way southbound from Lower Grosvenor Place to Eccleston Street, with a northbound route through Eccleston Street and Ebury Street. The south-western arm of Grosvenor Gardens had its flow reversed to run from north to south and the northern end of Ebury Street also became southbound only, the two combining to give a shorter route from the north to Buckingham Palace Road, which was used by Green Line coaches. The other major component of the scheme was the diversion of east-west routes based on alignments using Elizabeth Bridge eastbound and Eccleston Bridge westbound.

Thirty years later, after a few mollifying changes, these arrangements are so well settled that it could be easy to overlook the scale of disruption which they wreaked on bus and coach services. This was so serious as to provoke London Transport into taking out expensive advertisements in the evening papers, including full 'Where To Board Your Bus' maps. Southbound buses on the 2 and 36 groups, for example, were removed from moderately convenient southbound stops in Grosvenor Gardens (north side) to a remote and draughty site in Bressenden Place, the improvement gained by having a stop for northbound buses immediately outside Victoria station in Wilton Road, instead of at the top of Vauxhall Bridge Road, being small compensation. Eastbound routes 11, 39 and 46 were removed from their Grosvenor Gardens stop, a mere step from the station, to distant positions in Ebury Street and beyond Bressenden Place in Victoria Street, although they were unchanged in the other direction. Northbound routes towards Victoria Street were luckier as they could still serve stops at the station and then leave by a relatively short route through Allington Street and Bressenden Place. By their nature, terminating services were protected from the worst effects of the changes. Buses from the direction of Hyde Park Corner ran via Lower Grosvenor Place and Buckingham Palace Road to the bus station; those from Vauxhall Bridge Road were diverted via Gillingham Street and Wilton Road, gaining a setting down point more convenient for the station; and those from Victoria Street which used the standing area alongside Victoria garage, plus through 24s and 134s, ran via Vauxhall Bridge Road and Gillingham Street.

The inclusion of Eccleston Bridge in the east-west one-way system brought to an end its status as an unofficial coach station for the Green Line. Coaches making for southern destinations were evicted into Buckingham Palace Road, where a new series of stops was set up between Eccleston and Elizabeth Bridges. The complete revised route for southbound coaches was via Lower Grosvenor Place, Ebury Street, Grosvenor Gardens (West Side), Buckingham Palace Road, Elizabeth Bridge, St Georges Drive and Warwick Way. The northbound route from Eccleston Bridge was via Eccleston Street, Kings Road and Hobart Place, with the 727 continuing via Lower Grosvenor Place and Bressenden Place to reach Victoria Street.

A rare example of an LTMU scheme which brought buses closer to their objective came into being at Peckham on 17th October 1965. This made a clockwise gyratory of High Street (between Rye Lane and Clayton Road), Clayton Road, Hanover Park and Rye Lane (from Hanover Park to High Street). Although this lengthened the journeys for some buses, none were removed any significant distance from their main objectives and westbound buses from the New Cross direction actually got better placed stops in Hanover Park.

There were two minor projects favourable to buses during 1966. On 8th June an attempt was made to encourage general traffic to use Belgrave Road rather than Vauxhall Bridge Road by diverting northbound traffic via Bessborough Street and Belgrave Road for a period of six days, in the hope that drivers having learned the benefits of the alternative route would not return to their old habits. This did not work. A permanent arrangement was therefore instituted on 16th October, making the northbound carriageway of Bessborough Gardens 'Buses Only', forcing other traffic into Bessborough Street. Between these two stages, on 25th July, the terminal working for the new Red Arrow route 500 at Marble Arch was modified to include Tyburn Way, then an unused section of road which now also became 'Buses Only'.

The first 'major' traffic management scheme of 1966 was introduced at Archway on 14th August, although it was a pretty modest affair with a clockwise operation in Junction Road, Holloway Road and St Johns Grove and the denial of direct access from Junction Road to St Johns Way and from St Johns Way to Highgate Hill. Route 41 towards Tottenham ran instead via Holloway Road, Elthorne Road and Ashbrook Road and the 210 towards Golders Green via Holloway Road, St Johns Grove and Junction Road. The stand in Brookside Road also had to be abandoned and buses on routes 41 and 244 (plus 134 shorts) ran instead to Highgate garage, via Holloway Road and Pemberton Gardens, returning via Junction Road.

The completion of two further road building schemes brought changes to earlier one-way systems. On 8th October the southern extension of Exchange Road, Watford, was opened as far as King Street and northbound buses were diverted away from this section of High Street. On 13th November, the completed Euston underpass was opened to westbound traffic, having been in use eastbound since 29th April. Westbound routes 18, 27 and 30 had been diverted via Gower Street, Grafton Way and Tottenham Court Road from the earlier date to allow the preparations for the final stage to go forward. This enabled the westbound carriageway of Euston Road between Gower Street and Tottenham Court Road to be altered to take southbound traffic from Hampstead Road to Gower Street, in place of the direct movement in Gower Street which was severed at Euston Road by the underpass. Green Line route 714 was unique in using the underpass, thereby avoiding the detours, as it had no stops in the vicinity.

The one-way system including Tooley Street was enlarged significantly from 18th February 1967, with serious implications for route 70's ability to serve London Bridge station. An additional section of Tooley Street between Bermondsey Street and Tower Bridge Road was designated one-way eastbound and traffic in the opposite direction continued beyond Druid Street via Crucifix Lane and Bermondsey Street. However the use of Bermondsey Street applied only to route 47, as two other related changes caused route 70 to be altered more drastically. A scheme to remove southbound bus stops from Borough High Street had resulted in the reversal of the direction of travel through London Bridge station forecourt from 28th January and the diversion of southbound buses through the forecourt from 5th February. A ban on right turns from Borough High Street into Duke Street Hill was then instituted at the same time as the extension of the one-way system. Route 70 then had no alternative but to miss London Bridge station, and run via St Thomas Street, which it did in both directions, with eastbound buses regaining Tooley Street via Joiner Street.

The advent of the Greater London Council with its wider ranging traffic powers began to bear fruit for London Transport in 1968 with the introduction of two 'with-flow' bus lanes, the first to be designed specifically to give buses priority over other traffic as distinct from being allowed movements denied to others. The first was an experimental lane for southbound buses on Vauxhall Bridge which applied during the evening peak and resulted in significant improvements in the running of buses. The second was in Park Lane, approaching the Hyde Park Corner roundabout, which was less successful mainly because of conflicting movements of other traffic across the lane. These were the first two of four which had been proposed by the GLC in January 1967, the others being: Brixton Road northbound approaching Kennington Gate; and London Road, southbound, approaching Elephant & Castle. London Transport had responded to the new situation created by the formation of the GLC to set up its own bus priorities unit within the Central Bus operating department to deal directly with the officers in the Highways and Transportation department at County Hall. They had produced complementary proposals, starting with two important 'contra-flow' lanes, designed to undo the damage caused by the one-way systems in Baker Street and Piccadilly and had followed these up with extensive proposals for further bus priorities. One project which did attract approval but was being prepared at the end of 1969 was the contra-flow lane in Tottenham High Road. Otherwise, at the end of the 1960s, buses were still afflicted by appalling and worsening traffic conditions.

135

CHAPTER NINE

INDUSTRIAL RELATIONS

If the London Transport Executive had hoped that the drubbing it had experienced during the 1958 busmen's strike was some sort of catharsis which would lead to a period of equilibrium, it was to be sorely disappointed during the ensuing ten years. If anybody thought that the bus operating staff, having apparently burnt their fingers in calling the strike, would therefore become a docile, easily coerced, workforce, they were in for a nasty shock. Things may have been different if the Executive, later the Board, had been able to concentrate on the improvements in productivity which had been sought as part of the settlement of the strike but other events kept getting in the way. The negotiations had to be conducted in a period of seemingly intractable staff shortages and of catastrophic decline in passenger traffic, to which London Transport had little option but to respond by making matching reductions in service levels. These created a background of instability, fertile soil for the growth of resentment and feelings of insecurity among the staff and a perfect recipe for the volatility which was to upset the progress of good labour relations for over ten years.

Following the settlement of the strike, a Joint Working Party of London Transport and the Transport and General Workers' Union was formed to review ways of achieving economies in operation. The principal method envisaged by the Executive was the extension of one-man operation, including the lighter trafficked suburban services operated by Central Road Services. Negotiations during 1959 in respect of Central Road Services came to nothing, with no immediate prospect of any progress, and London Transport decided to try instead the idea of an efficiency bonus scheme for drivers and conductors. Proposals were submitted for approval to the British Transport Commission in December and its assent was received early in January 1960, clearing the way for a meeting with the Trade Union on 8th January. Agreement was reached at the meeting for the scheme to be submitted to the Joint Working Party for detailed consideration. Early in July the Working Party agreed on a scheme which the officers of the Union submitted to a Delegate Conference on 12th July, with a recommendation that it should be accepted. Not for the first nor last time, the long term benefits

foreseen by the officers of the Union were not recognised by the 'rank and file' garage representatives at the Conference, who rejected the scheme out of hand. A revised offer put to the Union on 18th September was similarly rejected.

Meanwhile, in the absence of progress on the bonus scheme some action had to be taken urgently to stanch the loss of staff to better paid jobs. A straightforward application for an increase in basic pay had been submitted by the Trade Union before these negotiations had started but had been rejected at the time by the Executive, which had pinned its faith in the bonus talks. In what was probably intended as an interim step, the claim was settled and increases of from 8 to 10 shillings

Above **Central to the embattled history of industrial relations in the 1960s was the crippling 1966 overtime ban when route 98B was permanently withdrawn. Valliant Coaches tried running it from 1st May but failed after four weeks. This Duple Britannia bodied AEC Reliance, seen at North Harrow on 7th May, had minimal destination equipment but had been provided with adequate board displays in the windscreen.** G. Mead

a week for garage inside staff, drivers and conductors were paid from 16th March. After the final rejection of the bonus plan, the Union submitted a further claim for a substantial increase in pay and improvements in working conditions. The earlier settlement had not resulted in any improvement in the staff position; on the contrary, the shortage had increased to a peak of fifteen per cent by September. The Executive therefore offered an increase of 18 shillings a week, plus improvements in conditions amounting to a further 7 shillings a week on earnings.

Such intermingling and leap-frogging of ordinary pay negotiations and the tenacious attempts by London Transport to achieve improvements in productivity were to be the hallmark of industrial relations in the 1960s. At each stage there were parallel settlements with garage maintenance staff and road operating supervisors, while the claims of workshop staff at Chiswick and Aldenham Works and of management and administrative grades, usually followed the lead of British Railways settlements. This account will concentrate on road services drivers and conductors as they were the most numerous and the most influential on the course of events.

At the end of 1960 the shortage had been reduced to eleven per cent of drivers but this was still substantially above the 8½ per cent of a year earlier and, although it was still improving, the poor standard of service on the road persisted. The Executive consequently decided to reduce services to a level more in line with the number of staff available in new schedules planned for 18th January 1961, but this move was deeply unpopular with the staff and there was potential for more strife. A deal was therefore struck under which the Trade Union undertook to ensure that staff would work additional overtime and on their rest days to make certain that duties were covered. At the ten worst affected bus garages and three trolleybus depôts, where this would not have been enough, local cuts were introduced on 18th January with the intention that they should be scheduled formally on 1st March. Thirty-five motor buses were removed from the peak requirement but the cuts in trolleybus services were confined to the off-peak and Saturdays. Although the worst excesses of 1960 were avoided during 1961, the situation was bad enough by the third quarter for further cuts to be imposed, purely for the reason of staff shortage, at twenty-eight garages, averaging 1.2 per cent over the fleet. These cuts were gradually restored as staff numbers improved.

Negotiations on the introduction of one-man operation to the Central Area were resumed in March 1961. The principle had been accepted by the staff, subject to a satisfactory agreement on rates of pay and the method of payment but these last three words were to provide the main obstacle to progress in subsequent talks. Discussions were still continuing in July when Brian Harbour, the Executive Member responsible for road services, widened the debate to embrace the experimental use of seventy-two seat double-deckers (RML), an experiment with standee buses on a central London route, the use of RMs to replace RTs, and the operation of

RF 555, on route 304 at Kimpton, was typical of most Country Bus single-deckers in being one-man operated, a well established practice in the Country Area. Ken Glazier

double-deck coaches (RMC). These talks were taking place at the same time as the Executive was seeking financial authority from the BTC for the purchase of 1340 RMs to replace 1488 RT type between 1963 and 1967, the financial justification for which was based on the assumption that for every ten RMs put into service, eleven RT type vehicles would be withdrawn.

The talks were still continuing over a year later when, in September 1962, Harbour added a proposal to adjust schedules to take account of a recent change in the PSV Regulations allowing the maximum speed of buses and coaches to be increased from 30 to 40mph. By this time the question of double-deck coaches had been settled and the first examples were already in service. The complete package of the remaining proposals was submitted to a Delegate Conference on 8th

October and was soundly rejected by 103 votes to three. It was then decided to divide the proposals into two separate phases: the introduction of OMO and the RT replacement programme in the first; and the experimental operation of 'one or two' standee buses in central London and the 40mph schedules in the second. A conditional improvement in the terms of the offer, including a reduction in working hours from forty-four to forty-two a week, was agreed by the Union's negotiating committee for submission to a Delegate Conference on 23rd October, where the proposals were again rejected. The Conference required the share of savings allotted to staff to be increased to forty-five per cent and that this should be allocated equally to all drivers, conductors and maintenance staff. These conditions were unacceptable to London Transport and the offer was withdrawn.

The idea of adopting seventy-two seaters as the future standard double-decker was first floated in July 1961 and grudging agreement was eventually forthcoming for their experimental operation on route 104. RML 896 is seen in Nether Street, North Finchley, in January 1962. M.C. Beamish

Meanwhile, the Executive's plans for the replacement of the RT family had been submitted to the Trades Unions at a Joint Sub-Committee convened to discuss technical developments, in January 1962. The Operating Manager (Central Road Services), Fred Lloyd, told them that approximately 350 vehicles would be replaced each year and that the new vehicles would be used to increase productivity in areas where recruitment of staff was difficult. Area traffic schemes would be prepared, based on the assumption that every eleven RTs would be replaced by ten RMs. The plans were discussed in detail at the joint management/Trade Union Bus Allocation Advisory Committee on 9th July 1962. This was the group which had so successfully overseen the post-war vehicle replacement programme, finishing its work in 1954. It had been reconvened in 1958 but so far had held only two meetings, both connected with the redeployment of redundant RFs. It now returned to the mainstream of the negotiating machinery.

The first scheme was to be in October 1962 and would cover routes 114, 140 and 158 at Edgware and Harrow Weald garages. The remaining one hundred or so RMs which would by then be available, would be allocated to route 73, replacing RT/RTL one-for-one, to test the hypothesis that the fourteen per cent increase in capacity might increase passenger traffic by a similar proportion. If this was successful, the service would be maintained. The Trade Union was cool. Staff were not prepared to accept the introduction of any Routemasters until the matter of productivity payments had been settled satisfactorily, not even the 'one-for-one' arrangement on route 73.

The introduction into service of RMs remained stalled throughout the summer but, in anticipation of the proposals being accepted, arrangements were made for the first specialised 'area scheme' to be scheduled as part of the Winter Programme on 10th October 1962. The mathematical relationship was honoured exactly, the seventy-seven RTs being covered by seventy Routemasters but pending the ratification of the agreement, which was expected to enable the Routemasters to go into service on 24th October, the attenuated schedules were augmented by the operation of unscheduled extras. The public's share of the benefits from the savings was new Monday to Saturday route 230A, which required two RTs and ran from Harrow Weald to Northwick Park, giving College Avenue, College Hill Road and the section of Kenton Lane as far as Christchurch Avenue their first bus service. With the rejection of the proposals, the unscheduled extras had to continue to operate until fresh schedules, restoring the seven withdrawn buses, could be implemented on 3rd January 1963. Ironically, Harrow Weald finished up running two extra buses as the 230A, having been introduced, could hardly be taken off again.

Right **New route 230A was scheduled for Harrow Weald RTs but an RLH sometimes appeared early in its life. RLH 71 is seen in College Hill Road on the first Saturday of operation.** Peter G. Mitchell

The introduction of new RMs was held up while the argument raged about the Executive's desire to use only ten to replace every eleven RTs. Yet, in the trolleybus conversion almost exactly that ratio had been applied for the number of RMs replacing larger trolleybuses, without any major industrial relations upset. RM 783, safely in service, is at Trafalgar Square on route N83, an extension of night route 543/643. E. Shirras

Harrow Weald was the unwitting eye of the industrial relations storm over future vehicle replacement policy. RT 153 in Imperial Drive, Rayners Lane on 6th October 1962, a week before the starting date originally set for Routemaster operation, was still carrying a Park Royal RT3 type body, complete with route number plate in the nearside pillar. Ken Glazier

Although the Monday to Friday services were restored in full, part of the cut on Saturdays and the entire reduction on Sundays was retained because the winter schedules for the rest of Central Buses had included mileage reductions of 3.4 and 2.5 per cent compared with Saturdays and Sundays in the previous winter. These cuts led to one-day protest strikes at Bromley, Catford and Dalston on the first Saturday and Southall on the second, while Edgware, with the added threat of the new RM schedules hanging over it, stayed out for three days from 13th to 15th October. In its winter programme on 24th October, the Country Bus and Coach department also made weekend cuts, of 1.26 and 2.6 per cent, but added the withdrawal of twenty buses on Mondays to Fridays (one per cent of mileage). It was claimed that the loss of traffic on Saturdays was caused by people switching to Fridays for their main shopping of the week, Friday traffic now reaching Saturday levels in some areas. The staff at Grays did not like the cuts, staged a one-day strike on 24th October and then banned overtime and rest day working. By this time there were over one hundred and thirty brand new RMs standing idle. London Transport was fast running out of storage space and realised that it could not go on waiting for an agreement indefinitely. It decided instead to use the new buses to replace RTs one-for-one, claiming that by concentrating them onto the busiest services the extra capacity could be used to encourage more people to travel. The sixty-four seat Routemaster now ceased to figure in the productivity discussions.

There then followed a series of meetings to consider a revised claim from the Trade Union for a substantial increase in pay and a reduction in the working week to forty hours. The latter was rejected but an increase of ten shillings was offered and a fresh attempt made to pursue the productivity proposals. This was rejected by the negotiating committee who referred the matter to the General Executive Council of the Union, who decided to submit the proposals to a Delegate Conference. The Conference continued the process of downward referral by calling for each garage to have its own separate vote. The majority decision was to accept the pay increase, which was duly paid from 3rd April, but to make no commitment on efficiency measures. The Board gave notice of its intention to pursue the matter. The Board then took another tack, offering a 'London Scarcity Allowance' of six shillings (Central) or five shillings (Country), which would be payable immediately. While agreeing to consider this, the Union submitted a new claim for an increase in pay and an extra week's holiday, linked to incremental increases of five shillings for every five years of completed service, the idea being to discourage wastage by making it worthwhile for people to stay longer. At a meeting on 11th October, the Board rejected the extra holidays and incremental payments but offered to consider general improvements in conditions if these were linked to efficiency improvements. The Negotiating Committee agreed to consider this but six days later submitted a revised claim for an increase of thirty shillings a week, plus either a five day week or the shortening of daily

hours, with particular regard to the urgent need to reduce weekend hours, and for an increase in annual holidays. A meeting was fixed for 1st November but before this could take place a general ban on overtime and rest day working was imposed. At the meeting Brian Harbour, in his swan song before retiring, agreed to consider the claim urgently in return for the Union's reconsidering the ban on overtime and rest day working.

The Government had become progressively more worried about the way things were developing and were anxious to demonstrate to an increasingly irritated public that urgent action was being taken to remedy the poor quality of service. Until now, the Minister had been content to stay out of the limelight, although he was clearly a party to all the important decisions made by the Board. He now took the initiative and set up a Committee of Inquiry under the chairmanship of Professor Henry Phelps Brown, who was Professor of the Economics of Labour at the London School of Economics, member of the National Economic Development Council and a former member of the Council on Prices, Productivity and Incomes. He was joined by four others of 'the great and the good' and their terms of reference were:

'To review the pay and conditions of the drivers and conductors of the . . . Board's road services in the light of the Board's manpower requirements, (its) statutory responsibilities, the working and operating conditions in London traffic and the likely repercussions of any changes on other employments, paying due regard to the possibilities of increasing the efficiency of (its) road services and to the considerations affecting national economic growth . . . '

At the request of both London Transport and the Transport and General Workers' Union, the committee's hearings were in public and took place on 5th and 6th December. In an interim report on 16th December, the committee recommended an immediate increase in basic pay ranging from eight shillings and sixpence for Country Bus & Coach conductors to fifteen shillings for a Central Bus driver. This was agreed and implemented on 18th December and the

overtime ban was lifted. The committee's final report was issued in June 1964. Its main conclusion was that busmen's earnings should be related to those of skilled and semi-skilled workers in London, rather than to the general average, and on this comparison London Transport drivers and conductors were not very high on the scale of actual pay. These comparisons also had to be qualified by the fact that busmen worked a complicated pattern of shifts and were required to work at weekends. The Committee's view was that these increasing disadvantages needed to be offset by higher pay and therefore recommended substantial improvements in pay and conditions, linked to the introduction of efficiency measures designed to improve the service. The report also introduced the concept of an annual pay review, the first of which would be due at the end of March 1965.

An agreement based on these recommendations was negotiated with the Transport & General Workers' Union and accepted by a Delegate Conference on 24th June. This covered an increase in pay of thirty-eight shillings for a standard forty-two hour week, paid in stages to coincide with the phased introduction of an efficiency payments scheme. This comprised a bonus on fares collected, a seating capacity bonus (which opened the way for larger capacity buses) and an increased safety allowance. A shorter working week of forty hours was also to be introduced as soon as practicable in 1965 and staff with at least five years service were to get an additional three days holiday. All these improvements taken together were equivalent to an increase of twenty-three per cent. There were also to be improvements in sick pay and pensions. In return, the staff accepted the introduction of one-man operation on suitable suburban routes in the Central Area, the extension of OMO in the Country Area, experiments with standee single-deckers in the Central Area and an experiment with front-entrance double-deckers. This set the stage for the new and revised orders for buses which is covered in more detail in chapter ten and for the more radical approach which was to emerge as the Bus Reshaping Plan.

Central Bus one-man operation was unshackled by Phelps Brown, leading to an immediate flush of conversions. The requirements of the duty roster sometimes led to conversions on Sundays only, as was the case with route 203, which changed over with the 237 on 5th July 1965. RF 417, at Staines West station, was one of the sixty-eight additional vehicles modified in the first half of 1965 to fulfil the expanded programme. Ken Glazier

The improvements helped to stem wastage at the end of the year, resulting in only a modest improvement in the number of drivers, and traffic was still in decline. Severe cuts were planned for the winter programme amounting to, in the Central Area, four per cent on Saturdays and seven per cent on Sundays, and on Country Buses two per cent on Saturdays and ten per cent on Sundays. A new note of conflict immediately entered relations between staff and management and the TGWU sought a meeting with Eric Ottaway, the new Board Member for road services, to discuss the staff position and the proposed service reductions. A Labour Government sympathetic to the needs of public transport had now been elected and the Union also suggested that there should be a joint meeting with the Minister to discuss problems and look for ways of making services more attractive. The meeting yielded important undertakings from Ottaway who not only promised to continue to strive for improvements in staffing levels but also agreed that there would be no service reductions on Mondays to Fridays during 1965 and no further reductions in weekend working in the spring and summer of 1965. What happened after that would depend on traffic trends. The Board also agreed to prepare plans to deal with the situation over the next year but pointed out that there would still be a need for overtime and rest day working for the foreseeable future. Ottaway also agreed to having reduced schedules during the summer months of June, July and August, when passenger demand was lower, so that more staff could take holidays in this period. The benefit to London Transport was that fewer staff would then be away during the busier times of year.

Just before the Government had set up the Phelps Brown Committee, a serious dispute had broken out which had a direct connection with the staff shortage. Since 1962 London Transport had been relying increasingly on private operators to provide the staff and coaches for its private hire work and for a while this had been tolerated by its own staff. However, matters came to a head in September 1963 in a dispute over the operation of a replacement bus service for the Northern City Line, while it was closed for work in connection with the Victoria Line, and the Board decided to employ Whitehall Motorways Ltd for the job. Under increasing pressure from both staff and public to concentrate on improving its mainstream bus services and in the face of the staff's continuing refusal to do other types of work, the Board announced, on 2nd April 1964, that private operators would be contracted to work special services to sporting events. From then onwards the same policy applied to Central Bus conducted coach tours, the Round London Sightseeing Tour and Private Hire work, which left the Private Hire RFs and RFWs with no work. Their last full season was 1963, although three RFWs were used by Country Buses in 1964. All thirty coaches (RF 1–15 and RFW 1–15) were sold, the RFs to a ready home market and all but five of the RFWs going to Ceylon.

Above **The summer of 1963 was the last for a generation that London Transport's own red double-deckers were to operate on the Round London Sightseeing Tour. It had been the custom to allocate newly overhauled buses to New Cross for the tour each season, like RT 3831 at the main picking up point then still in Buckingham Palace Road.** Malcolm Papes collection

Left **Country Buses had less difficulty than Central in covering its tours and private hire commitments and did not resort to sub-contracting. Red RT 3374, on loan from Central Buses, is dressed for an excursion from Dartford to Biggin Hill while standing alongside Reigate's 2RT2 trainer RT 137.**

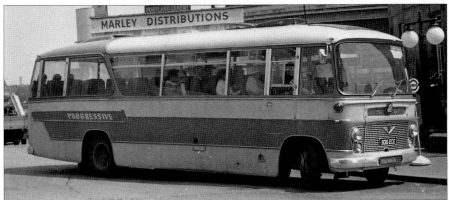

The idea of special summer schedules fell by the wayside and was doomed never to arise again; in fact there was no general summer programme in 1965. Agreement had been reached for the forty hour week to come into effect on 17th March, from which date staff were given a compensating payment for the additional two hours worked, and resources were devoted to the preparation of new schedules and rosters for introduction on 3rd October. Only three of the seasonal Sunday extensions were operated: routes 14 (to Hampton Court), 38 (to 'The Wake Arms') and 97 (Ruislip Lido) and only a handful of routes augmented. Their withdrawal at the end of the season marked the end of such operations. The special meetings about the Board's future plans continued at intervals until March 1965 and the Trade Union met the Minister on 11th December 1964. One of the clauses of the resulting agreement contained a condition that staff would not ban overtime and rest day working but in the event of such a ban occurring the Board reserved its rights 'to introduce measures to reduce mileage'. This was unacceptable to the Union who would not sign the agreement until this clause was removed and its sentiments expressed instead in an exchange of letters. The seeds of the bruising confrontations of 1966 were sown.

Above left **Football excursions were still popular when they were forcibly discontinued, as can be seen in this view of RTL 1347, alongside RTL 32.** Michael Rooum

Left **Typical of what was to appear on special services after 1963 was this Duple bodied Bedford SB owned by Progressive Coaches of Cambridge. It was sub-contracted to Valliant Coaches, hired by London Transport to operate the Wimbledon Tennis service in 1964.** H.E. Murrell

The summer service to London Airport on route 83 ran for the last time in the 1963 season, as pressure from staff to eliminate non-essential operations intensified. RT 1376 is seen at Golders Green. Ken Glazier

RT 3929, in Alton Road Roehampton before direct access to the A3 was severed, works the summer Sunday extension to Hampton Court on route 14 which did not return after the 1965 season. Ken Glazier

The Board's plans for 1966 were revealed to the Unions on 10th December 1965. Central Bus Sunday mileage was to be reduced by nine per cent in new schedules to be introduced from 23rd January, which would also contain area schemes. There would then be no further changes until the autumn but improved Sunday working conditions would be implemented between July and September. Ottaway also proposed that the Joint Working Party should review the conditions under which drivers and conductors operated, consider what changes were needed to reduce wastage (including the implications of a five day week) and review restrictive practices to see how they could be amended. When this was reported to a Delegate Conference on 16th December, delegates voted for a ban on overtime and rest day working from 23rd January in protest against the cuts. At further meetings in January, the Union was not impressed by the argument that there had been substantial improvements in pay and conditions in recent months and asked the Board to commit itself to the principle of a five-day week immediately. The Board was not prepared to do so until the Working Party had reported and reserved its right to adjust services, as required, in the meantime. The Union officers agreed to recommend that the ban should be lifted but the Delegate Conference on 23rd January refused to do so and sent the officers back to get the commitment to a five-day week.

The resulting mayhem, with an almost complete breakdown of services in those areas of worst staff shortage and long gaps in service everywhere, left the Board with no option but to exercise its right under the recent agreement to make reductions in service. Forty-four Central Bus routes, including such important central London services as the 9 and 52, were withdrawn temporarily from 30th January so that staff could be redeployed to maintain the remainder. Most significantly, Consent was given to private operators to operate on thirty-four sections of withdrawn route until the end of the ban. Despite the radical nature of this decision, London Transport drew back from blanket approval and operators were generally confined to sections of road not covered by other services. For example, route 27 was covered only between Teddington and Twickenham (by Conway Hunt) and the 52 only between Notting Hill Gate and Harrow Road 'Plough' (by Pulleine Coaches) and between Blackbird Cross and Burnt Oak (by Lewis-Cronshaw). Full details are in Appendix Three. Valliant-Cronshaw also ran some services on behalf of the North London Liberal Association over other sections of routes 83, 107 and 135 but as these did not receive Consent, no fares could be charged. Many of the vehicles used were coaches which had been delicensed for the winter and, although singularly unsuitable for bus work, introduced a pleasant aura of luxury into this troubled period. Other operators brought former London Transport vehicles into the arena, even including a GS which ran for a while on route 187. No financial support was provided by the Board for these services and many operators soon felt the pinch. Ironically, they also had difficulty in finding enough drivers, despite making liberal use of London Transport's own staff working on their rest days!

There was a flurry of meetings between the Board and the T&GWU culminating in an agreement to implement a forty-hour five day week from 31st December 1966, coupled with changes in conditions to allow the more economical deployment of staff. The overtime ban was withdrawn from 26th February and two-thirds of the withdrawn routes were reinstated two days later. Four (27A, 90, 116 and 135) had already come back at a reduced level in new schedules which started on 20th February at Enfield, Hounslow and Twickenham, where other services were also reduced on Mondays to Fridays and, more heavily, on Saturdays to the extent of twenty-seven buses and sixty rota duties. The unrest had provoked a big increase in the number of resignations as well as giving a boost to the loss of traffic and the restoration of the remaining routes was held in abeyance while the demand for them was assessed and the number of staff on books could be increased. All but two were restored on 20th March, the exceptions being the Ruislip to Rayners Lane section of route 98B (and the Sunday 98 to North Harrow) and the whole of the 235 between Richmond Station and Richmond Hill. There were also more service cuts on 20th March which were followed by further similar reductions on 18th April, 16th May and 10th July. Altogether, since January, 318 buses had been withdrawn on Mondays to Fridays (five per cent) and 299 on Saturdays (six per cent).

Left **Seen in Pond Street by South End Green, Seth Coaches' former GS 27 was probably about the right size for the loads likely to be carried between there and Maida Vale.** D.A. Ruddom Collection

Below left **Another former London Transport bus which helped out during the overtime ban was Wimbledon Coaches' Metro-Cammell bodied RTL 746, here somewhat underused in Burntwood Lane.** H.E. Murrell

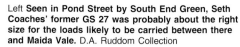

Below **Elms Coaches obtained consent to continue running route 98B after the overtime ban and its operation independent of London Transport was to continue until well into the 1980s. By the end of the 1960s, the coaches had been replaced by second hand buses, like this ECW bodied Bristol LS5G in Imperial Drive on 9th April 1969, which had been new to United Automobile Services in 1952.** H.E. Murrell

Short-term Consent was granted to Isleworth Coaches to continue to run the 235, which they did using an RTL, but there was no immediate taker for the 98B. Valliant Coaches started a service on 1st May but could not make a go of it and it was withdrawn again on 28th May. The Harrow Public Transport Users' Association, one of the more active and responsible groups representing passengers, who, ideally, would have liked the London Transport service restored, were determined to find someone to run it. Eventually they persuaded Elms Coaches to run a Monday to Saturday daytime service between Ruislip and North Harrow, which they shrewdly numbered 98B. Three one-man operated Harrington bodied Commer TS3s were used for a three month experiment, which proved to be successful enough to become permanent. London Transport even gave Consent to its extension to Rayners Lane, on condition that it ran non-stop so as not to compete with route 230.

Under the Phelps Brown rules, the annual review of pay took place at the end of March and London Transport was prepared to honour its commitment to pay a 6.6 per cent increase but was now confronted with a new hazard. In an attempt to halt the spiral of wages and prices chasing one another, the Government had set up the National Board for Prices and Incomes to review specific cases, with the particular aim of improving productivity, and the Minister had powers to impose its recommendations. Under what was known as the 'Early Warning system', London Transport was required to report the proposed settlement to the Government, which referred it to to the Prices and Incomes Board, whose Report No.16 was published in June. This agreed the 6.6 per cent increase but included two new productivity measures: one-man operation on the Green Line; and a relaxation in the rules on standing passengers, which allowed them to be carried outside the specified hours if undue hardship would otherwise be caused. The Union accepted the proposals but reserved its position on the question of sharing benefits from productivity. The first one-man operated Green Line route, the 724, started within a matter of days of the agreement, on 10th July.

On 20th July, the Prime Minister, Harold Wilson, announced a general standstill on prices and incomes until the end of the year, which would be followed by a six-month period of severe restraint. This was given statutory force in the Prices and Incomes Act 1966. During the period of severe restraint, increases in incomes would be justified only in exceptional cases and to a very limited extent. This threw some doubt over the introduction of the five day week at the end of the year but fortunately for all concerned, not least the travelling public, this was allowed to go ahead because it had been agreed before the freeze was announced. The supervisors were not so lucky. They found themselves caught by the standstill because they were still negotiating at the time and this left many of them with pay packets smaller than the people they were supervising. They staged a one-day protest strike on 20th January 1967 and officers of the Unions met the Minister of Transport, Mrs Barbara Castle, four days

later. She then accepted that a commitment to some increase had existed at the start of the freeze but not the amount, and opened the way for negotiations to take place on the basis of the starting date of any new scale being delayed six months (to December 1966).

The Board presented its radical 'Reshaping Plan' to the Trade Union on 16th September 1966 but lacked an agreement which would allow it to go ahead. Fresh proposals were therefore submitted to the Trade Union at the end of February 1967. Although their preparation had been steered by Eric Ottaway, he had died suddenly and tragically on 27th January at the age of sixty-two, while on London Transport business overseas. The loss of this visionary man at such a crucial stage was a severe blow to the Board. His place was taken on the Board by Ken Shave, who had only recently taken over the Chief Mechanical Engineer's job on the retirement of Bill Durrant. The proposed new agreement offered two levels of enhancement above basic rates for drivers of one-man buses (or

'driver/operators' as they were rather discordantly to be known). Drivers of single-deck flat fare buses would receive a 7½ per cent enhancement and those on double-deckers fitted with automatic fare collection equipment would get 10 per cent. The receipts bonus was also to be replaced by a productivity bonus designed to encourage the acceptance of high capacity buses and faster schedules and to provide an incentive to pick up passengers. This would have been based partly on the average capacity and miles per duty scheduled and partly on an index of the capacity actually used, either by garage or by route. Anthony Bull, the Vice Chairman and board member responsible for staff relations, presented the proposals to the Trade Union formally at a meeting on 22nd March. They agreed to negotiate providing the division of the proportions of the savings was open to negotiation and that agreement on one-man operation would not preclude pay increases for other staff. A Joint Study Group was set up to work out an agreement in detail.

Twickenham's RT 3739 arrives in Red Lion Street, Richmond on route 235, the other one of the two routes not restored by London Transport after their withdrawal during the overtime ban in 1966. A.B. Cross

Below Isleworth Coaches kept to ex-London Transport vehicles for its operation of route 235, which is all too evident on partially repainted former RTL 633, whose fleet name has been only half-heartedly painted over and whose fleet number it still bears. Colin Brown

At about this time 'A Group of Rank and File Busmen' published a pamphlet entitled 'Taking London For A Ride' in which they launched a strident attack on London Transport's policies. They attacked the management's 'alibis' of staff shortage, traffic congestion and declining passenger traffic as lies and excuses and claimed that the Board's policies of cutting services and introducing one-man operation were creating a vicious circle of decline. The authors also attacked the officers of the Transport and General Workers' Union for accepting the need for service cuts when the five-day week was agreed and described them as being strong on words and weak on action. The pamphlet called for no less than the abolition of the LTB and its replacement by an elected body, a halt to fares increases while a service plan was drawn up to meet passengers' requirements, a substantial wage increase before talks on productivity started and no further one-man operation until a satisfactory allowance had been agreed. The paper contained many sound arguments which echoed the views of many managers within London Transport and would not have looked out of place in official papers produced a few years later, but they were buried in a long rambling and repetitive document which opponents found easy to knock down. Its chief value is in showing the extent to which London busmen were disillusioned by not only the performance of the Board but also of the Labour Government and their own Union hierarchy, which helps to explain why these negotiations were so long drawn out and why the Union continually pushed for greater concessions from the Board.

By the end of May 1967, therefore, the Union had hardened its position and was prepared to negotiate only if all staff could benefit from the savings. On 28th June, the Union proposed a general review of all agreements to see what productivity improvements, other than OMO, could be made and tabled no fewer than thirty items for discussion. The matter was referred to a Joint Working Party which was to sit continuously to define areas of agreement and disagreement and report by mid-July. This resulted in a revised offer which was accepted by the Union officers for submission to a Delegate Conference on 17th August. Fortuitously, the Board had found that its expected savings from OMO on completion of the plan in 1982 would be £1 million greater than had been thought and they were able to use this to increase the proposed enhancements. The original offer of 10 per cent for Red Arrow and 15 per cent for suburban flat-fare drivers was not acceptable to the Union but a revised offer based on recent agreements in Liverpool and Manchester, which gave 20 per cent for single-deckers and 25 per cent for double-deckers, was. Productivity payments for two-man operators were to be based on a commission for the number of tickets sold, which would give each individual an extra ten shillings a week.

In 1967, during the prolonged negotiations about the Reshaping Plan, a group of 'Rank and File Busmen' produced this pamphlet, which captured the underlying feelings of unease and resentment which coloured labour relations during the 1960s.

The Delegate Conference remitted the proposals for decision at garage level, without a recommendation either way. The garages flatly rejected the proposals for two-man operators, with no hope that any amendment could make them acceptable. The OMO proposals were accepted in principle but the payments were still thought to be too low. The negotiating committee suggested a flat payment of 'more than £1' to all staff immediately as an advance on savings up to 1970 but this was not acceptable to the Board. The Union subsequently accepted the original proposals but were now seeking a straight increase in basic pay as well. When the Vice Chairman, Anthony Bull, met them again on 26th October, he told them that the Board could see no way of making any increase in wages which was not linked with productivity, as this was a clear requirement of Government policy. This was yet another inconclusive meeting.

Meanwhile on 25th July the Government had referred the whole question of productivity agreements in the bus industry, with particular reference to one-man operation, to the Prices and Incomes Board. Its Report No. 50, published in December contained a succinct review of the economic position of the bus industry and of its future prospects and opined that it was imperative that the industry should use its manpower more effectively. Of its eleven detailed proposals, four affected London Transport. It proposed that a weekly bonus of 10 shillings should be paid to all platform staff at garages where agreement for one man operation already existed, or could be negotiated; that the size of the bonus be reviewed annually in the light of actual gains from OMO; and that when the levels of savings became clearer, that the industry should consider how they might be distributed between platform staff, passengers and the operators. The recommended premium rates for OMO in London were: 15 per cent for Country Area single-deckers; 17½ per cent for Country double-deckers; 20 per cent for Central and Green Line single-deckers; 22½ per cent for Central and Green Line double-deckers; but this was conditional on the 'efficiency payments', which were at a higher level for OMO drivers than for conductors, being reduced to the same level. Proposals based on these recommendations were submitted to the Trade Union on 26th January 1968 but negotiations dragged on through the spring and early summer, with further meetings between the Union and the Minister of Transport and more attempts by the Delegate Conference to squeeze extra concessions.

TAKING LONDON FOR A RIDE

6d   the busmens' case

RTL 504

Agreement was reached in July and the Board announced that the first stage of Reshaping would take place on 7th September 1968, exactly a year later than planned.

That was not the end of the strife. The annual review of pay in April 1969 brought from the Transport and General Workers' Union, a claim for an extra 25 shillings a week, a seven per cent increase or, as the Union claimed, 3½ per cent over two years. On 2nd May the Union raised the claim to 10½ per cent, arguing that there had been no increase in basic pay for three years, sought a London Weighting allowance, a straight Sunday shift of 5½ hours and an increase in the premium for double-deck OMO of five per cent (17 shillings). London Transport offered 12 shillings (3½ per cent) on basic pay payable from 12th July and a 3½ per cent increase on the OMO premium for double-deckers but resisted the rest. The claim was amplified yet again in June, when the T&GWU asked for an increase in holidays and holiday pay for drivers and conductors. The Board revised its offer to include extra holidays and holiday pay and to increase the OMO premium to 17 shillings, and this went to a Delegate Conference on 3rd July. Far from accepting the offer, the Conference made threats of industrial action against schedules due to start on 19th July. Not only was there no progress at a meeting on 22nd July but the Union also went back on a provisional agreement for the introduction of double-deck one-man operation, saying that it would not proceed until agreement had been reached on a general wage increase. Official support was now given

by the Union to a ban on overtime and rest day working and an embargo was placed on training for one-man operation, a direct breach of the agreement.

The whole sorry tale of 1966 almost repeated itself. Plans were made for the withdrawal of Central Bus routes where an alternative facility was available, seventy on Mondays to Saturdays and forty-three on Sundays, the routes being much the same as in 1966. A different choice was made for Country Buses and Green Line coaches, where alternatives were fewer and Geoffrey Fernyhough considered it more important to protect his weekday traffic. These were to be withdrawn entirely on Sundays, with fewer withdrawals during the week. As in 1966, other operators were to be allowed to operate over the withdrawn sections but how many would have had vehicles available at the height of the summer season is a moot point. This plan was to operate from Saturday 26th July and got as far as the publication of press advertisements and the production of a glossy publicity leaflet. A settlement was reached in the nick of time, on 25th July, although some sporadic action did take place including unofficial strikes at some East End garages.

The culmination of ten years of discordant negotiations was the introduction of the first double-deck OMO service, route 233 from Croydon garage, on 22nd November. A passenger, money at the ready, hunches himself against the cheerless weather in the dreary surroundings of Roundshaw estate as he waits to board FRM 1, which replaced the pioneering Atlantean on 19th December 1969. E. Shirras

Fresh proposals covering the consolidation of penalty and premium payments, the payments for double-deck one-man operation and further productivity measures were submitted by the Trade Union to the 25th July meeting and this agenda was extended on 22nd September to include the rates for other forms of one-man operation. The draft agreement eventually produced, in October, also included holidays and holiday pay and proposals for discussions at sectional level on ways to improve productivity. On this seemingly harmonious note, the story of industrial relations in the 1960s came to an end but it was to be many years before there was to be anything resembling true harmony and the Board was still a long way from solving the problem of staff shortage, which had again worsened during 1969.

The advertisement which was prepared when the threat of another overtime ban arose at the end of July 1969.

London bus crews' overtime ban

Bus Route Changes

London Transport regrets that owing to a ban on the working of voluntary overtime and rest days by bus crews it will be necessary to withdraw, as from Saturday, July 26, a number of bus routes in order to maintain as good a service as possible on the remaining routes with the staff available. The Board apologises for the inconvenience caused to passengers who use these services. The routes to be withdrawn are listed here, but the precise position may vary with the circumstances at individual garages.

CENTRAL (Red) BUSES

Saturday

2, 6, 7, 9, 10, 19, 35, 36A, 39, 40, 40A, 42, 50, 61, 68, 78, 79A, 81, 81C, 85, 85A, 88, 89, 90B, 91, 98, 108B, 112, 115B, 116, 125A, 130A, 135, 135A, 142, 144, 149, 155, 158, 160, 162A, 164A, 166, 167A, 168, 170, 173, 183, 187, 194A, 207A, 210, 213, 216, 224, 226, 228, 240, 241, 255, 261, 274, 283, 284, 285, 287, E2, W4, 504.

Sunday

2B, 9, 27, 31, 35, 42, 58, 61, 77B, 78, 81, 83, 89, 90B, 105, 108A, 108B, 112, 115A, 125, 133, 134A, 135, 142, 158, 160A, 167A, 173, 183, 187, 197, 213A, 216, 224, 226, 228, 247, 273, 274, 279, 281, E2, W4.

Monday to Friday

4A, 8A, 9, 35, 36A, 39, 40, 46, 50, 51B, 56, 59A, 61, 70, 78, 79, 79A, 81, 81A, 81C, 85A, 88, 89, 90B, 91, 98A, 108B, 112, 116, 125, 130B, 135, 135A, 142, 144, 149, 155, 158, 162, 164A, 167A, 168A, 169A, 183, 187, 187A, 189, 194A, 207A, 210, 213, 216, 217A, 224, 226, 228, 234, 239, 240, 241, 245, 255, 274, 283, 284, 287, 289, 298A, E2, W4.

The frequency of buses on many other routes will be altered to provide as regular a service as possible. Every effort will be made to run first and last buses at normal times.

COUNTRY (Green) BUSES & GREEN LINE COACHES

Sunday

With the exception of certain special hospital and works journeys, all Country (green) Bus and Green Line coach routes will be withdrawn on Sundays, starting July 27.

Weekdays

Some routes may also be withdrawn or reduced. Details will be announced locally.

For further information please ask any bus inspector, or telephone your local garage or 01-222 1234.

145

CHAPTER TEN

NEW IDEAS FOR BUSES

It is perhaps not without significance for the history of London Transport's vehicle policy after 1964 that its Chief Mechanical Engineer (Buses), Mr A. A. M. ('Bill') Durrant, retired on 3rd July 1965. He had been in charge of bus mechanical engineering for the whole of the thirty-two years since the formation of the London Passenger Transport Board in 1933 and had held a similar position with the LGOC before that. He had been responsible for the development of the standard London bus from the STL to the RM and from the T to the RF. One of his last actions was to set in motion the development of the rear engined Routemaster, a project for which he had great enthusiasm. He was held in great respect both within London Transport and in the bus industry generally, admired as much for his boldness in grasping new concepts as for his diligence in ensuring that new designs were made to work before allowing them into production. It is tempting to speculate on how vehicle policy might have developed had he still been around at the end of the decade.

Trade Union acceptance in June 1964 of the Phelps Brown Report and London Transport's proposals based on its findings, opened the way for the Board to adopt larger buses and led to a thorough review of fleet renewal plans over the next ten years. During the long drawn out negotiations London Transport's official thinking about double-deckers had

changed rapidly from a desire to adopt the seventy-two seat version of the rear-entrance Routemaster as its standard to a conviction that there was a place for front-entrance buses in London. The RMF, described in chapter three, came part way through this change of direction and by the time the Board was in a position to take positive action, had already become a back number. At this stage it was believed that the scope for more one-man operation was limited to fifty-two complete routes and parts of seventeen others, requiring about six hundred buses, and that the remaining 4,600 vehicles in the RT and RM fleet would be replaced by 4,100 conductor-operated double-deckers. There were to be two basic types of bus: a seventy-two seat front entrance version of the Routemaster, the FRM, to replace RTs on routes which were to remain double-deck; and a thirty-six foot single-decker to replace the RFs and RLHs and for the conversion of some RT operated routes to one-man operation. There were also to be new coaches for the Green Line and, rather surprisingly, the programme also allowed for the purchase of a new type of twenty-six seater to replace the remaining GSs. This was considered worthwhile because the new seating capacity bonus made the twenty-six seater cheaper to operate than larger vehicles. The planned composition of the fleet in 1974 was:

	CENTRAL BUSES	COUNTRY BUSES & COACHES	TOTAL
XA	50	–	50
XF	–	8	8
FRM	2492	460	2952
RM	2121	–	2121
RML	424	100	524
RMC	–	69	69
RCL	–	43	43
RF	–	85	85
46str OMO	587	159	746
49str TMO	88	21	109
26str OMO	–	25	25
Coach	–	165	165
TOTALS	5762	1135	6897

The life expired fleet would be withdrawn between 1966 and 1974, starting with the RTWs and continuing with the Central Bus TMO RFs, GSs and RLHs in 1967, RTLs (by 1968), Green Line RFs (by 1969), Central Bus OMO RFs (by 1972), the last RTs in 1974 and, finally, the Country Bus RFs in 1975.

Above **XF 3, representing the new generation, overtakes the old, RM 382, at Moorgate during the exchange trials of the Atlanteans and Fleetlines, symbolising the change of direction in vehicle policy in the late 1960s.** Fred Ivey

The engineering department was wary about the rear-engined models then available and would have preferred to wait for the rear-engined Routemaster to be developed before carrying out any trials, but London Transport was under strong pressure to abandon what was seen by many as a costly adherence to purpose-built designs and to adopt instead standard manufacturers' products. This pressure came not only from politicians but also more damagingly for the Board's case, from some of its colleagues outside London, many of whom were highly critical of London Transport's insistence that there was something especially demanding about bus operation in the capital which justified carefully tailored designs. This was not entirely fair, at least so far as the mechanical specification was concerned, because no operator outside London had to cope with the long slogs of continual driving in heavy traffic which were already commonplace in London. Pressure also came in later years from the Leyland Motor Corporation, where Donald Stokes was aiming for the kind of standardisation which eventually led to the production of the Leyland National. The Board therefore decided to carry out its operational trials with standard manufacturers' products to test their suitability both operationally and from an engineering point of view.

As soon as the Phelps Brown agreement was ratified by the Delegate Conference, the Board decided that all Routemasters delivered from the middle of 1965 would be thirty-footers. The first fifty had already been authorised on 23rd October 1963, as these were to be a sixty-five seat extended version of the RMC intended for the replacement of RTs on the Romford and Grays coach routes, costing £8,100 each. The balance of 250 and a further 300 for delivery in 1966, were to be thirty-foot long buses. This interim arrangement was modified at the Board meeting on 8th July 1964 when a memorandum was approved for transmission to the Ministry of Transport seeking authority to purchase, at a net cost of £709,000, fifty Park Royal bodied Leyland Atlanteans and forty-five RMLs, for comparative service trials, in place of one hundred of the Routemasters already authorised. The same meeting authorised the purchase of eight Daimler Fleetlines, at £7,876 each, with similar Park Royal bodies but equipped with ticket machines and lockable doors at the foot of the stairs. These were for an experiment in the Country Area in which they were to operate with a conductor in peak hours and as one-man buses at other times. As the current Regulations did not allow one-man operation of double-deckers, the upper deck had to be sealed off when no conductor was carried so that it became a single-decker in the eyes of the law. Also approved on this occasion was the purchase of fourteen 36ft AEC Reliance coaches at an estimated cost of £6,080 each, for experimental operation on Green Line route 705.

Above **Noise abatement became an issue in 1963 with the publication of draft government regulations proposing the introduction of tough limits from 1968. After various preliminary experiments twenty-four AEC engined RMs were modified for service trials, one of them being RM 738, the only one fitted with these ungainly baffle plates which it retained until 1968. No permanent changes were made as a result of these tests.**
Capital Transport

Left **The 1964 fleet replacement plan assumed that the first of the post-war standard types to be withdrawn would be the RTW, as soon as 1966, although the whole class was at that time still in active service. Hackney's entire fleet was comprised of the type, including RTW 132 seen here at Blackwall Tunnel.**
W.R. Legg

Another early demise was planned for RLH 12 and the rest of the class in 1967, with routes like the 461A presumably being converted to forty-nine seat single-deckers. A.J. Wild

The background to the decision to buy fifty Atlanteans and only eight Fleetlines is of some interest in the light of subsequent events. It is almost certain that given a free hand the engineers at Chiswick would have preferred the Daimler Fleetline. They had done their homework and knew that it was giving better service than the Atlantean in many places outside London and, in any case, the new Chief Mechanical Engineer, Ken Shave, was a great enthusiast for the Gardner engine. These were the days before Daimler became part of the British Leyland group, whereas the ACV group, which included both AEC and Park Royal, had only recently 'merged' with the Lancashire concern. It was therefore possible to agree a modification to the existing contract to substitute fifty Atlanteans for fifty-five Routemasters, at roughly the same contract cost, without incurring any penalties. It would have been logical to have included the buses for the Country Bus experiment in the same deal but the number needed was small enough for the total cost to be below the limit of the Board's own financial authority. This gave the engineers the opportunity to persuade the Board to buy

Daimlers instead, so that they could be compared with the Atlantean with an eye to influencing future purchases.

It took a little longer for a decision to be made about the standee buses, possibly because the Board was waiting for AEC to announce its new rear engined single-deck model, which it did in the autumn of 1964. It was not until 9th December 1964, therefore, that the Board authorised the purchase of six rear-engined single-deckers at a cost of £6,827 each plus £5,700 in design and development costs, for operation on a new route between Victoria and Marble Arch. Also authorised was an order for nine forty-six seat one-man buses for the Country Area, at £6,350 each plus £2,800 for design and development, to replace an equal number of RFs. These became the XMA and XMB classes respectively.

By the time the 30ft Routemaster coaches went into production, the services at both Romford and Grays had been cut and the order was reduced from fifty to forty-three, the balance of seven being added to the RML order. The new vehicles, which were classified RCL, were in most essentials a

lengthened version of the RMC but they had a revised livery and a number of minor structural differences at the front end, aimed at improving their appearance. These changes had already been applied experimentally to RMC 1469 during a visit to the works between May and July 1964. The main bodywork changes were to the grille and bonnet assembly, which was a modified version of the new design already tried out on RMF 1254 in which the traditional triangular badge was incorporated at the top of the central strip of the radiator grille in place of the raised bullseye on the bonnet lid. The brake cooling grilles were omitted from the adjacent wing assemblies which were

The first RFs to go were to be the Green Line version planned to be replaced in 1969 by coaches of a type not yet determined in 1964. Godstone's RF 172 is seen curtailed just short of the full length of the 709. Colin Brown

extended downwards to make the bottom line continuous. The registration number plate was suspended, rather vulnerably as service experience was to prove, below the radiator grille. The route number and intermediate point indicator box at the front was made the same width as the destination box, giving the whole an improved appearance but with no apparent practical benefit. The now disused offside route number box and the raised bullseye symbols were removed and a new larger bullseye transfer, with LONDON TRANSPORT in block letters, was placed at the front of the between decks panels. On RMC 1469 the GREEN LINE fleetname, also in block letters, was placed immediately behind the bullseye but this was not visually satisfying and the RCLs carried the brand name in the orthodox position below the lower deck windows. Finally, the light green relief colour was replaced by a new shade of 'porcelain' green which was claimed to be brighter.

The RCLs were, at 8 tons, five hundredweight heavier than the RMCs and they were therefore powered by the larger 11.3 litre AV690 engine. Another minor difference was that their semi-automatic transmission did not have the option of being altered to fully automatic, but otherwise the specification of their running units was the same. Their greater length added to the already legendary stability of these vehicles to make them probably the most comfortable and smooth riding double-deckers ever produced.

RCL 2223 was the first to be licensed, for driver training, on 21st May 1965, and the first eighteen went into service on route 721 at Romford on 2nd June. The remainder followed on 16th June (ten for route 722), 1st July (nine at Grays for routes 723/A) and 14th July (one at Romford for the 726). As already described in chapter five, route 723B had been found unsuitable for the longer vehicle and the five which it could not use were licensed at Hertford for route 715A on 1st July.

The thirty-foot long Routemaster coaches were almost identical in overall appearance to the RMCs, the most important difference being the improved radiator grille and wing assembly. The symmetrical arrangement of route indicator boxes also gave the front a tidier look and the revised design for the fleet identity, with a large bullseye immediately beneath the front upper deck side window, was a notable concession to contemporary design thinking. The greater luminosity of the 'porcelain' green relief colour is also evident in this study of RCL 2227 at Aldgate. Capital Transport

XAs 2 and 3 seen in the finishing shops of Park Royal Vehicles Ltd, alongside the Grand Union Canal, where XA 3 still lacks its lights and trafficators. Capital Transport

As the RCLs went through the shops at Park Royal, cuckoos began to appear in the nest alongside them, in the form of the first of the Atlanteans (classified XA). The first four were delivered to London Transport on 14th June 1965 and little time was wasted before showing XA 2 off to the Press at Stockwell garage on 17th June, but it was to be some time before any appeared in service as deliveries were not completed until December. They were numbered XA 1–50 (CUV1C–37C; JLA38D–50D). Mechanically the Atlanteans were more akin to the RT than to the RM era, with beam axles and leaf springs, giving a poor ride at the front of the upper deck, and air pressure brakes. The engine was the 11.1 litre Leyland O.680, an enlarged version of the O.600 specified for the RMs, and the transmission was through a fluid flywheel and 'Pneumocyclic' gearbox, arranged to give automatic operation. Engine, fluid flywheel and gearbox were mounted as a unit transversely across the rear.

The seventy-two seat bodywork was a standard steel framed product based on those supplied to Birmingham and Nottingham and showed little allegiance to London Transport's usual standards of design. Like many first generation bodies on rear engined buses, the upper deck windows were shallower than those on the lower deck which combined with their uncompromisingly flat, severely upright, fronts and single skin domes to give the finished product a particularly graceless appearance. The 'cheap and cheerful' look was given extra emphasis by the patches on the front dome which were needed to support the bolts securing the grab rails across the windows. The flake grey relief band was much deeper than on earlier buses but, paradoxically, this merely seemed to make matters worse. A little more effort had been made at the rear which, in design terms, was the weak point of the rear engined layout. On most Atlanteans and Fleetlines produced up to that time the engine compartment projected like a pod under the rear lower deck window and the upper deck was cantilevered over the gap, the whole effect being disagreeably untidy. London Transport adopted a solution which had been pioneered by Northern Counties on bodywork supplied for Daimler Fleetlines and which Park Royal had used on a batch of seven Atlanteans for Stockton Corporation in May 1964. On these a marked improvement in appearance was achieved by fitting 'fairings' to cover the gap above the engine. Unfortunately, this arrangement created an even worse dirt trap, inaccessible to most bus washers, than already existed on this type of vehicle. A standard set of Routemaster style route and destination indicators was fitted at the front but, despite being intended for two-man operation, no side blinds were carried and only a route number box was installed at the back.

The Park Royal bodywork on the Atlanteans and Fleetlines was to the company's standard design with detailed improvements, notably the 'fairings' over the engine compartment which improved the appearance at the expense of creating a dirt trap, an idea first applied to a batch supplied to Stockton in 1964. The Atlanteans were stored at Fulwell until they were needed for service, which is where XA 9 posed on 2nd July 1965, soon after being delivered. The XAs were the first London Transport double-deckers to have only a route number box at the rear and no indicators of any sort on the nearside. Ken Glazier

London Transport's influence came into its own with a vengeance in the interior, starting with a new design for the platform area. One of the drawbacks of the front entrance layout on double-deckers was the bottleneck where the stairs landed in the 'throat' between the wheels. This reduced the flow of passengers to one stream, instead of the neat division into a separate flow for each deck which was possible on rear platform buses. London Transport, under the long-time influence of the Metropolitan Police, required fast loading times to avoid delays at busy stops in congested streets and single stream boarding and alighting would have been unacceptable. For this reason special attention had been given to the design of the platform and lower deck. The low floor which had been a major selling point for rear engined buses, also had the handicaps of deep wells with narrow passages over the axles, high pedestals for seats over the wheels and the need to lift the rear end of the lower saloon over the axle and transmission. This all allowed a lower overall height to be achieved, albeit with recourse to a section of lowbridge layout at the rear on the PDR1/1 Atlantean, but this was not essential in London where there were relatively few problems with height restrictions. The designers therefore decided to raise the lower saloon floor to a level where many of the intrusions could be eliminated and a slightly wider, less obstructed gangway created. The higher level continued onto the platform, which had two steps up from the kerb, rather than one. The staircase was also adjusted so that the bottom steps faced at an angle towards the front, so that passengers to and from the upper deck could, in theory, use the offside of the platform clear of those for the lower deck.

The interior finish reached a standard way above what could be seen in most contemporary buses outside London and at least matched the quality achieved by the few far-sighted operators who had adopted improved designs in recent years. The décor, based on the Routemaster scheme, used burgundy rexine for the side panels, Chinese green for the window surrounds and Sung yellow for the ceilings. Standard tubular framed seats with Routemaster style moquette added a final touch of quality to what was undoubtedly a pleasant and stylish interior. There were forty-one seats upstairs and thirty-one down, six fewer than on the standard provincial model, which enabled them to be spaced more generously and comfortably. One respect in which the XAs were superior to the Board's standard was the saloon lighting which, for the first time on a production London bus, was provided by fluorescent tubes, a feature which had become standard on most buses outside London long since.

The lower deck of XA 9, looking forwards. The high quality of the finish is evident and the slight angling of the bottom step of the staircase toward the platform can just be made out.
Ken Glazier

Production of bus Routemasters was resumed immediately after completion of the RCLs and the first, RML 2261 (CUV261C), was delivered to London Transport on 1st July 1965. The production version of the RML carried the bus version of the improved front end which had been introduced with the RCLs but was otherwise similar to the final batch of RMs. Ignoring the example set by the Atlanteans, they clung to tungsten bulb lighting right to the end of the production run but from August 1966 an attempt was made to make the lower saloons brighter by painting their ceilings 'magnolia' (or 'white' to the less sophisticated). This did not apply to the upper deck because the yellow colour helped to disguise the nicotine stains from cigarette smoke. There was one further experimental change to interior colours on three buses, RMLs 2674–2676, in the spring of 1967. These were finished in a scheme which resembled current practice on the Underground, where Professor Misha Black's bias towards variations of grey to indicate mechanical efficiency was just coming into vogue. The side panels and window surrounds on these three buses were coloured light grey, the ceilings white and the moquette was in blue and green. This scheme was never adopted on the RMLs but did become standard on many later vehicles. The three bodies retained the grey and blue décor at their first overhaul in 1974 (when they became RMLs 2678, 2676 and 2679 respectively) but at their next their side panels were repainted burgundy and their seats retrimmed with standard moquette. Other variations from the standard included 110 vehicles from which the interior illuminated advertisement panel was omitted (RMLs 2351–2560) and one hundred (RMLs 2561–2660) which were fitted with exterior illuminated panels. The absence of the interior panels was not apparently a sudden realisation that these were a redundant extravagance because all were later fitted with them.

Before either the RMLs or the XAs saw any service, the first of the Daimler Fleetlines was delivered to London Transport in August. The bodywork was the same as the Atlanteans, the only difference being the addition of a lockable door across the foot of the stairs for use when the bus was one-man operated. The chassis was a standard product with the 6LX 10.45 litre version of the Gardner engine, which developed 140bhp at 1,700rpm, but their semi-automatic gearboxes were also capable of being converted to fully automatic. The buses were numbered XF 1–8 (CUV51C–58C). As the RMLs and XAs were being stockpiled for the comparative trials it fell to the XFs to be the first of the new buses to enter service on 15th September 1965. They were allocated to East Grinstead garage where they replaced the RTs on route 424. They also worked on routes 435 and 438C. As the Regulations had not yet been changed to allow the experiment in composite operation to take place, they ran for the time being with conductors at all times.

Apart from their Country Bus livery, the only difference in appearance between the Fleetlines and the identically bodied XAs was the distinctive Daimler front wheel nut cover. Colin Brown

XF 5 leaves the canalside exit from the finishing area at Park Royal works, bearing a trade plate in its nearside windscreen. Judging by the number of people on board and the foreman-like man alongside the driver, this was probably a test run. Colin Brown

RML 2351 waits at the lights at Reigate Town Hall while an XA on comparison trial with the XFs follows on a short working of the 424. Roy Hobbs

XA 46 at the Northumberland Park terminus of route 67 following the swap of its RMLs with route 271. The vertical slant of the driver's windscreen and horizontal slant of both windscreens is particularly apparent at this angle.
Capital Transport

One hundred of the 1965 order for RMLs were allotted to the Country Bus department in two batches of fifty each (RML 2306–2355 and 2411–2460). The first thirty were intended for operation on routes 409, 410 and 411 from 3rd October 1965, coinciding with the introduction of new timetables in which frequencies were to be reduced to take account of the higher capacity of the new vehicles. As the delivery of green RMLs was running behind this schedule, some of the red ones had to be used to cover the shortfall, starting with the licensing of the first two (RML 2278 and 2279) as trainers at Godstone on 10th August. The first green RML (2306) arrived on 17th September but only thirteen were available for service on the first day, eleven at Godstone and one each at Reigate and East Grinstead. No fewer than seventeen red ones (RML 2278–2280, 2287, 2288, 2293, 2295–2305) had to be licensed as temporary cover at Godstone until they could be replaced in November. The remainder of the first green batch went to Northfleet, also in November, primarily for route 480 but they were also used on local works services.

The comparative trials between the RMLs and XAs started in November 1965. The first thirty-one production RMLs to be licensed for Central Bus service went into operation on routes 76 and 34B from Tottenham garage on 1st November, replacing RTWs, and the first Atlanteans went to Chalk Farm garage for route 24, where they replaced the incumbent RMs on Sunday 7th November. This allocation had not been made without a lot of argument with the Trade Union, who considered the route far too busy for an entirely untried bus. It wanted the XAs to be put onto a quieter route but this would have defeated the purpose of the experiment and London Transport stood firm. A consequential effect of the introduction of the Atlanteans was the reversion of route 45 on Sundays from RM to RTW. So unpopular were the RTWs that the Trade Union was prepared to contemplate the operation of XAs, in contradiction of its usual antipathy to mixing of types. Chalk Farm's Routemasters were transferred to Putney and Riverside garages for routes 74, 74A and 74B, replacing yet more RTWs. Another route whose RTWs had gone by this time was the 46 at Willesden which, together with RT operated route 33 at Upton Park, had received RMs made surplus by service changes on 1st September. Route 55 was similarly converted when its main Southall allocation was transferred into Hanwell on 3rd October 1965, Turnham Green's small allocation changing over at the same time.

The other pair of routes involved in the trials was the 67 from Stamford Hill garage and the 271 from Highgate. Stamford Hill was stocked with its RMLs on 1st December, over half coming from Godstone, and Highgate's XAs went into service on 1st January 1966. In both cases RMs were displaced, those from Stamford Hill going to Walworth and those from Highgate to Chalk Farm, replacing RTWs from route 45 in both cases. Despite the fact that these changes must have been part of a comprehensive plan, Chiswick appears to have shown its usual lack of foresight in transferring RMs out of Chalk Farm only a matter of weeks before putting some back.

Meanwhile, the fourteen AEC Reliance coaches for route 705, numbered RC 1–14 (CUV59C–72C), had been delivered. Their forty-nine seat Willowbrook bodies were built to the new maximum dimensions of thirty-six feet long by eight feet two-and-a-half inches wide, and their styling was based on the BET Federation standard bus body of the period, which was most notable for its peaked 'domes' and two-piece wrap-round windscreen. The saloon windows were of the panoramic type, the first three on each side being eight-feet long, with one shorter one which shared the rearmost bay with the hinged emergency exit door. Their most striking feature was a new attempt at finding a livery to brighten up the appearance of the vehicles while still retaining a link with the trading name. The main body colour was pastel grey and the Green Line connection was retained in a broad green band at waist level, at the front end of which an italicised version of the fleetname was carried. Traditional side boards were fitted above the second and third bays, coloured yellow with black lettering. The chassis was the 4U2RA version of the Reliance, with semi-automatic 'Monocontrol' gearbox and powered by the AH690 horizontal version of the 11.3 litre unit already in use on the RCLs. Internally, they were fitted with what might be described as 'semi-coach' seats, with high backs and headrolls, and the colour scheme was an attractive blend of blue, grey and white. These too were fitted with fluorescent lighting.

Sadly the high hopes invested in the RCs were very quickly dashed. They went into service from Dunton Green and Windsor garages on Sunday 28th November and immediately demonstrated the problems which were to beset London Transport with so many of the new vehicles tried in this period. Despite the fact that the Reliance was AEC's most successful single-deck model with a wealth of service experience behind it and a reputation for reliability, this batch began to give trouble from their first day in service, wrecking the operation of route 705 in the process, and never fully recovering themselves. They struggled on for two years before being replaced on the 705 by displaced RCLs on 2nd December 1967. They were then ignominiously delicensed for a thorough reassessment and, apart from a few which were used as duplicates on route 725 during 1968 and three which were allocated as late running spares for route 727 in February 1969, did not see main line service again until May 1968 when they were assigned to route 727. They were soon off the road once more and never ran again for London Transport.

Above right **The bodies supplied by Willowbrook for the RC class AEC Reliances were based on the styling of the contemporary BET Federation standard design. Other notable innovations were the new livery of pastel grey with a wide green waistband and, inside, coach type seats. RC 1 is seen at Eton when new into service.** Omnicolour

Right **When the RCs re-appeared intermittently on route 727 in 1969, they had been repainted in a more traditional colour scheme laid out in the style already used on the modernised RFs. RC 8 leaves the St Albans garage stop to set out on the remaining sixty-three miles of its journey to Crawley.** Colin Brown

The Atlanteans were also giving trouble and the engineering staff were at their wits' end to provide enough buses for service from day to day, despite having Leyland's own representatives on site to give advice and guidance. The source of the problem was the position of the engine, flywheel and gearbox in an environment where the heat built up when working in heavy traffic had little scope for escape. The fluid flywheels were particularly prone to expand to the extent that the crankshaft thrust bearings jammed. Engine failures also occurred frequently, the sight of an Atlantean with bonnet open and often an ominous pool of oil in the road becoming all too commonplace. When the Chiswick engineers enquired of established operators to find out where they were going wrong, they were astonished to find that their colleagues, some of them the very people who had been pressing London Transport to buy 'off-the-peg', were only too well aware of the problems, which they overcame by carrying high levels of spares. A crucial reason, not much aired at the time, was that London Transport's engineering organisation had been pared down to a bare minimum, geared as it was to the legendary reliability of the RT family, and simply was not equipped to cope with quite run-of-the-mill problems.

In contrast, the Fleetlines at East Grinstead were giving a much better account of themselves but London Transport could not be sure whether this was intrinsic or simply a result of the easier operating conditions. A secondary trial was therefore set up in April 1966 in which the eight XFs were exchanged for a like number of Atlanteans from Highgate. The second phase of the main trials started on 12th June, much to the relief of the engineering staff at Chalk Farm which received RMLs from Tottenham in exchange for its Atlanteans. A similar exchange between Highgate and Stamford Hill took place on 10th July when the XFs were returned to East Grinstead for the composite OMO experiment. On completion of the experiment, they were exchanged again, this time with XAs from Stamford Hill, which became the third garage to run them. They stayed there until June 1969.

The last and most revolutionary of the experimental new generation vehicles, the standee single-deckers for route 500, began to arrive during February 1966 (XMS 1–6, JLA51D–56D). The chassis chosen by London Transport was the new rear engined model which had been announced by AEC in the autumn of 1964. The standard bus, the Swift, was classified MP2R and had the new AH505 8.2 litre dry-liner engine, a slightly enlarged version of the AH471. There was also to be a distinct heavier-duty model called the Merlin, intended mainly for export, which was to have the larger AH691 11.3 litre dry-liner version of the 690 engine, rated at 147bhp at 1,800rpm. The specification included Monocontrol transmission, as used on the Routemaster, and air brakes as standard. As in the case of the Atlanteans and Fleetlines, the suspension came from an earlier era, comprising a beam axle rather than independent front suspension, and simple leaf springs rather then the coil type used on the Routemasters, which was to give the type a

reputation for rough riding. In the event the same basic chassis was used for both sizes of engine, the version with the AH691 engine being classified P2R and given the model name Swift 691, the name 'Merlin' being dropped. London Transport decided to have the larger engine but Chiswick had by now got used to the name Merlin and stubbornly continued to use it for the thirty-six footers throughout the time they were with London Transport.

All eight XFs originally had Gardner 6LX engines but, in 1967, XF 3 was fitted experimentally with a Cummins V6–200 9.6 litre unit, developing 140 bhp at 2,000 rpm. It was wider than the Gardner and gave the engine compartment the distinctive bulging appearance seen in this view at Horley on 25th February 1967. *Ken Glazier*

XMS 5 visited 55 Broadway on 4th March 1966 for an inspection by the Board, as yet unlicensed and carrying Trade Plates. The striking lines of the Strachan bodywork marked a styling departure by London Transport which was not carried through to the production buses. A notable feature of this scene which was to disappear within a few years, is the old, tile fronted, Electric Railway House alongside the Portland stone of the 1929 building. *Ken Glazier*

The choice of bodybuilder came as a surprise to seasoned observers who might have expected one of the Board's usual suppliers to be involved in such an important experiment where close contact and a good working relationship with the manufacturer were of such importance. Instead the contract was secured on the strength of its competitive price by Strachans (Coachbuilders) of Hamble, a name which had not been associated with bus bodywork for London since its predecessor had participated in the LGOC's vehicle renewal in the early thirties. The bodywork was based uncompromisingly on a box shape but was well designed and had a distinctive character which was not unattractive. The front was virtually flat with only a whisper of a curve but this was off-set by a deep two-piece windscreen, recessed on the driver's side, and satisfyingly complemented by a deep peaked 'dome' which incorporated a standard single aperture indicator box. There was a similar peaked 'dome' at the back but this aspect was marred by the insertion of a metal framed push out emergency exit in the centre of the rear window, effectively making three apertures and creating a crude effect. There was a wide front entrance and a separate exit of the same width ahead of the rear axle, both enclosed by double leaf folding doors. The centre doorway provided a happy design break between the forward two saloon windows and the 'two-and-a-bit' at the back whose bottom rail was higher, in line with the raised rear section of the saloon. On the offside the break was made by the hinged emergency exit door. They were finished in standard red with a deep flake grey relief band running all around the vehicle on which the fleetname appeared in red italicised capitals under the second window bay. There was an open style bullseye between the headlamps.

Inside the saloon the standard Routemaster colour scheme and moquette were used but the arrangements were like nothing seen before. All twenty-five seats were situated on the raised section at the rear and the area between the centre doors and front axle where most of the forty-eight standing passengers were to be accommodated, was completely bare. The most controversial feature was the fare collection system. Two milk-stool type turnstiles were situated between the wheel arches and these were unlocked by placing a sixpenny piece in one of two slots situated between them. As the driver was not to be involved in handling money on this service, a change giving machine was provided above the offside luggage pen. This did not survive long in service as its delicate machinery was prone to failure in the unsteady environment of a bus. There was a touch of the paradoxical that Barbara Castle should have been the Minister who inspected XMS 6 on 8th March, because she had made quite a name for herself in earlier years campaigning for the removal of turnstiles from ladies' lavatories. The six buses went into service on route 500, now branded 'Red Arrow', on 18th April 1966.

The nine buses for Country Buses (XMB 1–9, JLA57D–65D) arrived during April and May. They had the same chassis and bodywork as the XMSs but were designed for conven-

XMS 6 in service on route 500 at the Hilton Hotel, Park Lane, where the lower half of the bus stop sign shows the Red Arrow bullseye. Colin Brown

tional one-man operation and had seats for forty-six, twenty-one of them in the front section of the saloon, and no turnstiles. These did not have the rear emergency exit but had a neater looking two piece window instead. A new Country Bus colour scheme made its first appearance on these buses. The traditional Lincoln green was retained as the main body colour but the relief band, which was in the same position as on the XMSs, was a cheerful canary yellow which did a great deal to brighten their looks. The intention was that they should go to Addlestone for routes 427, 437 and 456, where they were to have started work on 29th May 1966. Unfortunately, this type of vehicle had not been covered specifically in the agreement which followed the Phelps Brown Report and the staff resolutely refused to operate them until such an agreement was forthcoming. The success of route

500 encouraged the Board to contemplate the introduction of a second route as quickly as possible and it decided to abandon the Country Bus experiment for the time being and convert eight of the nine XMBs (2–9) to standee layout instead. This was done in November 1966, the vehicles being renumbered XMS 7–14, but the new route did not materialise until the main Reshaping programme got under way in September 1968 and the buses were used instead as additional support for route 500 at Victoria. XMB 1 was retained by Country Buses for survey work but now renumbered XMB 15 and allocated a new registration NHX15E. After a false alarm in December 1967, when it was supposed to start work at St Albans on route 325, it eventually went into service at Tring with its third registration, SMM15F, which it had acquired when licensed in August 1967.

The modernisation programme carried out on 175 Green Line RFs in 1966 and 1967 satisfyingly blended the traditional lines of their early 1950s bodies with modern styling to achieve the good looking result shown by RF 163 at Heathrow when fresh out of the shops. Capital Transport

Competing for attention with these exciting new ideas was a development in the existing fleet which had been launched in March 1966. Because of the uncertain prospects for the Green Line, the Board had decided to rejuvenate a number of the existing fleet of RF coaches to tide them over until the likely direction of future events became more clear. RF 136 was to achieve immortal fame by being the vehicle chosen for the trial conversion, being taken into works in July 1965 and re-appearing in a startling new guise in March 1966. Although little more than a facelift, the changes to the exterior altered the appearance so radically that, apart from its size, it could have been taken for a new vehicle. The livery was changed to a style resembling that on the new Swifts, with a deep band of light green separating the traditional Lincoln green of the upper and lower parts. Two pairs of twin headlamps, one of the new style bullseye devices between them and a new vertically curved windscreen completed the effect. Internally, the contemporary fashion for grey was repeated, the moquette being the predominantly grey design with red lining which had been introduced with the RCLs, and the modernisation was finished off with fluorescent lighting. The completed vehicle went into service on route 705 from Dunton Green garage on 16th March 1966 but perhaps its reliability proved an embarrassing comparison with the RCs because it was moved to Tunbridge Wells for the 704 only five days later. The Board was so pleased with the result that, on 23rd March, it authorised the expenditure of £142,000 for the same treatment to be given to sufficient RFs to meet scheduled single-deck coach requirements. A further 174 were modernised between August 1966 and July 1967. The modernisation of the RFs was all the more remarkable for the fact that the vehicles had already covered around a million miles each, yet the expenditure was fully justified by the result. Alan Townsin recalls driving one a few months after overhaul and reflecting that, had he not known better, he would have thought it was only a few months old.

In the mainstream of events, RMLs continued to be put into service throughout 1966 but this was to be their last full year of production. Eric Ottaway had outlined his vision of the future to the Board at its meeting on 24th November 1965. Although the radical ideas of the Reshaping Plan did not feature, large-scale one-man operation did and he therefore proposed to stop Routemaster production at the end of the 1966 contract (at RML 2760). There was then to be a three year pause in vehicle replacement while a new vehicle could be developed. Technology had reached a point where automatic fare collection, ticket issue and ticket checking, way beyond the primitive coin operated turnstiles of the XMSs, was a serious possibility. Such systems were already being studied for use on the new Victoria Line, then being built, and Ottaway was confident that they could be adapted for use on a bus. Authority was therefore given by the Board on 23rd February 1966, for the purchase of eighteen experimental chassis from Leyland, at a projected cost of £90,000. Authority to purchase a like number of double-deck bodies from Park Royal Vehicles Ltd, at a cost of £123,000 plus £20,000 for design and development, was given on 27th July 1966. Each bus was therefore going to cost nearly £13,000, a fabulous sum at the time. It took until December for the Ministry to approve the project, which perhaps indicated some doubt in their minds about the practicability of the proposal.

Some idea of what was in mind for this revolutionary vehicle could be seen in a mock-up of the lower deck which was built in the experimental shop at Chiswick. This fascinating structure was designed to minimise delays at stops, a major contributor to fast boarding and alighting being the very low flat unobstructed floor which also speeded up movement through the bus. The low floor was to have been made possible by having a four-axle chassis with small wheels, an idea which Leyland also advanced in its single-deck 'Commutabus' project of 1967. As these two experiments came so close together it would seem that there had been some exchange of ideas between London Transport and Leyland. Although nothing came of either of these, the concept was to re-appear in the XRM project of the 1980s. Fare collection and ticket checking was intended to be fully automatic, based on a stored fare ticket. Passengers would board at the centre entrance where a reader would check the validity of the ticket and record the boarding fare stage before releasing the turnstile. If insufficient value remained in store, the passenger could top it up at this point. Another reader at the front exit would calculate and subtract the fare due before releasing the turnstile. Whether this would have worked in service may now never be known but experience with less complicated systems since then suggests not.

The day a No 7 caught fire
AND JAMMED TRAFFIC AT MARBLE ARCH

VISION

Picture by Daily Mail reader Mr. David Sharpe, of Frencklyn Gardens, Edgware, Middlesex

IT WAS a spectacular example of the old saying that there is no smoke without fire.

The smoke was noticed coming from under the bonnet by the driver of this No. 7 soon after leaving London Bridge.

He was taking the bus, with only a conductor in the back, to a Kensington depot because of engine trouble.

But at Marble Arch matters were taken out of his hands.

The driver described what happened: "Suddenly flames started pouring from beneath the bonnet.

"Soon the whole bus was blazing. Fortunately we were in the nearside lane so I could pull in fairly easily."

The driver said a passing motorist tried to put out the flames, but was beaten back by the heat.

Huge traffic jams built up, preventing fire engines getting through.

When they did arrive they had the blaze under control within ten minutes.

But by that time the No. 7 was a wreck.

End of the road for a No. 7. Flames from the engine engulf the bus. Soon it was a wreck.

End of the road for a No 7 bus

THIS is the end of the road for a No. 7 bus. It burns fiercely . . . only minutes after the driver and conductor leapt for safety when it burst into flames in a busy London street yesterday.

Massive traffic jams built up near Marble Arch as firemen fought the blaze.

They put the fire out within ten minutes—but by then the bus, which operates from London Bridge, was a write-off.

Earlier, the bus had been taken out of service because of engine trouble. So there were no passengers aboard when the fire started.

Flames lick doomed bus . . . "I don't know what happened," said driver

Left The flywheel fire which engulfed RM 1768 at Marble Arch on 30th July 1966 could stand as a symbol of London Transport's change of direction on vehicle policy, making a bonfire of all its earlier good intentions. To prevent similar overheating being repeated, all Routemasters were fitted with a fusible plug which operated when the oil temperature approached danger level.

The notion of a three year gap in vehicle replacement was soon abandoned as pressure to move more quickly, not least from the Government, became irresistible. The AFC vehicle was not intended to go into production before 1971 at the earliest, as it was not desirable for it to be bought in any quantity before decimalisation of the currency and, to bridge the gap, the Board was obliged to proceed with some form of single-deck one-man operation. A small programme for the purchase of one hundred and fifty single-deckers during 1967, at a cost of £1,215,000 (averaging £8,100 each), was therefore approved by the Board on 25th May 1966. There were to be a further twenty-five Red Arrows, sixty-four one-man operated Central Buses, thirty-six flat-fare Central Buses and seven for Country Buses. In the event this was modified to: sixteen Red Arrows (eight of the remainder being gleaned from the XMB conversions), forty-nine flat-fare for Central Buses, thirty-three one-man operated Country Buses and fifty-two one-man buses for the Central Area. It will be seen that this decision, which clearly related to the Reshaping Plan, was taken a month before the plan had been approved formally by the Board and four months before the public announcement on 14th September.

Once the RMLs needed for the comparative trials had been supplied, subsequent deliveries gradually spread themselves around the fleet, allocated to the busier routes where their capacity would be of the greatest value. Most of those in the Central Area already had RMs, which were then redeployed, ultimately to replace RTLs and RTWs, while in the Country Area the capacity was used to enable frequencies to be cut and economies made. The first routes to qualify were the 5 group and the 249/A, which brought RMLs to Poplar and West Ham on 1st February 1966 and Walthamstow on 13th February, West Ham being completed on 1st March. There was a nice coincidence here because the change of suffix letter on 1st January 1966 was the first under the new Greater London Council, and the new registrations allocated to London Transport (starting with JJD364D on RML 2364) used a former County Borough of West Ham mark. The displaced RMs went to Dalston and Riverside for route 11 which had held onto its RTWs for a surprisingly long time for a major central London route. At Dalston this removed a source of irritation, the staff there having objected to the allocation of no fewer than five types to the garage (RTL, RTW, RLH, RM and RF).

The standard RMs replaced at West Ham went to Dalston and Riverside to continue the process of replacing the RTW class, leaving only seventy-eight still scheduled for service after 1st February 1966. The handsome Victorian background in Victoria Street is now as much a memory as Dalston's RTW 301, photographed in November 1965. Ken Glazier

One of the first garages to get production RMLs as part of the normal fleet replacement programme was West Ham, most of whose allocation bore the new registration letters displayed on RML 2377 at Red Lion Square, a nice touch as this mark had belonged to the County Borough of West Ham before the Greater London Council had been formed in 1965. Routes 249 and 249A were converted at the same time and RML 2386 is seen at Walthamstow. Jim Blake

Left **Garston was one of the main beneficiaries of the second batch of green RMLs and the 306 one of the routes to which they were allocated. RML 2434 is seen at New Barnet.** Capital Transport

Below **Seen at the western extremity of busy cross-suburban route 37, Hounslow bus station, RML 2485 already had the kind of load which justified the allocation of seventy-two seaters.** Capital Transport

The first seven of the second Country Area batch went into service on route 363 at High Wycombe on 20th February, followed by Hemel Hempstead and a mass influx at Garston for new schedules on routes 306, 306A, 311, 347 and new route 347A starting on 20th March. Windsor (446 group) and Harlow (partial conversion of 396, 397 group, 804, 804A, 805 group and 806) took the remainder. The complexities of Country Bus scheduling ensured that the new buses appeared on many other routes too. The nineteen green RMLs which entered service in May were the last new double-deckers to be assigned to the Country department by London Transport. The vehicles displaced were RTs, some of which were on loan from Central Buses and were returned to them. Others were repainted red and transferred to Central Buses, where they ultimately replaced RTWs.

Red RMLs also went into service during May, on route 37 from Putney garage. The displaced RMs went to Brixton for route 95, where they had the historic duty of helping to topple the last RTWs, seventeen years after they had been London's first eight-foot wide motor buses, those on route 109 being displaced by spare RTs. The first of the major post-war classes had gone; next in line were the RTLs which had already been withdrawn from many garages. RMLs went next to Stockwell (route 37), Upton Park (15/100), Hackney and Willesden (6/A) and, on 1st November, Putney for route 14. The RMs displaced were transferred to routes 52 (replacing RTLs at Victoria and Willesden), 88 (RTs at Shepherd's Bush and RTLs at Stockwell), 165 (RTs at Hornchurch) and 174 (North Street). The displaced RTs were used to start the withdrawal of RTLs from Camberwell.

At this point production of RMLs ceased temporarily while Park Royal built sixty-five short wheelbase forward-entrance versions, adapted to tow a trailer, for British European Airways. Following trials beginning in August 1963, RMF 1254 had been operating on the airport service, fitted with a trailer, since 4th August 1964. With the arrival of BEA's own purpose built version, RMF 1254 was no longer needed and it was delicensed on 24th October 1966. Its sadly short and chequered career with London Transport was finally laid to rest on 24th November 1966, when it was sold to Northern General with whom it was destined to have a long and happier life.

Top **One of the routes to benefit from the inflow of RMLs in 1966 was the 88, which received some of the displaced standard type. There are examples from both garages in this photograph taken in South Lambeth Road, Stockwell's RM 1000 and Shepherd's Bush's RM 357.** Capital Transport

Centre **The RTW class ran in passenger service for the last time on Saturday 14th May 1966, by which time only Brixton garage had an allocation, principally for routes 95 and 109 but also for Sunday route 57A, on which RTW 313 is seen at work during 1965.** Capital Transport

Right **A rear view of a BEA Routemaster, showing the luggage trailer built by Marshalls of Cambridge on Rubery Owen single axles.** W.T. Cottrell

The move to double-deckers on the airport service came about because of the increasing size of aircraft and, before settling on the Routemaster, BEA had tried this AEC Regent V with the intention of carrying luggage on board. The Executive Express RF's elegance contrasts vividly with the unredeemed ugliness of the Regent's Park Royal body. *Colin Brown*

Below **FRM 1 in its original condition, photographed by the Research Department at Chiswick Works. Apart from having no opening windows, the upper deck was identical in design to a standard Routemaster, with one additional full length bay inserted. The front entrance and platform arrangements were similar to those on the Atlanteans and Fleetlines but a better rear end treatment was achieved by extending the saloon windows right through to the back wall.** *L.T. Museum*

While the fate of the forward-entrance Routemaster was being settled, London Transport had quietly taken delivery of its natural successor, the rear-engined front-entrance version FRM 1. Much mystery surrounds the development of this vehicle which had the misfortune to be conceived just at the time that AEC 'merged' with Leyland and born at the very moment that London Transport had settled on the Reshaping Plan as its future salvation. The idea of producing a rear-engined variant had originated from Southall at some time in 1962 or early 1963, when representatives from AEC had approached Bill Durrant informally with an outline proposal. At this time the Board had barely started to think about the possibility of operating front-entrance buses but Durrant secured the agreement of the Vice-Chairman to allow plans to be developed. The future prospects for such a vehicle became brighter in the wake of the Phelps Brown report in the spring of 1964 and a firm commitment was then made to the purchase of one proto-type. At this time the Reshaping Plan was not even a gleam in anybody's eye and it was confidently expected that over three thousand of the model would be required for two-man operation of the busier routes. AEC also had high hopes of it for sales outside London and strong interest was shown at an early stage by Sheffield Corporation in particular and operators such as Yorkshire Traction and Northern General. For this reason work was put in hand on three sets of parts but in the event only one vehicle was completed.

Left **Looking forward in the lower deck of FRM 1 after fitting of opening windows, it is possible to see the angling of the step up from the platform and the deft positioning of the grabrail to encourage passengers to board and alight in separate streams for the upper and lower decks. The 'Compass' fresh air grilles can be seen above the saloon windows between the rather clumsy looking fluorescent lighting tubes.** L.T. Museum

Below left **The lower deck looking towards the back. All but two of the thirty-one seats faced forward, the areas over the front wheels being occupied by the staircase on the offside and a parcel rack on the nearside. Note the provision in the staircase panel of a locker for the conductor's ticket machine and a rack for time cards and waybills, both indicative of the design's intended role as a crew operated vehicle.** L.T. Museum

Below right **The upper deck of FRM 1, looking towards the back. Apart from one inward facing single seat behind the stairwell, all seats faced the front, the two single seats being necessary to provide adequate circulating space at the top of the stairs.** L.T. Museum

The design team had started from the premise that as many as possible of the existing Routemaster parts should be used in the new vehicle and reached the creditably high proportion of sixty per cent. Like the standard Routemaster, the FRM was of aluminium alloy integral construction with independent coil spring front suspension, air suspension on the rear axle, power hydraulic brakes and a fully automatic 'monocontrol' gearbox. The transversely mounted rear engine was the AV691 11.3 litre unit, set to develop 150bhp at 1,800 rpm. The bodywork was unmistakably that of a Routemaster, the upper deck being virtually identical except for the additional bay dictated by its greater length. The front was distinguished by a new type of two piece windscreen inspired by Paris practice, which curved only in one plane from the dash panel into a recess at cantrail level. This was to become standard on future London buses. The back end was the neatest so far achieved on a rear-engined vehicle, with the rearmost lower deck window extending to the rear wall of the body, completely disguising the engine compartment when viewed from the side. At the back, the upper deck was again pure Routemaster and the engine compartment was neatly contained between the curved side panels, under a recess behind the rear saloon window. Route and destination indicators were slightly skimpy, with only a number and destination shown at the back, in line with a newly introduced policy, and no display at all on the nearside. At 31ft 10in and weighing 8 tons 10 cwt, the FRM was the longest and heaviest of the family but among the lightest of contemporary rear-engined designs despite the high quality of its finish.

Internally the seating, colour scheme and finishings were all to standard Routemaster specification but this was the first standard bus to be fitted with fluorescent lighting. The standard fresh air heating and cooling system was replaced on this bus by the 'Compass' sealed heating and ventilating system which supplied air through slots over the main side windows, as a result of which there were no opening windows on either deck. The grilles through which the air was drawn by two fans were at the rear end, one on each side. The arrangement of the staircase, platform and lower saloon floor was very similar to that used on the Atlanteans and Fleetlines.

Left **FRM 1 leaves Tottenham garage on what appears to be an engineering test run, leading an Atlantean on route 76. The 34B was a works service whose schedule was jointly compiled with the 76.** Capital Transport

Below **The fire in the engine compartment of FRM 1 in Princes Street on 31st August 1967 was dealt with quickly by the Fire Brigade who smashed the front upper deck window and opened the rear emergency window to allow smoke to escape. Judging by its appearance, their prompt action seems to have minimised damage to the engine.** A.B. Cross

FRM 1 was taken into stock on 4th July 1966 but by then the Board had already authorised the development of the AFC bus and the FRM's future was already in some doubt, although its technical specification would no doubt have formed the basis of the new vehicle. FRM 1 therefore languished, hidden from public view, until finally being presented to the Press at Victoria garage just before Christmas. It was a very subdued event and notable for being a purely London Transport occasion. AEC had not taken the opportunity to display its new model at the Commercial Motor Show, although the trade had expected them to do so, and it was now only too evident that the Leyland Motor Corporation was not interested in developing a rival to the Atlantean. Another six months elapsed before, on 23rd June, it was at last sent to Tottenham garage where it started work on route 76, alongside the XAs, three days later. Inevitably there were teething troubles which kept it in the garage much of the time but nothing so serious as the catastrophe which struck on 31st August when leaking flywheel oil caused the engine compartment to catch fire in Princes Street, in the heart of the City, filling the bus with smoke. As windows could not be opened, they had to be smashed by the fire brigade to disperse the choking fumes. It was taken to Chiswick where it remained until 1st December during which time it was fitted with standard Routemaster quarter drop windows, three downstairs and six up, which, apart from their practical advantages, immeasurably improved its appearance. It returned to Tottenham where it worked until 1st August 1969 when it was returned to Chiswick to be prepared for one-man operation. It reappeared in this form at Croydon on 19th December, replacing an Atlantean on the one-bus route 233 from Roundshaw estate.

While the Press was examining FRM 1 at Victoria in December 1966, a mile away at 55 Broadway its status as a back number was being underlined by the Board. At its regular monthly meeting on 21st December, it approved the detailed proposals for the early years of Reshaping and agreed to the purchase of 468 new buses in 1968, all of them single-deckers. There were to be 253 for Central Bus suburban flat fare (MBS), twenty for the Red Arrow (MBA type), ninety-four for Central Bus conventional one-man operation (MB), sixty-one for Country Bus town services (MBS) and fourteen for Country Bus conventional OMO (MB), but of outstanding interest was a proposal to purchase eighteen unspecified twenty-six seaters to replace the remaining GSs. When this was submitted to the Ministry of Transport it ran into an obstacle because the estimated cost of £3.8 million exceeded the amount in the Board's Capital Investment Programme but the spending had to be authorised before March 1967 if the Reshaping timetable was to be maintained. The Minister was also concerned that it exceeded the provisional spending authority but had persuaded the Treasury to increase the ceiling to £21 million so that the position could be regularised in time for orders to be placed. As prices were inclined to rise rather than fall, the number of buses which the authorised money could buy in this and subsequent years did not always match the forecast and in this case the number was marginally reduced to 450, the number of MBAs being increased to twenty-eight and the Country Bus MBSs to seventy-five, while the Country Bus MBs were deleted entirely. The plan to buy special buses to replace the GSs also fell out of the programme, never to be restored.

The delivery of RMLs resumed in March 1967 and the first went into service on route 14 from Holloway garage on 1st May. Putney then had a third intake, for route 74, followed by Riverside (route 74B), Hanwell and Uxbridge (207/A). The redeployed RMs went onto the 2 group at Cricklewood, Norwood and Stockwell and the 53 at Old Kent Road and Plumstead (AM). They were used ultimately to replace RTLs, whose numbers diminished rapidly until, by the end of 1967 only 229 remained licensed. The last garage to receive new Routemasters, starting on 11th November 1967, was Croydon where they were destined for the busy 130 group serving New Addington. It took three months to complete the changeover, as the rate of deliveries slowed down with the approaching end of production. The last Routemasters taken into stock were RML 2754 and 2756, which arrived on 8th February, the last to enter service being RML 2754 and 2755 at Croydon and, numerically the last, RML 2760 at Upton Park on 1st March 1968. There was no ceremony to celebrate this landmark, perhaps because it was not recognised as such at the time, although there was by now no project in being which might have continued the traditions embodied in the Routemaster.

Putney received a third tranche of RMLs in June 1967, this time for route 74. RML 2396, seen at Camden Town, was one from its second assignment. Colin Brown

RML 2760 taking part in a London Stores' promotion in Hyde Park in May 1968, two months after it had entered service on completion of RML deliveries. Capital Transport

Croydon was the last garage to receive new Routemasters in bulk and put two of the last three into service on 1st March 1968. The 130 group was to be the subject of the first major conversion to double-deck one-man operation within a few years but in 1968 it was still a high frequency two-man service from New Addington, the setting for this view of RML 2733.
Vectis Transport Publications

The one possible project, the low-floor, four-axle AFC vehicle, known affectionately within London Transport as 'the all-singing all dancing' bus, was formally abandoned by the Board with the joint agreement of Leyland and Park Royal on 28th February 1968, three weeks after the last RMLs arrived and almost exactly two years after the project had been launched. The manufacturers made no claim for preliminary design work but £4,116, which had been spent by London Transport on design development, was written down. Some of this money had been spent on the mock-up of the lower deck described earlier. Development of double-deck one-man operation had now moved into a new phase.

The new vehicle programme for 1969 had been approved at the Board meeting on 24th January 1968 for submission to the Ministry of Transport. The proposals included the first tentative step towards double-deck one-man operation, following a change in the law in July 1966, and comprised forty-six double-deckers and 481 single-deckers. There was as yet no agreement for their operation and none in sight, and neither had there been any service experience with the new buses, but the momentum of the programme was seen

as sacrosanct. The Chairman, Maurice Holmes, had doubts about making such a big commitment before any agreement had been secured and did not release the letter to the Ministry. At the 28th February meeting, with most of the first 150 buses in stock and lying idle and still no sign of an agreement with the Trade Union, the programme was again reviewed. Deliveries were in any case running several months late and those for 1968 were expected to spill over several months into 1969, so it was decided to limit the orders to the number which could be delivered in the remainder of 1969. The total was reduced to 211 single-deckers and forty-six double-deckers and the cost to £2,105,000, but the proposal was not to be sent to the Ministry until an agreement had been signed. This was subsequently reduced even further, to 198 single-deck and seventeen double-deckers, and the programme was approved by the Ministry in July.

Before, during and after these Board discussions, the composition of the proposed orders went through a number of changes. The first intention was to have 319 MBS and 131 MB but early problems with the manoeuvrability of these long vehicles prompted the idea that double-deckers should be used on flat-fare routes. The number of MBSs was then reduced to 232 and an order for seventy-one double-deckers added but it was not long before the desirability of flat-fares itself was being questioned and the concept of the 'split entrance' bus was born. This was a very much simplified and, so it seemed at the time, more practical form of automatic fare collection

than had been envisaged on the AFC bus, the idea being that passengers would normally pay their fares into a machine, which would issue a ticket and release the turnstile. The machine would be capable of issuing up to three values of ticket and this led to the related idea of a 'coarsened' fare scale in sixpenny steps, so as to make the machine available for the maximum possible number of journeys. Passengers making longer distance journeys, needing change or who had some reason for not wanting to use a turnstile, would pay their fares to the driver in the conventional way. At this point the order was altered again to contain 302 'split-entrance' single-deckers but still with a reduced number of seventeen double-deckers.

The decision to reduce the size of the programme coincided with another to change to shorter single-deckers to overcome the operational problems being encountered by the thirty-six footers. Future orders were therefore to be for the 33ft 6ins long Swift 505 but it was too late to amend the specification for the first fifty, which were to remain MB type. The remainder of the revised order for single-deckers comprised fifty conventional OMO and fifty 'split entrance' buses for Central Buses and forty-eight conventional OMO single-deckers but with separate entrance and exit doors for Country Buses. Even at this stage, Chiswick could not completely shake off its allegiance to the name 'Merlin' and classified these SM and SMS, retaining the basic type letter M, as though this were a short Merlin, rather than the more logical SB and SBS.

The first 150 MB family vehicles differed from subsequent deliveries in having a lower driving position, which was to lead ultimately to their early demise, and were given the type designation 3P2R by AEC. On these production vehicles, the AH691 engine was rated at 165bhp, rather than the 147bhp of the experimental batch. They all had bodywork by MCW of Birmingham to the same basic design which had a softer, perhaps less uncompromisingly modern, look than the Strachans batch. The box shape was retained and the front end was still flat but the peaks were omitted from the domes and all corners were rounded. The windscreen was of the type which had first appeared on FRM 1, and the rear window was a single piece with an inserted emergency exit. The Country version retained the split window of the prototype. The Red Arrow vehicles (MBA 16–31; coded 1MB2) had the same layout as the experimental XMSs, and the Country Bus vehicles (MB 81–113; 1MB1) were similar to the XMB but with one seat fewer. The suburban flat-fare buses (MBS 32–80; 1MB1/1) had the same internal layout as the Red Arrows but a different fare collection system which took account of the need to accept both child and adult rates. The new machine had been developed jointly by London Transport and Setright Registers and was known as the Setright coin acceptor and ticket cancelling machine. It could take up to three values of coin in any combination and was capable of being set for any one value in 3d steps between 3d and 7s 9d. There was one machine on each side above the wheel arches, one of which was fitted with a device to check prepaid tickets. The fifty conventional OMO buses for Central Buses (MB 114–165; 1MB3) were front entrance/exit fifty-seaters laid out in orthodox style. In all cases the interior colour scheme and finishings were the same burgundy and magnolia as on Routemasters but for the seat moquette there was a surprise reversion to the RT design, although the leathercloth trim was red rather than brown to match the rest of the décor. There were still large quantities of this material in stock and the rapid decline in the RT fleet had made much of it surplus. Externally, the colours and layout of the liveries were the same as on the experimental vehicles but the grey relief band was shallower and did not run around the front. They were all allocated matching SMM-F registrations but most were re-registered VLW-G before entering service.

The second tranche had the higher driving position specified by London Transport and the model designation was 4P2R. The four individual types were spread over seven number batches: MBA 166–193 (Red Arrow: 2MB6); MBS 194–269 and 439–615 (Suburban Flat-Fare 2MB6/1); MBS 270–303 and 398–438 (Country Bus standee 2MB6/2); and MB 304–397 and 616–665 (Central Bus conventional OMO 2MB5/1). The mechanical specification was the same as on the first 150 but there were two experimental vehicles. MBA 36 had Voith transmission and MB 165 was fitted with air suspension. MCW again supplied the bodywork and the design and interior layout was the same as on the first batch, except for the Country Bus MBSs which did not have turnstiles. Instead two

The turnstiles on the MBAs were simple coin operated machines which accepted only sixpenny pieces through slots on the central pedestal, highlighted for the benefit of users by the arrow on the small dividing perspex panel. The red 'Ambla' plastic covering of the seats in the rear section of the saloon signals that this is one of the second batch of MBAs (166–193), the only Swifts fitted with this material. The space between the turnstiles and the centre doorway was completely empty of seats, on both the MBAs and, at first, the MBSs. L.T. Museum

The interior of a Country Bus MB differed from the Central Bus version in having a centre exit door, complete with a Used Ticket box, and a luggage rack over the front section on the nearside. The two-piece rear window, also unique to Country Buses, closes this rearward view of the spacious and airy interior. L.T. Museum

Autoslot MkIIA passenger operated ticket issuing machines were carried, one behind the driver which accepted 3d coins and one on the nearside which took 3d and 6d coins. On MBS 277–286 the machines were the later Autoslot V which printed the ticket at the time of issue. Despite the absence of turnstiles the standing capacity was only forty-one, giving a total capacity of sixty-six, which became the standard for Country Buses irrespective of size or layout of the bus.

Externally, the only difference was the higher position of the driver's signalling window but MBA 18 was finished in an experimental polyurethane paint. This was also

used for the magnolia coloured ceilings on five of the MBSs. Internally, the MBAs broke with tradition by having seats covered with red ambla PVC supplied by ICI but thankfully this lapse in quality proved to be only a temporary aberration and MBS 194–269 reverted to RT type moquette, which also appeared on MBS 439–456 and 547–615. The remainder, starting with the first Country Bus batch (MBS 270–303) had an entirely new interior scheme in which the main side panels were blue, the window finishings grey and the ceilings white. There was also a new design of moquette continuing the blue theme, interwoven with green.

Unlike their Central Bus equivalents, the Country Bus 'conventional OMO' MBs had centre exit doors and were therefore virtually identical to the MBA and MBS classes externally. They consolidated the move to a new green and yellow livery, which was carried through to the roundel on the front dash. MB 86, seen in its home town, was one of eleven which went into service on route 447, ahead of final agreement of the Reshaping proposals, on 9th March 1968, the first complete changeover to the class.
Colin Brown

Delivery of MB family vehicles began in October 1967 and the whole of the first order for 150 was in stock by March 1968, the second batch following without a break until the last arrived in October 1969. As the buses piled up and a settlement with the Trade Union seemed as far off as ever, the engineers began to get anxious about their lack of operational experience. A concession to allow some very limited operation was therefore negotiated, which enabled MBA 18 to go into service on route 500 at Victoria in February. Characteristically, Country Buses was able to be a little bolder and made the first complete changeover to MB on route 447 from Reigate

on 9th March 1968 with eleven MBs (81–89, 91 and 92). These received the allocated SMM-F registration letters, as did MBS 32–35, 37, 38, MB 81–92 and 97 but, although many more were delivered bearing that mark, the rest were to appear with either VLW-G (to 546), WMT-G (616–624) or AML-H (the rest).

Although a settlement was reached with the Trade Union at the beginning of July 1968, there was no immediate rush to get the new buses into service because it was now possible to secure a considerable saving in capital outlay by a further delay. Under Section 32 of the Transport Act 1968, the Government was able to pay grants covering twenty-five per cent of the purchase price of new buses, provided they met a standard specification, and this was to be payable on buses first registered on or after 1st September 1968. Although the MB family did not fully conform, because their entrance doors were of sub-standard width, there was provision in the Act for dispensation on minor items on vehicles ordered before 8th July 1968 and it was therefore worthwhile waiting until the qualifying date before licensing them.

The dam broke on Saturday 7th September 1968, when 144 of all three Central Bus types, including forty-four from the second batch and almost the whole of the first batch, suddenly flooded onto the roads in the much delayed and enlarged first stage of Reshaping. The size of the programme, which also involved mass withdrawals and transfers in the established fleet as well as introducing new complications onto the buses such as ticket machines and turnstiles, put an unprecedented strain on engineering resources which were overwhelmed by the problems which multiplied on that day. A number of the new buses had been stored in the open during what had been an unusually wet summer and a number suffered corrosion which affected gearboxes, brakes and door mechanisms. Later, some had to be withdrawn for rectification. The virtual collapse of the services on the first day, particularly in Wood Green and Walthamstow, which was not solely due to the mechanical problems, earned the MB family a reputation for unreliability which was not altogether deserved but which was to colour official thinking for some years ahead.

Above **Brand new into service on one of the new Red Arrow routes introduced in September 1968, MBA 19 is seen at Victoria station.** Colin Brown

The orderliness of the rear end of the new standard single-deck bodywork was disfigured by the unsymmetrical emergency exit window whose unpainted metal frame looked like an afterthought. MBA 18 is in Wilton Road, leaving Victoria on a busy peak journey. Colin Brown

Just as this cataclysm was hitting London Transport, Ralph Bennett was appointed as a member of the Board from 16th September. Ralph Bennett had had a distinguished career in the municipal field, lately as General Manager at Manchester. While at Bolton, in 1963, he had enthused the industry with a new design of body for the Atlantean which had the kind of flair and style which had been largely absent from rear-engined designs up to then. More recently at Manchester he had been responsible for the new generation 'Mancunian' design which again had set new standards. He was a proponent of the double-decker and had also shown enthusiasm for the fare box as a means of speeding up boarding on one-man buses. His appointment raised hopes in many people that he would bring with him new ideas on vehicle design and operating practices but, when first appointed, his areas of responsibility were in planning with no direct line of responsibility to the operational side of the business. This did not stop him from speaking his mind and he took the opportunity of a discussion on vehicle policy, at the Board meeting on 14th January 1969, to suggest that London Transport should consider buying some Manchester type Atlanteans. This was resisted by Ken Shave, who had replaced Ottaway as the member responsible for road services, because too many modifications would be needed for London service. Features which met with his disapproval included the cab layout and the very large windscreen which would have been vulnerable to accidental damage and cause drivers problems at night because of excessive reflection. The driver's controls were also significantly different from London Transport's contemporary standard and might not have found favour with drivers. Finally, the entrance layout was based on the use of Autoslot fare collection equipment and would require extensive modification to accommodate the split-entrance layout. Bennett nevertheless hoped that the new double-deckers would present a modern image.

He had an opportunity to express his views again when the design for the new double-decker was submitted to the Board on 18th March 1969 and compared with photographs of the latest Sheffield and Manchester double-deckers and of FRM 1. The details of the design are not known but some idea of what it may have looked like can be divined from the two main decisions recorded at the meeting, which asked for a less domed roof and the retention of some rounding at the rear. This suggests that it might have had a fairly orthodox front with a more severely upright rear. The indicator arrangements were presumably similar to those on FRM 1, as the Board decided that there should be a number on the nearside to help people in queues when a bus pulled up behind another. Unfortunately, this was not thought through thoroughly and a later modification to include a destination blind, following pressure from the public, was to prove fruitless once the staff had got used to the idea of not having one.

The design was relevant to the £3.8 million programme for 1970 which had been agreed at the previous week's meeting. This required

There were no standee buses for Country Buses in the first series of Swifts but there were seventy-five in the second order. A small yellow label at the bottom of the windscreen, reading 'AUTOFARE BUS', is all that draws attention to the mechanised fare collection system on MBS 303 at the Firbank Road terminus of route 391. J.G.S. Smith

the purchase of three hundred single-deckers (SMS) and one hundred double-deckers (DMS), all of the as yet untried split-entrance type. The total number of vehicles now on order to follow on from the MBs was 448 single-deckers and 117 double-deckers, none of which was destined to enter service before the end of 1969. The bodywork contracts were shared between traditional supplier Park Royal Vehicles Ltd and Marshalls of Cambridge, who had not previously supplied new vehicles to the capital but had done a considerable amount of work on the rehabilitation of the London Transport fleet immediately after the Second World War and had become

Centre **The decision to adopt the 33ft version of the Swift for future orders came too late to influence the first fifty which therefore materialised as fifty-seat MBs for Central Buses. One of these, photographed at Blackbird Cross during the summer of 1969, was MB 619 which was also unusual in being one of the nine with WMT-G registrations.** J.G.S. Smith

Above **One of the last batch of seventy-seven MBSs, MBS 493 first saw service on 14th June 1969, allocated to West Ham garage for the Stratford circular route S1. During their first few weeks in service, new OMO buses carried inspectors to help speed things along and two can be seen talking to the driver on this occasion.** Captial Transport

XA 39 at Roundshaw estate on London Transport's first double-deck one-man route 233. G. Mead

Early operational experience with the MBSs generated the hardly surprising revelation that the absence of seats in the front part of the bus was unpopular, particularly with older passengers and those laden with shopping or children. A programme was therefore started in May 1969 of adding seven single seats in the standing area, five forward facing on the offside and one forward and one rearward facing on the nearside. This reduced the standing capacity to thirty-four and the total capacity to sixty-six and was eventually applied to all vehicles in the class, the last being modified in April 1970.

Ten vehicles delivered in the summer of 1969 (MBS 550–559) were modified to include an experimental set of the new 'split-entrance' fare collection equipment. These had no turnstile on the offside, as passengers boarding this way were to pay the driver, but the by now familiar barrier was present on the nearside. It was attached to a machine which accepted 3d, 6d and 1s coins and, when the appropriate button was pressed, could issue tickets for up to six values: 6d, 1s or 1s 6d adult and 3d, 6d and 9d child. To help passengers know which was the correct fare, an elaborate illuminated display was placed above the machine, showing the fare to up to fifteen fare stage points. The driver had to remember to set the current stage number using a rotary console. This remarkably sophisticated machine was also designed to allow a second transaction to start while the first passenger was going through the turnstile. The buses were given the type code 2MB6/3.

A problem which had arisen with the XMSs and MBAs on Red Arrow service was that they were fitted with machines which could accept only one value of coin, unlike the MBSs whose machines were capable of accepting three values. It was therefore decided to replace the entire Red Arrow fleet with modified MBSs and to convert the existing Red Arrow buses to forty-six seat conventional OMO pattern, at a total cost of £50,000 plus £8,000 for the Ultimate ticket machines. Fifty-eight MBSs had their additional seats removed from the standing area, were reclassified MBA and entered service at Hackney, Victoria and Walworth on 19th September 1969. The modified buses, which were recoded 2MB6/5, were MBA 518, 523, 536–547 and 572–615. The modified XMSs and MBAs, reclassified MB, re-entered service between January and July 1970.

The final vehicle modification made during the Board's tenure of office was in preparation for the introduction of one-man operated double-deckers. During October and November, the Atlanteans and FRM 1 were withdrawn from Stamford Hill and Tottenham garages where they were replaced by surplus RMs. Most of the XAs were earmarked for flat fare operation at Croydon and Peckham and were to be the first London Transport buses fitted with fare boxes, in this case of the American designed Johnson type. None of these re-appeared before the end of 1969 but XA 22 made history on 22nd November when it entered service on route 233 between West Croydon and Roundshaw estate as London's first one-man operated double-decker, replacing an RF.

Top **Fifty-eight MBSs with no work in prospect on suburban flat fare services, were modified for use as Red Arrows in the summer of 1969 because their machines could accept more types of coin than the original MBAs. MBA 607 in its reformed guise at County Hall, displays one of the odder characteristics of the MB family, their propensity to build up a patch of oily grime on the offside front corner.** John Fozard

Centre **On the ten experimental 'split entrance' buses, the 'PAY AS YOU ENTER' signs were augmented with the exhortation '3d, 6d and 1/- COINS ONLY PLEASE' and made more prominent by being printed in black on a yellow label. The equipment seems to be giving trouble to the passengers waiting to board MBS 557 in Twickenham.** P.J. Relf

a major supplier of single-deck bodywork to BET companies. Marshalls were allotted fifty of the 1969 batch (SM 1–50; 1SM2) and seventy-five for 1970 (SMS 149–223; 1/1SM4). Park Royal were to build the rest: SMS 51–100 (1SM1) and Country Bus SM 101–148 (1SM3/1) for 1969, SMS 224–448 (1/1SM1/1) for 1970 and all 117 DMSs. At the request of the National Bus Company, the purchase of a further ninety single-deckers for London Country Bus Services at a cost of £742,000 was authorised on 6th May 1969. These had MCW bodies, were numbered SM 449–538 and coded 1/1SM5, although never owned by London Transport.

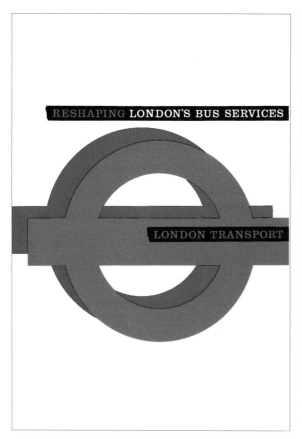

Left **Front cover of the Reshaping Booklet published in September 1966.**

Above **Flat fare equipment demonstration at Lower Edmonton, June 1969.**

CHAPTER ELEVEN

RESHAPING LONDON'S BUSES

What came to be known as the Reshaping Plan had its origins in one of the recommendations of the Chambers Committee of Inquiry in 1954. There was a school of thought at the time that the solution to all London Transport's ills was the operation of 'shuttle' services, a term which was never defined and which could mean different things to different people. There was also a slightly romanticised notion, nurtured by jolly experiences on continental holidays, that flat fares and standee buses were the ideal combination for an efficient bus service. The Chambers Committee were not so easily convinced but saw special services of this type as making sense where there were large numbers of people travelling between two points, usually from a railway station to a centre of employment, and suggested that London Transport should carry out an experiment, possibly at a flat fare and using either double-deckers or 'standee' single-deckers. The Committee dismissed one-man operation as impracticable, except in country areas, because of the combination of graduated fares with the frequent and intensive boarding and alighting experienced in London. This was in line with London Transport's thinking at the time, although its attitude was to change slightly in favour of one-man operation on suburban routes after the 1958 busmen's strike. None of these modest ideas, nor

London Transport's actions in the intervening years, prepared the world for the whirlwind of the revolutionary ideas which suddenly burst on the scene in 1966.

Chapter nine records how the management of London Transport started the 1960s with the fairly modest targets of using larger double-deck buses and extending one-man operation to lightly trafficked suburban routes but then rapidly slipped step by step to the concept of ultimate universal one-man operation and the widespread application of flat fares. As late as 1964 the vast majority of routes were expected to remain two-man, but operated with front-entrance double-deck buses, and the idea of employing one-man buses on any but the quietest of routes still seemed far from anybody's mind. Plans being drawn up at that time saw the scope for the extension of one-man operation as limited to fourteen single-deck and thirty-eight lightly trafficked double-deck routes, as well as parts of seventeen others. The buses were to be fifty-seat single-deckers, which would also be used in two-man form on the busier single-deck services. The rest of the RT and RM fleet would be replaced by seventy-two seat front-entrance double-deckers. The proposals had barely reached the desks of the Board members before circumstances were to change fundamentally and irrevocably.

The first formal indication of the move

towards one hundred percent one-man operation was given in a report by Eric Ottaway to the Board meeting on 24th November 1965, in which he outlined the future direction of Road Services policy. He perceived no slackening in the trend of lost traffic, despite the fact that fares had not increased since July 1964, but there had been some improvement in staffing and if this continued it would be possible to introduce the special summer schedules originally planned for 1965 during the summer of 1966. Area schemes were to continue as the basis for improving efficiency and reducing costs but there was a limit to what these schemes could do if traffic losses continued unabated. One-man operation was therefore the best option if some way could be found of increasing the speed of boarding, perhaps by collecting fares automatically. He therefore proposed to stop Routemaster production at the end of the 1966 contracts, after which there would be a gap of three years during which a new vehicle equipped for automatic fare collection (the AFC bus described in chapter ten), would be designed and developed. Ottaway also suggested that there was scope for a substantial reduction in the amount of work done at Aldenham, possibly to the extent of cutting the space used by about one-third. The report also contained a review of the future of the Green Line network, which is covered in chapter five.

The idea of a three year moratorium on new vehicles was to survive for less than six months because the need for economy had become so pressing that the Board could no longer contemplate such a long wait before harvesting the fruits of one-man operation. The Bus Reshaping Plan was therefore presented to the Board on 22nd June 1966 and approved as a policy, although the money to buy the first one hundred and fifty buses had been authorised a month earlier. The Plan, at this stage still very loosely defined, was presented to the Transport & General Workers' Union on 13th September 1966 and made public at a Press Conference the following day. An eighteen page leaflet describing the plan was published on the same day.

The published plan put forward four main aims: to alleviate the effects of traffic congestion by shortening routes; to reduce staff shortages by extending one-man operation throughout the fleet; to use the available space on buses more effectively in peak hours by allowing a high proportion of standing passengers on short routes; and to introduce new methods of fare collection. The justification for shortening routes was based on statistical evidence which showed that forty-five per cent of passenger journeys were of less than one mile and eighty per cent of less than two. These figures were often repeated but had an important flaw which was not recognised for some time: because longer distance travellers, by definition, remain on the bus for longer, the proportion of passengers on the average bus who were making journeys of less than two miles was closer to fifty-seven per cent. Also, on many routes the shorter distance journeys overlapped each other and did not fall into neat one or two mile compartments.

The plan included the expected expansion of both Red Arrow operation in central London and one-man operation in the suburbs and envisaged little immediate change to the main trunk routes, although some would be shortened. The important new feature, thought breathtakingly bold and imaginative by some, foolhardy and ill-thought out by others, was the proposal to establish no fewer than forty networks of 'satellite' routes around major suburban centres. These were to be operated by what the Board soon preferred to call 'multi-standing' one-man buses on which a flat fare would be charged. Longer suburban routes would also be one-man operated but would retain their graduated fares while the shortened trunk routes would continue to be operated by RTs and Routemasters with a conductor collecting fares. The authors of the plan recognised that it implied some inconvenience to some passengers, notably that there would be more need to change from bus to bus. To make this process as easy and comfortable as possible, therefore, it was proposed to have interchange stations at the hubs of these networks, either for bus to bus only or to include bus to Underground or suburban train. Unfortunately, to enable such facilities to be provided, the co-operation of other authorities was essential and in the event this was to be found wanting. There was also no continuing financial provision for the construction of the new interchanges and this important element was

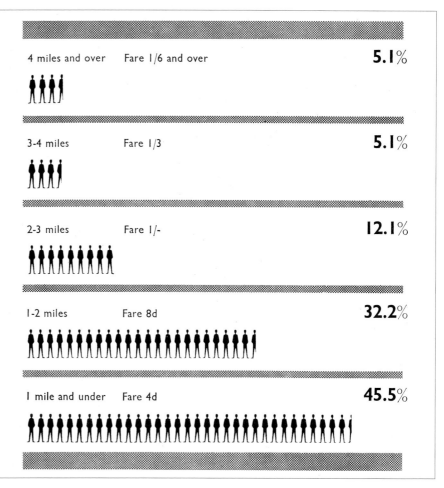

4 miles and over	Fare 1/6 and over	**5.1**%
3-4 miles	Fare 1/3	**5.1**%
2-3 miles	Fare 1/-	**12.1**%
1-2 miles	Fare 8d	**32.2**%
1 mile and under	Fare 4d	**45.5**%

This table printed in the published document was used to justify the shortening of routes but was flawed in using passenger journeys, rather than passenger miles, as the basis of comparison. Each silhouette figure represents 500,000 passengers.

to prove to be a major weakness of the plan.

There was reference in the plan to the need to develop equipment for the automatic collection of graduated fares, possibly by means of a stored fare ticket which could be used on both bus and Underground. The implied intention was that the trunk routes would be converted to one-man operation once such a system had been perfected. As seen in chapter ten, authority had by then been given for the development of a new AFC bus but this did not survive beyond the mock-up stage and was formally abandoned in February 1968.

Very little was said in the document about the future of Country Buses and Green Line coaches because the radical restructuring elements of the plan were essentially a Central Bus brainchild. The Country Bus route network was intended to remain much the same and Green Line was to continue to provide an express service with, perhaps, some new cross-country connections. Interestingly there was not such a clear intention to achieve one hundred per cent one-man operation in the Country area, where it was merely described as to be 'much extended' but in the case of Green Line coaches the commitment was unequivocal.

A more detailed plan for the first two years was approved in principle by the Board on 21st December 1966, the same meeting at which approval was given to the 1967/1968

vehicle purchasing programme. The Central Bus plan was to be carried out in two phases. The first phase would concentrate on establishing the Red Arrow, Satellite and 'conventional' OMO suburban routes between 1967 and 1974, and would require the purchase of 2,777 new single-deckers. The second would begin in 1971 and would require double-deck buses for the trunk services. Country Buses were to follow a similar pattern, except that double-deckers would not appear until 1974. The RT family would be replaced by 1974 (Central) and 1977 (Country) and the Routemasters would be taken out between 1974 and 1979.

The scheme was estimated to turn a loss of £4.2 million in 1966 into a profit of £3.2 million when fully realised. In the light of subsequent events it is significant that Ottaway was keeping an open mind on how the plan might develop, particularly in relation to flat fares. He told the Board that a universal standard flat fare might not be appropriate and that the system had to be roughly equitable to all passengers. How the plan would unfold after the first two years would depend particularly on experience with flat fares. Within two months of having set the plan in motion, Eric Ottaway died. It can be only a matter of conjecture whether or not events would have turned out more happily if he had been spared to stay at the helm.

Any thought of operating one-man buses on busy routes through the West End, like the 39, other than on short haul feeder routes, was far from the corporate mind of London Transport at the beginning of the 1960s. RTW 306 is in Victoria Street in more settled times, when the VC10 was the latest Jet marvel for Ghana Airways. R.D. Hyslop

Plans drawn up in 1964 envisaged the replacement of the RT family on most routes by front-entrance seventy-two seaters with conductors but with some parts of routes converted to fifty-seat single-deck one-man operation. Route 134's RTs would have been replaced by FRMs on the London end, leaving the outer end to single-deckers. Alan B. Cross

This monumental shake-up of the network and in operating practices was to be accompanied by an important change in the way Central Bus services were managed. Parallel with the work on the Reshaping Plan, Ottaway had engaged a team of management consultants to examine the local management structure of the Central Bus department, with the aim of increasing local autonomy and accountability for the planning and operation of bus services. The current structure was much the same as that inherited from the LGOC in 1933 and was designed within a framework which required highly centralised decision making. The District Superintendents were little more than advisers on most matters, had limited disciplinary powers and their responsibility for service control was confined to their own areas, which sometimes caused havoc on routes passing through several districts. In the modified structure, a new post of Area Traffic Manager (ATM) was created with overall responsibility, including negotiating with the Police and Local Authorities, for all physical matters such as bus stops, routeings, terminal workings and stands within a defined geographical area, and direct operational responsibility for the full length of a specified group of routes. For the bigger, more complicated routes, the latter was to be achieved by a system of 'route control' under which Area Traffic Inspectors were to be responsible for the control and supervision policy for whole routes or groups of routes, both inside and outside their Area. Unlike the District Superintendents, the ATMs had no responsibility for garage operating matters and were therefore free to concentrate on operation on the road. To cover this part of the former Superintendents' responsibilities, the post of Chief Depôt Inspector was abolished and a new more senior grade of Garage Manager introduced at each garage.

Fourteen Areas were created to replace the former nineteen Districts, four each in the South and East Divisions and three each in Central and West. The Divisional structure was also changed to support the new arrangements, the most significant being that the

Central Division, which had until now had no garages under its control, became a fully fledged organisation with responsibility for thirteen garages. The Divisional Superintendents were given the new title 'Divisional Operating Manager', in recognition of their new status and a new post of Divisional Garage Manager was created to take responsibility for the Garage Managers. At Head Office level, the Traffic Office continued to provide the administrative support to the ATMs for matters relating to bus routeings, stands and stops but no longer took the lead, as full responsibility was devolved to Area level. The new organisation came into being on 10th April 1967, in time for the original planned launch of Reshaping but with an extra year to settle down before being faced with that particular test. These changes did not apply to the Country Bus and Coach department where the District Superintendents already enjoyed a considerably greater degree of autonomy than their Central counterparts and were well practised in exercising it.

In the meantime Phelps Brown had unblocked the passage to conventional one-man operation in the Central Area and their first one-man operated buses for fifteen years took to the roads on 18th November 1964. The RFs which had been modified for the original abortive plan in 1959 were used on routes 201, 206, 216 and 250 and on the two routes which followed on 27th January 1965: 237 and 251. An additional sixty-eight RFs were modified during the first half of 1965 and these were used for the next phase of conversions, including the first from double-deck. On 3rd October 1965, the Loughton to Epping section of route 20 was converted from RT to RF OMO on Sundays to Fridays under the number 20B, the first indication that the spread of OMO would sweep away forever the artificial division of numbering between single- and double-deck routes which had existed with only minor, temporary infringements, since 1934. The Saturday service on route 20 remained unchanged because it was not possible to roster the full amount of OMO work at Loughton garage on that day. Route 20B

was introduced as an RT operated route on Saturdays at the end of 1966 when the new five day week agreement made it possible. Route 254 also changed over on 3rd October, as did the Barking to Ilford (via South Park Drive) section of route 129 which became new route 291 on 4th October. The programme continued on 23rd January 1966 (215, 215A and 264) and 7/8th August 1966 (121 and 234A). The 121 remained RT on Saturdays and the Hackbridge end of the 234A was transferred to the 234. One of the benefits claimed for the economies of one-man operation was that it would enable wholly new routes to be tried and the first example was RF operated route 136 which started on 8th August 1966. It ran on Mondays to Fridays only between Harrow-on-the-Hill and South Harrow stations, opening up new ground through Harrow village. In passing, it is of interest to note that this number had remained unused since 1940 and in latter years had been allocated to the British Transport Film Unit for use as a spurious number in films. These were the last Central Bus conversions before the onset of Reshaping two years later.

Country Buses, flush with spare buses thrown up by service cuts, had been pushing ahead with orthodox conversions to one-man operation, using RFs, but now began to turn attention to double-deck routes in a big way, starting on 4th November 1964 with Hertford's route 327. Routes 429/439 followed on 3rd October 1965 but a more significant change on that day was the conversion of route 336 which brought about the withdrawal of the first of the lowbridge RLH class. The Watford to Hemel Hempstead section of route 318 lost its RTs in favour of one-man operated RFs from 20th March 1966 and a similar conversion of the Dunstable to St Albans part of route 343 (renumbered 342) followed on 15th May. The big five day week programme on 31st December 1966 saw the conversion of routes 323, 374, 391, 391A, 431 group, 447 group, 460 and 854 (which was pointlessly renumbered 493). This eliminated two-man operation of single-deckers, except for a few odd workings.

The first conversion of a double-deck route to one-man single-deckers occurred on 3rd October 1965 when part of route 20 went over to RF operation. RF 503 is seen in Loughton. Capital Transport

Practical preparations for the new age had also been in progress, although the first experiments had evolved from an earlier phase of planning when only limited one-man operation had been foreseen. The comparative trials of Atlanteans against RMLs in central London were intended to help determine the best vehicle layout for double-deckers operating with a conductor and were to take place on two pairs of routes so that different operating characteristics could be tested. One pair was to be in central London (routes 24 and 76) and the other in the inner suburbs (67 and 271). In making the selection, London Transport was faced with one of the drawbacks which was to bedevil the Reshaping Plan when its original choice of route 7 was found to be impracticable because the larger buses would not fit into Middle Row garage. Route 76 was substituted. Under the June 1964 agreement with the Trade Union, it had been intended to carry out a further experiment by introducing reduced schedules on one pair of routes, to test this approach

against the 'one-for-one' arrangement which had applied since 1962. However, this was dropped before the experiment started.

The first Atlanteans started work on route 24 from Chalk Farm garage on 7th November 1965, with Highgate's route 271 following on 1st January 1966. The RMLs went to Tottenham for the 76 on 1st November and Stamford Hill for the 67 on 1st December. Eight of Highgate's XAs were exchanged for East Grinstead's Fleetlines in April, for a separate engineering experiment. The next phase took place from 12th June when Tottenham's RMLs were exchanged with Chalk Farm's XAs, and a similar swap was made between Stamford Hill and Highgate, except that the XFs returned to East Grinstead. Apart from a further experimental exchange of XFs with XAs from Stamford Hill on 14th May 1967, this was how things remained until Reshaping was well under way. Apart from the engineering information gleaned from these trials, the main finding was that buses with doors were too slow for central

London operation for as long as a conductor had to be carried. Hence the provision in the Reshaping Plan for the continued operation of RMs and RTs until an AFC bus could be developed. On the engineering side the superiority of the RML was proved beyond doubt, its reliability being excellent and its fuel consumption, at 7.8 miles to the gallon, the best of the bunch. Of the two rear engined models, the Fleetlines had shown a higher degree of reliability, though still not approaching that of the Routemaster, and also turned in a significantly better fuel consumption at 7.4 mpg, compared with the Atlantean's 6.6.

The Country Bus contribution to these ideas was an experiment in so-called 'composite' operation of double-deckers on routes which carried heavy peak loads, making them unsuitable for one-man operation at those times, but were more lightly loaded at other times. The idea was that a conductor would be carried in the normal way during peak hours but for the rest of the time the bus

Route 291 was the quiet Ilford to Barking via South Park Drive portion of otherwise busy route 129, which changed to driver only operation on 4th October 1965, using thirty-nine seaters like RF 384. A.B. Cross

would be one-man operated. The route chosen for the experiment was the 424 between Reigate and East Grinstead and its eight Daimler Fleetlines were the first of the new buses to go into service, on 15th September 1965, nearly two months before the Atlanteans. At the time there was no legal basis for the experiment and London Transport had to seek dispensation but this was slow in coming and the XFs were destined to operate for thirteen months as two-man buses before a change of law in 1966 allowed the operation of one-man double-deckers, enabling the trial to start on 2nd October that year. To comply with the Agreements, the upper deck had to be sealed off when the bus was operating without a conductor and this was done by means of a door which could be locked across the foot of the stairs. The experiment ultimately proved a failure because it was uneconomic and the process of switching between modes proved cumbersome in operation because East Grinstead garage was not on the line of route and the relief point was not at a terminus. Either the changeover had to take place on route, obliging some passengers to come down from the upper deck, and causing delays while the door was locked and the ticket machine installed, or the buses had to change over at Stone Quarry Estate, thereby incurring dead mileage. It was also uneconomic because, under the terms of the Schedules Agreement, it was not possible to roster conductors or 'driver/operators' to work only during peak hours. London Transport therefore had to resort to employing the more highly paid 'driver/operators' (the cumbersome title for those who drive one-man buses) for both driving and conducting duties. The experiment was discontinued after six months and route 424 reverted to two-man operation, still using the XFs, on 1st April 1967. The whole idea was in any case in the process of being overtaken by events because the new legislation allowed fully fledged one-man operation of suitably designed double-deckers and its introduction awaited only an agreement with the staff.

Top **One-man operation using RFs was already well established on Country Buses but following the Phelps Brown agreement some of the more lightly used double-deck routes came under consideration. The scheduling agreement with the Trade Union required minimum layovers of five minutes to give drivers time to complete waybills and change blinds. To avoid accruing excessive amounts of layover, routes 429 and 439 were combined into one route which passed through Dorking twice, giving rise to the very detailed blind displayed on RF 643.**
Colin Stannard

Centre **Route 336 had been the first route to have RLHs, in 1950, and was now the first to lose them with the change to driver-only RFs. RLH 4, one of Amersham's original allocation, pulls away from the Rickmansworth station stop on 2nd September 1961 with a load which could comfortably fit into a GS, let alone an RF.**
P.J. Relf

Right **A more surprising conversion from double-deck was Grays local route 323, which changed over on 31st December 1966. RF 149, a former Green Line coach downgraded to bus status in October 1965, is seen at Chadwell St Mary near the end of London Transport's reign, on 9th August 1969.** J.G.S. Smith

As things turned out, the most significant experiment and the one which attracted the greatest attention was the Red Arrow, which was launched with much acclaim on 18th April 1966. Apart from the basic idea of a short haul, flat fare, standee service, several other new theories were tested on route 500. There was only one intermediate stop on the peak hour service between Victoria and Marble Arch, at the Hilton Hotel, and buses ran empty towards Victoria in the morning and Marble Arch in the evening peak. Between the peaks the route was altered to run in a loop via Grosvenor Square, Hanover Square and Oxford Street to serve the shops. Such variations of route and the idea of 'dead' running may have been commonplace outside London but in the Metropolis they were revolutionary. There was no evening service at first and the route ran only on Mondays to Fridays. There was a special design of Bus Stop sign with a white bullseye bearing the Red Arrow symbol in red against a black background.

The new service was a great success, although the unreliability of the change-giving machines was one point of contention. Another was the 'dead' running which irritated the considerable number of people making journeys against the main flow who were often left standing by an empty Red Arrow to await the vagaries of routes 2, 16 and 36. This arrangement was therefore discontinued from 18th July, although for a while the

Hilton Hotel stop was not served on these journeys. A limited early evening service was introduced on the off-peak loop from 13th November 1967. Another problem encountered by the 500 was the congestion at Marble Arch where it turned by making a complete circuit of the roundabout. Tyburn Way was at that time unused and London Transport sought permission for the 500 to use it to by-pass the congestion. The authorities were persuaded eventually and Tyburn Way became London's first stretch of bus only road from 25th July 1966. Special signs were erected reading 'Route 500 Only', as the concession was strictly confined to that route. The success of the 500 not only encouraged London Transport to contemplate extending the network but was also instrumental in persuading them of the merits of similar operations in the suburbs.

There should have been an experiment with conventional one-man operation of the new XMB class buses in the Country Area but this never took place because it was not specifically covered by the agreement reached following the Phelps Brown Report. As already recorded in chapter ten, all but one of these was converted to Red Arrow layout during November 1966. These provided useful relief to the original six vehicles on route 500 but it had also been hoped that they might be used to start a second route, between Waterloo and Mansion House in peak hours, with an off-peak service to Portman Square.

However, this too was not covered by the 'Phelps Brown' agreement and all further development had to await a settlement with the Trade Union.

Preparations for a pilot satellite scheme were launched by the Traffic Committee on 6th June when a sub-committee was set up to make proposals for flat fare operation in 'a suburban area', which was not specified although the inclusion of the Divisional Superintendent (East) among its members suggests that Wood Green had already been selected. Towards the end of 1966, a programme was drawn up for 1967 which envisaged the introduction of Red Arrow routes 501, 502 and 503 in March, the Wood Green Satellite scheme and Red Arrows 504, 505 and 506 in October, and the first stage of conventional one-man operation (still referred to at this time as XMB) in December. The first MB routes were to be the 10A, 21A, 35B, 79, 79A, 81 and 84. What might be described as 'conventional' reviews were also included in this programme, covering Area Schemes for Addington, Woolwich and Cricklewood and the review of RML operation on routes 6, 6A, 15 and 37. It is interesting to note that, in these early stages of planning, the satellite routes were to be numbered in a series from 600 upwards and it was not until March 1967, when the first detailed proposals were discussed, that the decision was made to use prefix letters related to the area of operation.

The possible network of Red Arrow services shown in the Plan included several which did not fructify, including routes to Paddington, from Charing Cross to Victoria, Waterloo to the City via Blackfriars Bridge, King's Cross to Oxford Circus and a route through Leicester Square.

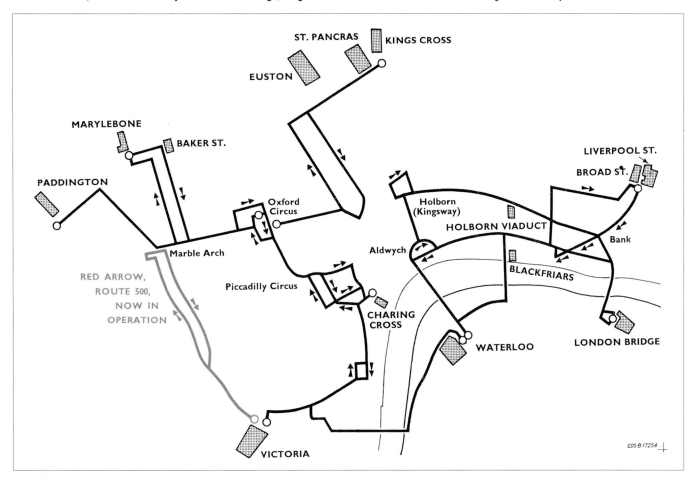

Meanwhile, very little had happened to schedules or service patterns since the introduction of the five-day week on 31st December 1966, which had affected every schedule in the fleet and coincided with major cuts in service. Central Buses cut 186 buses on Mondays to Fridays, 315 on Saturdays and eighty-one on Sundays, while Country Buses shed twenty-six double-deckers and six GSs on Mondays-Fridays, off-set by the addition of twelve OMO RFs, twenty-four double-deck, eight single-deck and six GSs on Saturdays, the Sunday figures being twenty, three and two respectively. There were also cuts on Green Line amounting to seventeen Monday to Friday runnings, seven on Saturdays and twelve on Sundays.

There were many complete or partial route withdrawals. Central Buses dispensed entirely with eight routes (4, 20, 26, 33, 74A, 265, 268 and 282), although in some cases parts were covered by changes to other services, and withdrew a further sixteen on Saturdays and ten on Sundays. To cover sections of some of these routes, three new routes were created on Saturdays and another three on Sundays and another ten routes were given weekend variations. On the other hand, the 6, 256 and 257 reverted to a standard route pattern on Saturdays. There were also many minor withdrawals, either over part of the route or for

only part of the day, too numerous to mention here but involving twenty-two routes. There was also a minor 'scheme' involving the withdrawal of route 285 between Raynes Park and Haydons Road and the extension of route 200 from Wimbledon to Haydons Road and then onwards to Mitcham via Phipps Bridge Estate. Country Buses withdrew routes 315 (except for some peak journeys), 315A and 854A, five others on Saturdays and fifteen on Sundays, although some short sections of these were covered by the extension of other routes. As already noted, there was also a programme of conversions to one-man operation.

The Central Bus cuts proved to be rather too severe and unscheduled extras were introduced on no fewer than ninety-five routes in the early part of 1967. The maximum number of additional buses reached was 192, of which 142 were incorporated into new schedules introduced on 15th June 1967. These included the introduction of new route 295 between East Acton and Hammersmith, restoring the link from Westway which had been lost when route 72 was diverted via Ducane Road, and the long delayed extension of route 195 to Charville Lane Estate. Other than this, and another couple of schemes a year later, only a handful of schedule changes took place, during 1967 and the first eight months of 1968, most of them straightforward

minor cuts or connected with alterations to running time. Planning had not stood still while the arguments with the Trade Union had been going on however. By the time agreement was reached there were no fewer than fifty-four proposals waiting to be implemented, seven of them area schemes involving many routes.

There were two changes on 17th June 1968 which affected route structures. Route 21A was withdrawn between Sidcup and Woolwich, becoming a much foreshortened Sidcup Station to Farningham service, and the daytime service on route 182 was withdrawn outright. A local service was introduced on route 21 between Eltham and Sidcup garage and a few extra journeys were added to the 161 between Woolwich and Eltham, but otherwise the service was just cut. The night service on the 182 was renumbered N82 but ran only between New Cross and Woolwich. The other restructuring involved the 98 group which was reduced from three wide headway to two rather stronger routes. The 98B and 198 were both withdrawn and the 98 was intermediately diverted via Oak Farm Estate and extended to Uxbridge, with a double run at Hillingdon Station. The other bits were picked up by new route 98A which ran from Ruislip to Hayes, with a peak hour extension to Hatton Cross.

Below In the schedule changes on 17th June 1968, route 50 began its retreat from Addiscombe, being cut back to Streatham garage on Mondays to Fridays and replaced by new route 289 between Addiscombe and Thornton Heath. Before the change, in August 1967, RT 2098 is seen at the Vauxhall Bridge Road end of the lengthy route. Alan B. Cross

Right The number 33 moved abruptly from east London to its former haunts between Hounslow and Kensington on 31st December 1966. The east London version had started only just over four years earlier as a localisation of route 5, soon after which RT 3018 was photographed in Becontree. Peter G Mitchell

Below right The changes to the 98/198 group of routes on the same date involved the withdrawal of the 198 and the introduction of a new 98A. The middle part of Long Lane, Hillingdon, lost its bus service as a result. RT 2841 is seen at Uxbridge, the northern terminus of the 198.

Reshaping was launched with such a big splash on 7th September 1968 that its ripples were to be found all over London, the whole of the 1967 programme plus some other items having been compressed into this one programme. There were three major schemes, a number of other conversions to one-man operation and some conventional alterations to other routes which taken together involved over a thousand buses, a sixth of the scheduled fleet. Six more Red Arrow routes were introduced plus a Saturday variant of one, all but one of them serving Waterloo, three Victoria, and one each Charing Cross, Holborn Viaduct, Marylebone and Liverpool Street stations. They were: 501 (Waterloo, Holborn, Bank, Aldgate, Mondays to Fridays); 502 (Waterloo – Fleet Street – London Wall – Liverpool Street – Bank – Fleet Street – Waterloo, Mondays to Fridays); 503 (Victoria – Westminster – Waterloo, Daily); 504 (as 502 but via Bank both ways, Saturdays until 14.30); 505 (Waterloo – Charing Cross – Oxford Street – Portman Square, extended peaks to Marylebone station, Mondays to Fridays); 506 (Victoria – Piccadilly Circus – Pall Mall – Victoria, Mondays to Fridays; and 507 (Waterloo – Lambeth Bridge – Victoria, Mondays to Saturdays). Walworth garage was allocated twenty-five MBAs for routes 501 and 505, Hackney nine for routes 502 and 504 and Victoria nine, in addition to the existing spare XMSs, for the 503, 506 and 507. The spread of allocations, rather than a more efficient concentration at one location, was dictated by the twin needs of spreading the benefits around as many garages as possible and avoiding making too many conductors redundant at any one garage.

Carving this network from the heart of the central London route system caused considerable upheaval with many long established through routes disappearing for all time. Other routes had their services substantially cut. Routes which lost inner London sections were the the 23, which was withdrawn between Aldgate and Marylebone (replaced by the 501 and 505), the 46 and 70 between Waterloo and Victoria via Lambeth Bridge (507) and the 76 (except during Monday to Friday peak hours) from Victoria to Waterloo via Westminster Bridge (503). Route 11 was also reduced substantially between Aldwych and Liverpool Street. The 46 also lost its outer end beyond Neasden, being replaced by a new 297 which ran from Willesden to Perivale, also replacing part of the 79/A. Although the 297 was being set up for one-man operation, it was RT operated by Alperton garage for the time being. Route 6A was withdrawn altogether (502/504) and the number was attached to a new Saturday service from Hackney Wick to Oxford Circus with a morning extension to Marylebone. Route 60 disappeared in a chain reaction to the introduction of route 505. It was covered between Cricklewood and Oxford Circus by a new RM operated 8B, which continued to Tottenham Court Road station, and between Cricklewood and Colindale by a peak hour extension of route 245 from West Hendon, to which point it had otherwise been cut back. The Stanmore end of the 245 was taken over by route 251, extended from Burnt Oak on Mondays to Saturdays.

One of the many through connections lost with the establishment of the Red Arrow network was the one supplied by route 46 across Victoria. RM 2162 had just emerged from Bressenden Place into Victoria Street when photographed a few years before the Waterloo end was lopped off.
Colin W. Routh

XMS 14 at Victoria on route 506 which replaced shortworkings on route 38 between Victoria and Piccadilly Circus. The Red Arrows carried white-on-blue blinds as they did not observe all stops and were regarded as express buses.
W.T. Cansick

The number 8B re-appeared on Mondays to Fridays in the first stage of Reshaping to replace the Cricklewood to Oxford Circus section of route 60, with an extension to Tottenham Court Road and Bloomsbury. Cricklewood's RM 174 was photographed in Edgware Road on 13th February 1969, while working the off-peak operation to Tottenham Court Road. Colin Stannard

Above **Envisaged as a forerunner to many new bus stations in the suburbs as interchange points under the Reshaping Plan, the one at Turnpike Lane is seen under construction. The bus station was ready in time for the first day of the Wood Green scheme, unlike the one at Walthamstow.**

Left **Construction of the new roof at Turnpike Lane station was nearing completion on 13th July 1968 when RT 724 was photographed displaying the intermediate point blind for the northern section which was to become route 298 in the Wood Green scheme. The additional loading islands and other trappings needed were yet to appear and the vertical bracket awaits the new route signs.** Mick Webber

Facing Page **Layout and artist's impression of a bus and Underground interchange station. Nowhere in the Reshaping report was it explained where the land was to come from for these projects, nor how they were to be funded. This proved to be a major weakness.**

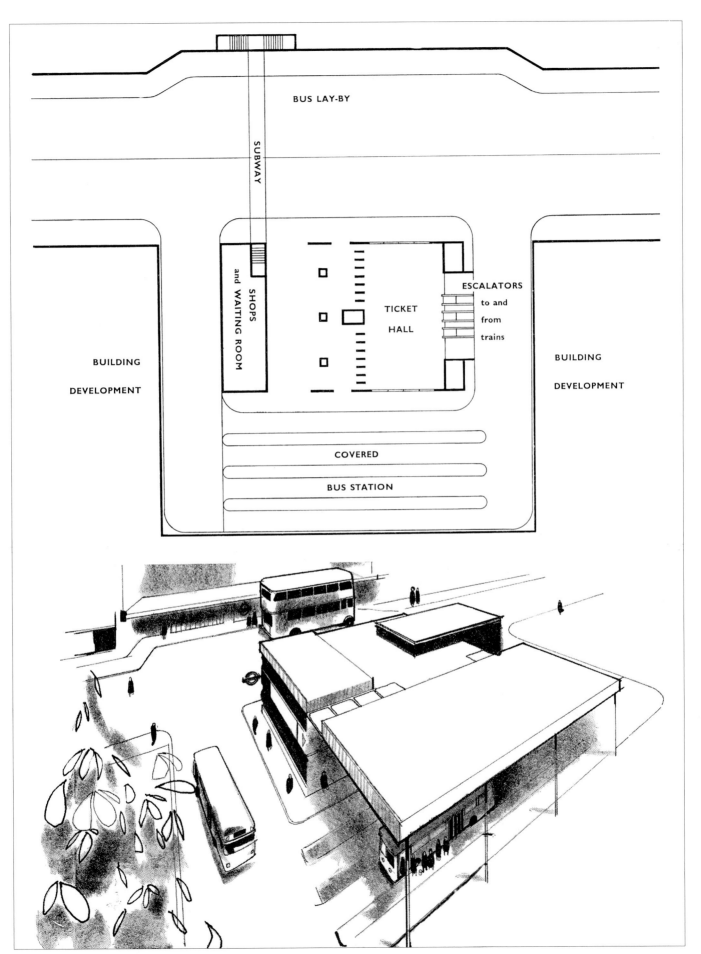

BUS LAY-BY

SUBWAY

SHOPS and WAITING ROOM

TICKET HALL

ESCALATORS to and from trains

BUILDING DEVELOPMENT

BUILDING DEVELOPMENT

COVERED

BUS STATION

The first of the projected 'satellite' schemes was introduced on this day at Wood Green, a year after it was supposed to have started as the pilot. There were four basic routes conforming exactly to those announced in March 1967 but these were joined by two Saturday only variants to bring the total to six. It had been decided that the flat fare routes would be numbered in local series using prefix letters to identify the area and those at Wood Green were numbered from W1 upwards. They were: W1 Edmonton 'Cambridge' – Turnpike Lane Station, extended Monday to Friday off-peak, Saturdays and Sundays to Wood Green; W2 Alexandra Park ('Victoria') – Turnpike Lane Station extended Monday to Friday off-peak, Saturdays and Sundays to Wood Green also extended express from Alexandra Park to Finsbury Park, Monday to Friday peak hours; W3 Finsbury Park Station to Northumberland Park Station (Mondays to Fridays and Sundays); W4 Winchmore Hill – Wood Green, extended to Turnpike Lane station except during Monday to Friday peak hours; W5 Finsbury Park – Alexandra Palace – Wood Green – Turnpike Lane, Saturdays only; W6 Northumberland Park – Wood Green – Turnpike Lane, Saturdays only. The W1 replaced shorts on the 144, 217 and 231, the W2 replaced the Turnpike Lane to Alexandra Park section of route 217 and 231 and the express service on the 212, the W3 was the 233 renumbered and the W4 replaced the 141 north of Wood Green. The W5 and W6 were Saturday variants of the W3 designed to take passengers to the heart of the shopping area, as were the off-peak extensions of the others. This noble idea soon crumbled to dust when the immense increase in the number of buses using the High Road caused severe congestion. The turning of buses in Wood Green garage also created problems and the extensions of the W1 and W2 were therefore withdrawn after only a week.

Trunk route 269 was withdrawn altogether and the 275 between Walthamstow and Enfield. They were replaced between Tottenham and Enfield Town by route 123 which was withdrawn from Manor House, diverted via Bruce Grove and Westbury Avenue and extended to Enfield. The original plan had been to extend the 275 shorts from Winchmore Hill to Enfield, so that it would have worked Woodford Bridge to Enfield at all times but this was changed in connection with the opening of the first section of the Victoria Line. The southern end of the 269 was covered as far as Palmers Green by an increased service on route 29 which was itself withdrawn north of Cockfosters on Mondays to Fridays and Southgate on Sundays. Route 29B was also withdrawn. To cover these various bits and pieces a new 298 was introduced on Mondays to Saturdays between Turnpike Lane and South Mimms, with journeys to Cranborne Road and Borehamwood, in readiness for its ultimate conversion to one-man operation. The 29A was renumbered 298A. Because of the increased frequency on route 29, the 127 was cut back from Victoria to Warren Street station and the 168A from Turnpike Lane to Finsbury Park station. A plan to split route 221 at Turnpike Lane, which would have involved changes to routes 17, 76, 168A and 259, was dropped in order to reduce the work load on the Schedules Office.

The first of the new interchange centres was opened at Turnpike Lane station from the same date. The fact that there was a large existing bus stand alongside the station, provided as an interchange facility when the Piccadilly Line was first extended north of Finsbury Park in 1932, probably weighed heavily in the choice of Wood Green for the pilot scheme. The layout drawings in the Reshaping booklet certainly bear a striking resemblance to Turnpike Lane. The bare open parking area had been laid out with loading platforms, which were narrow and proved to be a tight squeeze for waiting passengers, and a simple roof had been provided over the waiting area which was linked by new canopies to the station entrance. Ironically, the loading islands in Turnpike Lane which had direct links by subway to the Underground station, were removed as part of this project. Originally used by trams, they had been taken over in 1938 by the replacing buses which had continued to use them until the present time.

The scheme brought with it a number of new practices which had not been aired in the policy document and were a distinct liability for the users of the services. Having established the bus interchange, London Transport decided that there would be no bus stops at the kerbside within about a quarter of a mile, the idea being that people would make their way to the bus station. Unfortunately, many of these people were returning shoppers, laden with purchases, who had previously been able to board a bus near the shops. Then there was the fare structure. Passengers making short distance journeys were expected to use the flat fare routes, leaving the other services to longer distance travellers. To ensure that this happened, a minimum fare of 9d was applied during the evening peak on routes 29, 123, 298 and 298A between Wood Green and Palmers Green and a similar restriction imposed on routes 144, 217 and 231 as far as 'The Cambridge'. Another restriction was that Rover tickets could not be used on flat fare buses because this would have required the driver to freewheel the turnstile and the Commercial Department saw this as laying the system open to misuse. This did not matter too much where there were alternative routes, but users of such tickets on the former 233 and on the 217/231 between Turnpike Lane and Alexandra Park were now denied them. There was no reference to any of this in the otherwise good publicity leaflets and all these things helped to build up resentment.

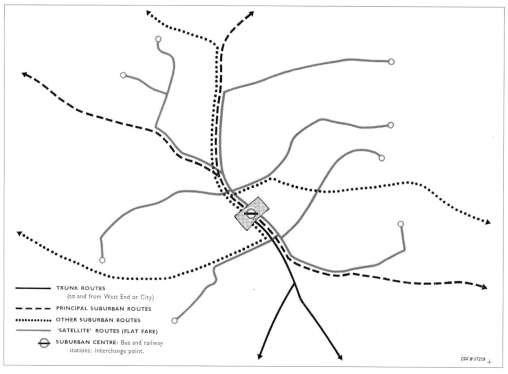

A diagram from the Reshaping booklet showing a typical pattern of route through a suburban centre as envisaged in the plan. Though not identified in the booklet, the map is clearly based on the Wood Green scheme.

TRUNK ROUTES
(to and from West End or City)
PRINCIPAL SUBURBAN ROUTES
OTHER SUBURBAN ROUTES
'SATELLITE' ROUTES (FLAT FARE)
SUBURBAN CENTRE: Bus and railway
stations: interchange point.

CDS-8-17219

THE NEW FLAT-FARE BUSES
How to use the machines

COIN IN HERE (6d or 3d bit)
COIN REJECT LEVER
ENTER SIGN
CHILDREN'S BUTTON

REJECTED COIN

ADULTS
1. Put in your 6d. bit. The driver can give you change.
2. There is no ticket. Just push through the gate when the ENTER sign on the machine lights up.

CHILDREN (Under 14 years of age)
1. First press the Children's Button.
2. Then put in your 3d. bit.
3. There is no ticket. Just push through the gate when the ENTER sign on the machine lights up.

DON'T press the coin reject lever unnecessarily. It will only return your coin - it will NOT open the gate.
DON'T put money in while the ENTER sign is lit.

Above left **MBS 80 on the first day of suburban flat-fare routes. Route W4 replaced the 141 north of Wood Green.** G.F.Walker

Above **This poster was displayed to help passengers understand the more complicated arrangements for paying at turnstiles on the MBS flat-fare buses. An audible signal sounded when the Children's button was pressed, alerting the driver who was supposed to check the authenticity of the client, but most found themselves engaged on more pressing duties most of the time.** L.T. Museum

Left **Saturday only W5 gave a service to the heart of the Wood Green shopping centre from the Finsbury Park end of the former 233 but proved transient. Along with its companion W6 it gave way to a restored through service on route W3 after 15th March 1969, on which day MBS 60 was photographed in Station Road, Wood Green after application of 'coin-in-the-slot' symbols.** A.B. Cross

There was nothing radical about route 298, which was one of the 'new' routes created for the Wood Green Reshaping scheme, as it was merely the long-established localised northern end of route 29 under a new number. RT 4011 is in Greyhound Lane, South Mimms, almost at the northernmost extremity of the route, Clare Hall Hospital. J.G.S. Smith

The driving force for the third big scheme which started on 7th September was the opening of the first section of the Victoria Line between Walthamstow Central and Highbury on the previous Sunday, 1st September. The network in this part of north-east London was completely restructured to supply feeder services and to reduce the extent of parallel running between bus and Underground but the service planners had few precedents to guide them on the effects of comprehensive integration on this scale. Major restructuring had never before taken place to coincide with the opening of a new line but comprehensive planning was fashionable in the 1960s and a large part of the financial case for the Victoria Line had been based on the assumption that passengers would transfer from bus to rail and that bus services would be reduced. Unlike pre-war and early post-war practice, when the service changes generally came after the passengers had changed their habits, in this case there was to be an element of coercion.

Although it might have seemed a classic case for a 'satellite' scheme, many feeder journeys to Walthamstow Central came from some distance away and were not suited to the economical application of a flat fare. Most of the new feeder routes therefore continued to have graduated fares and there was only one flat fare route, the W21. This was a circular operation through Wood Street, Highams Park, Chingford Mount and Chingford Road, replacing parts of routes 35, 35B and 257 and providing direct links from Highams Park and Wood Street to the Underground. It was an immensely complicated scheme and there was no case of a straight conversion to one-man operation, although three conventional OMO routes, operated by MB class fifty seaters, emerged. The 235 did not feed the Victoria Line but was an entirely new route which ran from Chingford Hatch to Chigwell Station, picking up parts of truncated or withdrawn routes 35, 35B, 236, 10 and 10A, and was allocated to Leyton garage. The rump of route 275 between Woodford

Top **Work in progress on the new bus station at Walthamstow Central on the day of the opening of the Victoria Line, 1st September 1968.** Capital Transport

Centre **The stand at Abridge was not suitable for the longer MB class, forcing the curtailment of the 235 at Chigwell and the creation of the lame duck 167A. A characteristically empty RT 1863 was frozen by the photographer in a landscape typical of the route which captured the essence of its lack of potential.** Colin Stannard

Right **Route 38A was a true relic of an earlier age, still thrusting out almost to the limits of Central Bus operation from Victoria to Loughton and was ripe for the localisation which came with Reshaping. RT10-bodied RTL 1475 is seen in August 1967 at Loughton station.**

Bridge and Walthamstow Central and the 276, which covered the northern end of the 278 from Walthamstow Central to Yardley Lane Estate, were the other two MB operated routes, both allocated to Walthamstow. Another new feeder was numbered 20 but was in effect the Loughton station to Leyton section of route 38A extended to Walthamstow Central, the rest of the 38A being absorbed into the 38. This restored a parent to routes 20A and 20B, which had been orphaned in 1966.

Routes 6B, 10A, 35B, 38A, 249, 249A, 257 were withdrawn completely and many others were shortened. The 35 was withdrawn between Shoreditch and Chingford and diverted via Hackney Road to Hackney station to cover that section of the 257, the 38 was withdrawn between Walthamstow garage and Chingford and diverted in Hackney to follow the 38A route via Graham Road instead of Hackney Downs, the 41 was withdrawn between Tottenham Hale and V&A Docks and the 210 and 236 between Leytonstone station and Leyton. The route of the former 35 through Dalston and Lea Bridge Road was covered by a new RT operated route 48 from London Bridge to Whipps Cross, the 38 and 249 north of Walthamstow and the 35/B north of Chingford Hatch by the extension of routes 69 and 191 respectively to Chingford station, the 41 east of Tottenham Hale and the Manor House section of the 123 by new 241 between Victoria & Albert Docks and Manor House. Route 10A was covered between Chigwell and Abridge by new RT operated route 167A which ran as a circular via Chigwell, Buckhurst Hill, Loughton and Debden. The seemingly more obvious idea of running the 235 further north could not be adopted because it was not possible to turn a one-man bus at Abridge. Finally, this was the day when the long-established stand at the 'Royal Forest Hotel' was abandoned, together with the intervening uninhabited grassy slopes of Epping Forest, and all routes cut back to Chingford Station, where a new stand had been created.

Top **The Loughton to Leyton section of route 38A was replaced on 7th September 1968 by new route 20 which continued to Walthamstow Central to connect with the new Underground service. RT 3783 is seen leaving Walthamstow a few weeks before MBs were introduced onto the route on 14th June 1969.** Colin Stannard

Right **Having been used in both the tram and trolleybus conversions for services that soon atrophied, the number 48 was attached to an important innovation in the first stage of Reshaping, giving it the chance to survive for at least thirty years. There was still evidence of the wartime bombing of London Bridge station when RT 2383 was photographed arriving from Walthamstow, long before the extensive new bus station was built.** Colin Stannard

MB 143 at the temporary Walthamstow Central terminus in Stainforth Road prior to completion of the new bus station. G.F. Walker

A new bus station was built alongside the entrance to Walthamstow Central station, in Selborne Road which had to be closed to general traffic. It was a simple arrangement of purpose built shelters alongside the kerb on the south side of the road. These were of an unusual design with wing-like overlapping sections of sloping roof extending in each direction from a central 'V'-shaped section which was surmounted by a combined London Transport/British Rail totem. The bus station was not ready on the first day and buses had to use a temporary stand in Stainforth Road for some time.

Below **The new bus stand at Chingford station opened for business with Reshaping when route 69 was extended from Chingford Mount to cover the 38 and 249, both of which were cut back to Walthamstow Central. This reunited the numbers 69 (RT 1828) and 179 (RT 1873) which had once shared the stand at Grove Park, until 1958 when that version of the 69 became 36B.** J.G.S. Smith

A careful study of the scheme shows that a great deal of ingenuity went into ensuring that many of the old established links were preserved, while honouring the principle of route shortening. For example, the 48 retained all the connections previously given by the 35 from London Bridge to Leyton, while also covering the Hackney Downs route of the 38 and the Clapton to Whipps Cross links of the 38A. The 35 in turn gave the old 257 connections between London Bridge and Hackney, leaving route 256 to provide those from Shoreditch and Hackney Road across to Walthamstow. Unfortunately, all its good points were engulfed in such a catastrophic start that they mostly went unremarked. Not only were the vehicles themselves in poor condition after their lengthy enforced hibernation but there were also all the problems which are intrinsic to a conversion to one-man operation. The drivers were faced with having to drive unfamiliar vehicles on subtly different routes and every one of them was new to the job of knowing the fares and issuing tickets. The passengers, accustomed to the relative tranquillity of travelling on a bus with a conductor, were now faced with having to have their money ready, in the correct coins for flat fare buses, with manipulating their belongings while they paid their fares and perhaps having to cope with an unfamiliar turnstile. The turnstiles had their own problems, sometimes jamming, sometimes refusing to accept the proffered coins and sometimes objecting to misuse by passengers. The extra length and width of the vehicles also increased their chances of being baulked by badly parked cars, particularly on corners. All these factors working together in a programme covering so many buses ensured disaster and the standard of service on that day, in Wood Green and on the Red Arrows as well as at Walthamstow, gave Reshaping a bad name from which it never recovered. It is easy to see in retrospect that it would have been wiser to phase the changes over a

longer period and London Transport certainly learnt that and many lessons from this baptism of fire but with the political and financial pressures which faced those making the decisions at the time, it is hardly surprising that they were anxious to make up for lost time.

Two new routes unconnected with the major schemes also started on 7th September, the more important being the first motor bus service for Hampstead village, MB operated route 268 (Golders Green – Finchley Road station, where it ran as a loop, so as to avoid having to allocate five minutes layover at both ends). An earlier plan to extend route 226 and convert the whole to MB had been abandoned in favour of a more local route. This was the culmination of a long fought campaign, first by Hampstead Council and latterly by Camden, for a service to the village. A proposal to extend route 2A from Swiss Cottage to Golders Green via Fitzjohns Avenue, which had been shown by surveys to be worthwhile, had reached an advanced stage some years

earlier but had run foul of objections to double-deckers in the village. Requests from the Potters Bar Public Transport Sub-Committee for a more local service were also the genesis of a new circular route 284 which linked Potters Bar station with Darkes Lane, High Street and Mutton Lane, using one RF. There were also three more OMO conversions which used RFs, routes 218 and 219 at Kingston and the Richmond to Hammersmith section of route 90C which was renumbered 290.

All the changes on 7th September together added thirty-two OMO RFs, thirty-four MBs, forty-nine MBAs and fifty-nine MBSs to the schedules in exchange for the withdrawal of 135 double-deckers and twenty-three TMO RFs. Many of the displaced buses were RMs and these were used to convert routes 29, 35 and 171, removing RTs from Tottenham garage in the process. The buses ultimately withdrawn were RTLs and they disappeared completely from Bow, Hackney, Poplar and West Ham garages.

Above **Route 268 was part of the public's share in the savings from single-manning and introduced motor buses to Hampstead village for the first time. It was an immediate success. MB 145 was photographed at Golders Green on the first day.** G.F. Walker

Left **Route 90C, captured in this 1964 view of RT 2833 in Butterwick, Hammersmith, had been a Sunday only variant which covered the Richmond to Hammersmith section of the 71. A Monday to Saturday service was introduced over this section from 11th November 1967 in preparation for its conversion to RF OMO as route 290 in the September 1968 programme. Ironically, the Sunday operation continued but under the number 90A to Yeading.** A.B. Cross

Route 82 had the rare distinction of crossing over itself three times where Brunel Road and Rotherhithe Street passed above Rotherhithe Tunnel, but this feature was lost after 25th October 1968 when the route ran for the last time. Lights aglow in the gloom and demonstrating by its emptiness why route 82 would soon disappear, RTL 1613 has just come under the river through Rotherhithe Tunnel whose distinctive arch can be seen to the left of the flats.
A.B. Cross

The busy part of route 82 was replaced by flat-fare routes P1 and P2, each working one way around the Rotherhithe loop and also covering route 202. MBS 253, one of ten allocated to New Cross, is at the stop for Surrey Docks station in Redriff Road, alongside the immensely capacious wooden queue shelter which bore testimony to the importance of both the docks and route 82 as a means of access to them in days gone by.
P.J. Relf

The first major change in south-east London took place on 26th October and included no flat-fare routes. As things turned out, this was to be the typical pattern in the south, where no comprehensive flat-fare networks were destined to be introduced. MBs were used for route 21A, which was withdrawn from Sidcup station, where there were no facilities for turning 36ft buses, and extended to Well Hall via New Eltham regaining a section lost only as recently as June, the loss of the cross-Sidcup links having aroused considerable opposition. MBs were also used for the 126, whose conversion was not so straightforward. The Traffic Commissioner had refused permission for thirty-six footers to operate from Riefield Road into Lingfield Crescent, Falconwood, on the Sunday only extension to Welling and this section was therefore exchanged with the 160A via

Eltham Park and Rochester Way. It was also extended to Bexleyheath, so that drivers could have access to the amenities at the garage, to improve the efficiency of the time and duty schedules and to enable train connections to be given at Beckenham Junction, Bromley South and Welling. The 126 was to have been converted earlier, using RFs, but the consequential increase in buses would have required the removal of fourteen buses from Bromley garage and it had to wait until extra parking space could be laid out on the other side of Lower Gravel Road.

The main scheme in this area was concerned with the modifications which were being made to the old Blackwall Tunnel now that the new bore was in operation. To ease the sharp bends and widen the effective carriageway, the roadway was lifted to a level which would prevent the operation of double-

deck buses when it re-opened. The 108/228 groups of routes were therefore remodelled so that a much shortened 108 could be one-man operated using MBs. The 108 became Bromley-By-Bow to Blackheath 'Royal Standard', the 108B became the daily route between Crystal Palace and Blackheath, with peak journeys to Blackwall Tunnel, and the Surrey Docks to Eltham service was covered by a modified 108A, which no longer went through the tunnel. The 228 was cut back to Well Hall and the 228A was withdrawn. Eleven MBs were allocated to Sidcup, thirteen to Bromley and nine to Poplar.

The other Thames tunnel at Rotherhithe was unsuitable for any type of modern bus because it was restricted to vehicles no more than 7ft 6ins in width and therefore lost its service altogether from 26th October. The freehold section of route 82 south of the river,

The loss of RTLs from Cricklewood and Stonebridge garages, in the wake of the schedule changes on 26th October 1968, removed their distinctive roar from the North Circular Road symphony in which RTL 1433 is participating.

Although given priority over the AECs for early withdrawal, the RTL class nevertheless completed nearly twenty years of service in London, before being phased out once and for all on 29th November 1968. All were at Willesden on routes 176 and 226. There were thirteen Leylands still licensed on the last day, including RTL 1526, seen here in Willesden Lane on route 176. The very last RTL (543) ran on this route. Colin Stannard

along Rotherhithe Street, was incorporated into one of two new flat-fare routes which also replaced RF-operated route 202. The P1 was a direct replacement of the 202 from New Cross and the P2 covered the 82 from St Mary Church Street, both continuing from Surrey Docks to the Bermondsey loop, the P1 anti-clockwise and the P2 clockwise. As this was not a true satellite scheme, it had been the sensible intention to retain the number 202 for the unchanged route and use 202A for the replacement of route 82. Such continuity would have helped passengers to come to terms with the changes more easily but unfortunately it was decreed instead that flat fare buses should have a clear identity which differentiated them from ordinary services. New Cross garage was allocated ten MBSs for the two routes.

Twenty-six double-deck and seven TMO RF

runnings were dropped from the schedules as a result of the complete programme, replaced by seven MBSs and twenty-eight MBs. The heavy loss of work from Poplar to south London garages was compensated by the re-allocation of route 40 from West Ham. It was now the turn of Cricklewood and Stonebridge to lose their RTLs, leaving a mere twenty of the class to continue operating on routes 176 and 226 from Willesden garage for one more month until the next stage of Reshaping made them redundant also. The last of London's Leyland RTs ran on 29th November 1968 and it fell to RTL 543 to fulfil that solemn task, just a couple of days short of twenty years since the first production examples had gone into service at Sidcup.

Squeezed between this helter skelter activity by Central Buses, the Country Bus department at last made a start on its version

of Reshaping on 23rd November, which was also the day on which the first conversions of Green Line routes to one-man operation took place. Routes 305 and 305A were converted to one-man operation using the forty-five seat two door version of the MB which was peculiar to Country Buses. The services to West Wy-combe, Horn Hill and Woburn Common were all withdrawn and the main road service on route 455 reduced to a few morning peak journeys, also operated by MBs. The Penn to Beaconsfield section of route 363 was restored to a separate existence under its old number 373 and converted to MB. Amersham needed a mere two and High Wycombe six MBs for this, which included some journeys on the 362/A and the Sunday service on route 353. At Reigate the first Autofare buses were introduced on route 430 on this day, six MBSs being allocated for the purpose.

Route 65A was an amalgamation of the Sunday service on route 265 with shorts on the 65 in October 1963. It became daily as part of the welter of changes associated with the five day week from 31st December 1966 and disappeared again in the Ealing flat-fare scheme of November 1968. RT 2381, seen here at Richmond station on a quiet Sunday afternoon, carries an RT10 body. Ron Wellings

The changes instituted on 30th November included the second of the comprehensive satellite schemes, which also proved to be the last in anything like the form envisaged by the original plan. Five of Ealing's principal local routes were shortened or split to create a small network of three flat-fare routes but significantly, there was no central terminal point and no specially built interchange. In fact the only places where all three routes came together were West Ealing and Greenford. Route E1 replaced route 83 and the peak hour extension of route 255 between Brentford (Half Acre) and Hanwell, then continued via Ealing Broadway to pick up the route of the 211 as far as Greenford. The E2 ran between the same outer terminals and was simply the 97 renumbered, while the E3 was the Chiswick to Greenford section of route 55 renumbered. Two new RT operated local routes were set up in readiness for eventual conversion to one-man operation, one of which covered some new ground and represented the passengers' share of the redeployed savings. Route 273 ran from Ealing Broadway to Ruislip, covering the 65 as far as Argyle Road and then the 97 and 211, while the 274 opened up yet another route between Ealing Broadway and Greenford, bringing buses for the first time to the full length of Argyle Road and to Drayton Green Road. It continued beyond Greenford to Hayes (Bourne Avenue) to cover the part of route 55 omitted from the E3. Hanwell garage operated on all three flat-fare routes and was allocated thirty-six MBSs, while Turnham Green received thirteen for its share of route E3.

Other changes in the same area, not directly connected with the flat-fare scheme, included splitting route 232 to give two shorter routes, five and a half years after being joined together. The 232 was replaced north of Yeading (Northolt in peak hours) by a new conventional OMO route 282 from Mount Vernon Hospital/Northwood to Yeading, where it diverged to run to Greenford. This had not been its intended southern terminus, which was to have been at Southall Town Hall, giving a rather better overlap with the 232, but the Traffic Commissioner would not give route approval. The option of making a straight conversion of the whole 232 instead, was considered but rejected because it would have left the route longer than was desirable. Fourteen MBs were allocated to Southall. As well as losing its Ealing Broadway to Argyle Road section outside peak hours, the 65 was withdrawn between Chessington Zoo and Leatherhead and intermediately diverted via Copt Gilders, absorbing the 65A. The Leatherhead service was covered by extending route 71 from Kingston on Mondays to Saturdays and introducing it on Sundays between Kingston and Leatherhead. Both remained RT operated at this stage.

A London Co-operative Society self-service shop, long since superseded by a Multi-Bite pizza and burger bar, and a convertible Morris Minor parked outside, provide a suitable period background to RT 4022 turning onto the stand at Bourne Avenue, Hayes, recently ceded to the 274 by route 55. Designed for eventual conversion to one-man operation, the 274 opened up new territory in Argyle Road and Drayton Green Road as well as replacing the western end of route 55 in the Ealing flat-fare scheme of 30th November 1968. J.H. Blake

The northern and southern ends of route 232 which had been joined as recently as 1963 were severed again in the Ealing scheme, the northern end being covered by route 282 on which MB 331 is seen at Yeading. J.G.S. Smith

There were two other isolated conversions on 30th November, both to conventional one-man operation using MBs. Route 143 shed the Archway to Farringdon Street projection which it had acquired in the trolleybus conversion, to revert to its former terminals at Hendon Central and Archway. Between East Finchley and Archway Road it exchanged routeings with the 17, to avoid the awkward corners on the route via The Bishops Avenue. To cover the section south of Archway extra buses were operated on route 17, and route 168A was diverted via Farringdon Road instead of Grays Inn Road. Further north, the conversion of route 242 was complicated by the need to withdraw the Sunday only 242A and switch the southern terminus of the 205 from Chingford to Upshire, but it did provide the scope in the rota for route 284 to be introduced on Saturdays. Highgate garage was allocated thirteen MBs and Potters Bar sixteen, one of which was used to replace the RF on the 284.

Altogether on 30th November, forty-four MBSs and thirty-eight MBs were added to the peak vehicle requirement and the double-deck schedule was reduced by seventy. The Routemasters displaced from the 55 and 143 went to Abbey Wood and Catford to replace RTs on the busy 180, followed by Hackney and Poplar for the 106. The last of the RTLs having been cleared out, it was now the turn of RTs to be withdrawn and the choice fell on those without saloon heaters.

The bruising early experiences with Reshaping were reviewed by the Board on 18th December and a committee was set up, comprising the Vice Chairman (Anthony Bull), Ralph Bennett and Ken Shave, with a remit to carry out a thorough review and make recommendations as to the further implementation of the plan. They had to consider the extreme unpopularity of standee buses in the suburbs, particularly among old people and those with young children or laden with shopping. To give some alleviation to their plight

it was quickly decided to fit some seats in the front part of these buses. Peak hour users had also suffered from the severe loss of regularity which accompanied the introduction of OMO buses, as so graphically experienced on 7th September, and seventy-two per cent of all complaints were concerned with this. Another matter which was becoming an increasing problem was the difficulty in obtaining route approval for 36ft-long vehicles in many places. They eventually reported on 29th July 1969 that there was less scope for flat-fare operation than had been thought and recommended scaling down the intake of flat-fare buses in favour of the new concept of 'split-entrance' operation. By releasing extra passenger space, this layout made it possible to switch to the shorter, 33ft 6in version of the Swift without loss of capacity.

Route 143's brief flirtation with central London came to an end on 30th November with the introduction of MBs between Archway and Hendon Central. A different kind of one-man operation was being celebrated during the preceding summer, when the yacht 'Lively Lady', in which Sir Alec Rose had sailed around the world single-handed, was on display at Holborn Circus, as RM 1120, destination already set for its next trip, made its way to Shoe Lane to reach the stand at Stonecutter Street. A.B. Cross

The largely rural 242 route was an obvious early candidate for one-man operation under the Reshaping Plan. MB 354 is seen at Northaw. Capital Transport

The first changes of 1969 were made by Country Buses in a large programme on 15th February. Thirty-five 'Autofare' MBSs went into service, eleven at Two Waters garage for Hemel Hempstead town services 314/A/B/C and 344, a similar number to St Albans for routes 325, 354, 391 and 391A, ten to Garston for routes 346/A/B and three to Hatfield for Welwyn Garden City town service 324. Hatfield also received five MBs for conventional one-man operation on routes 315, 340, 340A and 340B, a surprising choice in the case of the 340 group operations in the New Towns, and Garston six for routes 318 and 335. Half the buses allocated to routes 318 and the 340 group continued to be RTs and a similar mixture of two-man and one-man operation had already been applied at Amersham and High Wycombe. This could never have been done in the Central Area where even the use of the officially allocated type of bus was rigorously enforced, let alone mixing the two types of operation on one route. This was expressly outlawed by the schedules agreement and was to lead to many a twist and turn to make the

route pattern fit the restriction. RFs displaced from Two Waters and St Albans were found new work at Dunton Green and Dartford where routes 402 and 486 changed over to one-man operation and at Garston where one replaced the GS on route 309. This left only two GSs scheduled for service, one each at Northfleet (route 451) and Garston (336A), of which only the latter was left by the end of the year. There was also a significant spread of Sunday only one-man operation by the use of RFs on eight routes.

Country Buses had a rather smoother run than Central Buses with their conversions and had even escaped censure on the use of the coarsened fare scale on the 'Autofare' buses, but their luck ran out at Hemel Hempstead. The loss of the 9d fare was keenly felt in that town and objections were lodged with the Traffic Commissioner who eventually ruled that the 9d rate should be re-instated, which London Transport did from 20th July. As the ticket machines issued either 6d or 3d tickets, passengers were obliged either to visit both machines for one transaction or take three 3d

tickets. This resistance was not repeated elsewhere but it was in any case a transitory victory as the whole fare scale went into 6d steps at the end of the year.

Twenty more MBSs and four MBs went into service with Country Buses from 15th March, the new 'Autofare' operations being on routes 400, the 446 group and the 484 group from Windsor garage (eleven) and on the 495 and 496 from Northfleet (nine). Crawley took three MBs for the otherwise RF operated 434/473, to pay for their extension from Crawley to Horsham in place of route 405, and Dorking took one for route 449. The last MB family buses used in a Country Bus conversion went to Harlow which was allocated six 'Autofare' MBSs for routes 804/A/B from 22nd March. The two remaining conversions made use of surplus RFs, starting with route 468 from Leatherhead garage on 14th June. London Transport's very last Country Area conversion took place at Grays on 4th October, when nine RFs replaced the same number of RTs on the much eroded 371 group.

Unlike the upheavals of Central Bus Reshaping, most Country Bus conversions to one-man operation took place on the existing routes. The big programme on 15th February 1969 included putting MBs onto part of route 318, although the use of MB 105 on the Abbots Langley to Watford section seems a rather quixotic choice since this was probably the busiest part of the service. Roy Marshall

When route 434 was extended from Crawley to Horsham on 15th March 1969, to recover possession of the section which route 405 had appropriated twelve years earlier, three MBs were allocated to Crawley to bolster the RFs already on the route. Red MBS 379 is seen on the first day. A.B. Cross

Central Buses had resumed their activities on 22nd March with a further assault on the network in the Morden area, in which the RF class figured prominently. They were used for the single-manning of the outer ends of routes 80 and 80A which were simultaneously restored to their pre-1939 terminal at Morden, although running via Collingwood Road and Sutton Common Road rather than St Helier. The northern end between Belmont and Tooting continued as a two-man operated route but was given the new number 280, leaving the established numbers to the altered rumps. The routes were to have terminated at Sutton garage as originally planned but this was found to be too expensive because it would have created too high a proportion of Saturday work to fit the rota. The solution was to extend them to Morden over the 213A, the section onwards to Wimbledon not being replaced. On Sundays, the 213A was diverted to Belmont and the 213 was withdrawn. Morden was also the focus of a new flat-fare route M1, which combined the Raynes Park to Morden section of the 118 with the Hackbridge end of route 151, both routes being cut back to Morden. Twelve RFs were allocated to Sutton for the 80/A, its first for over seven years, and ten MBSs to Merton for the M1.

On the same day as the Morden area changes, there was another major casualty of the continuing shrinkage in the size of the fleet. Rye Lane garage at Peckham, which had opened only seventeen years earlier to house tram replacement buses on the Grove Park routes, was closed. Its work transferred to Camberwell (route 13) and Peckham (12, 36A and 36B), with route 188 moving from Peckham to Camberwell as part of the re-shuffle.

Above **Routes 80 and 80A returned to Morden after a thirty year absence, albeit by a different route which brought them past Morden South station, the scene of this view of RF 439.** Colin Stannard

Left **The main Belmont to Tooting section of routes 80/A was retained as a double-deck route when the outer ends were converted to OMO but absurdly renumbered 280. The name Amen Corner, not seen since the withdrawal of trams in 1951, makes an interesting come-back on the blind of RT 345 seen at Belmont (California) terminus.** Colin Stannard

Rye Lane garage, a structure only eighteen years old, closed after traffic on 21st March 1969, finally capitulating to the surplus of garage space which had existed in south east London for many years. RM 1386 was photographed in Vauxhall Bridge Road during the previous summer. D.D. Kirk

A major flat-fare scheme had been planned for introduction in the Croydon area on 22nd March but had to be deferred because the Traffic Commissioner would not grant route approval. His objections concerned: the turn from Portland Road into Doyle Road, Norwood Junction; obstruction caused by parked cars in Zion Road and Zion Place, Thornton Heath; the turns into and out of Dingwall Road; and the islands on Spurgeon's Bridge, Croydon. This was a good example of the sorts of problems encountered when London Transport tried to introduce 36ft-long buses into old road networks. The belief at the time was that the necessary road works to remedy the first two problems could be completed in time for routes C1 and C2 to start in June but that the C3 would have to wait until the autumn, when a new roundabout at Spurgeon's Bridge was due to be ready. Unfortunately, there was a dispute with the local authority about who should pay for some of the work and, in the event this scheme died in the womb. Croydon was spared the MBS, and the flat-fare buses which eventually arrived in the town in April 1970 were double-deck Atlanteans on entirely different routes. Instead of a fleet of MBSs, Croydon's contribution to Reshaping at this stage was reduced to the use of a single OMO RF to inaugurate Roundshaw Estate's first bus service on 31st May. Numbered 233, it ran to West Croydon bus station and included an unusual non-stop section from Stafford Road/Mollison Drive to West Croydon, eventually using the new flyover.

Meanwhile, an addition had been made to the list of Central Bus flat-fare routes with the straight substitution of MBSs for RTs on route 212 (renumbered W7) from 10th May. From the same day Bromley's MB fleet expanded by eight for the conversion of route 138.

Some changes were made to the Red Arrow network on 14th June, notably in response to the high operating costs and poor use being made of route 505. The service to Marylebone station was transferred to a new route 508 which ran in a loop from Oxford Street via Piccadilly Circus, Cambridge Circus and Charing Cross Road, in the hope of drumming up some fresh trade in the West End. The idea of a loop working had been inspired by the success of the one on route 506 and the intention had been to introduce one on route 505 also, using Portman Street, Portman Square and Orchard Street but this was not approved. Instead, the 505 was altered to run all day (except evenings) between Waterloo and Marble Arch. The terminal working for routes 503 and 507 at Waterloo was also improved by their use of the taxi road for inward journeys and for their main picking up point, instead of York Road, and this too became a loop working.

The 508 proved to be another flop and ran for only four months, its last day being 24th October. The Red Arrow drivers were in a special grade for which no other work existed at Walworth garage, and the buses were of a unique design which could be used only on Red Arrow services, so London Transport was faced with having to find employment for the displaced staff and buses. They did so by creating another new route, 509, which ran

The first important modification to the inaugural Red Arrow network was the division of route 505 into two, creating a new 508 whose main selling point was a big loop around the West End. MBA 176 has just left the northern terminus, Marylebone station and has completed the wide sweep out of Harewood Avenue to make this angled approach to the stop outside the Great Central Hotel. E. Shirras

from Victoria to the South Kensington museums fast to Sloane Square via Kings Road and Sloane Street, then in a one-way loop via Knightsbridge, Royal Albert Hall, Queens Gate, Cromwell Road and Brompton Road back to Victoria. The hope was that it would encourage new shopping and museum traffic, as well as catering for the heavy peak hour movement between Victoria and Knightsbridge. What was left of route 46 was withdrawn, the intermediate routeing between Notting Hill Gate and Kensal Rise via Westbourne Park and Harrow Road being lost for good. The service level north of the Royal Albert Hall was maintained by localising the Mill Hill service on route 52 to start from Palace Gate, thereby providing extra buses between there and Willesden.

With the failure of the 508 after only four months, the buses and drivers were given new employment on route 509 which served the heavy Victoria to Knightsbridge peak demand, before continuing in a loop around the South Kensington museums. MBA 600, one of the conversions from MBS, approaches Victoria in Buckingham Palace Road. Colin Stannard

There were only five more conversions using the MB type, all during 1969. Route 20 changed over on 14th June, using MBs from Loughton garage, and was extended to Epping in place of the relatively new 20B. Similar changeovers followed on 21st July (route 297 from Alperton garage on Mondays to Fridays only until 25th October when the Saturday service followed suit) and 23rd August (route 84 from Potters Bar and 122A, Plumstead). The 84 was cut back to work only between New Barnet and St Albans, its Arnos Grove end being covered by route 34 which was removed from the section via Lyonsdown Road to New Barnet and diverted via Great North Road to Barnet Church. Lyonsdown Road was covered by the 260, which was withdrawn from Barnet Church and diverted to New Barnet station, with a Sunday extension to Chesterfield Road in place of the 134A, which was otherwise re-placed by extra 134s. On conversion, the 122A lost its Sunday extension from Woolwich to Crystal Palace. The very last Central Bus MB conversion was on 25th October, at Alperton garage on routes 79/A, which had two altera-tions to accommodate the longer buses. At Colindale the 79 now turned at the round-about in Colindale Avenue, while on journeys to Northolt the route through Perivale be-came one-way, because of obstruction caused by parked cars. In order to balance the roster at Alperton, it was necessary to introduce route 297 on Saturdays and to create some Sunday OMO work. This was done by split-ting route 83 to run from Golders Green to Alperton using RMs, and Wembley (Empire Pool) to Ealing Broadway, renumbered 83A, using MBs. By this time 158 of the class were scheduled for operation on Mondays to Fri-days. Two routes which should have got MBs, but never did, were the 217 and 217A. These should have been included in the October 1969 programme but had to be dropped when the turn from Sewardstone Road into Farm Hill Road was found to be unsuitable.

The programme of 14th June also saw the introduction of three more flat-fare routes, none of them part of a network. At Harrow, plans for a system of three or four routes radiating from the Met station were held over to await the 'split-entrance' era but the straight changeover of route 230, renumbered H1, did take place, enabling the withdrawal of the first Central Bus RLHs. The other two were also direct switches, Enfield's 128 be-coming the W8 and West Ham's 272 the S1. Twenty-six MBSs were needed, seven at En-field, nine at Harrow Weald and ten at West Ham. Only two more of this type of route were to be introduced using MBSs, neither of them during 1969, and London Transport was to be left with a rag-bag of isolated flat-fare operations until the revolutionary changes of the early 1980s brought them in from the cold.

The changes surrounding the conversion of route 84 caused the disappearance of Sunday route 134A, a product of the upheavals which followed the 1958 bus strike. RT 3717 works a rare short·at the 'Black Bull', Whetstone in September 1962.
Peter G Mitchell

In the days before hell broke loose with the arrival of crush loading single-deckers on the W8, RT 357 went about its business in Silver Street, Enfield with serenity.
Colin Stannard

When routes 79/A were converted on 25th October 1969 it was necessary to find some Sunday OMO work for the roster, this being done by creating a new Sunday route 83A between Wembley and Ealing and cutting the 83 back to Alperton. MB 655 is seen at the Empire Pool, Wembley. E. Shirras

The quieter section of route 111 south of Hanworth was replaced by new route 211 in August 1969 when the 'split-entrance' experiment was introduced, but unlike its 'high tech' progenitor with its brand new Swifts, it was operated conventionally with a driver issuing tickets, and the rolling stock comprised seventeen year old Regal IVs. An RM on route 33 follows RF 392 down Hounslow High Street as it heads for the Monday to Friday terminus at Hampton station.
Jim Blake

Introduced with a flat fare of one shilling, Airport Express route A1 provided a fast link between Hounslow West station and Heathrow Airport pending the extension of the Piccadilly Line. MBS 569 leaves the forecourt of Hounslow West station. J.G.S.Smith

The successor to the flat fares concept was tried out for the first time at Hounslow on 23rd August 1969 when ten MBSs fitted with 'split-entrance' equipment were put into service on routes 110 and 111 amidst a huge burst of publicity. Immense efforts were made to 'educate' passengers through detailed instructions in leaflets and on notices posted at stops and on the buses about how to use the machines. Inspectors were put on the buses in the early days of operation to give help and guidance and there was also further help on the machine where an elaborate display showed the fare payable to up to fifteen fare stages. This need for 'education' demonstrated only too clearly the weakness of the system. For as long as it was possible to buy a ticket and get change from the driver, the vast majority of passengers steered clear of the perils of the machinery, forcing London Transport to spend years of management, supervisory and planning effort in a futile attempt to persuade them otherwise. The machines soon revealed their unhappy propensity to fail in service, often placing users in embarrassing situations which discouraged them from trying again. Nevertheless, the system was to play a crucial rôle in persuading staff to accept one-man

operation of high capacity vehicles, including double-deckers, and for this reason, if no other, was destined to become the standard arrangement for more than a decade. The route pattern of the 110 and 111 was simplified as part of the experiment, the section of the 111 south of Hanworth being hived off into a new Monday to Saturday RF OMO route 211 between Hounslow and Hampton (extended on Saturdays to Kingston).

In the same group of changes, employment was found for a few more of the spurned MBSs on a new express service between Hounslow West and Heathrow Airport Central, which was introduced following a direction from the Board, an extremely rare event. Numbered A1, it was intended as a kind of 'pre-Metro' providing a fast link from the Underground to the airport until the Piccadilly Line could be extended. A flat fare of one shilling was charged to both adults and children and, apart from the modifications to the coin acceptors, the buses were standard MBSs with turnstiles. To keep the operation within the definition of a stage carriage there had to be a fare below one shilling and this was rather cheekily provided on garage runs between Hounslow West and Hounslow. Route 81A and the extension of route 91 on

Mondays to Fridays from Hounslow West to Heathrow were withdrawn and the Sunday services on routes 81 and 117 were brought into line with the Monday to Saturday pattern. The A1 had taken a long time to get into operation as it was first proposed early in 1968 as a double-deck operation using XAs, but this was held up by the continuing productivity negotiations. There was a fall-back plan to use RMs temporarily from 27th April 1968 but this was never implemented and by the time double-deck OMO had been agreed, there had been a change of heart.

The opening of the third stage of the Victoria Line from Warren Street to Victoria on 7th March 1969 should have been accompanied by another round of the economies, amounting to the withdrawal of 120,000 miles a year, which were an essential part of the financial case for the line. Following experience of the September 1968 changes, these had been deferred so that the changes in travel patterns and levels of demand could be studied. However, when reviewing current financial performance at its meeting on 24th June, the Board pointed out that the economies were part of the budget and called for the process to be accelerated so that economies could be made as soon as possible.

The Oxford Street to Marylebone section of route 508 was the first to be converted back from one-man to two-man operation when that route was withdrawn after 24th October 1969. It was incorporated into new route 55, which came all the way from Walthamstow Central, covering various bits and pieces of routes 38, 170 and 256. RT 1828 passes the 'Baker's Arms', Leyton on a sunny November day, shortly after the route started. J.G.S. Smith

The first Central Area lowbridge buses to yield to the single-decker were the RLHs at Harrow Weald working on route 230, which became the H1. MBS 504 is seen at North Harrow. J.G.S. Smith

The first stage of the alterations, which concentrated on the Walthamstow – Hackney – central London corridor, came into operation on 25th October 1969. Route 38, which linked both extremities of the line, was again shortened and simultaneously localised to run Victoria – Clapton/Bloomsbury – Leyton Green. Its outer end was covered by a new RT operated route 55 which ran between Walthamstow Garage and Bloomsbury, with a Monday to Friday extension to Marylebone to replace the 508 Red Arrow (mentioned earlier in connection with the introduction of route 509). It also replaced parts of routes 170, which was cut back from Leyton to Shoreditch and withdrawn in the evenings, and 256, cut back from Moorgate to Hackney. The Newham scheme introduced on the same day made its contribution by including substantial reductions on routes 10, which were somewhat irrelevant, and 25, including its withdrawal between Victoria and Oxford Circus in the evenings and on Saturdays and Sundays. The latter was partly compensated by the introduction of Red Arrow 500 at weekends on its off-peak routeing. The second and more drastic stage did not take place until the following January.

This final major programme for the year, which included further weekend cuts and withdrawals, removed another thirty-nine RTs from Central Buses' peak vehicle requirement, bringing the total for the year to 197. In the Country Area the reduction was 110, eighteen of which had been replaced by redundant RMCs (see chapter five). During the full year the number of RTs licensed for service in the whole fleet diminished by 280, the vehicles withdrawn from passenger service being those not fitted with saloon heaters, which included a considerable number of the remaining roofbox bodies of both RT10 and Saunders types. The fourteen RTs made surplus at Grays on 4th October were transferred to the staff bus fleet to start the final removal of RTLs. A similar move was started on 1st November when a start was made on eliminating the RTWs from the training fleet. The twenty-four green RTs on staff duties were transferred officially to Central Bus stock on 19th November in readiness for the change of ownership of the green fleet to the National Bus Company on 1st January 1970.

London Transport entered the field of double-deck one-man operation in a very timid fashion on 22nd November 1969, when the RF on route 233 was replaced by an Atlantean. XAs should also have started on route P3 (173 renumbered) on the same day but the schedules were deferred until the New Year. A week later, RF operated route 136 was extended on Mondays to Fridays from Harrow station to Harrow Weald garage to give a bus service for the first time to Harrow View and Courtenay Avenue, both originally earmarked for flat fare route H3. This had been made possible by the recent completion of a bridge over the London Midland main line, linking the two roads. Taken together, these two events mark a fitting close to the only full year of Reshaping, as London Transport prepared to move away from the wholesale use of high capacity standee single-deckers back to double-deckers, having already abandoned the concept of flat-fare satellite networks. Apart from the principle of single-manning, little was left of the original plan, but a great deal had been achieved in a remarkably short time. Had the pilot scheme at Wood Green gone into operation in 1967, as originally intended, there would have been an extra year for assessment and more tranquil reflection, and the story may then have had a very different ending.

CHAPTER TWELVE

POSTLUDE

The 1960s had been a troubled time for London Transport, with an unrelentingly disputatious staff, ever worsening traffic conditions and the drift of passengers away from public transport turning into a veritable torrent, enough one would think to justify the full-time attention of its senior management. Yet, the undertaking was subjected to unprecedented political scrutiny and two major reorganisations during that ten year period, the second and more fundamental of which occupied much of the time and energy of the Chairman, several members of the Board, Chief Officers and their supporting staffs during the second half of the decade. The first hint of a possible move in the direction of local government control came in the report of the Royal Commission on Local Government in 1961. Although the Commission had not been asked to review transport, it nevertheless suggested that some machinery was needed which would enable roads, railways and buses to be reviewed together on a comparable basis. The example quoted was a comparison of the costs and benefits of a new tube line with those of a new road. The machinery which then existed was steered by the Ministry of Transport, through its London

Transport Commission, but this was little more than an advisory body and the Royal Commission suggested that this could be accomplished more effectively through the agency of the proposed Greater London Council. No action was taken on this proposal in the 1962 Act which set up the London Transport Board.

The election of a Labour government in October 1964 and the concurrent creation of the Greater London Council, whose boundaries included most of the Central Bus operating area, gave new stimulus to the idea of co-operation. Following preliminary negotiations with the Board, the Minister announced on 25th June 1965 that the Board had been asked to set up a joint working party with the GLC to consider what traffic management measures and traffic restraint were needed to improve the attractiveness of bus services. This resulted in the measures described in chapter eight, including the introduction of bus lanes. Meanwhile the Select Committee on Nationalised Industries had been examining London Transport and issued its report on 2nd September 1965. It was a reasonably favourable report which reached the conclusion that London Transport could,

in time, provide an efficient, economic and adequate service, provided it was allowed to invest in modern automated equipment to facilitate one-man operation, that staff relations were improved and that buses were given some measure of priority.

Above **London Transport in transition. One of the places where Reshaping made its biggest initial impact was Victoria, where this aerial view shows the number of MBAs almost matching the total of double-deckers, six compared with the two RTs and five Routemasters. Also new to the scene, in the bottom left of the photograph, were the two entrances to the Victoria Line ticket hall, which opened in March 1969, but the overall canopy had to await the largesse of the Greater London Council, from whom it was a greeting present.** LT Museum

Right **One of the perversities of Reshaping was that Central Buses were tackling some heavily used central London routes while Country Buses continued to operate RTs on less intensely busy services. Potters Bar's MB 355 rubs shoulders with St Albans's RT 3117 on 2nd November 1969, just over two months after route 84 lost its own RTs and two months before Country Buses were transferred to London Country Bus Services.** N. Rayfield

This all culminated in a policy statement by the Minister to the House of Commons on 9th December which called for a halt to the deterioration of London's transport by making the positive improvements necessary. Action was to be taken to ensure the best use of scarce road space, to improve public transport, to discourage the use of private cars and to find a more equitable way of paying for London's transport in all its forms.

The first step was the establishment of a Transport Co-ordinating Council for London, with representatives from the Ministry, the GLC, London Transport, British Railways, the London Boroughs and the Trades Union Congress, which met for the first time on 3rd March 1966. Although this was a helpful move, the Council had no executive powers and was to prove largely ineffective because its members had conflicting powers and responsibilities. The Government then made provision for financial support of up to £16 million a year up to the end of 1968, to be given to London Transport from public funds, while a fundamental re-appraisal of the rôle of public transport in London was carried out. A Joint Review was then set up under the control of the Ministry of Transport, to examine the Board's financial needs and its main operating and management problems. The first meeting took place on 31st August 1966 and the detailed review was carried out with the help of outside consultants.

By now there was a new Minister of Transport, the redoubtable and energetic Barbara Castle, who was to invest the proceedings with an extra dose of vigour and imagination. In July 1966, she issued a White Paper on Transport Policy (Cmnd 3057) which proposed the establishment of 'Conurbation Transport Authorities', under local government control, which would have responsibility for highways, traffic and public transport, with a duty to integrate public transport. These proposals, which were in line with those submitted to the Minister by the Board in June, were intended to include London, although the Government was concerned that London's

problems were unique in their size and complexity. Ironically, it was the policy for conurbations outside London that was to be watered down, with the eventual establishment of Passenger Transport Authorities lacking the general powers envisaged for the CTAs and with only slender connections with the local authorities. The approach adopted in London was also different, but was closer to the original theory. The proposals were made public in a joint statement by the Minister of Transport and the Leader of the Greater London Council on 15th December 1967 and their main provision was that the GLC would become the statutory transport planning authority for London. It was to be given wide powers covering highways, traffic and public passenger transport and was to have policy and financial control over a new London Transport Executive, which would replace the Board and whose members it would appoint. It was not to be involved in the day-to-day running of the undertaking, which was to remain the responsibility of the Executive. Wider highways and traffic powers were to be given to the Council, so that policy and planning could be unified. As ever, British Railways was omitted from the new arrangements, except that fares were to be subject to consultation with the GLC. No reference was made at this stage to any special treatment for the Country Bus and Coach department but it was subsequently agreed between the Minister and the GLC that, as its operations were outside the scope of the GLC's other powers, it should be transferred to a new company, London Country Bus Services Ltd, whose unusual geographical base was described by the new Minister, Richard Marsh, as resembling a demented Polo mint. This would become a subsidiary of the new National Bus Company which was being set up under separate legislation, the Transport Act (1968), which also established the PTAs and PTEs. The opportunity to set up a regional transport authority, whose geographical scope would have been more in keeping with the transport needs of the area, was lost for all

time, possibly because the GLC did not want to share its new-found powers with other councils and possibly because it did not want to be faced with subsidising essential services outside Greater London.

The 1968 Act included a number of important financial matters which applied to London as well as the rest of the country. One of the most important was the provision of grants, normally twenty-five per cent, towards capital expenditure on new buses, providing these met standard specifications approved by the Minister, which were aimed at improving the efficiency of bus manufacture and encouraging the spread of one-man operation. These applied to conforming vehicles registered on or after 1st September 1968. The revenue side of the account was also to be given help by a fuel grant, which started at the rate of 9d a gallon on 1st January 1969 and was expected to reduce the Board's annual costs by £1 million. Provision was also made for local authorities to have powers to contribute to the cost of rural services and for the government to make 'infrastructure' grants, up to seventy-five per cent of the cost on railway projects and twenty-five per cent on bus stations.

The Transport (London) Act, giving statutory force to the transfer of responsibility from the Minister to the GLC, received the Royal assent in the summer of 1969 and came into force on 1st January 1970. The London Transport Board ceased to exist on 31st December 1969, bringing to an end Herbert Morrison's great creation. On the face of it, London Transport was ending the 1960s in much more optimistic circumstances and in a stronger financial and strategic position. The 1970s were indeed to prove a much more positive and fruitful ten years, but the organisational changes which had been hammered out in the last few years of the 1960s turned out to bear the seeds of the ultimate demise of bus operation by London Transport. Herbert Morrison's belief that it was wiser to keep the business out of the hands of politicians was about to be proved true.

APPENDIX ONE
THE SCHEDULED FLEET 1960–1969

The following tables show the maximum number of buses and coaches of each type which were *officially* allocated for scheduled service on 31st December each year.

TYPE	1960	1961	1962	1963	1964	1965	1966	1967	1968	1969
CENTRAL BUSES										
RT	3426	3393	3317	3055	2820	2945	2877	3038	2951	2775
RTL	1231	1218	1077	1056	988	826	448	227	–	–
RTW	476	471	497	461	429	175	–	–	–	–
RLH	29	28	26	27	27	27	23	23	23	16
RM	437	842	1243	1590	1905	2041	1925	1990	1974	1996
RML	–	15	19	19	19	63	244	404	415	417
FRM	–	–	–	–	–	–	–	1	1	1
XA	–	–	–	–	–	30	46	37	32	–
XF	–	–	–	–	–	–	–	8	8	–
DOUBLE DECK TOTAL	5999	5967	6179	6208	6188	6112	5563	5728	5404	5205
TD	19	16	–	–	–	–	–	–	–	–
RF (TMO)	202	198	204	176	146	120	93	93	63	64
RF (OMO)	–	–	–	–	24	60	84	85	116	128
XMB	–	–	–	–	–	–	5	5	14	–
MB	–	–	–	–	–	–	–	–	102	158
MBA	–	–	–	–	–	–	–	–	40	55
MBS	–	–	–	–	–	–	–	–	110	175
SINGLE-DECK TOTALS	221	214	204	176	170	180	182	183	445	580
MOTOR BUS TOTALS	5820	6181	6383	6384	6358	6292	5745	5911	5849	5785
TROLLEYBUSES	631	200	–	–	–	–	–	–	–	–
CENTRAL TOTALS	6451	6381	6383	6384	6358	6292	5745	5911	5849	5785
COUNTRY BUSES										
RT	*707	709	700	710	699	629	538	539	523	424
RLH	38	38	36	36	23	16	16	16	15	15
RML	–	–	–	–	–	46	93	93	94	94
RMC	–	–	–	–	–	–	–	–	–	18
XF	–	–	–	–	–	8	§8	–	–	7
XA	–	–	–	–	–	–	–	7	7	†3
DOUBLE-DECK TOTALS	745	747	736	746	722	699	655	655	639	561
T	1	1	–	–	–	–	–	–	–	–
RF (TMO)	27	27	27	26	16	17	4	5	9	5
RF (OMO)	134	130	148	152	167	183	217	217	213	233
RFW	1	1	1	1	–	–	–	–	–	–
RW	3	3	3	–	–	–	–	–	–	–
MB	–	–	–	–	–	–	–	–	15	31
MBS	–	–	–	–	–	–	–	–	5	61
GS	55	57	35	31	26	23	15	10	3	–
SINGLE-DECK TOTALS	221	219	214	210	209	223	236	232	241	320
COUNTRY BUS TOTALS	966	966	950	956	931	922	891	887	880	891
GREEN LINE										
RT	87	85	70	72	56	17	10	10	1	1
CRL/RMC	1	1	47	61	61	59	60	55	57	45
RCL	–	–	–	–	–	39	39	38	38	38
DOUBLE-DECK TOTALS	88	86	117	133	117	115	109	103	96	84
RF (TMO)	251	254	192	167	168	138	137	134	49	1
RF (OMO)	–	–	–	–	–	–	8	20	78	137
RC	–	–	–	–	–	12	12	–	3	†2
SINGLE-DECK TOTALS	251	254	192	168	168	170	157	154	130	140
GREEN LINE TOTALS	339	340	309	300	285	285	266	257	226	224
COUNTRY BUS & COACH TOTALS	1305	1306	1259	1256	1216	1207	1157	1144	1106	1112
GRAND TOTALS	7756	7687	7642	7641	7574	7499	6902	7055	6955	6900

* includes up to 17 RTL   § 'composite' one-man operation   † official allocation - none were actually licensed.

LIST OF LONDON TRANSPORT BUS AND TROLLEYBUS ROUTES
Operating on 1st January 1960

ROUTE NUMBER	ROUTE DETAILS

CENTRAL BUSES

1   Marylebone Stn - Surrey Docks Stn via Euston Rd, Tottenham Crt Rd, Trafalgar Sq, Waterloo, Bermondsey; extended to Lewisham (Rennell Street) Mon to Fri peak hours, Sat afts and eves and Suns via Deptford Bdy and Lewisham Rd. Also extended Sat afts, eves and Suns from Marylebone to Willesden (L.T. Gar, Pound La) via Maida Vale and Kilburn. *(Early morning jnys Mons to Fris also operate Lewisham to Catford Gar.)*

2   Golders Grn (L.T. Stn) - Crystal Palace (Parade) via Swiss Cottage, Baker St, Victoria, Stockwell, Brixton, Railton Rd, Herne Hill, W. Norwood and Elder Rd.

2A Golders Grn (L.T. Stn) - W. Norwood ('Rosendale') via 2 to Brixton, Effra Rd, Herne Hill and Robson Rd. (Mons to Sats.)

2B Golders Grn (L.T. Stn) - West Norwood (L.T. Gar) via route 2 to Brixton, then Tulse Hill (Suns); extended Sun afts and eves to Crystal Palace (Parade) via Elder Rd.

3   Camden Town (Camden Gdns) - Crystal Palace (Parade) via Albany St, Oxford Circus, Whitehall, Lambeth Bdg., Kennington, Brixton, Herne Hill and Croxted Rd.

4   Finsbury Park (Station Pl) - Surrey Docks (Osprey St) via Highbury, Islington, Aldersgate, St Pauls, Blackfriars, Elephant & Castle and Rotherhithe. (Mons to Fris; also Sats until end of midday peak.)

5   Bloomsbury (Red Lion Sq) - Barking (L.T. Gar) via Clerkenwell, Commercial St, Limehouse, Poplar and E. Ham.

5A Clerkenwell Grn - W. India Dock (Ming St) via 5 to Limehouse, W. India Dock Rd. (Mons to Fris.)

6   Kensal Rise Stn - Hackney Wick (Eastway) via West Kilburn, Maida Vale, Oxford St, Strand, Bank, Shoreditch and Hackney Rd; extended Mon to Fri peak hours and Sat afts to Leyton (Town Hall) via Ruckholt Rd.

6A Waterloo Stn - Hackney Wick (Eastway) via Aldwych and route 6. (Mon to Sat peak hours and Sat mornings); extended Mon to Fri peak hours and Sat midday peak to Leyton Town Hall.

7   Acton (Gunnersbury La) - Oxford Circus via E. Acton, Wormwood Scrubs, Ladbroke Gve, Westbourne Park Rd, Paddington and Marble Arch (Mon to Sat); extended Mon to Fri until end of eve peak, Sat morning and midday peak via Holborn and Bank to London Bdg. Stn.

8   Old Ford ('Lady Franklin') - Neasden (Dog La) via Bethnal Grn, Liverpool St Stn, Holborn, Marble Arch, Kilburn and Willesden (Mons to Sats); extended Mon to Fri peak hours to Wembley Trading Estate via Blackbird Cross and Wembley Park. *(Operates in two sections: Old Ford to Willesden/Kilburn Park Stn to Neasden or Wembley.)*

8A Old Ford ('Lady Franklin') - London Bdg Stn via Liverpool St Stn and Monument. (No service Mon to Fri eves, Sun afts and eves.)

8B Old Ford ('Lady Franklin') - Alperton (L.T. Stn) via 8 to Blackbird Cross, Wembley Park Dr and Wembley Central. (Suns.)

9   Mortlake (L.T. Gar) - Liverpool St Stn via Hammersmith, Hyde Pk Cnr, Strand and Bank; diverted at Bank Suns and extended to Becontree Hth (Lay-By) via Aldgate, Poplar, Barking and Longbridge Rd.

10 Abridge ('Blue Boar') - London Bdg Stn via Woodford Bdg, Wanstead, Stratford and Aldgate; extended: Mons to Sats, except eves, to Victoria Stn (S.R. Forecourt) via Borough Rd and Lambeth Bdg.

11 Liverpool St Stn - Shepherds Bush (Wells Rd) via Bank, Strand, Victoria, Fulham Bdy and Hammersmith.

12 South Croydon (L.T. Gar) - Oxford Circus via Croydon, Addiscombe, Norwood Junction, Penge, Forest Hill, E. Dulwich, Peckham, Walworth Rd, Lambeth North and Trafalgar Sq; extended Mons to Sats to Harlesden ('Willesden Junction Hotel') via Notting Hill Gate, Shepherds Bush, E. Acton La and Park Royal. *(Operates in two sections: South Croydon - Oxford Circus/Dulwich ('Plough') - Harlesden but some garage jnys work Elmers End or Peckham to Park Royal/ Harlesden.)*

Route 9 remained intact throughout the 1960s, apart from losing its Sunday extension to Becontree Heath in September 1968. It saw RTWs only on Saturdays until the spring of 1963 when the whole allocation was replaced by RMs. Dalston's RTW 119 is seen at Butterwick, Hammersmith. M. Dryhurst

13 London Bdg. Stn - Golders Grn (L.T. Stn) via Cannon St, Trafalgar Sq, Oxford St, Finchley Rd. (Mons to Sats).

14 Hornsey Rise ('Favourite') - Putney (Oxford Rd) via Holloway, King's Cross, Tottenham Court Rd, Piccadilly, Knightsbridge and Fulham Rd; part service diverted Suns at Putney High St and extended to Kingston (Bus Stn) via Putney Heath and Roehampton; further extended summer Suns to Hampton Court (Vrow Walk).

15 E. Ham ('White Horse') - Ladbroke Gve ('Eagle') via Poplar, Aldgate, Bank, Strand, Oxford St, Paddington and Westbourne Gve; diverted Suns at Ladbroke Gve Stn and extended to Kew Grn ('Coach & Horses') via E. Acton, Acton and Gunnersbury La. *(On Suns operates in two sections: E. Ham - E. Acton/Poplar, market hours, or Aldgate - Kew Grn.)*

16 Victoria Stn (S.R. Forecourt) - Sudbury Town (L.T. Stn) via Marble Arch, Cricklewood, Neasden, Nth Wembley. *(After morning peak Mon to Fri operates in two sections: Victoria - Neasden/Kilburn Park - Sudbury.)*

18 Edgware (L.T. Stn) - Wembley (Empire Pool) via Belmont, Harrow, Sudbury; diverted Suns at Wembley Triangle and extended to London Bdg Stn via Harrow Rd, Paddington, King's Cross, Grays Inn Rd, Ludgate Circus and Southwark Bdg.; also extended Mon to Fri peak hours from Edgware to Aldenham L.T. Works via Watford By-Pass.

18B Harlesden ('Willesden Junction Hotel') - London Bdg Stn via route 18 Mons to Sats (not eves).

19 Finsbury Pk (Plimsoll Rd) - Upper Tooting (Tooting Bec L.T. Stn) via Highbury, Islington, Bloomsbury, St Giles's Circus, Piccadilly, Sloane Sq, Battersea, Clapham Junction, Battersea Rise and Trinity Rd.

20 Leytonstone ('Green Man') - Epping Town ('Cock') via Wanstead, Woodford and Loughton; extended Sun afts to St Margarets Hospital.

20A Leytonstone ('Green Man') - Debden Bdy via 20 to Loughton, then Chester Rd and Jessel Drive.

21 Moorgate (Finsbury Sq) - London Bdg Stn (Mon to Sat); extended daily to Sidcup (L.T. Gar) via Borough, Old Kent Rd, New Cross Gate, Lewisham, Eltham and New Eltham; further extended Suns to Farningham ('Bull') via Swanley and Kingsdown.

21A Woolwich (Parsons Hill) - Farningham ('Bull') via Eltham and route 21 (Mons to Sats). *Woolwich to Eltham (Well Hall Stn) service operates peak hours and Sats until early eve only.*

22 Putney Common ('Spencer Arms') - Homerton ('Clapton Park Tavern') via New Kings Rd, Sloane St, Piccadilly, Shaftesbury Av, Holborn, Bank, Dalston Junction, Graham Rd and Dunlace Rd.

23 Becontree Heath (Lay-By) - Aldgate (L.T. Stn) via route 9 (Mons to Sats); extended (except eves and Sat afts) to Marylebone Stn via Bank, Holborn, Oxford St, Baker St.

23C Creekmouth (Electric Supply Works) - Barking (Blakes Cnr) via River Rd and Ripple Rd; extended Mon to Sat peak hours to Becontree (Chittys La) via Bennetts Castle La. *Irregular works jnys only.*

24 Hampstead Heath (South End Grn) - Pimlico (Grosvenor Rd) via Malden Rd, Camden Town, Tottenham Court Rd, Whitehall, Victoria and Belgrave Rd.

25 Victoria Stn (S.R. Forecourt) - Becontree Heath (Lay-By) via Bond St, Holborn, Bank, Aldgate, Stratford, Ilford and Green La; also operates Mon to Fri peak hours Dagenham East Stn - Dagenham (Fords) via Ballards Rd, with some through jnys to/from the main route.

26 Aldgate (Minories Lay-By) - Leyton ('Bakers Arms') via Stratford, Leytonstone and Whipps Cross.

27 Archway (L.T. Stn) - Teddington Stn via Camden Town, Hampstead Rd, Marylebone, Paddington, Kensington, Hammersmith, Kew, Richmond, Twickenham and Cross Deep; extended summer Suns to Hampton Court via Bushy Park.

28 Golders Grn (L.T. Stn) - Wandsworth (High St, Armoury Way) via West Hampstead, Kilburn, Westbourne Park, Kensington, West Kensington, Fulham Bdy and Wandsworth Bdg.

29 Victoria Stn (S.R. Forecourt) - Sth Mimms (Blanche La) via Whitehall, Tottenham Crt Rd, Camden Town, Manor Hse, Wood Grn, Palmers Grn, Southgate, Cockfosters and Potters Bar; extended Sun afts, also jnys Mon to Fri and one jny Sats, to Clare Hall Hospital; one jny each peak Mon to Fri diverted at 'White Hart' and extended to Borehamwood ('Elstree Way Hotel') via Barnet By-Pass. *Operates in two sections Mons to Sats: Victoria - Cockfosters/Turnpike La -Sth Mimms or Borehamwood.*

29A Turnpike La (L.T. Stn) - Oakwood (L.T. Stn) via 29 to Southgate and Chase Rd (Mons to Sats).

30 Roehampton ('Earl Spencer') - Hackney Wick (Eastway) via Doverhouse Rd, Putney, Fulham Palace Rd, Old Brompton Rd, Hyde Park Cnr, Marble Arch, Baker St, King's Cross, Islington, Highbury, Hackney and Morning Lane.

RT 3774 approaches the East Street junction from Ripple Road, Barking, on route 23C which kept going throughout the decade while all around it changed constantly. A.B. Cross

A product of the third stage of the trolleybus conversion, route 32 soon withered and finally expired in November 1964. RTL 1093 is at the Leytonstone 'Green Man' junction, with the road to Whipps Cross going off to the left. A.B. Cross

31   Camden Town ('Britannia') - Chelsea ('Stanley Arms') via Swiss Cottage, Kilburn, Westbourne Park, Kensington and Earl's Court.

32   Victoria Stn (S.R. Forecourt) - Wanstead (Woodbine Place) via route 25 to Stratford, then Leytonstone (Mons to Sats). *(No service Mon to Sat eves Bow Rd (Fairfield Rd) to Wanstead, nor Sats after the midday peak, Victoria to Bow.)*

34   Barnet (Chesterfield Rd) - Walthamstow ('Crooked Billet') via Barnet Church, Meadway, New Barnet, Longmore Av, Whetstone, Arnos Gve and Edmonton (Mons to Sats).

34B   Brimsdown (Power Stn) - Walthamstow ('Crooked Billet') via Green St, Ponders End, Edmonton and North Circular Rd (Mon to Fri peak hours). *(Evening service works mainly Brimsdown - Ponders End; no through service southbound.)*

35   Clapham Common (Old Town) - Chingford Hatch (Friday Hill) via Brixton, Camberwell, Elephant & Castle, London Bdg, Shoreditch, Dalston, Pembury Rd, Clapton, Leyton and Highams Park.

35A   Clapham Common (Old Town) - Chingford ('Royal Forest Hotel') via route 35 to Highams Park, Larks Hall Rd (Summer Suns).

36   W. Kilburn (Claremont Rd) - Hither Grn Stn via Malvern Rd, Royal Oak, Paddington, Victoria, Camberwell, New Cross Gate, Lewisham, Catford, Sangley Rd and Torridon Rd.

36A   W. Kilburn (Claremont Rd) - Brockley Rise ('Chandos') via 36 to New Cross, Malpas Rd and Brockley Rd (Mons to Sats).

36B   W. Kilburn (Claremont Rd) - Grove Park Stn via 36 to Catford, Bromley Rd and Downham Way. *No service Sats W. Kilburn - Victoria (Vauxhall Bdg Rd).*

37   Peckham (L.T. Gar) - Hounslow (L.T. Gar) via E. Dulwich, Herne Hill, Brixton, Clapham, Clapham Junction, Wandsworth, Putney, Richmond, St Margarets, Isleworth.

38   Victoria Stn (S.R. Forecourt) - Chingford ('Royal Forest Hotel') via Piccadilly, Bloomsbury, Islington, Essex Rd, Dalston, Pembury Rd, Clapton, Leyton, Walthamstow and Chingford Mount; extended Summer Suns to Epping Forest ('Wake Arms') via Rangers Rd and Epping New Rd.

38A   Victoria Stn (S.R. Forecourt) - Loughton Stn via 38 to Dalston, then Graham Rd, Clapton, Leyton, Whipps Cross, Woodford and Buckhurst Hill.

39   Southfields Stn - Charing Cross, Trafalgar Sq via Replingham Rd, Wandsworth, Clapham Junction, Battersea Bdg, Royal Hospital Rd, Victoria and Whitehall (Mons to Sats); extended Mon to Fri, except eves, and Sats, except afts and eves, plus some garage jnys, to Camden Town (Camden Gdns) via Tottenham Court Rd.

40   Wanstead (Woodbine Place) - Camberwell Grn via Blake Hall Rd, Forest Gate, Green St, Upton Park, Poplar, Aldgate, London Bdg, Elephant & Castle and Walworth Rd; extended Mon to Fri peak hours and Suns to Herne Hill (Post Office); further extended Suns to Norwood Junction Stn via W. Norwood and Upper Norwood. *(On Mon to Fri works: Wanstead - Aldgate/ Wanstead Flats - Herne Hill/ Poplar -Camberwell.)*

41   Archway (L.T. Stn) - Tottenham Hale ('White Hart') via Crouch End, Turnpike La, West Green and Tottenham; extended Mon to Fri peak hours to Ilford Stn via Forest Rd, S. Woodford and Gants Hill.

42   Aldgate (Minories Lay-By) - Camberwell Grn via Tower Bdg, Bricklayers Arms, Old Kent Rd and Albany Rd; extended Mon to Fri peak hours and Sat shopping hours to Herne Hill Stn via Loughborough Junction and Milkwood Rd.

43   London Bdg Stn - Friern Barnet ('Orange Tree') via Moorgate, Islington, Archway and Muswell Hill Bdy (Mon to Fri, except eves, and Sat, except afts and eves).

44   London Bdg Stn - Mitcham ('Cricketers') via Southwark Bdg Rd, Lambeth Rd, Vauxhall, Battersea, Wandsworth and Tooting; extended Suns to Wallington (Belmont Rd) via Hackbridge and Carshalton Stn.

45   Sth Kensington (L.T. Stn) - Farringdon St (Farringdon Av) via Beaufort St, Battersea, Clapham Jnc, Cedars Rd, Clapham, Stockwell, Brixton, Camberwell, Elephant & Castle and Blackfriars Bdg.

46   Alperton (L.T. Stn) - Willesden (L.T. Gar) via Wembley, Wembley Park Dr, Blackbird Cross and Neasden La (Mons to Sats); extended, except Mon to Fri eves, Sat afts and eves, to Waterloo Stn via Staverton Rd, Kensal Rise, Harrow Rd, Westbourne Park, Notting Hill Gate, Kensington, Sloane St, Pimlico Rd, Victoria and Lambeth Bdg.

47   Shoreditch Church (Calvert Avenue) - Bromley (L.T. Gar) via London Bdg, Rotherhithe, Deptford Bdy, Brookmill Rd, Lewisham, Downham and Bromley Market Place; extended Suns to Farnborough ('George & Dragon').

48   Waterloo Stn - N. Woolwich (Free Ferry) via Aldwych, Bank, Aldgate, Poplar, Canning Town and Silvertown. *Operates: Waterloo - N. Woolwich Mon to Fri peak hours; Waterloo - Poplar Mon to Fri between peaks; Aldgate - N. Woolwich Sat peak hours and early Sun a.m.; Aldgate - Poplar Sun market hours.*

49   Crystal Palace (Parade) - Shepherds Bush Grn via Beulah Hill, Streatham Common, Tooting Bec, Clapham Jnc, Battersea Bdg, Oakley St, Sydney St, Sth Kensington, Harrington Rd, Gloucester Rd, Kensington High St and Holland Rd: extended Sun to Harlesden ('Willesden Junction Hotel') via route 12.

50   Addiscombe ('Black Horse') - Stockwell (L.T. Stn) via St James's Rd, Thornton Hth Pond, Streatham and Brixton (Mons to Sats); extended Mon to Fri peak hours to Victoria Embankment (Horse Guards Ave) via Vauxhall, Lambeth Bdg and Millbank.

51   Farnborough ('George & Dragon') - Sidcup Stn via Farnborough Hill, Orpington, Cray Av, Foots Cray; extended Mon-Fri peak hours, Sats and Suns, to Blackfen ('The Woodman') via Willersley Av and Wellington Av; extended Sats and Suns to Welling Stn via Westwood La and Hook La; also extended Sun afts from Farnborough to Bromley (L.T. Gar).

51A   Green St Green ('Rose & Crown') - Sidcup Stn via Orpington and route 51 (Mons to Fris); extended Mon to Fri except eves to Eltham (Well Hall Stn) via Blackfen.

51B   Orpington Stn - Sidcup Stn (Mon to Fri peak hours and two Sat jnys); extended Mon to Fri peak hours to Eltham (Well Hall Stn) via route 51A.

51C   Green St Green ('Rose & Crown') - Welling Stn via routes 51A and 51 (Sat).

52   Victoria Stn (S.R. Forecourt) - Mill Hill ('Green Man') via Hyde Park Cnr, Kensington Church, Notting Hill Gate, Ladbroke Gve, Kensal Rise, Willesden, Neasden, Kingsbury Grn, Burnt Oak and Deans La; extended Mon to Fri peak hours and Suns to Borehamwood (Drayton Rd) via Selvage La, Barnet Way, Stirling Corner, Manor Way and Shenley Rd; further extended Suns to Rossington Av via Theobald St and Leeming Rd.

52A   Colindale (L.T. Depôt) - Borehamwood (Rossington Avenue) via Burnt Oak and route 52. *Also Express buses Colindale - Borehamwood (Brook Rd) Mon to Fri peak hours.*

53   Camden Town (Camden Gdns) - Plumstead Common (Warwick Terrace) via Albany St, Regent St, Westminster, Elephant & Castle, Old Kent Rd, Deptford, Blackheath, Charlton Village, Woolwich and Burrage Rd; extended Suns to Erith ('Prince of Wales') via Kings Highway, Okehampton Crescent, Bedonwell Rd, Parsonage Manor Way and Carlton Rd.

54   Selsdon (Farley Rd) - Woolwich (General Gordon Place) via Selsdon Rd, South Croydon, Park La, Shirley, Elmers End, Beckenham, Southend Pond, Lewisham, Blackheath and Charlton Village; extended Mons to Sats to Plumstead Common ('The Woodman').

55   Chiswick (Swimming Pool) - Hayes (Bourne Av) via Grove Park, Turnham Grn, Acton, Popes La, Northfields, Hanwell, Church Rd, Greenford, Yeading, Hayes Stn and Dawley Rd. *On Mons to Sats operates in two sections: Chiswick -Greenford/Chiswick Stn - Hayes.*

56   Poplar (Blackwall Tunnel) - Limehouse ('Eastern Hotel') via Manchester Rd and W. Ferry Rd.

57   Victoria (Vauxhall Bdg Rd) - Tooting Bdy via Vauxhall, Brixton, Streatham and Southcroft Rd (Mons to Sats).

57A   Sth Croydon (L.T. Gar) - Victoria (Vauxhall Bdg Rd) - via W. Croydon, Whitehorse Rd, Thornton Hth, Green La, Streatham and route 57; extended Summer Suns to Camden Town (Buck St) via Marble Arch, Baker St and The Zoo. *NOTE: The summer extension had continued to Hampstead Heath via route 24 in 1959.*

59   W. Hampstead (West End Grn) - Chipstead Valley (Rectory La) via St Johns Wood, Lords, Baker St, Oxford Circus, Trafalgar Sq, Lambeth Bdg, Kennington, Brixton, Streatham, Thornton Heath Pond, Croydon, Purley and Coulsdon (Suns).

59A   W. Hampstead (Sherriff Rd) - Streatham (L.T. Gar) via St. Johns Wood, Lisson Gve, Rossmore Rd, Baker St and route 59 (Mons to Fris); extended peak hours to Thornton Heath (L.T. Gar).

61   Eltham (Well Hall Stn) - Bromley Nth Stn via New Eltham, Chislehurst, Orpington and Locksbottom.

62   Little Heath ('Haw Bush') - Barkingside ('Old Maypole') via Barley La, Goodmayes, Longbridge Rd, Barking, Rippleside, Becontree Stn, Valence Av, Chadwell Hth, Whalebone La, Rose La and New North Rd (Mons to Sats); extended Mon to Fri to Gants Hill (L.T. Stn); further extended off-peak to Ilford Stn (York Rd).

62A   Little Heath ('Haw Bush') - Chigwell Row ('Maypole') via route 62 to Chadwell Heath, then Whalebone La and Romford Rd (Suns).

63   King's Cross Stn - Honor Oak ('Forest Hill Tavern') via Farringdon Rd, Blackfriars, Elephant & Castle, Old Kent Rd, Trafalgar Av, Peckham and Peckham Rye; extended Mons to Sats to Crystal Palace (Parade) via Wood Vale, Underhill Rd and Sydenham Hill.

64   W. Croydon Stn - Addington (Featherbed La) via Park La, South Park Hill Rd, Croham Rd and Selsdon.

65   Ealing (Argyle Rd) - Leatherhead (L.T. Gar) via Castlebar Hill, Montpelier Ave, Eaton Rise, Ealing Bdy, S. Ealing, Brentford, Kew, Richmond, Kingston, Surbiton, Hook and Leatherhead Rd.

The Elmers End allocation added to route 64 in the trolleybus conversion of July 1960, lasted only until May 1962 when it switched to Thornton Heath. Elmers End's RM 355 threads its way across London Road, West Croydon from Station Road to Tamworth Road. A.B. Cross

Hounslow's RT 369 is working the Kensington to Hounslow service on route 73, which was really the 33 in disguise, the two having been combined in November 1958. It recaptured its true identity from 31st December 1966, although the through Sunday service remained as route 73. *John Gascoine*

66 Leytonstone ('Green Man') - Hornchurch Stn via Eastern Av, Romford, Victoria Rd, Slewins La, Butts Grn Rd and Station La; morning and late aft jnys extended to Hacton Drive Mon to Sat and additionally all afternoon on Weds and Suns.

66A Harold Hill (Dagnam Park Dr) - Romford (North St L.T. Gar/'Parkside Hotel', early am and late pm) via Petersfield Av, Faringdon Av, Gallows Cnr, Gidea Pk Stn and Victoria Rd; extended Mon to Fri peak hours and Sats to Collier Row (Clockhouse La).

68 Chalk Farm (L.T. Stn) - Sth Croydon (L.T. Gar) via Camden Town, Euston, Waterloo, Elephant & Castle, Camberwell Grn, Denmark Hill, W. Norwood, Upper Norwood, Whitehorse La, Whitehorse Rd and W. Croydon.

70 Eltham (Southend Crescent) - Waterloo Stn via Rochester Way, Blackheath, Westcombe Hill, Greenwich, Surrey Docks, London Bdg and Southwark St (Mons to Sats); extended Mon to Fri peak hours and Sat mid-evenings to Victoria Stn via Lambeth Bdg.

71 Hammersmith (Brook Grn) - Kingston (L.T. Bus Stn) via Chiswick La, Chiswick Bdg, Richmond, Petersham, Ham Common, Lock Rd, Dukes Av, Tudor Dr and Kings Rd (Mons to Sats); extended Sats to Sunbury Stn via Hampton Court, Hampton Stn and Sunbury Village.

72 Esher ('Windsor Arms') - E. Acton (Ducane Rd) via Kingston By-Pass, New Malden, Kingston Vale, Roehampton, Hammersmith, Shepherds Bush and Westway (Mons to Sats); extended Mon to Fri peak hours to Park Royal (Stadium) via Gypsy Corner.

72A Tolworth ('Toby Jug') - E. Acton (Erconwald St) via route 72 to Shepherds Bush, Ducane Rd (Suns).

73 Stoke Newington (Northwold Rd) - Hounslow (L.T. Gar) via Newington Grn, Islington, King's Cross, Tottenham Court Rd, Oxford St, Hyde Park Corner, Kensington, Hammersmith, Barnes, Richmond, Twickenham and Whitton. *Operates in two sections Mons to Sats: Stoke Newington - Richmond/Kensington, Palace Gate - Hounslow.*

74 Camden Town (Buck St) - Putney Hth ('Green Man') via The Zoo, Marble Arch, Knightsbridge, Cromwell Rd, Earl's Court, Fulham Palace Rd and Putney; extended Mons to Sats to Putney Hth ('Telegraph Inn').

74A Marylebone Stn - Kingston Vale (Beverley Bdg) via Baker St, route 74 to Putney, then route 14 (Mon to Fri peak hours).

75 Woolwich (Market Hill) - W. Croydon (Stn) via Charlton Village, Blackheath, Lee Grn, Brownhill Rd, Catford, Sydenham, Penge and Anerley.

76 Victoria Stn (S.R. Forecourt) - Tottenham ('Swan') via Westminster, Waterloo, Blackfriars, Queen Victoria St, Bank, Moorgate, New North Rd, Baring St, Stamford Rd, Dalston, Stoke Newington and Stamford Hill; extended Mon to Fri peak hours to Lower Edmonton Stn; two aft jnys further extended to Brimsdown (Stn/Power Stn) via Ponders End and Green St. Mon to Fri peak hour service also operates Victoria to Liverpool St Stn via London Wall, Blomfield St, returning via Old Broad St.

77 Euston Stn - Tooting ('Mitre') via Aldwych, Whitehall, Lambeth Bdg, Vauxhall, Clapham Junction and Earlsfield (Mons to Sats); also Tooting Bdy - Wallington (Belmont Rd) via Mitcham, Hackbridge Cnr, Carshalton and Parkgate Rd (Mons to Sats).

77A King's Cross (Stn, York Way) - Raynes Park ('Junction Tavern') via Euston, route 77 to Clapham Junction, Wandsworth, Durnsford Rd, Gap Rd, Wimbledon and Hartfield Rd (Mons to Sats); extended Mon-Fri a.m. peak hours to Worcester Park Stn via New Malden and Malden Rd.

77B Euston Stn - Tooting ('Mitre') - as route 77 but via Millbank and Vauxhall Bdg (Suns).

77C King's Cross (Stn, York Way) - Raynes Park ('Junction Tavern') as route 77A but via Westminster Bdg and Albert Embankment (Suns).

78 Shoreditch (Calvert Av) - Dulwich ('The Plough') via Liverpool St Stn, Aldgate, Tower Bdg, Grange Rd, Dunton Rd, Old Kent Rd, Peckham Pk Rd, Rye La and Barry Rd.

The association of route 81 with Windsor, spanning more than fifty-one years, came to an end in October 1963 when the weekend extension beyond Slough was withdrawn. RT 2703 occupies the time-honoured stand in Castle Hill surrounded by the ancient stonework of the castle outbuildings. R. Butler

79	Colindale (L.T. Stn) - Perivale (Dawlish Av) via Hay La, Kingsbury, Preston Rd, Wembley, Alperton, Bilton Rd and Aintree Rd (Mons to Sats). *Mon to Fri eves between North Wembley ('Preston Hotel') and Alperton (L.T. Stn) only. On Sats operates an anti-clockwise loop via Horsenden La, Dawlish Avenue, Aintree Rd.*
79A	Edgware (L.T. Stn) - Perivale (Dawlish Av) via Whitchurch La, Honeypot La, Kingsbury and route 79 (Mons to Sats); extended Mon to Sat peak hours and Mon to Fri lunch times to Northolt ('Target Inn', Church Rd) via Western Av. *On Sats operates a clockwise loop via Dawlish Av, Horsenden La and Bilton Rd.*
80	Tooting Bdy (Longmead Rd) - Lower Kingswood ('Mint Arms') via Mitcham, St. Helier, Sutton, Belmont and Reigate Rd.
80A	Tooting Bdy (Longmead Rd) - Walton-On-The-Hill ('Chequers') via route 80 to Burgh Heath, Dorking Rd (return Tadworth Rd) and Chequers La.
81	Hounslow (L.T. Gar) - Slough Stn via Hounslow West, Harlington, Colnbrook and Langley; diverted Sat and Sun afts at Slough 'Crown' and extended to Windsor (Castle Hill) via Eton. *(On summer Suns operates to Windsor all day.)*
81A	Hounslow (L.T. Gar) - Langley (Sutton La, Hawker's Factory) via Hounslow West, Harlington, Colnbrook By-Pass and Sutton La (three peak hour jnys Mon to Fri).
81B	Hounslow (L.T. Gar) - London Airport Central via Hounslow West, Harlington and airport tunnel.
82	Stepney (Branch Rd) - Rotherhithe (St Marychurch St) via Rotherhithe Tunnel, Lower Rd, Redriff Rd and Rotherhithe St.
83	Golders Grn (L.T. Stn) - Ealing Bdy Stn via Hendon, The Burroughs, W. Hendon, Kingsbury, Wembley Pk, Wembley, Alperton and Hanger La; extended summer Suns to London Airport Central via Sth Ealing, Great West Rd, Hounslow West and Harlington (see route 112). *On Mons to Sats operates in two sections: Golders Grn - Alperton/W. Hendon (Wembley Empire Pool Mon to Fri off-peak) - Ealing Bdy.*
84	St Albans (L.T. Gar) - Arnos Gve (L.T. Stn) via South Mimms, St. Albans Rd, Barnet and Whetstone; extended Suns to Walthamstow ('Crooked Billet') via route 34. Some Mon to Sat jnys operate to and from New Barnet Stn via Stn Rd. Some Mon to Fri jnys work to or from Palmers Grn (Green Lanes), Edmonton 'Cambridge' or Walthamstow 'Crooked Billet'.
85	Putney Bdg (L.T. Stn) - Kingston (L.T. Bus Stn) via route 14 (Mons to Sats).
86	Limehouse ('Eastern Hotel') - Upminster Stn via Devons Rd, Bow, Stratford, Ilford, Romford, Roneo Corner and Hornchurch; extended Mons to Sats to Upminster Park Estate via Hall La and Avon Rd.
87	Brentwood ('Yorkshire Grey') - Rainham (White Post Cnr) via Brook St, Harold Wood, Gallows Cnr, Romford, Roneo Cnr, Becontree Hth, Barking, Rippleside and Dagenham. Also operates Mon to Fri peak hours Fords - Rainham (War Memorial) and Fords - Becontree Hth; Sat jnys Fords - Barking (L.T. Gar).
88	Acton Grn ('Duke of Sussex') - Mitcham ('Cricketers') via Shepherds Bush, Marble Arch, Piccadilly Circus, Whitehall, Great Smith St, Vauxhall, Stockwell and Tooting; extended Mon to Fri peak hours, Sat shopping hours and Suns to St Helier (Rose Hill); further extended Suns to Belmont ('California') via Sutton.
89	Lewisham (Rennell St) - Welling ('Guy, Earl of Warwick') via Blackheath and Shooters Hill.
90	Kew Gardens Stn - Staines (Clarence St) via Richmond, Twickenham, Hanworth, Sunbury and Ashford Common (Mons to Sats).
90A	Kew Gardens Stn - London Airport Central via Richmond, Twickenham, Hanworth, Feltham, Hatton Cross and Harlington (summer Suns).
90B	Kew Gardens Stn - Yeading ('White Hart') via route 90A to Harlington, Hayes, Church Rd, Lansbury Dr and Kingshill Av.
90C	Hammersmith (Brook Grn) - Staines (Clarence St) via route 71 to Richmond, then route 90 (Suns).
91	Wandsworth Bdg Tavern - London Airport Central via North End Rd, Hammersmith, Turnham Grn, Wellesley Rd, Great West Rd, Hounslow W and Harlington (Mons to Sats but no eve service Hounslow W - London Airport).
92	Southall (L.T. Gar) - Wembley Empire Pool via Greenford Rd, Greenford Stn, Sudbury Hill and Sudbury (Mon to Fri off-peak and Sats). Some peak hour jnys work Southall or Greenford to Greenford Stn or Sudbury Hill.
92A	Southall (L.T. Gar) - Wembley Trading Estate via route 92 to Wembley, then private road (Mons to Sats except eves).
92B	Southall (L.T. Gar) - North Wembley ('Preston Hotel') via 92 to Wembley, then 79 (Suns).
93	Putney Bdg (L.T. Stn) - Epsom Stn via Wimbledon, Sth Wimbledon, Morden, North Cheam and Ewell; extended

Buses for the intermittent 100 came from Upton Park's allocation on route 15, hence the incorrect 'via' blind and route number plate on RTW 267 seen leaving Barking. Although the route, then numbered 623, replaced the Beckton trams in February 1929, the tarred-over tracks are still clearly present over thirty years later.
C. Carter

summer Suns to Dorking (Bus Stn) via Leatherhead and Mickleham.

94   Petts Wood Stn - Lewisham (Rennell St) via Bromley Common, Bromley, Grove Park and Lee Grn; extended Sat afts to Brockley Rise ('Chandos') via Adelaide Av.

95   Tooting Bdy (Coverton Rd) - Cannon St Stn via Southcroft Rd, Streatham, Brixton, Kennington, Borough and Marshalsea Rd (Mons to Sats).

95A   Tooting Bdy (Coverton Rd) - London Bdg Stn via route 95 to Borough, Borough High St (Sun); extended Sun market hours to Poplar (Blackwall Tunnel) via Aldgate and Limehouse.

96   Dartford (Market St) - Woolwich (Parsons Hill) via Crayford, Bexleyheath, Welling, Wickham La and Plumstead; extended Mon to Sat peak hours to Woolwich Rd (Victoria Way).

97   Brentford (Half Acre) - Ruislip (L.T. Stn) via Northfields, Ealing Bdy, Pitshanger La, Greenford and Yeading; extended summer Suns to Ruislip Lido.

98   North Harrow (L.T. Stn) - Hounslow (L.T. Gar) via Headstone La, Hatch End, Pinner, Eastcote Rd, Ruislip, Ickenham, Long La, Hayes End, Hayes and Bath Rd (Sats and Suns).

98A   Hounslow (L.T. Gar) - Hillingdon (L.T. Stn) via route 98 to Hayes End, Windsor Av and Granville Rd (Mons to Fris); extended peak hours to Ruislip (L.T. Stn).

98B   North Harrow (L.T. Stn) - Hayes Stn via route 98 (Mon-Fri); extended peak hours to Feltham Stn via route 90B.

99   Woolwich ('Earl of Chatham') - Erith ('Prince of Wales') via Plumstead and Upper Belvedere.

100   Barking (St Pauls Rd) - Beckton (Gas Works) via Gascoigne Rd and Jenkins La (Daily jnys at shift times).

101   Wanstead (Woodbine Place) - Nth Woolwich (Free Ferry) via Aldersbrook Rd, Manor Park, E. Ham and Royal Albert Dock. *On Mons to Sats normally operates in two sections: Wanstead-Royal Albert Dock/Manor Park Stn - Nth Woolwich.*

102   Golders Grn (L.T. Stn) - Chingford ('Royal Forest Hotel') via Temple Fortune, Hampstead Gdn Suburb, E. Finchley, Muswell Hill Bdy, Bounds Grn, Bowes Rd, Palmers Grn, Edmonton, Hall La, Chingford Mount, New Rd and Larks Hall Rd; extended summer Sat and Sun afts and eves to High Beach via Epping New Rd, Earls Path and King's Oak Rd.

102A   Golders Grn (L.T. Stn) - Chingford Hatch (Friday Hill) via route 102 to New Rd, Hatch La (Suns).

103   North Romford (Chase Cross) - Rainham (War Memorial) via Pettits La, Eastern Av, Romford, Oldchurch Rd, Rush Grn, Rainham Rd, Dagenham East and Dagenham Rd.

105   Shepherds Bush (Wells Rd) - Hayes Stn (Blyth Rd) via Wood La, Westway, Perivale, Greenford, Mornington Rd, Cornwall Rd, Allenby Rd, Carlyle Avenue, Southall, Western Rd and North Hyde Rd; extended Mon to Fri peak hours to Hayes North (Goshawk Gdns) via Church Rd and Kingshill Avenue. *Journeys towards Hayes North broken at Hayes Stn.*

106   Finsbury Park (Station Pl) - Becontree (Chittys La) via Blackstock Rd, Brownswood Rd, Stoke Newington, Clapton, Bethnal Grn, Roman Rd, Mile End, Limehouse, Poplar, E. Ham and Barking By-Pass, Movers La, Barking Bdy, Longbridge Rd, Becontree Av and Bennetts Castle La (Mons to Sats).

106A   Finsbury Park (Station Pl) - Dagenham (Kent Av) via route 106 to E. Ham and Barking By-Pass, Rippleside and Ripple Rd (Suns).

107   Queensbury (L.T. Stn) - Ponders End (Durants Rd) via Camrose Avenue, Edgware, Edgwarebury La, Stanmore Circus, Elstree, Borehamwood, Balmoral Dr, Arkley, New Barnet, Oakwood and Enfield Town (Mons to Sats); extended Mon to Sat peak hours and Mon to Fri lunchtimes to 'The Alma' via Nags Head Rd; some jnys further extended to Ponders End Stn.

107A   Enfield Lock (RSA Factory) - Enfield Chase Stn via Ordnance Rd, Ponders End and Enfield Town; extended Mon to Fri, except peak hours, and Suns to Oakwood (L.T. Stn); further extended Suns to Edgware (L.T. Stn) via route 107.

108   Bromley-By-Bow (Edgar Rd) - Crystal Palace (Parade) via Blackwall Tunnel, Westcombe Hill, Blackheath, Lewisham, Catford and Lower Sydenham.

108A   Bromley-By-Bow (Edgar Rd) - Eltham (Southend Cres) via route 108 to Blackheath, Delacourt Rd, Rochester Way and Well Hall.

109   Purley (High St) - Victoria Embankment via Croydon, Thornton Hth Pond, Streatham, Brixton and Kennington; continuing Mons to Sats and early Sun mornings in a two-way loop via Lambeth Nth, Westminster Bdg, Victoria Embankment, Blackfriars Bdg and Elephant & Castle. On Suns continues from Kennington to Horse Guards Av via Westminster Bdg.

110   Hounslow (L.T. Gar) - Twickenham Stn via Hanworth Rd, Powder Mill La and Staines Rd.

111 Cranford ('Berkeley Arms') - Hanworth ('Brown Bear') via Heston, Hounslow East and Hanworth Rd; extended Sat afts to Twickenham Stn via Staines Rd. Also extended Mon to Fri peak hours from Cranford to London Airport Central.

112 Palmers Grn (Green Lanes) - Ealing Bdy Stn via Nth Circular Rd; *operates in two sections Mon to Fri: Palmers Grn - Stonebridge Park extended peak hours to Park Royal (L.T. Stn)/ Finchley 'Manor Cottage Tavern' (peak hours) or Brent (L.T. Stn) - Ealing Bdy. (NOTE: Summer Sun extension to London Airport Cent not re-instated in 1960 - see route 83.)*

113 Oxford Circus - Edgware (L.T. Stn) via Baker St, Swiss Cottage, Hendon Central, Mill Hill and Edgwarebury La.

114 Edgware (L.T. Stn) - Rayners La (L.T. Stn) via Whitchurch La, Stanmore, Harrow Weald, Harrow, Lascelles Av, Porlock Av, Sth Harrow and Kings Rd.

115 Wallington (Belmont Rd) - Croydon Airport via Hackbridge, Mitcham, Streatham, Thornton Hth Pond and Purley Way; extended Mon to Sat to Whyteleafe (Upper Warlingham Stn) via Purley. *Operates in two sections Mon to Fri peak hours: Wallington - Croydon Airport/Thornton Hth (L.T. Gar) - Whyteleafe.*

116 Hounslow (L.T. Gar) - Staines (Moor La) via Staines Rd and Bedfont; extended summer Suns to Old Windsor ('Bells of Ouzeley') via Staines Bdg, The Causeway and Windsor Rd.

117 Hounslow (L.T. Gar) - Egham Stn via Hounslow Hth, Feltham, Lower Feltham, Ashford, Staines, The Causeway and The Avenue.

118 Raynes Park ('Junction Tavern') - Clapham Common (Old Town) via Grand Dr, Hillcross Av, Morden, Wandle Rd, Mitcham, Mitcham Common, Greyhound La, Streatham and Poynders Rd.

119 Bromley Nth Stn - Croydon (Park La) via Hayes La, Hayes, West Wickham and Shirley.

120 Hounslow Hth ('Hussar') - Southall (Town Hall, Cambridge Rd) via Hounslow Central, Lampton and Heston; extended Mon to Fri peak hours to Hayes Stn (Blyth Rd) via 'The Grapes' and Coldharbour La.

121 Ponders End (Enfield L.T. Gar) - Chingford Stn via Ponders End Stn and Lea Valley Rd.

122 Woolwich ('Earl of Chatham') - Bexleyheath (L.T. Gar) via Plumstead, Wickham La, Long La, Pickford La and Crook Log.

122A Woolwich ('Earl of Chatham') - Erith ('Prince of Wales') via Plumstead, Okehampton Cres, Bedonwell Rd, Parsonage Manor Way and Carlton Rd (Mons to Sats).

124 Forest Hill Stn - Eltham (Southend Cres) via Woolstone Rd, Catford, Sangley Rd, Torridon Rd, Verdant La, Northover, Grove Park, Dunkery Rd and Mottingham; extended Mon to Fri peak hours and Sun afts to Blackfen ('Woodman'); further extended Sun afts to Bexley Hospital via Bexley and Dartford Rd. *On Mons to Fris operates in two sections: Forest Hill - Eltham/Catford - Blackfen.*

125 Golders Grn (L.T. Stn) - Southgate (L.T. Stn) via Hendon, Holders Hill, Woodside Pk, Nth Finchley, Whetstone, Russell La and Osidge La (no service Suns Golders Grn -Woodside Pk, Cissbury Ring); extended Mon to Sat peak hours, Mon to Fri early eves, Wed and Sat afts, and Suns to Highlands and Sth Lodge Hospital via Winchmore Hill Rd and Eversley Pk Rd; further extended Suns to Winchmore Hill (Capitol) via Green Dragon La.

126 Beckenham Junction Stn - Plumstead Common ('Woodman') via Wickham Rd, Hayes La, Westmoreland Rd, Bromley, Grove Park, Grove Park Road, Mottingham, Eltham, Riefield Rd, Falconwood, Welling, Edison Rd and Swingate La.

128 Chase Farm Hospital - Lower Edmonton Stn via Lancaster Rd, Baker St, Enfield Town, Village Rd and Church St.

129 Claybury Bdy - Ilford Stn (York Rd) via Clayhall Av, Barkingside and Gants Hill; extended Sun afts to Little Hth ('Haw Bush') via Seven Kings and Barley La.

130 New Addington (Homestead Way) - Streatham (L.T. Gar) via Arnhem Dr, Lodge La, Shirley Inn, East Croydon, George St, Thornton Hth Pond, Galpins Rd, Wide Way and Greyhound La. *(Also express buses Mon to Fri peak hours New Addington (Homestead Way) - East Croydon Stn.)*

130A Thornton Hth (High St) - New Addington (Parkway) via Brigstock Rd, Thornton Hth Pond and route 130 to Lodge La, Headley Dr and Gascoigne Rd; extended Mons to Fris, except evenings, in a two-way loop via Arnhem Dr and King Henry's Dr to Headley Dr.

131 Kingston (S.R. Stn) - Walton-on-Thames (Manor Rd) via Hampton Court, East Molesey, West Molesey and Terrace Rd.

132 Eltham (Well Hall Stn) - Bexleyheath (L.T. Gar) via Blackfen, Danson Rd and Crook Log; extended Mon to Fri except eves, and Sat shopping hours to Erith ('Prince of Wales') via Erith Rd.

133 Sth Croydon (L.T. Gar) - Liverpool St (Finsbury Circus) via West Croydon, Whitehorse Rd, Thornton Hth, Melfort Rd, Streatham, Brixton, Kennington, Elephant & Castle, London Bdg and Moorgate; on Suns diverted at Moorgate and extended to Hendon Central (L.T. Stn) via Islington, Holloway, Archway, East Finchley, East End Rd and Hendon La.

134 Pimlico (Dolphin Square) - Potters Bar (L.T. Gar) via Victoria, route 24 to Camden Town, Kentish Town, Archway, Muswell Hill Bdy, Friern Barnet, Whetstone and Barnet (no service Mon to Fri off-peak Pimlico - Victoria); extended Mons to Sats to Potters Bar Stn via Church Rd and Darkes La. *(On Mon to Fri operates in two sections: Pimlico or Victoria - Friern Barnet/Archway - Potters Bar.)*

134A Victoria Stn (Wilton Rd) - Barnet (Chesterfield Rd) via route 134 to Whetstone, then route 34. (Suns)

135 Forty Hill ('Goat') - Brimsdown Stn via Chase Side, Enfield Town, Ponders End and Green St; works journeys extended to Brimsdown Power Stn daily.

137 Crystal Palace (Parade) - Oxford Circus via Crown Point, Leigham Court Rd, Streatham Hill Stn, Kings Av, Clapham Common, Cedars Rd, Chelsea Bdg, Sloane St and Marble Arch; extended Mon to Fri except evenings and Sat except afts and evenings, to Archway Stn via Great Portland St, Warren St and Camden Town.

138 Bromley Nth Stn - Coney Hall via Westmoreland Rd, Pickhurst La, Hayes and Kingsway (Mons to Sats).

139 Gants Hill (L.T. Stn) - Dagenham Dock via Whalebone La, Becontree Hth, Heathway and Chequers La (Mons to Sats). (No service Sat eves 'Church Elm' - Dagenham Dock.)

140 Mill Hill (Bunns La) - London Airport Central via Watling Av, Burnt Oak, Queensbury, Kenton, Harrow, Sth Harrow, Northolt, Yeading, Hayes and Harlington.

142 Watford Junction Stn - Edgware (L.T. Stn) via Bushey, Stanmore and Edgwarebury La; extended Mons to Sats except eves to Kilburn Park (L.T. Stn) via Colindale and Cricklewood.

143 Archway Stn - Hendon Central Stn via Highgate Stn, Aylmer Rd, The Bishops Av and route 133 (Mons to Sats).

144 Turnpike La (L.T. Stn) - Ilford Stn (York Rd) via Westbury Av, Great Cambridge Rd, Edmonton, 'Crooked Billet', Waterworks Corner and Gants Hill.

145 Chingford ('Royal Forest Hotel') - Dagenham (Kent Av) via Woodford Wells, Gates Corner, Gants Hill, Ilford, Green La, Bennetts Castle La, Porters Av, Becontree Stn, Hedgemans Rd and Heathway; works journeys extended/diverted Mons to Sats to Fords or Dagenham Dock.

146 Bromley Nth Stn - Downe (High St) via Hayes La, Keston and Downe Rd.

147 Redbridge (L.T. Stn) - East Ham ('White Horse') via The Drive, Ilford, Little Ilford La, Browning Rd and East Ham High St (Mons to Sats); extended Mon to Sat peak hours to Royal Albert Dock; some journeys further extended Mon to Fri peak hours to Nth Woolwich (Free Ferry).

RT 3769 and RT 4611 are seen in a traffic-free Sutton High Street on routes 164, which survived the 1960s unmolested, and the 156, which disappeared altogether in October 1961. *A.B. Cross*

148   Leytonstone ('Green Man') - Dagenham (Kent Av) via Gants Hill, Ilford, Green La, Bennetts Castle La, Parsloes Av and Heathway; works journeys extended/diverted to Fords or Dagenham Dock.

148A   Leytonstone ('Green Man') - Dagenham (Kent Av) via Redbridge, The Drive, Ilford and route 148 (Suns); some early and late journeys extended to Fords.

150   Lambourne End ('Beehive') - Ilford Stn via Chigwell Row, Manford Way, New North Rd, Barkingside and Gants Hill; extended Suns to E Ham ('White Horse') via route 147.

151   Hackbridge (Reynolds Close) - Morden (L.T. Stn) via Greenwrythe La and Middleton Rd; extended Mon to Fri peak hours to Nth Cheam ('Queen Victoria').

152   Mitcham ('Cricketers') - Feltham Stn via Western Rd, Colliers Wood, Sth Wimbledon, Kingston Rd, Kingston By-Pass, Hampton Court Way, Hampton Court, Bushy Park, Teddington, Hampton Hill and Hanworth.

153   West Hampstead (West End Grn) - Plumstead (L.T. Gar) via 59 to Oxford Circus then 53 (Suns).

154   Crystal Palace ('White Swan') - Sutton Grn via Anerley, Norwood Junction, Selhurst, West Croydon, Waddon, Stafford Rd, Park La, Carshalton, Ringstead Rd and Benhill Av; extended Mons to Sats to Morden (L.T. Stn) via St. Helier Av; and Suns to Sutton (L.T. Gar).

155   Wimbledon Stn (St George's Rd) - Victoria Embankment loop via Sth Wimbledon, Tooting, Clapham, Kennington then Lambeth Nth, Westminster Bdg, Blackfriars Bdg and Elephant & Castle or the reverse.

156   Morden (L.T. Stn) circular both ways via Nth Cheam, Cheam, Sutton, Collingwood Rd, Reigate Av and St. Helier Av. Some Mon to Fri early morning journeys operate St. Helier -Sutton Common Rd ('Woodstock') via Morden.

157   Crystal Palace ('White Swan') - Raynes Park ('Junction Tavern') via route 154 to Park La, Carshalton Stn, Wrythe La, St Helier, Morden and Martin Way.

158   Watford Junction Stn - Ruislip Lido via Bushey Hth, Harrow Weald, Harrow, Bessborough Rd, Sth Harrow and Ruislip Manor.

159   West Hampstead (West End Grn) - Thornton Hth (Clock Tower) via route 59 to Streatham and Green La (Mons to Sats); extended Sat afts to Sth Croydon (L.T. Gar) via Whitehorse Rd, West Croydon and Brighton Rd.

160   Catford (St Dunstan's College) - Welling ('Guy, Earl of Warwick') via Brownhill Rd, Westhorne Av, Middle Park Av, Kingsground, Eltham, Eltham Pk Stn, Rochester Way and Bellegrove Rd.

161   Chislehurst (War Memorial) - Woolwich (Parsons Hill) via Mottingham, Eltham and Woolwich Common; extended Mon to Fri peak hours to Greenwich Church via Woolwich Rd; also extended Mon to Fri peak hours, plus garage journeys daily, from Orpington to Sidcup (L.T. Gar) via Perry St and Sidcup High St.

161A   Petts Wood Stn - Woolwich (Parsons Hill) via Chislehurst and route 161 (Mons to Sats); extended Mon to Fri peak hours to Greenwich Church.

163   Victoria Embankment (Horse Guards Av) - Woolwich (General Gordon Pl) via Westminster Bdg, Kennington, Camberwell, New Cross, Greenwich and Woolwich Rd (Mons to Sats but no Mon to Fri eve service Victoria Embankment to Camberwell Grn); extended, except eves to Plumstead Com (Warwick Terrace) via Burrage Rd.

163A   Camberwell Grn - Woolwich (General Gordon Pl) via route 163 (Suns); extended aft and eve to Woodlands Estate (Flaxton Rd) via Griffin Rd, Plumstead Com and Garland Rd. *(Two early morning journeys extended from Camberwell Grn to Kennington ('Horns').)*

164   Morden (L.T. Stn) - Epsom Stn via St Helier, Sutton, Banstead Village, Drift Bdg and Alexandra Rd.

164A   Morden (L.T. Stn) - Tattenham Corner Stn via route 164 to Banstead and Tattenham Way.

165 Havering Park (Hunters Grove) - Rainham (War Memorial) via Collier Row, Romford, Hornchurch Rd, Abbs Cross Rd, Elm Park, Mungo Park Rd and Cherry Tree La.

166 Thornton Hth (High St) - Chipstead Valley Rd (Rectory La) via Brigstock Rd and route 59 (Mons to Sats).

167 Debden Bdy - Ilford Stn (York Rd) via Rectory La, Loughton, Buckhurst Hill, Roding La, Chigwell and Barkingside.

168 Putney Hth ('Green Man') - Victoria Embankment (Horse Guards Av) via West Hill, Wandsworth, Clapham Junction, Vauxhall and County Hall (Mon to Sat); extended Mon to Fri and Sat until lunchtime to Farringdon St (Farringdon Av). Also night service and early Sun journeys Wandsworth (Town Hall) - Farringdon St.

169 Barkingside (Forest Rd) - Barking Bdy via Horns Rd, Ley St, Ilford and Ilford La; journeys extended Mon to Fri peak hours to Remploy Factory via Thames View Estate.

169A Barkingside (Forest Rd) - Bow (Fairfield Rd) via 169 to Ilford and route 25 (Mons to Sats); extended Mon to Fri peak hours to Mile End Gate (Cambridge Rd).

170 Wandsworth (High St, Armoury Way) - Leyton Grn via route 44 to Vauxhall, Westminster Bdg, Temple Stn, Bloomsbury, Shoreditch, Hackney, Clapton and Lea Bdg Rd; (no Sunday service Wandsworth - Bloomsbury); extended to Leyton Downsell Rd Sat shopping hours, also some morning peak journeys Mon to Fri.

171 Tottenham (Bruce Grove) - Forest Hill Stn via Philip La, St Anns Rd, Manor House, Newington Grn, Essex Rd, Islington, Rosebery Av, Grays Inn Rd, Chancery La, Waterloo, County Hall, Elephant & Castle, Camberwell, New Cross Gate and Brockley.

172 Archway (L.T. Stn) - West Norwood ('Thurlow Arms') via Highbury, Islington, Bloomsbury, Temple Stn, Westminster Bdg, Kennington, Brixton, Effra Rd and Herne Hill; extended Suns to West Norwood (L.T. Gar).

173 Peckham (L.T. Gar) circular both ways via Rye La, Nunhead La, Evelina Rd, Ivydale Road, Cheltenham Rd and Peckham Rye.

174 Noak Hill ('Pentowan' Mons to Sats/Tees Dr daily) -Dagenham (Kent Av) via Whitchurch Rd, Hilldene Av, Gallows Corner, Romford, Roneo Corner, Dagenham Rd, Oxlow La and Heathway; works journeys extended daily to Fords Foundry. *Also Express service Mon to Fri peak hours Harold Hill (Gooshays Dr) - Romford Stn.*

175 Ongar (Moreton Rd) - Dagenham (Kent Av) via Stapleford Abbots, Havering, Collier Row, Romford, Roneo Corner, Becontree Hth and Heathway; part of service diverted at 'Chequers' and extended Mons to Sats to Poplar (Blackwall Tunnel) via route 106A; part of service diverted daily at 'Chequers' to Fords.

176 Willesden (L.T. Gar) - Forest Hill ('Railway Telegraph') via Kilburn, Maida Vale, Marylebone Rd, Tottenham Court Rd, Charing Cross, Waterloo, Elephant & Castle, Camberwell Grn and East Dulwich (Mons to Sats); extended Mon to Fri off-peak and Sat (after 9.30 a.m.) to Catford (L.T. Gar) via Stanstead Rd and Bromley Rd.

176A Cannon St Stn - Dulwich ('Plough') via Marshalsea Rd, Borough, Elephant & Castle and route 176 (Mon to Fri peak hours); some journeys extended to Forest Hill ('Railway Telegraph'). One aft jny from Catford (L.T. Gar).

177 Abbey Wood (L.T. Gar) - Victoria Embankment via Plumstead, Woolwich, Greenwich, New Cross Gate, Old Kent Rd and Elephant & Castle; continuing Mon to Fri, Sat peaks and am, and early Sun am in a two-way loop via Lambeth Nth, Westminster Bdg and Blackfriars Bdg On Sat afts and eves and Suns (except early morning 'press' journeys), service terminates at Horse Guards Av via Westminster Bdg.

177A Abbey Wood Estate (Grovebury Rd) - Woolwich (Parsons Hill) via Eynsham Dr, Basildon Rd and Plumstead.

178 Clapton Pond (Millfields Rd) - Stratford (Maryland Stn) via Homerton High St, Hackney Wick, Lee Conservancy Rd, Eastway and Carpenters Rd (Mons to Sats, except late evenings). *(Lowbridge buses.)*

179 Grove Park Stn - Finsbury Pk (Station Pl) via Downham Way, Catford, Stanstead Rd, Brockley Rise, New Cross Gate, Old Kent Rd, Elephant & Castle, Ludgate Circus, St Pauls, Aldersgate, Islington and Highbury.

Another product of trolleybus conversion stage three which rapidly withered was the 169A, which was just hanging on as a peak only service from Stratford to Barkingside by 1969. RTL 199 is at Stratford heading for its original western terminus at Mile End Gate. A.B. Cross

180 Lower Sydenham Stn - Woolwich (Parsons Hill) via Southend La, Catford, Lewisham and Greenwich (Mons to Sats); extended Mon to Fri peak hours to Plumstead Common (Warwick Terrace) via Burrage Rd.

181 Victoria (Vauxhall Bdg Rd) - Streatham (L.T. Gar) via Vauxhall, Stockwell, Clapham, Tooting and Southcroft Rd.

182 Cannon St Stn - Eltham (Well Hall Stn) via Marshalsea Rd, Borough, Old Kent Rd, New Cross Gate, Lewisham and Lee Grn (Mons to Sats but no service Mon to Fri evenings, Sat afts and evenings Cannon St - New Cross Gate); extended Mon to Fri peak hours and Sats until lunchtime to Woolwich (General Gordon Place). Some journeys operate Sun mornings and evenings New Cross Gate - Woolwich.

183 Golders Grn (L.T. Stn) - Northwood Stn via Brent St, Hendon Central, West Hendon, Kingsbury, Kenton, Harrow, Nth Harrow and Pinner.

184 Brockley Stn (Revelon Rd) - Victoria Embankment via Peckham Rye, Goose Grn, Camberwell Grn and Elephant & Castle; continuing Mon to Fri, Sat peaks and a.m., and early Sun a.m. in a two-way loop via Lambeth Nth, Westminster Bdg and Blackfriars Bdg On Sat afts and eves and Suns (except early morning 'press' journeys), service terminates at Horse Guards Av via Westminster Bdg.

185 Victoria (Vauxhall Bdg Rd) - Blackwall Tunnel (South Side) via Vauxhall, Camberwell Grn, East Dulwich, Forest Hill, Catford, Lewisham and Greenwich.

186 Woolwich (General Gordon Place) - Crystal Palace (Parade) via Well Hall Circus, Westhorne Av, Lee Grn, Lewisham, Adelaide Av, Brockley Rise, Forest Hill, Kirkdale and Westwood Hill; extended Mons to Sats to Victoria (Vauxhall Bdg Rd) via route 2B.

187 Sth Harrow (L.T. Stn) - Hampstead Hth (South End Grn) via Whitton Av, Alperton, Park Royal Stn, Chase Rd, Harlesden, Wrottesley Rd, Doyle Gardens, Kensal Rise, W Kilburn, Maida Vale, Circus Rd, Ordnance Hill, Adelaide Rd, Englands La and Haverstock Hill. *On Mons to Fris operates in two sections: Sth Harrow - W Kilburn/Park Royal Stn -Hampstead Hth.*

188 Greenwich Church - Aldwych via Surrey Docks, Rotherhithe, Tower Bdg Rd, Elephant & Castle and Waterloo; extended, except Sat afts and evenings to Chalk Farm (L.T. Stn) via route 68.

189 Clapham Common (Old Town) - Sth Wimbledon (L.T. Stn) via Nightingale La, Burntwood La, Plough La and Haydons Rd; extended Mons to Sats to Raynes Park ('Junction Tavern'); further extended Mon to Fri peak hours to Worcester Pk Stn via New Malden and Malden Rd.

190 Thornton Hth (High St) - Old Coulsdon ('Tudor Rose') via route 166 to Coulsdon, Marlpit La and Chaldon Way.

191 Edmonton (Goodwin Rd) - Chingford Hatch (Friday Hill) via Bounces Rd, Fore St, Angel Rd, Hall La, Chingford Mount and Larks Hall Rd (Mons to Sats).

192 Lewisham (Rennell St) - Woodlands Estate (Flaxton Rd) via route 89 to Shooters Hill, Eglinton Hill, Woolwich and route 163A (Mons to Sats).

193 Thames View Estate (Bastable Rd) - Chadwell Hth (Wangey Rd) via Barking Bdy, Ilford and Seven Kings; extended Sat afts to Hornchurch (L.T. Gar) via route 86.

194 Forest Hill Stn - Croydon Airport via Lower Sydenham, Penge, Anerley, Elmers End, West Wickham, Shirley, Croydon and Denning Av.

194A Beckenham Junction Stn - Croydon (Katherine St) via Village Way, West Wickham and Shirley (Mons to Sats); extended Sat afts to Croydon Airport.

195 Woolwich (Parsons Hill) - Eltham (Well Hall Stn) via route 96 to Bexleyheath, Bexley and Blackfen.

196 Tufnell Park (Hotel) - Norwood Junction Stn via Brecknock Rd, Kings Cross, Euston, route 68 to Beulah Hill and Sth Norwood Hill (Mons to Sats).

197 Norwood Junction Stn - Caterham Valley ('Old Surrey Hounds') via Woodside Grn, Addiscombe, Dingwall Rd, Croydon, Purley and Whyteleafe.

198 Uxbridge (L.T. Stn) - Hayes Stn (Blyth Rd) via Honeycroft Hill, Hillingdon and route 98 (Mons to Sats); extended Mons to Fris to Hounslow West (L.T. Stn).

199 Waterloo Stn - Farnborough ('George and Dragon') via route 1 to Lewisham then route 47 (Mons to Sats).

The official allocation of RTWs to route 185 ceased at the beginning of 1960 but Walworth had enough spare for it on Sundays until the class was withdrawn. RTW 425 is seen in Vauxhall Bridge Road. A.B. Cross

§200 Wimbledon Stn and Copse Hill (Coombe La) via Wimbledon Hill and Ridgway.

§201 Hampton Court Stn - Kingston (Bus Stn) via Imber Court, Thames Ditton, Effingham Rd, Surbiton, Claremont Rd, Lingfield Av and Villiers Rd.

§202 New Cross (Clifton Rise) - Rotherhithe (Canal Bdg) via Trundleys Rd, Surrey Docks, Hawkstone Rd and Rotherhithe New Rd; on Mons to Sats continues in a loop (both ways) via St James's Rd and Galleywall Rd back to New Cross.

203 Staines (Bridge St) - Stanwell Village (War Memorial) via Town La; extended Mons to Sats to Twickenham Stn via Hatton Cross, Hounslow, Hall Rd, Whitton, Percy Rd and Staines Rd.

203A Ashford Stn - Twickenham Stn via Town La, Clare Rd and route 203 (Mon to Fri).

204 Hayes Stn (Clarendon Rd) - Uxbridge (L.T. Stn) via Botwell La, Judge Heath La, Colham Grn, Hillingdon Hospital and Kingston La; extended Mon to Fri peak hours and Suns to Ruislip (L.T. Stn) via Park Rd, Swakeleys Rd and Ickenham.

205 Chingford ('Royal Forest Hotel') - Hammond St ('Rising Sun') via Sewardstone, Waltham Abbey, Waltham Cross and Cheshunt.

§206 Hampton Court Stn - Claygate (Holroyd Rd) via Imber Court, Lower Green Rd, Esher, Hare La and Coverts Rd.

§208 Clapton Pond (Millfields Rd) - Bromley By-Bow ('Seven Stars') via Homerton High St, Kenworthy Rd, Hackney Wick, Parnell Rd, Fairfield Rd and Bow Church.

209 Harrow Weald (L.T. Gar) - Sth Harrow (L.T. Stn) via Long Elmes, Hatch End, Elm Park Rd, Pinner, Cannon La, Rayners La Stn and Scott Cres (Mons to Sats).

§210 Finsbury Park (Wells Terrace) - Golders Grn (L.T. Stn) via Stroud Grn, Hornsey Rise, Archway Stn, Highgate Village and Hampstead La.

§211 Ealing Bdy Stn - Greenford (Windmill La) via Gordon Rd, Drayton Bdg Rd and Greenford Av.

§212 Finsbury Park (Wells Terrace) - Muswell Hill Bdy via Stroud Grn, Crouch End and Park Rd. *Also Express service Mon to Fri peak hours. (NOTE: Converted to double-deck 6.1.60.)*

§213 Kingston (Bus Stn) - Belmont ('California') via Norbiton Stn, Coombe La, Trapps La, New Malden, Worcester Park, Cheam, Sutton, Park Hill and Carshalton Beeches.

§215 Kingston (Bus Stn) - Ripley (Post Office) via Portsmouth Rd, Esher, Church Cobham and Wisley.

§215A Kingston (Bus Stn) - Downside Common via Portsmouth Rd, Church Cobham and Downside Rd (Mons to Sats).

§216 Kingston Stn - Staines (Bridge St) via Hampton Court, Hampton, Sunbury Village, Sunbury, Felthamhill Rd and Convent Rd.

217 Muswell Hill ('Victoria Hotel') - Upshire (Princesfield Rd) via Turnpike La, Westbury Av, Great Cambridge Rd, Waltham Cross, Waltham Abbey and Broomstickhall Rd (Mons to Sats).

§218 Kingston (Bus Stn) - Staines (Bridge St) via Esher, Hersham, Walton-on-Thames, Shepperton Stn and Laleham.

§219 Kingston (Bus Stn) - Weybridge Stn via Esher, Hersham, Queens Rd, Weybridge and Heath Rd; extended Mon to Fri peak hours, with some journeys on Sats and Suns, to Vickers Works via Caneswood Hill.

§222 Uxbridge (L.T. Stn) - Hounslow Central (L.T. Stn) via Cowley, West Drayton, Sipson Rd and Bath Rd. *(NOTE: Temporarily operating in two sections while West Drayton station bridge is rebuilt: Uxbridge - West Drayton Stn/ West Drayton (Warwick Rd) - Hounslow.)*

223 West Drayton Stn - Uxbridge (L.T. Stn) via Falling La, Colham Grn and route 204; extended Mons to Sats to Ruislip (L.T. Stn) via route 204.

§224 West Drayton (Warwick Rd) - Laleham (Broadway) via Harmondsworth, Colnbrook, Horton, Wraysbury, Staines and Worple Rd. *(Temporarily withdrawn Uxbridge (L.T. Stn) - West Drayton Stn during bridge rebuilding.)*

§224A West Drayton (Warwick Rd) - Mill Rd via Swan Rd (Mons to Sats). *Temporarily curtailed, as route 224.*

§224B West Drayton (Warwick Rd) - Stockley Estate (Mulberry Parade) via Porters Way (Mons to Sats). *Temporarily curtailed, as route 224.*

225 Eastcote La ('Eastcote Arms') - Northwood Stn via Eastcote, Field End Rd and Northwood Hills; extended Sun early afts to Mount Vernon Hospital.

226 Golders Grn (L.T. Stn) - Cricklewood Bdy (Ash Grove) via The Vale and Pennine Dr; extended Mons to Sats to Harlesden ('Willesden Junction Hotel') via Anson Rd, Dollis Hill, Willesden and Robson Av; further extended Mon to Fri peak hours to Park Royal Stadium via Acton La.

A lifetime's association with single-deckers came to an end for route 212 on 6th January 1960 when its RFs were replaced by RTs following the strengthening of Muswell Hill station bridge. RF 398 is seen in Stroud Green Road.

§227 Crystal Palace (Parade) - Chislehurst ('Gordon Arms', Edward Rd) via Penge, Beckenham, Shortlands, Bromley and Bickley.

228 Eltham (Well Hall Stn) - Chislehurst ('Gordon Arms', Edward Rd) via Avery Hill, Halfway St, Sidcup and Perry St.

229 Orpington Stn - Woolwich (Parsons Hill) via St. Mary Cray Estate, Foots Cray, Sidcup, Faraday Av, Murchison Av, Arbuthnot La, Townley Rd, Bexleyheath, Erith, Belvedere, Abbey Wood and Plumstead; extended Mon to Fri peak hours to Woolwich Rd (Victoria Way).

230 Rayners Lane (L.T. Stn) - Northwick Park Stn via Nth Harrow, Headstone Dr, Wealdstone, Christchurch Av and Kenton La. *(Lowbridge buses.)*

231 Muswell Hill ('Victoria Hotel') - Forty Hill ('The Goat') via 217 to Gt Cambridge Rd, then 135.

232 Hounslow (L.T. Gar) - Greenford ('Civil Engineer') via Hounslow West, Norwood Grn, Thornecliffe Rd, Southall and Lady Margaret Rd.

233 Finsbury Park (Clifton Terrace) - Northumberland Park Stn via Stroud Grn, Ferme Park Rd, Middle La, Alexandra Palace, Wood Grn, Perth Rd, White Hart La and Northumberland Park.

234 Wallington (Beddington Gardens) - Selsdon (Farley Rd) via Woodcote Grn, Purley, Mitchley Av and Sanderstead.

§234A Hackbridge Corner (Elm Rd) - Purley (Old Lodge La) via Wallington, Woodcote Grn and Purley.

235 Richmond Stn - Richmond Hill (Friars Stile Rd) via Church Rd (Mons to Sats and summer Suns).

§236 Leyton (Hainault Rd) - Finsbury Park (Plimsoll Rd) via Fairlop Rd, Grove Grn Rd, Hackney Wick, Victoria Park Rd, London Fields, Albion Dr, Queensbridge Rd, St Marks Rise, Shacklewell La, Mildmay Grove, Grosvenor Av and Highbury Barn; extended Mon to Fri peak hours to Stroud Grn ('The Stapleton').

§237 Hounslow (L.T. Gar) - Chertsey Stn via Hounslow Hth, Hounslow Rd, Feltham, Sunbury, Shepperton and Chertsey Rd.

238 Becontree (Chittys La) - Canning Town (Woodstock St) via Bennetts Castle La, Barking and route 5; extended Mon-Fri peak hours to North Woolwich (Free Ferry) via route 48.

240 Golders Grn (L.T. Stn) - Mill Hill Bdy (Station Rd) via Hendon, Holders Hill Rd, Mill Hill East and The Ridgeway.

§240A Mill Hill East (L.T. Stn) - Edgware (L.T. Stn) via Engell Park, Page St, Bunns La, Mill Hill Bdy and Hale La.

241 Sidcup (L.T. Gar) - Welling Stn via route 51 (Mons to Fris).

242 Epping Forest ('Wake Arms') - Cuffley Stn via Waltham Abbey, Waltham Cross and Cheshunt; extended Mons to Sats to Sth Mimms (Blanche La) via Northaw, Potters Bar and Mutton La.

242A Upshire (Princesfield Rd) - Potters Bar (L.T. Gar) via route 217 to Waltham Abbey and route 242 (Suns).

244 Winchmore Hill (Capitol Cinema) - Muswell Hill Bdy via route 125 to Southgate, Powys La, Bounds Grn and Alexandra Park Rd (Mons to Sats); extended Mon to Fri peak hours to Archway (L.T. Stn) via Highgate Stn.

246 Hornchurch Stn - Noak Hill (Tees Dr) via Emerson Park, Ardleigh Green Rd, Squirrels Hth Rd, Harold Wood Stn and Gooshays Dr (Mons to Sats); diverted Mon to Sat peak hours at North Hill Dr and extended to Gidea Park Stn via Straight Rd and Upper Brentwood Rd.

247 Brentwood ('Robin Hood and Little John') - Collier Row ('White Hart') via Warley, Harold Wood, Ardleigh Grn Rd, Gidea Pk Stn, Brentwood Rd, Romford and Collier Row La.

247A Harold Hill (Gooshays Dr) - Collier Row ('White Hart') via Harold Wood Stn and route 247 (not summer Suns); extended Mons to Sats to Gants Hill (L.T. Stn) via Romford Rd, New Nth Rd and Barkingside; further extended Sat shopping hours to Ilford Stn (York Rd)

247B Harold Hill (Gooshays Dr) - Chigwell Row ('Maypole') via 247A to Romford Rd (summer Suns).

248 Cranham (Moor La) - Upminster (Hall La) via St Mary's La and Upminster Stn. *(Lowbridge buses.)*

248A Corbets Tey ('Huntsman and Hounds') - Upminster Stn (Mon to Fri peak hours). *(Lowbridge bus.)*

§250 Hornchurch (L.T. Gar) - Epping Town (Grove La) via Romford, Collier Row, Stapleford Abbots, Abridge, Theydon Bois and Ivychimneys.

§251 Burnt Oak (Edgware Rd) - Arnos Grove (L.T. Stn) via Mill Hill Bdy, Highwood Hill, Totteridge and Whetstone.

252 Sth Hornchurch (Wood La) - Collier Row (Lowshoe La) via Elm Park, Rainham Rd, Romford and Mawney Rd. *(NOTE: from 20.1.60 school journeys extended Mon to Fri to Lodge La (Stapleford Gardens).)*

§254 Loughton (L.T. Stn) - Buckhurst Hill (L.T. Stn) via Oakwood Hill, Debden, Church Hill, Loughton Stn and Valley Hill; extended Mons to Sats to Sth Woodford (L.T. Stn) via Roding Valley.

260 Cricklewood (L.T. Gar) - Waterloo Stn via Kilburn, Marble Arch, Oxford Circus and Trafalgar Square (Mons to Fris); extended Mon to Fri peak hours to Surrey Docks Stn via route 1.

263 Coulsdon Nth Stn - Clockhouse Farm Estate via The Avenue and Grove La (Sat shopping hours).

§264 Kingston Stn - Hersham Grn via Hampton Court, Hampton, Staines Rd, Sunbury, Upper Halliford, Walton-on-Thames, Bowes Rd, Ambleside Av, Rydens Rd and Molesey Rd (Mons to Sats).

265 Chessington (Copt Gilders Estate) - Kingston (Bus Stn) via Stokesby Rd, Bridge Rd, Hook, Surbiton, Claremont Rd and Villiers Rd; extended Mon to Fri peak hours to East Acton (Brunel Rd) via Richmond, Kew and route 15. Also operates Mon to Fri off-peak and Sats Kew Grn ('Coach & Horses') - East Acton.

270 Teddington Stn - Hammersmith Bdy via route 27 (Mons to Sats); extended Mon to Fri, and Sat until lunchtime, to Kensington (Palace Gate).

277 Cubitt Town (Stebondale St) - Smithfield via West Ferry Rd, Limehouse, Mile End, Lauriston Rd, Hackney, Dalston Junction, Essex Rd, Islington, Goswell Rd and St John St.

§ - single-deck route

Route 229 was at its maximum extent at the beginning of 1960, following its extension in the first stage of the trolleybus conversion. RT 464 is seen mid-route at Bexleyheath Market Place. A.B. Cross

284   Charing Cross (Trafalgar Square) - Popar (Aberfeldy St) via Piccadilly Circus, Shaftesbury Av, Bloomsbury and route 5; one journey extended to Barking Bdy.

285   Grove Park Stn - Charing Cross (L.T. Stn) via route 36B to New Cross and 177 via Blackfriars.

286   Brockley Rise ('Chandos') - Charing Cross (L.T. Stn) via route 171 to Elephant & Castle, Blackfriars, Victoria Embankment.

287   Charing Cross (L.T. Stn) circular via Westminster, then route 155 to Tooting, Southcroft Rd, Streatham and route 109 via Westminster (one way only). Also Charing Cross circular via Blackfriars and route 109 to Streatham, Tooting and route 155 via Blackfriars.

288   Farringdon St (Farringdon Av) - Wandsworth (Armoury Way) via Victoria Embankment and route 170.

289   London Bdg Stn - Southall (Brent Rd) via route 7 to Marble Arch, 12 to Shepherd's Bush, Acton and Ealing.

290   Edmonton (Park Rd) - Pimlico (Grosvenor Rd) via Tottenham, Stamford Hill, Manor House, route 29 to Camden Town, Eversholt St, Euston Rd and 24.

291   Willesden (L.T. Gar) - Liverpool St Stn via Harlesden, Harrow Rd, Paddington Grn, Marble Arch, Trafalgar Square and route 11.

292   Archway (L.T. Stn) - Charing Cross (Trafalgar Square) via route 172 to Aldwych, Strand.

294   Cricklewood (L.T. Gar) - Liverpool St Stn via route 260 to Trafalgar Square and route 11.

295   Becontree Hth (Lay-By) - Charing Cross (Trafalgar Square) via route 23 to Aldgate, Monument, Bank, Holborn, Shaftesbury Av and Piccadilly Circus.

296   Leyton (L.T. Gar) - Waterloo Stn via route 38A to Rosebery Av, Farringdon Rd, Fleet St and Aldwych.

297   Turnham Grn (L.T. Gar) - Liverpool St Stn via Hammersmith, Dawes Rd, Fulham Bdy, route 14 to Piccadilly Circus and route 291.

298   Hornchurch (L.T. Gar) - Charing Cross (Trafalgar Square) via route 86 to Bow, Aldgate and route 295. Operates Sat night/Sun mornings Hornchurch - Holborn Circus.

SPECIAL SERVICES (CENTRAL ROAD SERVICES)

BEA   West London Air Terminal (Cromwell Rd) and London Airport (non-stop). *Operated on behalf of British European Airways Corporation.*

C   Hounslow Central (L.T. Stn) - Clare Hall Hospital via Busch Corner, Gunnersbury Av, Ealing Com, Hanger La, Alperton, Wembley Park and Burnt Oak. (Limited Stop; Weds and Suns).

PLA   Custom House Stn and Manor Way Stn (Mons to Sats). *Operated on behalf of the Port of London Authority.*

'Special'   Wimbledon Stn - Wimbledon Stadium via Alexandra Rd (non-stop). Operates Mon evenings for Speedway meetings, Wednesday and Fri evenings when dog racing takes place.

'Express'   Plaistow Stn - West Ham Stadium via Prince Regent's La (when events take place; non-stop).

'Greyhound Express' Romford Stn - Chadwell Hth stopping only at Romford Stadium. (Tues and Sat evenings).

RACE SPECIALS (All to Hurst Park, Kempton Park or Sandown Park from points shown.)

P   Tottenham Grn, Finsbury Pk, Camden Town and Baker St.

R   Barking (Fair Cross L.T. Gar), Manor Park Bdy, Mile End and Aldgate.

S   Lewisham (Rennell St), New Cross and Camberwell Grn.

T   Peckham (L.T. Gar), Clapham Common (The Polygon), Tooting Bdy and Morden (L.T. Stn).

U   Shepherd's Bush (The Grampians), Hammersmith Bdy and Putney Bdg.

V   Kingston (Wood St) and Hampton Court Stn to Hurst Park only.

W   Kingston (Bus Stn) to Sandown Park only (Sats only).

COUNTRY BUSES

NOTE: There were many minor variations on Country Bus routes, often involving only one or two journeys. To simplify presentation, only the main operations are shown here. Many routes had no service on Sunday mornings; these are not distinguished unless there is a variation during the day.

301   Aylesbury (Kingsbury Sq) - Watford Junction Stn via Tring, Boxmoor and Kings Langley.

301A   Ovaltine Works - Watford Junction Stn (Works jnys Mon to Fri).

301B   Hemel Hempstead (Bus Stn) - Watford Junction Stn via Two Waters, Kings Langley and Watford By-Pass (Works jnys Mon to Fri).

301C   Hemel Hempstead (Bus Stn) - Durrants Farm Estate via Two Waters, Boxmoor and Berkhamsted; diverted Mon to Fri peak hours and one journey Sats to Tring (L.T. Garage); also extended Mon to Fri peak hours, with some Sat and Sun jnys to Hemel Hempstead (St Pauls Rd).

301D   Ovaltine Works - Watford Junction Stn via By-Pass (Works jnys Mon to Fri).

302   Longlands (Windmill Rd) - Watford Heath (Memorial) via Hemel Hempstead Town Centre, Two Waters, Watford High St, Bushey Stn and Pinner Rd.

303   New Barnet Stn - Hitchin via Potters Bar, Bell Bar, Hatfield, Welwyn Garden City and Stevenage.

303A   New Barnet Stn - Hitchin via Welham Green and route 303.

#304   St Albans (City Stn) - Whitwell (Post Office) via Wheathampstead and Kimpton; extended Sat and Sun afts and eves to Hitchin (St Mary's Sq); on Sat afts, diverted in St Albans to St Julians, Park St or Colney St.

305   Beaconsfield ('Saracen's Head') - Gerrards Cross ('Packhorse') via The Chalfonts; extended Sat afts and eves to Uxbridge (L.T. Stn).

305A   Gerrards Cross ('Packhorse') - Chalfont Common (Post Office) via Chalfont St Peter and Leachcroft Estate (Mons to Sats); extended Sat afternoons to Horn Hill (Church).

306   Leavesden (Works, peak hours, Ganders Ash other times) - Borehamwood (Elstree Way/Warwick Rd) via Gammons La, Watford, Bushey Heath and Elstree; extended, except late evenings Mons to Sats and Sun mornings to New Barnet Stn via route 107.

306A   New Barnet Stn - Leavesden (Ganders Ash) as 306 but via Little Bushey (Mons to Fris).

#307   Boxmoor Stn - Harpenden (Masefield Rd) via St John's Rd, Hemel Hempstead, Lybury La and Redbourn.

#307A   Apsley Mills - Harpenden (Masefield Rd) via Hemel Hempstead and route 307 (Works jnys Mons to Fris).

#307B   Chaulden (Lower Sales) - Hemel Hempstead (Bus Stn) via St John's Rd (Sat shopping hours).

#308   Hertford (Bus Stn) - Cuffley Stn via Brickendon, Epping Green and Newgate St.

#308A   Hertford (Bus Stn) - Little Berkhampsted ('Five Horseshoes') via 308 to Epping Grn (Mons to Sats).

#309   Chorleywood (Furze View) - Harefield (Hill End, St Mary's Rd or Truesdale Dr Mons to Sats, 'Kings Arms' or Hospital Suns) via Heronsgate, Rickmansworth and Woodcock Hill.

310   Hertford (Sele Farm Estate) - Enfield Town (Cecil Rd) via Ware, Hoddesdon, Waltham Cross and Gt Cambridge Rd.

310A   Rye House (Old Highway) - Enfield Town (Cecil Rd) via Hoddesdon and route 310.

311   Shenley ('Black Lion') - Watford (Chilcott Rd) via Radlett, Aldenham and Bushey; extended to Leavesden (Works or Ganders Ash) Mon to Fri peak hours, Mon to Sat afts and eves.

312   Little Bushey (Oundle Avenue) - Cassiobury Estate (Langley Way) via Watford High St.

313   Enfield Town (Cecil Rd) - St Albans (L.T. Garage) via Potters Bar and London Colney; extended during summer months to Whipsnade Zoo via Markyate.

314A   Warners End (Birch Green) - Bennetts End via Gadebridge or Boxted Rd, Town Centre, St Albans Hill then a two-way loop via Leys Rd, Barnacres Rd and Belswains La.

314B Warners End (Birch Green) - Maylands Avenue (Rotax or Cleveland Rd) via 314, Town Centre and Adeyfield Rd (Mon to Sat peak hours).

315 Kimpton (Lawn Av) - Welwyn Garden City (Black Fan Rd), via Welwyn (Mon to Fri peak hours).

#316 Chesham Bdy - Hemel Hempstead (Bus Stn) via Codmore Cross, Bovingdon and Boxmoor; extended Sat afts and early eves to St Pauls Rd. *(Operated jointly with Rover Bus Services, who also work via Latimer and Flaunden.)*

#316A Apsley Mills (Clock) - Hemel Hempstead (Bathurst Rd) via Two Waters (Works jnys Mon to Fri).

#317 Two Waters (L.T. Gar) - Berkhamsted Stn via Hemel Hempstead, Great Gaddesden and Ringshall (Mons to Sats).

#317A Two Waters (L.T. Gar) - Little Gaddesden ('Bridgewater Arms') via Nettleden (Mon to Sat).

318 Hemel Hempstead (Bus Stn) - Abbots Langley (Hazelwood La) via Bovingdon, Sarratt, Croxley, Watford and Garston. (Watford, Clarendon Rd - Abbots Langley only, on Sun mornings.)

318A Bucks Hill ('Cart and Horses') - Abbots Langley (Hazelwood La) via Croxley and route 318.

318B Garston (L.T. Gar) - North Watford (Maytree Crescent) (school jny Mon to Fri).

#319 Garston (L.T. Gar) - Chipperfield ('Two Brewers') via Abbots Langley and Kings Langley (Mons to Sats); some Mon to Fri peak jnys extended to Sarratt ('Wheatsheaf').

#319A Garston (L.T. Gar) - Two Waters (L.T. Gar) via Nash Mills (Mon to Fri works jnys).

#319B Two Waters (L.T. Gar) - Chipperfield via Kings Langley (Mon to Fri jnys).

#319C Garston (L.T. Gar) - Two Waters (L.T. Gar) via Apsley Mills (Mon to Fri works jnys).

#319D Garston (L.T. Gar) - Langleybury School via Abbots Langley (school jnys).

320 Warners End (Martindale Rd) - Hemel Hempstead (Bus Stn) via Chaulden, Boxmoor and Two Waters; extended Mons to Sats to Adeyfield (Vauxhall Rd) via Adeyfield Rd (peak hours and lunchtimes via Maylands Av); also extended Mon to Sat peak hours and Mon to Fri eves Warners End to Gadebridge.

321 Luton (Park Sq) - Uxbridge (L.T. Stn) via Harpenden, St Albans, Garston, Watford and Rickmansworth. *(Normally works: Luton - Maple Cross/St Albans or Garston - Uxbridge.)*

321A Luton (Park Sq) - Rickmansworth (Berry La Estate) via 321 and Church La.

#322 Hemel Hempstead (Bathurst Rd) - Watford Junction via Belswains La, Kings Langley Stn and Huntonbridge.

#322A Warners End (Birch Green) - Watford Junction via Gadebridge, Town Centre and 322 (Suns pm).

#322B Watford Junction - Kings Langley ('The Nap') via 322 to Kings Langley Stn (Sats).

323 Woodside Estate (Buxton Rd) - Purfleet Stn via Southend Rd, Grays and West Thurrock (works jnys Mons to Sats).

323A Nutberry Corner - Purfleet Stn via Socketts Heath and 323 (works jnys Mons to Fris).

323B Stifford Clays (Whitmore Av) - Grays (War Memorial) via Stifford Long La and Rectory Rd; extended Sat afts, also works jnys Mons to Sats, to Purfleet Stn via 323.

324 Welwyn Garden City (Knightsfield) - Station via 'Cherry Tree', Heronswood Rd, Howlands and Ludwick Way; (some jnys complete the circuit to Knightsfield).

325 New Greens Estate (High Oaks) - Cottonmill Estate via Batchwood Dr, St Peters St, Prospect Rd and Maynards Dr and back; or via Townsend, St Peters St, Maynards Dr, Prospect Rd and back.

§325A St Albans (Firbank Rd) and Cottonmill Estate (anti-clockwise) (Mon to Fri peak hours).

326 Micklefield Estate (Woodside Rd North) - Mill End Rd (Dashwood Av) via Wycombe Marsh, Bowerdean Cross Rds, High Wycombe Stn, Desborough Rd and Green St; some morning jnys extended Mons to Sats to Sands (Sherwoods Corner). Also operates from New Bowerdean Rd Mon to Fri peak hours and evenings, Sats and Suns, normally to Castle St. *(Operated jointly with Thames Valley routes 26/26A.)*

327 Hertford (Bus Stn) - Nazeingwood Common (Church Rd) via Ware, St Margarets, Hoddesdon and Broxbourne.

328 Woodside Estate (Buxton Rd) - Aveley (Usk Rd) via Southend Rd, Grays, North Stifford and Belhus Estate; extended Mon to Sat peak hours to Rainham (War Memorial) via Wennington; some jnys also extended Mons to Fris from Woodside Estate to Orsett (High Rd).

328A Purfleet Stn - Woodside Estate (Buxton Rd) via Aveley and route 328. *(Mon to Sat peak hours); only two jnys Mon to Sat in reverse direction; one from Orsett on Thursdays.)*

328B Sth Ockendon (Ockendon Stn) - Purfleet Stn via Stifford Rd and Aveley (Mon to Sat peak hours).

RT 1000 in Watford on Country Bus route 306, which covered the same roads as Central Bus route 107 for half its length. A.B. Cross

When Harlow garage opened in May 1963, the related extension of the 339 from Epping to the New Town made the continued operation of the Coxtie Green spur, on which RT 3649 was photographed in October 1962, impracticable and it was surrendered to Eastern National.
Ken Glazier

#329   Hertford (Bus Stn) - Woolmer Green via Bramfield and Datchworth Green; extended Mon to Sat to Nup End via Knebworth.

#329A   Datchworth (Church) - Hitchin (St Mary's Sq) via Knebworth, Nup End, Langley and St Ippolytts (Tues and Sats).

330   Welwyn Garden City (Howlands via Hollybush La or Great Ganett via Cole Green La) - Hemel Hempstead (Bus Stn) via Valley Rd, Stanborough, Stone House Corner, Oaklands, St Albans and Leverstock Green.

330B   St Albans (L.T. Garage) - Hatfield Technical College (School Days Only).

331   Hertford (Bus Stn) - Buntingford ('Jolly Sailors') via Ware, Wadesmill, Standon Stn, then either West Mill, or Braughing and Hare St.

#332   Amersham (L.T. Garage) - Quill Hall Estate (Grove Rd) via Stanley Hill (school days only).

#333   Hertford (Bus Stn) - Bengeo (Parker Av) via Port Hill; jnys extended Mons to Sats to Chapmore End.

#333B   Hertford (Bus Stn) - Ware Park Hospital via Bengeo.

334   Hemel Hempstead (Bus Stn) - Maylands Av (Cleveland Rd) via Belswains La and Bennett Gate (Mon to Sat peak hours, also Mon to Fri lunchtimes and evenings).

334A   Hemel Hempstead (Bus Stn) - High St Green via Belswains La and Bennett Gate (Mon to Fri peak hours).

335   Watford (Leavesden Rd) - Windsor (Bus Stn) via Rickmansworth, Chenies, The Chalfonts, Gerrards Cross, Wexham St, Slough and Eton.

336   Watford (Leavesden Rd) - Chesham ('Nashleigh Arms') via Rickmansworth, Chenies and Amersham Stn.

#336A   Rickmansworth Stn - Loudwater Estate Office via Loudwater La and Troutstream Way or the reverse (Mons to Sats).

#337   Dunstable (Square) - Hemel Hempstead (Bus Stn) via Whipsnade Heath, Gaddesden Row and Water End; extended Mons to Sats to Boxmoor Stn via St John's Rd. During summer months operates via Whipsnade Zoo.

338   St Albans (L.T. Gar) - Harperbury Hospital via London Colney; extended Wed and Sun afternoons to Radlett (Station Rd). Some jnys run via Napsbury Hospital, numbered 338A.

339   Epping (L.T. Gar) - Brentwood Stn via North Weald, Ongar and Kelvedon Hatch; extended, except Sun am and eves to Warley ('Headley Arms'). A separate spur also

works Coxtie Green ('White Horse') - Brentwood or Warley.

340   New Barnet Stn - Welwyn Garden City Stn via Potters Bar, North Mimms, Stone House Corner and Stanborough (Mon to Sat peak hours).

340A   Potters Bar (Whaley Rd) - Hatfield Technical College (school days only).

340B   New Barnet Stn - Hatfield (L.T. Gar Suns; Stn Mons to Sats) via Potters Bar, North Mimms, South Hatfield and Roe Green; extended Mon to Sat peak hours to Birchwood Estate (Longmead) or Welwyn Garden City Stn via Oldings Corner and Longcroft Green; also extended Sat afternoons Hatfield to Hitchin via Welwyn Garden City and route 303.

341   Marshalswick Estate (Sherwood Av) - Hertford (Bus Stn) via St Albans, Hatfield, Mill Green and Essendon Mill.

341A   Marshalswick Estate (Sherwood Av) - South Hatfield (Hazel Grove) via St Albans, Stone House Corner and Roe Green (Sat and Sun afts).

343   Brookmans Park Stn (Blue Bridge Rd) - Dunstable (Square) via North Mimms, Colney Heath, Oaklands, St Albans and Markyate; extended Mon to Fri peak hours and Sat morning to AC-Delco Works.

#343A   Studham ('Red Lion') - Dunstable AC-Delco Works (Mon to Sat peak hours).

345   Bushey and Oxhey Stn - Napsbury Hospital via Watford and Garston (Limited Stop Weds and Suns).

346   Kingswood (North Orbital Rd) - Oxhey Estate (Hallowes Cres) via The Harebreaks, Watford, Bushey Arches and Hayling Rd.

346A   Kingswood (North Orbital Rd) - Oxhey Estate (Heysham Dr) via 346 and Prestwick Rd.

346B   Oxhey Estate (Hallowes Cres) - Oxhey Estate (Heysham Dr) via Carpenders Park Stn (Mon to Fri peak hours).

346D   Oxhey Estate (Hallowes Cres) - Aldenham Rd (Bushey Mill La) (Schoolchildren only).

346E   Oxhey Estate (Heysham Dr) - Garston (St Michaels School) (Schoolchildren only).

347   Hemel Hempstead (Bus Stn) - Uxbridge (L.T. Stn) via Bedmond, Garston, Watford, Bushey, Northwood, Harefield and Denham.

347A   Watford (Gaumont Cinema) - Bushey and Oxhey Stn via St Albans Rd, Watford By-Pass and Bushey Technical School (Limited Stop School Days only).

#348 Chesham Moor - Buckland Common ('Rose & Crown') or St Leonards via Bellingdon.

#348A Chesham Bdy - Pond Park Estate via Hivings Hill and Upper Belmont Rd (Mons to Sats).

349 Grays (War Memorial) - Shell Haven (Shell Cottages) or Coryton (Mobil Oil Co.) via Socketts Heath, Stanford-le-Hope and Corringham (Works jnys daily).

#350 Bishops Stortford (Havers La Estate) - Hertford (Bus Stn) via Little Hadham, Widford, Wareside and Ware; extended, except late evenings and Sun mornings, to Potters Bar (Whaley Rd) via Cole Green, Essendon and Brookmans Park; further extended Mon to Fri peak hours and Sat, except evenings to New Barnet Stn.

#350A As 350 but via Hunsdon and St Margarets; on Suns only one jny to Potters Bar.

§#352 Dunstable (Square) - Dagnall (#Weds, #Fris and §Sats); extended Sats to Berkhamsted Stn via Ringshall and Northchurch.

353 Berkhamsted Stn - Windsor (Bus Stn) via Chesham, Chesham Bois, Amersham, The Chalfonts, Gerrards Cross, Stoke Common, Slough and Eton.

354 St Albans (Chestnut Dr) circular both ways via Fleetville, St Peters St and Sandpit La.

#355 Harpenden (Church Green) - Borehamwood (Cowley Hill) via Wheathampstead, St Albans, Radlett, Allum La, Eldon Av and Hartforde Rd; also operates Harpenden - Pickford Hill Estate.

357 Grays (L.T. Gar) - Tilbury (Iron Bridge) via Nutberry Corner, Socketts Heath, Little Thurrock and Dock Rd (Mon to Sat peak hours).

358 St Albans (L.T. Gar) - Borehamwood (Drayton Rd) via London Rd, Napsbury and Shenley. On Sats also operates St Albans (L.T. Gar) - Sheephouse Farm Estate.

#359 Amersham (L.T. Stn) - Aylesbury (Kingsbury Sq) via Great Missenden and Wendover. *(Operated jointly with United Counties Omnibus Co.)*

360 Luton (Park Sq) - Caddington via Farley Green.

362 High Wycombe (Queen Victoria Rd) - Ley Hill ('Crown') via Hazlemere, Holmer Green, Amersham and Chesham.

362A As 362 but via Widmer End (Suns).

363 Penn (Post Office) - Totteridge via Hazlemere, High Wycombe and Wycombe Marsh.

#364 Hitchin (St Mary's Sq) - Flamstead Village via Preston, Breachwood Green, Cockernhoe, Vauxhall Works, Luton, Woodside and Markyate.

#364A Hitchin (St Mary's Sq) - Kensworth ('Farmer's Boy') via 364 to Markyate; extended summer months to Whipsnade.

#365 Luton (Park Sq) - St Albans (City Stn) via Newmill End and Wheathampstead.

366 High Wycombe (Queen Victoria Rd) - Widmer End (Primrose Hill) via Terriers (Mons to Sats).

367 Tilbury Docks ('The Ship') - East Tilbury (Bata Shoe Factory) via Civic Sq and Chadwell St Mary (Mon to Fri peak hours, peak direction only; Bata employees only).

368 Grays ('Queen's Hotel') - East Tilbury (Bata Shoe Factory) via Chadwell St Mary (Mon to Fri peak hours, peak direction only; Bata employees only).

369 Aveley (Usk Rd) - South Ockendon Stn via Belhus Estate (Mon to Fri peak and Sat shopping hours).

370 Tibury Ferry (Riverside Stn) - Romford (London Rd L.T. Gar) via Chadwell St Mary, Grays, The Ockendons, Upminster and Hornchurch.

370A Tibury Ferry (Riverside Stn) - Purfleet Stn via Chadwell St Mary, Grays and Stonehouse Corner (works jnys Mons to Sats).

371 Rainham (War Memorial) - Tilbury (Feenan Highway) via Tunnel Garage, Aveley, Stonehouse Corner, Grays and Dock Rd.

371A Purfleet Stn - Tilbury (Feenan Highway) via Grays and 371 (NOT Sat afternoons).

371B As 371 but via Sandy La, Aveley, instead of Tunnel Garage (Mons to Sats).

#372 Welwyn Garden City (Lemsford La) - Coopersale St ('Theydon Oak') via Hertingfordbury, Hertford, Ware, Roydon, Epping Green and Epping; some jnys extended Mons to Sats to Coopersale Common (Gernon Bushes).

#373 Penn (Post Office) - Beaconsfield ('Saracen's Head') via Knotty Green; Mon to Fri afternoon jnys extended to Holtspur (North Dr).

374 Aveley (Tunnel Garage) - Linford ('George & Dragon') via Uplands Estate, Stonehouse Corner, Grays, Chadwell St Mary and East Tilbury.

377A Boxmoor Stn or Apsley Mills - Friars Wash via Two Waters, Hemel Hempstead and Cupid Green (works jnys, Mon-Fri); one eve jny Sat and Sun Two Waters (L.T. Gar) - Cupid Green (Brocks factory).

377B Apsley Mills - Friars Wash via St Albans Hill or Bennetts Gate and Cupid Green (works jnys Mons to Fris).

378 Apsley Mills - Boxmoor (Wharf Rd) or Warners End (Martindale Rd) via Two Waters (works jnys Mons to Fris and Suns).

379 Tilbury Docks ('The Ship') - Chadwell St Mary ('Cross Keys') via Civic Sq and Feenan Highway (works jnys Mons to Sats).

There was no official allocation of lowbridge buses to the 353 but they appeared occasionally and RLH 42 seems to be working a summer duplicate from Windsor to Chalfont St Giles, an unusual intermediate destination for this route. Amersham lost its RLHs in October 1965 when route 336 became RF one-man operated. A.B. Cross

#381 Roydon (Temple) - Toothill ('Green Man') via Epping Green, Epping and Colliers Hatch (Mons to Sats).

#382 St Albans (L.T. Garage) - Codicote ('Red Lion') via Fleetville, Woodstock Rd, Lemsford and Welwyn (Mons to Sats).

#383 Hitchin (St Mary's Sq) - Purwell La Estate or Weston via Walsworth and Willian.

#384 Letchworth Stn - Hertford (Bus Stn) via Graveley, Stevenage, Walkern, Dane End, Tonwell and Ware.

#384A Great Munden (Schools) - Hertford (Bus Stn) via Dane End and 384 (Mons to Sats).

#384B Letchworth Stn - Stevenage (Bus Stn) via Letchworth Gate (Mon to Fri peak hours).

385 Croxley Green (Manor Way) - Mill Way Estate (Park Av) via Whippendell Rd, Queens Av, Watford Junction and Bushey Mill La; extended Mon to Fri peak hours to Aldenham L.T. Works (Elstree Hill) via Watford By-Pass. Some peak hour jnys run to or from Holywell Estate.

385A Holywell Estate (Tolpits La) - Garston (L.T. Gar) via Hagden La, Queens Av, Watford Junction, Bushey Mill La and Meriden Estate (Mons to Sats, except evenings). Some peak jnys start from Croxley Green (Manor Way) or Watford (Met Stn).

385B Croxley Green (Manor Way) or Watford (Met Stn) or Holywell Estate - Aldenham Works via North Watford (Mon to Fri peak hours).

#386 Bishops Stortford (Havers La Estate) - Hitchin (St Mary's Sq) via Little Hadham, Standon, Braughing, Buntingford, Cottered, Walkern, Stevenage, Titmore Green and Great Wymondley. Operates throughout on Sats; B. Stortford - Buntingford Thursdays; Buntingford - Hitchin Tuesdays.

#§387 Tring (Beaconsfield Rd) - Aldbury (The Pond) via Tring Stn (Mons to Sats).

#388 Sawbridgeworth (Knight St) - Welwyn (Prospect Pl) via Gilston, Stanstead Abbotts, Ware, Hertford and Tewin; extended Mon to Fri peak hours and Sat a.m. peak to Mardley Hill ('North Star'); some jnys diverted Mons to Sats at Welwyn North to Welwyn Garden City Stn via Tewin Rd.

389 Hatfield (Manor Rd) - Sth Hatfield (Hazel Grove South) via Barnet By-Pass (Mon to Fri peak hours).

#390 Hertford (Bus Stn) - Stevenage Stn via Stapleford, Watton, Aston, Bragbury End and Broadwater; double-deck service also operates Hertford - Watton Stn (closed) Mons to Sats.

§391 Tyttenhanger ('Plough') - St Albans (L.T. Gar) via Hill End; extended Sun eves and Mons to Sats to Firbank Rd; also extended Mon to Sat peak hours and Sat afts to Sandridge (Church).

§391A Hill End Hospital - New Greens Estate (Woollam Cres) via St Peters St and Townsend.
NOTE: Some Mon to Fri peak jnys on 391 and 391A run to/from Hill End Stn.

392 Stevenage Stn - Bus Stn via Haycroft Rd, Popple Way and Six Hills Way (Mons to Sats).

392A Bandley Hill - Stevenage Stn via Bedwell, Cuttys La and Bus Stn; part diverted at High St and extended to Hitchin (St Mary's Sq) via Little Wymondley Mons to Sats, except evenings.

#393 Welwyn Garden City (Lemsford La) - Old Harlow ('Green Man') via Hertford, Hertford Heath, Hoddesdon, Broxbourne, Lea Side Nursery, Gt Parndon and First Av.

#394 Great Missenden Stn - Hyde Heath (Meadow Way) via Ballinger, Chartridge, Chesham and Copperkins La; one journey Weds and Fris and part of Sat and Sun service intermediately diverted via Swan Bottom between Lee Common and Chartridge.

#394A Great Missenden Stn - Chesham Moor via 394 to Chesham, Waterside (Mons to Sats).

395 Hertford (Bus Stn) - Ware (Fanshawe Crescent).

395A Hertford (Bus Stn) - Fanham Common via Musley Hill, Fanhams Rd (return Cromwell Rd).

396 Epping (L.T. Gar) - Bishops Stortford ('Bricklayers Arms') via Thornwood, Old Harlow and Sawbridgeworth. Some jnys operate via Epping Stn.

396A Harlow (Hare St) - Harlow Stn via First Av; extended Mon to Sat peak hours, Mon to Fri lunchtime and Sat afts and eves to Bishops Stortford ('Bricklayers'); some jnys work via Burnt Mill roundabout and/or Templefields.

#397 Chesham Bdy - Tring (L.T. Gar) via Hawridge and Wigginton; operates TO Chesham Moor only Mon to Fri peak hours and Sats.

#398 Beaconsfield ('Saracen's Head') - Amersham (L.T. Gar Suns; Quill Hall Estate, Grove Rd, Mons to Sats) via Coleshill.

#398A Quill Hall Estate (Grove Rd) - Winchmore Hill via Coleshill (Mon to Sat jnys).

399 Bulphan (Church) - Grays (War Memorial) via Orsett and Socketts Heath; extended Mons to Sats and two jnys Suns to (one from) Uplands Estate via Stonehouse Corner; evening jnys Mons to Sats further extended to Aveley (Tunnel Garage).

400 Britwell (Wentworth Av) - Wexham Court Farm Estate circular via Farnham Rd, Slough and Upton Lea (Mons to Sats); operates Slough Stn - Wexham Court Farm Estate (circular) Suns.

401 Sevenoaks (Bus Stn) - Upper Belvedere ('Eardley Arms') via Otford, Farningham, Sutton-at-Hone, Dartford, Bexley, Bexleyheath and Long La; diverted during peak hours and extended to Lower Belvedere (Railway Place); some works jnys continue to Crabtree Manor Way or Belvedere Generating Stn.

401B Swanley (L.T. Garage) - Eynsford ('Castle') via Farningham (garage jnys for R.401).

402 Bromley North Stn - Sevenoaks (Bus Stn) via Farnborough, Knockholt and Dunton Green; extended Mon-Fri (except evenings), Sat shopping hours and Suns, to Tonbridge Stn. Works jnys also operate Mon-Fri Fort Halstead - Sevenoaks.

403 Tonbridge Stn - West Croydon (St Michaels Rd) via Sevenoaks, Westerham, Chelsham, Sanderstead Stn and Park La; extended Mon-Fri (except evenings) and Sat to Wallington (Belmont Rd) via Waddon and Beddington. (No service Tonbridge - Sevenoaks winter Suns.)
Also express service Mon-Fri peak hours (peak direction only) Chelsham - West Croydon.

403A Warlingham Park Hosp - Wallington (Belmont Rd) via Chelsham and 403 (Mon-Fri peaks, Wed afts, Sats and Suns).

403B Farleigh ('The Harrow') - Wallington (Belmont Rd) via Chelsham and 403 (Mon-Fri peaks and Sats).

#404 Sevenoaks (Bus Stn) - Shoreham Village via Otford and Twitton.

405 West Croydon (St Michaels Rd) - Horsham (Carfax) via Coulsdon, Redhill, Crawley and Faygate.

405A Roffey Corner - Horsham (Carfax) via Littlehaven.

406 Kingston Stn - Redhill (Market Pl) via Tolworth, Ewell, Epsom, Tadworth and Kingswood.

406A Kingston Stn - Tadworth Stn via 406 and Merland Rise.
Also Express service Mon-Fri peak.

§406C Kingswood (Windmill Press) - Reigate (L.T. Gar) via Reigate, Redhill, Earlswood and Meadvale (works jnys Mon-Fri).

406E Epsom Town - Epsom Downs (Derby Stables Rd) via Ashley Road, Chalk Lane, Woodcote Road and South Street. Race Days only. *(Route reversed after 3 pm, except on Derby Day.)*

406F Epsom Station - Epsom Downs (Derby Stables Rd) via route 406E. Race Days only.

408 Guildford (Bus Stn, Onslow St) - Chelsham (L.T. Garage) via Effingham, Leatherhead, Epsom, Cheam, Sutton, Beddington and 403.

408A Guildford (Bus Stn, Onslow St) - Merrow (Bushy Hill).

409 West Croydon (Station Rd) - Forest Row ('Swan') via Purley, Coulsdon Common, Caterham, Godstone, Lingfield and East Grinstead.

410 Bromley North Stn - Reigate ('Red Cross') via Bromley Common, Biggin Hill, Westerham, Godstone and Redhill.

411 West Croydon (Station Rd) - Reigate ('Red Cross') via 409, Godstone and 410 (Mon to Sats).

The route served by the 430 was one of the oldest established in Reigate, where RT 3454 is seen, its ancestor having started in 1920. A.B. Cross

#412 Dorking North Stn - Sutton ('The Volunteer') via Wotton Hatch and Holmbury St Mary.

#413 Brasted (Rectory La) - Chipstead (Square) via Ide Hill, Sevenoaks and Bessels Grn. Peak hour jnys also operate to/from Sundridge Hospital.

#413A Four Elms (Cross Roads) - Chipstead (Square) via Ide Hill and 413 (Mon to Sat).

414 West Croydon (St Michaels Rd) - Horsham (Carfax) via Coulsdon, Redhill, Reigate, Betchworth, Dorking and Capel.

415 Guildford (Bus Stn, Onslow St) - Ripley (Post Office) (Mons to Sats); curtailed Burpham (Sutton Hill) between peaks.

#416 Esher ('Windsor Arms') - Tadworth Stn via Oxshott, Leatherhead and Headley; on Suns diverted at Pebblecombe to Boxhill (Greenacres).

417 Windsor (Bus Stn) - Langley ('The Harrow') via Eton, Slough and Langley Rd; extended peak hours to Meadfield Rd or Colnbrook (Sutton La). Also operates Windsor (Thames St) - Old Windsor Hospital Wed and Sun afternoons.

418 Kingston Stn - Bookham Stn via Berrylands, Tolworth, West Ewell, Epsom, Ashtead Stn, Leatherhead, Great Bookham then a two-way loop via Little Bookham and Church Rd.

418A As 418 but not via Ashtead Stn (occasional jnys only).

#419 Epsom (Brettgrave) - Langley Vale (Harding Rd) via Long Grove, Epsom and Woodcote.

420 Woking Stn - Sheerwater (Lambourne Cres) via Albert Drive (Mons to Sats); extended Mon to Sat peak hours to West Byfleet Stn.

421 Sevenoaks (Bus Stn) - Heverham (Farmhouse) via Bat & Ball, Otford and Kemsing.

#422 Boxhill (Greenacres) - Leatherhead Stn via Pebblecombe and Mill Way (some jnys via Headley Court RAF Hospital) (Mons to Sats); some morning jnys extended to Oxshott or Esher.

423 Longfield (Essex Rd) - Swanley (L.T. Gar) via Watchgate, Dartford, Wilmington, Dartford Hth and Birchwood.

423A Watchgate (Ladywood Rd) - Wells Factory via Dartford and Joyce Grn (Mon-Fri peak hours).

423B Watchgate (Ladywood Rd) - Littlebrook Power Stn via Dartford and Littlebrook Manor Way (Mon-Fri a.m. peak).

423D Watchgate (Ladywood Rd) - Wilmington (P.O.) (Sat shopping hours; occasional jnys Mon-Fri).

424 Reigate Stn - East Grinstead (Stone Quarry Estate) via Woodhatch, Duxhurst (not Suns) or Irons Bottom, Horley, Smallfield, Snow Hill (not Suns) or Crawley Down and Felbridge. Also: Crawley (Bus Stn) - East Grinstead via Three Bridges and Crawley Down (Mon to Sat peak hours).

#425 Dorking North Stn - Guildford (Bus Stn, Farnham Rd) via Westcott, Gomshall, Albury and Shalford.

#426 Crawley ('George') two-way circular via Three Bridges, Tinsley Grn, Horley, Charlwood and Ifield.

426A Ifield Stn - Pound Hill (Grattons Dr (not Suns) or Hillcrest Close) via Ewhurst Rd, West Green Dr, Town Centre, Mitchells Rd and Gales Dr.

#427 Woking Stn - Addlestone Stn via Maybury Inn, Pyrford, Byfleet and New Haw; extended Mons to Sats except eves to Weybridge ('Ship'); some jnys further extended to 'Lincoln Arms'.

#428 East Grinstead (Bus Stn, King St) - Dormansland ('Plough') via Felcourt and Lingfield.

429 Dorking (Bus Stn) - Newdigate (Village Corner) via Brockham and Parkgate; some Mon-Fri jnys start from Newdigate via Holmwood.

430 Redhill Stn - Reigate ('Red Cross') via Woodlands Rd, Woodhatch and South Park; some jnys extended Mons to Sats to Reigate Station.

431 Sevenoaks (Bus Stn) - Orpington Stn via Dunton Green, Knockholt Pound and Chelsfield; some jnys extended to Kelvin Parade.

431A Sevenoaks (Bus Stn) - Orpington Stn via Knockholt and Green St Green (occasional jnys).

431B Knockholt Pound - Fort Halstead via Halstead (works jny Mon-Fri).

431C Knockholt Stn - Fort Halstead via Halstead and Polhill (works jny Mon-Fri).

431D Orpington Stn - Fort Halstead via Green St Green, Knockholt Stn and Polhill (works jnys Mon-Fri).

#432 Guildford (Bus Stn, Onslow St) - Great Bookham ('Old Crown') via Horsley and Effingham Jnc; runs via Bookham Stn Mon to Sat peak hours.

#433 Ranmore (Dog Kennel Grn) - Coldharbour ('Plough') via Dorking (no service winter Suns).

434 Crawley ('George') - Edenbridge ('Swan' or 'Albion') via Copthorne, Crawley Down, East Grinstead and Dormansland, then alternate jnys via Troy Town.

436 Staines (Bridge St) - Guildford (Bus Stn, Onslow St) via Chertsey, Addlestone, Woodham, Sheerwater, Woking, Send and Burpham.

436A Staines (Bridge St) - Ripley (Post Office) via 436 to Send.

#437 Woking Stn - Weybridge ('Ship') via Maybury Inn, Byfleet and Addlestone (Mons to Sats); some jnys extended to 'Lincoln Arms'.

438 Crawley (Bus Stn) - East Grinstead (Bus Stn, King St) via Manor Royal, Tinsley Grn, Copthorne and Snow Hill (Mon to Fri works jnys. One eve peak jny via Crawley Down.)

438A Crawley (Bus Stn) - East Grinstead (Bus Stn, King St) via Brighton Rd, Tinsley Grn, Copthorne and Crawley Down (Sat works jny).

438B Three Bridges Stn - Gatwick Rd (Rutherford Way) via Crawley (Mon to Fri works jnys).

438C Crawley (Bus Stn) - East Grinstead (Bus Stn, King St) via Manor Royal, Tinsley Grn, Copthorne and Snow Hill (Mon to Sat works jnys).

439 Newdigate (Village Corner) - Redhill Stn via Dorking, Brockham, Leigh, Reigate and Wray Com.

#439A Reigate (L.T. Gar) - Merstham ('The Feathers') via Wray Common (Mon to Fri jnys).

#440 Woldingham (The Ridge) - Redhill (Market Place) via Caterham, Chaldon and Sth Merstham; extended Mons to Sats to Salfords (Monotype) via Earlswood; extended Suns Redhill to Reigate (L.T. Gar) via Blackborough Rd.

#440A Woldingham (The Ridge) - Redstone Estate via 440 to Redhill, Philanthropic Rd (Mons to Sats).

441 Staines Central Stn - High Wycombe (Guildhall) via Pooley Grn, Egham, Englefield Grn, Burfield Rd or Straight Rd (Old Windsor), Windsor, Slough, Farnham Rd and Beaconsfield. Part service diverts at Hedgerley Corner to Hedgerley Hill or Village.

441A Windsor (Castle Hill) - Britwell (Wentworth Av) via Slough and Salt Hill (Suns).

441B Beaconsfield ('Saracen's Head') - Langley Village via Slough (Mon to Fri jny).

441C Staines Central Stn - Englefield Grn (Larchwood Dr) via Egham.

441D Staines Central Stn - Virginia Water Stn via Pooley Grn and Egham (school days).

443 Staines (L.T. Gar) - Ascot ('Horse & Groom') via Virginia Water (Mon to Fri jny and race days).

#445 Windsor (Castle Hill) - Datchet Common ('Rising Sun') via Eton and Pococks La (Mons to Sats).

446 Slough Stn - Farnham Rd ('George') via Elliman Av and Whitby Rd.

446A Slough Stn - Farnham Rd ('George') via Elliman Av, Manor Park and Villiers Rd.

446B Windsor (Bus Stn) - Slough Trading Estate via Salt Hill (Mon to Fri peak and Sat a.m. peak).

§447 Redhill Stn - Merstham (Delabole Rd) via Doods Rd, Reigate, Meadvale, Earlswood, Redhill and Frenches Rd.

§447A/B Reigate (L.T. Gar) - Merstham (Delabole Rd) via Main Rd (A) or Blackborough Rd (B) (jnys).

#448 Guildford (Bus Stn, Onslow St) - Peaslake (War Memorial) via Merrow and Gomshall; jnys extended Mons to Sats to Ewhurst ('Bulls Head'). (Operated jointly with Tillingbourne Valley.)

#448A Guildford (Bus Stn, Onslow St) - Pewley Way via Addison Rd (Mons to Sats).

449 Chart Downs Estate - Dorking (Bus Stn) via Deepdene Av; jnys extended Mon to Fri to Goodwyns Farm Estate; extended Sat afternoons Dorking to Holmwood ('Holly & Laurel').

#450 Dartford (L.T. Gar) - Gravesend (Clock Tower) via Greenhithe, Betsham and Southfleet Stn.

#451 Gravesend (Clock Tower) - Hartley Court via Southfleet and Betsham (Mon-Fri and Sat a.m.).

#452 Dartford (L.T. Gar) - West Kingsdown ('Portobello') via Greenhithe, Westwood and Longfield (Sat and Sun).

453 Warlingham (The Green) - Caterham ('Clifton Arms') via Westhall Rd, Whyteleafe Rd and Buxton La.

454 Chipstead (The Square) - Tonbridge Stn via Bat & Ball, Sevenoaks and Sevenoaks Weald. (Occasional journeys via Sevenoaks station numbered 454A.)

455. High Wycombe (Frogmoor) - Uxbridge (L.T. Stn) via Beaconsfield and Gerrards Cross.

455A West Wycombe ('Swan') - High Wycombe (L.T. Gar)/High Wycombe (Frogmoor) - Wooburn Common ('Royal Standard') via Holtspur (Mon to Sat jnys).

#456 Woking Station - Addlestone Stn via Pyrford, W. Byfleet and Woodham extended Mon to Sat, except eves, to Weybridge ('Ship'); one Sat jny further extended to 'Lincoln Arms'.

456B Addlestone (L.T. Gar) - Vickers Works via Woodham, W. Byfleet and Byfleet (works jnys Mon-Fri).

457 Uxbridge (L.T. Stn) - Windsor (Castle Hill) via Iver Heath (some via 'Stag & Hounds'), George Green and Uxbridge Rd. (Journeys via Upton Lea numbered 457A.)

457C Pinestead - Uxbridge (L.T. Stn) via Iver Heath (works jnys Mon-Fri).

457D Pinewood - Windsor (Bus Station) via Upton Lea (works jnys Mon-Fri).

§458 Uxbridge (L.T. Stn) - Slough Stn via Cowley, Iver, Shreding Green and Langley.

#459 Uxbridge (L.T. Stn) - Richings Park Estate ('Tower Arms') via Iver Heath and Iver (Mon to Sat).

460 Staines (Central Stn) - Slough Stn via Hythe End, Wraysbury and Datchet.

461 Walton (Odeon) - Chertsey (Church) via Weybridge and Addlestone; extended Mon to Sat, except eves, to Staines (Bridge St).

461A Walton (Odeon) - Ottershaw via Addlestone; extended Mon to Sat, except eves, and Suns to Botleys Park (Holloway Hill).

#462 Leatherhead Stn - Addlestone (L.T. Gar or 'Dukes Head') via Fetcham, Cobham, Vickers Works and Weybridge; extended Mon to Sat, except eves, to Chertsey (Church); further extended Mon-Sat peak hours, Wed and Sat afts, to Staines (Bridge St).

462B Walton (Odeon) - Vickers Works via Weybridge Stn (works jnys Mon-Fri.)

462C Vickers Works TO Ottershaw only (one jny Wed and Fri).

463 Walton (Odeon) - Guildford (Bus Stn, Onslow St) via Addlestone, Woodham Church, Woking, Send and Merrow.

#464 Westerham ('Kings Arms') - Holland (Coldshott) via Crockham Hill, Chart, Oxted and Hurst Green; school jnys extended to Staffhurst Wood Church; (some journeys operate via Pollards Oak Crescent). Journeys also operate Oxted (Barrow Green Rd) - Holland.

#465 Edenbridge ('Star') - Holland (Coldshott) via Crockham Hill and 464.

466 Staines (Bridge St) - Knowle Hill ('Stag & Hounds') via Egham and Stroude (Mon to Sat).

467 Horton Kirby (Westminster Mills) or Wilmington (Hazel Rd) - Sidcup Stn via Sutton at Hone, Wilmington, Dartford, Heath La, Princes Rd, Crayford, Bexley and North Cray. (Horton Kirby covered jointly with 491.)

467A Dartford (Bow Arrow La) - Sidcup Stn via St Vincents Rd and 467 (Sun afts).

468 Chessington Zoo - Epsom Stn via West Ewell and Ewell; extended Mon-Fri peak hours and Sat afts to Leatherhead (L.T. Garage); further extended Mon-Fri peak hours to Effingham (Woodlands Rd).

469 Staines (Bridge St) - Virginia Water Stn (jnys to 'Wheatsheaf' Mon-Fri) via Pooley Grn, Thorpe Lea and Thorpe.

470 Dorking (Bus Stn) - Chelsham (L.T. Gar) via 93 to Epsom and 408; extended, except Mon-Fri peak hours and Sats, to Warlingham Park Hospital; and Sun afternoons to Farleigh ('The Harrow').

#471 Orpington Stn (circular, both ways) via Green St Green, Pratts Bottom, Knockholt Pound, Scotts Lodge and Cudham.

472 Leatherhead (L.T. Garage) - Netherne Hospital (limited stop) via 408 to Carshalton, Park La and Woodcote Green (Weds and Suns).

#473 Crawley ('George') - Dormansland ('Plough') via Rowfant, Turners Hill and 434 (Mon to Sat).

475 Crayford Ness - Belvedere (Crabtree Manor Way) via Slade Green, Perry Street, Barnehurst and Northumberland Heath (works jnys Mon-Fri).

476 Tilgate (Canterbury Rd) - Langley Green via Southgate Av, Town Centre and Martyrs Av, return Langley Dr; extended Mon-Fri peak hours and lunchtimes to Ifield (The Parade).

476A Pound Hill (Hillcrest Close) - Ifield (The Parade) via Manor Royal and Langley Green (works jnys).

476B Tilgate (Canterbury Rd) or Pound Hill (Hillcrest Close) - Gatwick Airport Stn via Town Centre, Manor Royal and Gatwick Rd (works jnys).

The former Hants & Sussex Horsham - Lambs Green - Crawley service was never operated by any other class than the GS in London Transport days. The 852 was withdrawn in October 1965. Eric Surfleet

477   Chelsfield ('Five Bells') - Dartford (Henderson Drive) via Orpington, St Mary Cray, Swanley and Hextable; works jnys extended Mon to Sat to Littlebrook Power Stn.

477A   Chelsfield ('Five Bells') - Dartford (Joyce Green Hospital) via 477 and Joyce Green La; works jnys extended to Wells Factory Mon to Sat.

478   Swanley (St Mary's Estate) - West Kingsdown ('Portobello') (Mon to Sat) extended Mon-Fri peak hours to Wrotham (The Square) via Farningham.

480   Denton ('Milton Ale Shades') - Erith ('Wheatley Arms') via Gravesend, Swanscombe, Dartford, Crayford and Slade Green.

480A   Denton ('Milton Ale Shades') - Rosherville (Mon-Fri lunchtimes).

#481   Epsom Stn - Wells Estate (Mon to Sat).

#482   Caterham Stn - Smallfield Hospital (limited stop) via Godstone and Redhill (Thurs and Suns).

484   Farnham Rd ('George') or Trading Estate (Dover Rd) - Langley Village ('Harrow') via Salt Hill, London Rd and High St (Mon to Sat).

484A   Farnham Rd ('George') or Trading Estate (Dover Rd) - Datchet (Green) via Salt Hill, London Rd and Ditton Rd (Mon-Fri peak hours and Sats).

484B   Farnham Rd ('George') or Trading Estate (Dover Rd) - Colnbrook (Sutton La) (Mon-Fri peak hours).

#485   Edenbridge ('Star') - Westerham ('Kings Arms') via Crockham Hill.

486   Dartford (Fleet Estate) - Bexleyheath (Market Pl) via Dartford, Burnham Rd and Crayford; extended Mon to Sat, except eves, to Upper Belvedere ('Eardley Arms') via Long La; further extended Mon-Fri peak hours to Lower Belvedere (Railway Pl). Works jnys also operate Mon-Fri Crayford Ness - Dartford (L.T. Gar) via Slade Green and Crayford.

487   Swanscombe (Alkerden La) - Gypsy Corner via Northfleet, Wrotham Rd and Cross La; extended Mon to Sat to Singlewell (Hever Court Estate).

487A   Swanscombe (Alkerden La) - Rosherville (Mon-Fri lunchtimes).

488   Swanscombe (Eglinton Rd) - Kings Farm Estate via Northfleet, Wrotham Rd, Cross La and Kings Dr.

488A   Kings Farm Estate - Rosherville (Mon-Fri lunchtimes).

#489   Ash ('White Swan') - Gravesend (Clock Tower) via Hartley, Longfield, Westwood and Southfleet.

#489A   Hook Green (Aborfield House) - Gravesend (Clock Tower) via Longfield and 489.

#490   Gravesend (Clock Tower) - Hartley Court via Southfleet, New Barn and Longfield.

491   Horton Kirby (Westminster Mills) (see 467) - Lower Belvedere (Railway Pl) via Wilmington, Dartford, Shepherds La, Chastillian Rd, Crayford, Perry Street, Barnehurst, Brook St and Picardy St; works jnys extended Mon to Sat to Crabtree Manor Way or Belvedere Generating Station.

493   Englefield Green (Larchwood Dr) - Botleys Pk (St Peters Hospital) limited stop via Egham, Pooley Grn, Stroude, Virginia Water and Thorpe (Weds and Suns).

#494   Oxted Stn (West Side) - East Grinstead (Bus Stn, King St) via Tandridge, Crowhurst and Lingfield.

495   Christianfields Estate - Northfleet (Church) via Echo Sq, Parrock St, Pelham Rd, Colyers Rd, Waterdales and Springhead Rd; extended Mon to Sat peak hours, also occasional jnys to 'Plough'.

495A   Christianfields Estate - Rosherville (Mon-Fri lunchtimes).

496   Kings Farm Estate - Northfleet ('Plough') via Sun La, Parrock St, Pelham Rd and Vale Rd.

496A   Waterdales - Rosherville (Mon-Fri lunchtimes).

497   Dover Road Schools - Gravesend (Clock Tower) via Old Rd West and Darnley Rd (Mon to Sat peak hours and afts).

498   Gravesend (Clock Tower) - Coldharbour Estate via Darnley Rd, Dashwood Rd, New House La and Hardens Rd; extended Mon to Sat peak hours and lunchtimes, Sat afts and Suns to Painters Ash Estate; further extended Mon to Sat peak hours to Northfleet ('Plough') via Springhead Rd.

499   Dartford (L.T. Gar) - Bow Arrow La via East Hill and St Vincents Rd (Mon to Sat).

801   Longmeadow - Stevenage Stn via Marymead, Monks Wood and bus station (works jnys via Six Hills Way and Gunnels Wood Rd); diverted at High St and extended Mon-Fri peak hours, Sats and Sun afts to Hitchin (St Mary's Sq) via Lt Wymondley. (Some jnys continue to Hitchin Stn.)

801A   as 801 but via Stevenage Stn to Hitchin (Mon-Fri peak hours).

802   Bandley Hill - Stevenage Industrial Area circular via Bedwell, Monks Wood (some direct via Six Hills Way), High St, Popple Way and Bedwell. (Some jnys to/from Bus Stn) (works jnys Mon to Sat).

803   Welwyn Gdn City Stn - Uxbridge (L.T. Stn), Express, via Valley Rd, Oldings Cnr, 330 to St Albans, then 321 (Mon-Fri peak hours).

804   Bush Fair - Harlow (Bus Stn) via Tye Grn and Second Av (Mon to Sat); extended Mon-Fri peak hours to Pinnacles via Fourth Av.

805   Canons Gate (Hobtoe Rd) - Potter Street (Fullers Mead) via Hodings Rd, First Av, Bus Stn, First Av, Howard Way, Tillwicks Rd and Southern Way; extended Sat to Epping (L.T. Stn) via 396 (also garage jnys to Epping L.T. Gar). Peak jnys also work to/from Pinnacles.

805A   Harlow Stn - Potter St (Fullers Mead) via Templefields and Tillwicks Rd (works jnys Mon to Sat).

806   Harlow Stn - Canons Gate (Hobtoe Rd) via Templefields and Bus Stn (works jnys Mon to Sat).

#807   Letchworth Stn - Stevenage (Bus Stn) via Letchworth Gate and Weston (works jnys Mon to Sat); jnys extended Mon-Fri to Gunnels Wood Rd.

808   Longmeadow - Hitchin (Old Park Rd, for Lister Hospital) via Marymead, Bedwell, Bus Stn and Lt Wymondley (Suns). (Limited stop, for passengers to Lister Hosp only.)

811   Hitchin (St Marys Sq) - Longmeadow via 811 (Tuesdays); limited stop Hitchin - Stevenage

851   Three Bridges Stn - Smallfield Hospital via Gales Dr, Crawley, County Oak and Horley (limited stop Three Bridges to Horley) (Suns).

#852   Horsham (Carfax) - Crawley (Bus Stn) via Faygate, Lambs Grn and Ifield (Mon to Sat).

853   Pound Hill (Hillcrest Clo) circular via Crawley, Manor Royal and Gatwick Rd (works jnys Mon-Fri).

853A   Pound Hill (Hillcrest Clo) - Gatwick Airport Stn via Crawley, Manor Royal and Gatwick Rd (works jnys Mon to Sat).

853B   Pound Hill (Hillcrest Clo) - Gatwick Airport Stn via Gatwick Rd (works jnys Mon-Fri).

854   Chelsfield Stn - Ramsden Est (Petton Gve loop) via Warren Rd, Orpington and Spur Rd (Mon to Sat).

854A   Chelsfield Stn - Green St Green ('Rose & Crown') (works jnys Mon-Fri)

§   single-deck route two-man operated
\#   single-deck route one-man operated

TROLLEYBUSES

513 Hampstead Heath (South End Grn) - Parliament Hill Fields (Swain's La) via Malden Rd, Prince of Wales Rd, Royal College St, King's Cross, Grays Inn Rd, Holborn Circus, Farringdon Rd, King's Cross, Royal College St and Kentish Town (Mon to Sat and early am Suns); On Sundays, except early morning, returns to Hampstead Heath via Prince of Wales Rd and Malden Rd. Also night service Hampstead Hth -Hampstead Hth via Grays Inn Rd or Farringdon Rd.

517 Nth Finchley ('Tally Ho!') - King's Cross Stn via E. Finchley, Archway, Holloway and Caledonian Rd; extended Mon to Sat and early am Suns to Holborn Cir via Grays Inn Rd (return Farringdon Rd).

521 Nth Finchley ('Tally Ho!') - King's Cross Stn via Bounds Grn, Wood Grn, Finsbury Pk and Caledonian Rd; extended, except Sat afts and eves to Holborn Circus via Grays Inn Rd (return Farringdon Rd).

543 Wood Grn (Redvers Rd) - Shoreditch Church via Bruce Grove, Stamford Hill and Dalston Jnc (Mon to Sat); extended, except Mon-Fri eves and Sat afts and eves to Holborn Circus via Clerkenwell and Grays Inn Rd (return Farringdon Rd). Early am jnys Suns operate Stamford Hill (Amhurst Pk) - Holborn Circus.

557 Chingford Mount (New Rd) - Liverpool St Stn via Leyton, Clapton, Cambridge Hth and Shoreditch.

601 Twickenham (Junction) - Tolworth (Kingston By-Pass) via Fulwell, Teddington, Hampton Wick, Kingston, Penhryn Rd, Surbiton Cres, St Marks Hill and Ewell Rd.

602 The Dittons (St Leonards Rd), circular one way via Brighton Rd, Surbiton, Kingston, Norbiton, Park Rd, Kings Rd, Richmond Rd and Kingston.

603 Tolworth ('Red Lion'), circular one way via Surbiton and the reverse of 602.

604 Wimbledon Stn - Hampton Court (Vrow Walk) via Worple Rd, Raynes Pk, West Barnes La, New Malden, Norbiton and Kingston.

605 Wimbledon Stn - Teddington (Savoy Cinema) via 604 to Kingston and Hampton Wick; extended Suns to Twickenham (Junction) via 601.

607 Shepherds Bush Grn - Uxbridge (Frays River Bdg) via Acton, Ealing, Southall and Hayes End.

609 Moorgate (Finsbury Sq) - Barnet Church via Islington, Holloway, Archway and North Finchley.

611 Moorgate (Finsbury Sq) - Highgate Village (South Gve) via New North Rd, Highbury, Holloway and Archway.

613 Reverse of 513 (Mon to Sat and early am Suns).

615 Moorgate (Finsbury Sq) - Parliament Hill Fields (Swain's La) via Islington, King's Cross and 513.

617 Reverse of 517 (Mon to Sat).

621 Reverse of 521.

623 Woodford ('Napier Arms') - Manor House (L.T. Stn) via Forest Rd, Broad La and Seven Sisters Rd.

625 Woodford ('Napier Arms') - Wood Green (Redvers Rd) via Forest Rd, Chesnut Rd, Tottenham and Lordship La; extended Mon-Fri peak hours to Winchmore Hill ('Green Dragon') via Palmers Grn. (No service Mon-Fri peak or eves 'Napier Arms' to Walthamstow (Beacontree Av.)

626 Clapham Junction (Meyrick Rd) - Acton (High St) via Wandsworth, Putney Bdg Rd, Fulham Palace Rd, Hammersmith, Shepherds Bush, Scrubs La, Harlesden and Horn La. (Mon-Fri peak hours).

627 Tottenham Court Rd (Maple St) - Waltham Cross via Camden Town, Finsbury Pk, Tottenham, Edmonton and Ponders End (Mon to Sat). Early am jnys operate Suns Tottenham Crt Rd - Edmonton (Town Hall) but only one throughout.

628 Clapham Junction (Meyrick Rd) - Harlesden (Craven Park) via 626 to Jubilee Clock (not Mon-Fri peak hours).

629 Tottenham Court Rd (Maple St) - Enfield Town (Cecil Rd) via 29 to Palmers Grn and Winchmore Hill.

630 West Croydon (Station Rd) - Harrow Rd (Scrubs La) via Mitcham Common, Tooting, Wandsworth and 626. Also evening jnys Mon, Wed, Fri Tooting - Wimbledon Stadium via Garratt La and Wimbledon Rd; and night service Tooting (Longmead Rd) - Hammersmith Bdy.

639 Moorgate (Finsbury Sq) - Hampstead Heath (South End Grn) via Islington, King's Cross, Crowndale Rd, Camden Town, Chalk Farm, Ferdinand St and Malden Rd.

641 Moorgate (Finsbury Sq) - Winchmore Hill (Green Dragon La) via New North Rd, Baring St, Southgate Rd, Newington Grn, Manor House, Wood Grn and Palmers Grn.

643 Reverse of 543 (Mon to Sat except Sat eves).

645 Barnet Church - Canons Park (Stanmore Circus) via North Finchley, Golders Grn, Childs Hill, Cricklewood, Colindale and Edgware.

647 Stamford Hill (Amhurst Pk) - London Docks (Dock St) via Shoreditch, Commercial St and Leman St.

649 Liverpool St Stn - Waltham Cross via Dalston Jnc, Tottenham, Edmonton and Ponders End.

649A Liverpool St Stn - Wood Grn (Redvers Rd) via Dalston, Tottenham, and Lordship La (Suns).

653 Aldgate (Minories Bus Stn) - Tottenham Court Rd (Maple St) via Whitechapel, Bethnal Grn, Hackney, Clapton, Stamford Hill, Manor House, Holloway and Camden Town.

655 Hanwell (Depôt) - Brentford (Half Acre) via Boston Manor; extended, except Sun am and eves to Hammersmith Bdy ('Hop Poles') via Chiswick; further extended Mon-Fri peak hours to Clapham Junc (Meyrick Rd) via 626; also extended Mon-Fri peak hours Hanwell to Acton Vale (Bromyard Av) via Ealing.

657 Shepherds Bush Grn - Hounslow (Wellington Rd Nth) via Goldhawk Rd, Chiswick, Brentford and Isleworth.

659 Waltham Cross - Holborn Circus via 627 to Holloway, Caledonian Rd, King's Cross and Farringdon Rd (return Grays Inn Rd).

660 North Finchley ('Tally Ho!') - Hammersmith Bdy ('Hop Poles') via Golders Grn, Cricklewood, Willesden, Harlesden, Acton, Askew Rd and Paddenswick Rd. Journeys also operate Mon-Fri early am peak Paddington Green - Acton Vale (Bromyard Av) via Harlesden and Acton.

662 Paddington Green - Sudbury ('Swan') via Harrow Road, Harlesden and Wembley.

666 Edgware (Station Rd) - Hammersmith Bdy ('Hop Poles') via Colindale, Cricklewood and 660.

667 Hammersmith Bdy ('Hop Poles') - Hampton Court (The Green) via Chiswick, Brentford, Twickenham, Fulwell and Hampton Hill.

669 Nth Woolwich (Free Ferry) - Stratford Bdy via Silvertown, Canning Town, Hermit Rd, Upper Rd and Plaistow.

679 Waltham Cross - Smithfield via 627 to Holloway, Islington and St John St. Also jnys Mon-Fri pm peak Waltham Cross - Tottenham Hale via Chesnut Rd. Also three early jnys Mon to Sat Archway (L.T. Stn) - Smithfield (t/buses ex route 627, whose number they normally carried).

685 Walthamstow ('Crooked Billet') - Canning Town (Hermit Rd) via Billet Rd, Blackhorse La, Markhouse Rd, Leyton High Rd, Crownfield Rd, Cannhall Rd, Dames Rd, Forest Rd, Forest Gate, Green St and Barking Rd; extended Mon to Sat peak hours, also late evening jnys Mon-Fri, to Silvertown Stn; further extended Mon-Fri peak hours to North Woolwich (Free Ferry).

687 Walthamstow ('Crooked Billet') - Victoria and Albert Docks via 685 to Forest Gate, Upton La, Stopford Rd, Clegg St, Balaam St, Newbarn St and Freemasons Rd.

689 Stratford Bdy, circular one way via West Ham La, Portway, Plashet Gve, High St Nth, East Ham Town Hall, Barking Rd, Upton Pk, Green St and Plashet Rd.

690 Reverse of 689.

697 Chingford Mount (New Rd) - Victoria and Albert Docks via Leyton, Crownfield Rd, Maryland, Stratford, Plaistow, Balaam St, Newbarn St and Freemasons Rd.

699 Chingford Mount (New Rd) - Victoria and Albert Docks via 697 to Plaistow, Greengate St and Prince Regents La.

GREEN LINE COACHES

701 Gravesend (Clock Tower) - Ascot ('Horse & Groom') via Dartford, Crayford, Bexleyheath, Welling, Shooters Hill, Deptford, New Cross, Old Kent Rd, Elephant & Castle, Lambeth Rd, Millbank, Belgrave Rd, Victoria (Eccleston Bdg), Hyde Park Cnr, Kensington, Hammersmith, Chiswick, Brentford, Hounslow, Bedfont, Staines, Egham and Virginia Water.

702 Gravesend (Clock Tower) - Sunningdale Stn via 701 to Virginia Water, Fort Belvedere.

703 Wrotham (The Square) - Amersham (L.T. Gar) via Farningham, bus 21 to New Cross, 701 to Hyde Pk Cnr, Marble Arch, Paddington Grn, Harlesden, Wembley, Harrow, Northwood, Rickmansworth and Chorleywood.

704 Tunbridge Wells (Coach Stn) - Windsor (Bus Stn) via Tonbridge, Sevenoaks, Knockholt, Farnborough, Bromley, Catford, Lewisham, New Cross, route 701 to Chiswick, Great West Road, Bath Road, Colnbrook, Slough and Eton.

705 Sevenoaks (Bus Stn) - Windsor (Bus Stn) via Riverhead, Westerham, Westerham Hill, Keston, Hayes, Bromley and 704.

706 Westerham Stn - Aylesbury (Kingsbury Square) via Tatsfield, Chelsham, Sanderstead, South Croydon, bus 109 to Brixton, Vauxhall Bdg, Belgrave Rd, Victoria (Eccleston Bdg), Hyde Pk Cnr, bus 16 to Cricklewood, Colindale, Edgware, Stanmore, Bushey, Watford and bus 301.

707 Oxted Stn (Gresham Rd) - Aylesbury (Kingsbury Square) via Titsey Hill, Chelsham and 706.

708 East Grinstead (Bus Stn, King St) - Hemel Hempstead (Bus Stn) via bus 409 to Caterham Stn, 197 to South Croydon and 706 to Two Waters.

709 Chesham ('Nashleigh Arms') - Caterham ('Clifton Arms') via Amersham Stn, Amersham (L.T. Gar), Chalfonts, Gerrards Cross, Uxbridge, trolleybus 607 to Shepherds Bush, Notting Hill Gate, Lancaster Gate, Sussex Gardens, Marylebone Rd, Portland Pl, Oxford Circus, Trafalgar Sq, Westminster Bdg, bus 109 to Purley, Coulsdon, Marlpit La and Old Coulsdon; garage and changeover jnys extended via 409 to Godstone (L.T. Garage).

710 Amersham (L.T. Gar) - Crawley (Bus Stn) via 709 to Coulsdon, then bus 405.

711 High Wycombe (L.T. Gar) - Reigate (L.T. Gar) via Beaconsfield, Oxford Rd, Uxbridge, 709 to Kennington, bus 155 to Tooting, 80 to Lower Kingswood and Reigate Hill.

712 Dorking (Bus Stn) - Luton (Park Square) via bus 93 to South Wimbledon, 155 to Stockwell, Vauxhall Bdg, Belgrave Rd, Victoria (Eccleston Bdg), Hyde Pk Cnr, Marble Arch, Baker St, Finchley Rd, Golders Grn, Hendon Central, Mill Hill Bdy, Stirling Cnr, Furzehill Rd, Borehamwood, Brook Rd, Aycliff Rd, Theobald St, Radlett, Shenley, London Colney, St Albans and Harpenden.

713 Dorking (Bus Stn) - Dunstable (The Square) via 712 to St Albans, Redbourn and Markyate.

714 Dorking (Bus Stn) - Luton (Park Square) via Leatherhead, Chessington, Hook, Ewell Rd, Surbiton, Kingston, Richmond, bus 73 to Marble Arch, Baker St, King's Cross, York Way, Brecknock Rd, Tufnell Park, Archway, North Finchley, Barnet, bus 84 to St Albans and Harpenden.

715 Guildford (Bus Stn, Onslow St) - Hertford (Bus Stn) via bus 415 to Ripley, Cobham, Esher, Kingston By-Pass, Roehampton, Hammersmith, Shepherds Bush, bus 12 to Oxford Circus, Portland Pl, Albany St, Camden Town, Camden Rd, Isledon Rd, Finsbury Pk, trolleybus 629 to Enfield and bus 310.

715A Marble Arch (Bayswater Rd) - Hertford (Bus Stn) via 715 to Finsbury Pk, trolleybus 627 to Waltham Cross, Hoddesdon and Hertford Hth.

716 Chertsey (Bridge) - Hitchin (St Mary's Sq) via bus 461 to Walton, 131 to Kingston, 714 to Baker St, 712 to Golders Grn, trolleybus 645 to Barnet, bus 303 to Stanborough, Great North Rd, Welwyn and 303.

716A Woking (Car Park, Commercial Rd) - Stevenage (Bus Stn) via bus 436 to Addlestone and 716.

Double-deck duplication was a prominent feature of Green Line operations in the first half of the sixties when traffic was buoyant. St Albans's RT 2319 is in the familiar surroundings of Eccleston Bridge, Victoria, after the new shelters had been erected. *Gerald Mead*

717 Victoria (Eccleston Bdg) - Welwyn Garden City (Cole Green La) via Hyde Pk Cnr, 716 to Potters Bar, Brookmans Park, Welham Grn, Barnet By-Pass, South Hatfield, Cavendish Way, St Albans Rd, Great North Rd, Valley Rd and Ludwick Way.

718 Windsor (Bus Stn) - Harlow New Town (Centre) via Old Windsor, Englefield Grn, Egham, Staines, Ashford, Sunbury, Kempton Park, Hampton Court, Kingston, Roehampton, Putney, Fulham Bdy, Harwood Rd, Kings Rd, Cremorne Rd, Cheyne Walk, Royal Hospital Rd, Victoria (Eccleston Bdg), Hyde Park Cnr, Marble Arch, Baker St, Albany St, route 715A to Tottenham, Forest Rd, Walthamstow, Chingford Mount, Chingford, Woodford Wells, Buckhurst Hill, Loughton, Epping, Potter Street, Southern Way, Tillwicks Rd and First Av.

719 Victoria (Eccleston Bdg) - Hemel Hempstead (Bus Stn) via Hyde Park Cnr, Marble Arch, bus route 8 to Blackbird Cross, Fryent Way, Kingsbury, Honeypot La, Stanmore, Bushey, Watford, bus 347 to Leverstock Grn, Longlands and Adeyfield Rd.

720 Aldgate (Minories Coach Stn) - Bishops Stortford ('Bricklayers Arms') via bus 10 to Leytonstone, 20 to Epping and 396.

720A Aldgate (Minories Coach Stn) - Harlow New Town (Centre) via 720 to Potter Street and 718.

721 Aldgate (Minories Coach Stn) - Brentwood (London Hospital Annexe) via bus 25 to Stratford, 86 to Romford, Gallows Corner, Harold Park and Brook Street.

722 Aldgate (Minories Coach Stn) - Corbets Tey ('Huntsman & Hounds') via bus 25 to Becontree Hth, Rush Green, Oldchurch Hospital, Hornchurch and Upminster. Part of service operates Mon-Fri to Hornchurch Stn.

723 Aldgate (Minories Coach Stn) - Tilbury Ferry (Riverside Stn) via bus 23 to Barking, 87 to Rainham, Purfleet, Grays and Chadwell St Mary. (*NOTE: diverted via Movers La and Alfreds Way 7 June 1961.*)

723A Aldgate (Minories Coach Stn) - Grays (War Memorial) via bus 23 to Barking, Movers La, Alfreds Way, Rainham, Sandy La, Mill La, Aveley, Belhus and Nth Stifford.

723B Aldgate (Minories Coach Stn) - Tilbury Ferry (Riverside Stn) via 723 to Grays, Dock Rd (Mon to Sat).

725 Gravesend (Clock Tower) - Windsor (Bus Stn) via Dartford, Crayford, Bexley, Sidcup, Chislehurst, Bromley, Beckenham, Elmers End, Addiscombe, West Croydon, bus 408 to Cheam, Worcester Park, New Malden, Norbiton, Kingston and 718.

726 Romford (Market Pl) - Whipsnade Zoo: limited stop via 721 to Aldgate, [Bank, Holborn, Grays Inn Rd, Euston Rd non-stop], Baker Street, route 716 to Barnet, 714 to St Albans and 713 to Markyate (summer months only). One Sun jny starts from Harold Hill (Petersfield Av, Retford Rd) via Petersfield Av, Gooshays Dr, Hilldene Av and Straight Rd.

APPENDIX THREE
OVERTIME BAN - ROUTES WITHDRAWN FROM 30TH JANUARY 1966

MONDAYS TO FRIDAYS: 2A, 4A, 5A, 9, 13, 26, 27A (off-peak), 33, 45, 52, 56, 59A, 74B, 79, 79A, 89, 90, 97, 98B, 108B, 116, 125, 133A, 135, 149 (Victoria -Liverpool St section), 151, 155, 162, 169B, 187A, 188, 189, 207A, 228, 230, 235, 240, 253A, 261, 265, 266, 268, 282, 285.

SATURDAYS: 2A, 9, 13, 26, 27, 29A, 36A, 40B, 52, 79, 79A, 89, 90, 97, 98, 116, 125, 135, 151, 155, 159A, 160, 162A, 168, 187, 188, 191, 207A, 213, 230, 234, 234A, 235, 240, 245A, 253A, 261, 265, 266, 268, 282, 285.

SUNDAYS: 27, 45, 52, 52A, 77B, 89, 90C, 98B, 113, 116, 125, 135, 151, 160A, 187, 188A, 213, 230, 234, 234A, 240, 259, 266, 268, 285.

INDEPENDENT OPERATIONS

On the following sections of route, where there was no other London Transport service, the Board granted short term Consents to allow Independent companies to operate and charge fares.

	SECTION	OPERATOR
9	Hammersmith Bdy - Mortlake (Mon-Sat)	Conway Hunt
27	Twickenham Stn - Teddington Stn (Sats & Suns)	Conway Hunt
52	Burnt Oak - Blackbird Cross (Mon-Sat)	Lewis-Cronshaw
	Harrow Road ('Plough') - Notting Hill Gate	Pulleine Coaches
56	Poplar - Cubitt Town ('Queens Hotel') (Mon-Fri)	Popular Coaches
79	Wembley Central - Queensbury (Mon-Sat)	Valliant Direct Coaches
89	Bexley Stn - Blackfen ('Woodman') (Mon-Sat)	Thames Weald (numbered B1)
	Welling Cnr - Blackheath Stn (Mon-Sat)	Thames Weald (numbered B2)
90	Staines - Hanworth ('Hope & Anchor') (Mon-Sat)	Fountain Coaches
97	Ealing Bdy - Greenford ('Red Lion')	Valliant Direct Coaches
98/B	Pinner - Ruislip	Worldwide Coaches
116	Staines - Minimax Corner	Hall's Coaches
125	Whetstone - Southgate (daily)/ Winchmore Hill (Suns)	Southgate Coaches

151	Belmont Stn - Carshalton Middleton Rd/St Helier Av - Hackbridge	Paynes Coaches Carshalton Belle
160/A	Catford - Welling	Pulleine Coaches
162	Wanstead - Forest Gate (Mon-Fri)	Modern Travel
162/A	Barking - Mayesbrook Pk (Mon-Sat)	Leighton Coaches
169B	Barkingside - Hainault Industrial Estate (Mon-Fri peaks)	Super Coaches
187	Hampstead Hth - Maida Vale Alperton Stn - South Harrow (Sat & Sun)	Seth Coaches Lessway Coaches
189	Clapham Sth - Sth Wimbledon (Mon-Fri)	Wimbledon Coaches
230	Rayners La - Kenton Library (Mon-Fri, except eves & Sats)	Valliant Direct Coaches
234	Wallington - Selsdon (Sats & Suns)	Coachmaster Tours
234A	Purley (Fountain) - Old Lodge Lane (Sats & Suns)	Capital Coaches, Sutton
235	Whole route (Richmond Stn - Friars Stile Rd) (Mon-Sat)	Isleworth Coaches
240	Mill Hill Bdy - Golders Grn (Mon-Sat)	Lewis-Cronshaw
245A	Golders Green - Cricklewood (Sats)	Lewis-Cronshaw
261	Arnos Grove - Barnet (Chesterfield Rd)	Finsbury Coaches
	Barnet Church - Chesterfield Rd (Mon-Fri peaks)	Twentieth Century Coaches
265	Kingston - Copt Gilders	Happy Wanderer Coaches
285	Kingston - London Airport Central	Conway Hunt

Operation of these services started on various dates between 31st January and 18th February, and ceased when the London Transport service was restored. There were also many routes, or sections of routes, which were operated by hired coaches, without Consent and therefore without charging fares, by several local Liberal Party Associations and at least one private individual.

APPENDIX FOUR
PROPOSALS FOR ONE-MAN OPERATION FOLLOWING PHELPS BROWN REPORT : JUNE 1964

In the wake of the 'Phelps Brown' settlement in June 1964, the following routes were assessed to be suitable for conversion to one-man operation, either in whole or in part. The thirty-nine seat RF was considered suitable for fourteen routes, while the remainder were to have new thirty-six footers seating fifty. This is the full list.

RF THIRTY-NINE SEAT

ROUTES ALREADY ANNOUNCED:
201, 206, 215, 215A, 216, 218, 219, 237, 250, 251, 254, 264.

ROUTES ADDED IN JUNE 1964:
202, 234A.

FIFTY SEAT SINGLE-DECK

WHOLE ROUTES:
20, 20A, 21A, 62, 79, 79A, 82, 84, 90, 92, 92A, 98, 98B, 108B, 110, 111, 120, 126, 189, 192, 198, 203, 203A, 204, 209, 213, 213A, 223, 226, 230, 230A, 232, 235, 244, 246, 261, 282, 283.

ROUTES SUITABLE ONLY IN PART:
10, 29, 29A, 29B, 65, 71, 72, 77, 89, 107, 113, 115, 131, 134, 142, 255, 285.

224